AF567023

THE BEST COMPUTER PAPERS OF 1971

Edited by Orlando R. Petrocelli

Acknowledgment

The papers in this volume have been selected and honored as prize-winning papers by the various award committees of the respective societies. The editor and the publishers decided, therefore, that it would be an important contribution to the state of the art if all of the papers were included in one volume, making them readily accessible to those who wish to broaden their current awareness of new developments in the computer industry.

The editor wishes to acknowledge with sincere appreciation the invaluable contributions and cooperation of the following professional societies in helping to make this innovative book possible:

- American Federation of Information Processing Societies, Inc. (AFIPS)
- Association for Computer Machinery (ACM)
- The British Computer Society (BCS)
- Institute of Electrical and Electronics Engineers, Inc. (IEEE)
- Numerical Control Society (NCS)
- Simulation Councils, Inc. (SCI)
- International Federation for Information Processing (IFIP)
  (Selected by an independent panel, not by IFIP)

February 10, 1972 O. R. Petrocelli

Published simultaneously in Canada by Book Center, Inc.

Library of Congress Catalog Card Number: 72-77255
International Standard Book Number: 0-87769-127-4

First Printing

Printed in the United States of America

Contents

List of Contributors

ISAAC L. AUERBACH, President, Auerbach Corporation
Technological Forecast 1971

ALGIRDAS AVIŽIENIS, Jet Propulsion Laboratory, California Institute of Technology; and Department of Computer Science, University of California at Los Angeles
The STAR (Self-Testing And Repairing) Computer: An Investigation of the Theory and Practice of Fault-Tolerant Computer Design

D. BARTON, Computer Laboratory, University of Cambridge, Cambridge, England
The Automatic Solution of Systems of Ordinary Differential Equations by the Method of Taylor Series

LOUIS J. BONA, Senior Staff Engineer, Digital Simulation Section, Technical Facilities Division, National Aviation Facilities Experimental Center, Federal Aviation Administration, Atlantic City, N.J.
Air Traffic Control System–Digital Simulation Facility

D. C. BOSSEN, IBM Laboratories, Poughkeepsie, N.Y.
Optimum Test Patterns for Parity Networks

A. P. ERSHOV, Computing Center, Siberian Division, Academy of Sciences of the USSR, Novosibirsk, USSR
Theory of Program Schemata

PETER L. GARDNER, IBM United Kingdom Laboratories Limited, Winchester, Hants, England
Functional Memory and Its Microprogramming Implications

J. GECSEI, Staff Engineer, IBM Corporation, San Jose, Cal.
Evaluation Techniques for Storage Hierarchies

GEORGE C. GILLEY, Jet Propulsion Laboratory, California Institute of Technology; and Department of Computer Science, University of California at Los Angeles
The STAR (Self-Testing And Repairing) Computer: An Investigation of the Theory and Practice of Fault-Tolerant Computer Design

JAMES GIPS, Computer Science Department, Stanford University, Stanford, Cal.
Shape Grammars and the Generative Specification of Painting and Sculpture

LEO P. KADANOFF, Brown University
From Simulation Model to Public Policy: An Examination of Forrester's "Urban Dynamics"

EDWARD E. KIRKHAM, Associate Director, Technical Engineering, Kearney and Trecker Corportion
Developments in DNC

FRANCIS P. MATHUR, Jet Propulsion Laboratory, California Institute of Technology
The STAR (Self-Testing And Repairing) Computer: An Investigation of the Theory and Practice of Fault-Tolerant Computer Design

R. L. MATTSON, Manager, Storage System Analysis, IBM Research, San Jose, Cal.
Evaluation Techniques for Storage Hierarchies

A. ORTONY, Research Fellow, Computing Unit, University of Surrey, Guildford, Surrey, England
A System for Stereo Viewing

D. L. OSTAPKO, IBM Laboratories, Poughkeepsie, N.Y.
Optimum Test Patterns for Parity Networks

A. M. PATEL, IBM Laboratories, Poughkeepsie, N.Y.
Optimum Test Patterns for Parity Networks

JOHN B. PETERSON, Manager, Applications Engineering, Numerically Controlled Products, Sundstrand Machine Tool
Computer-Aided Manufacturing for the 70's

E. R. REESE, President, Digital Automation Corp., Irvine, Cal.
Computer and Numerical Control–A Shotgun Marriage

DAVID A. RENNELS, Jet Propulsion Laboratory, California Institute of Technology
The STAR (Self-Testing And Repairing) Computer: An Investigation of the Theroy and Practice of Fault-Tolerant Computer Design

JOHN C. REYNOLDS, Systems and Information Science, Syracuse University
GEDANKEN−−A Simple Typeless Language Based on the Principle of Completeness and the Reference Concept

JOHN A. ROHR, Jet Propulsion Laboratory, California Institute of Technology
The STAR (Self-Testing And Repairing) Computer: An Investigation of the Theory and Practice of Fault-Tolerant Computer Design

DAVID K. RUBIN, Jet Propulsion Laboratory, California Institute of Technology
The STAR (Self-Testing And Repairing) Computer: An Investigation of the Theory and Practice of Fault-Tolerant Computer Design

D. R. SLUTZ, Research Staff Member, IBM, San Jose, Cal.
Evaluation Techniques for Storage Hierarchies

GEORGE STINY, Los Angeles, Cal.
Shape Grammars and the Generative Specification of Painting and Sculpture

I. L. TRAIGER, San Jose, Cal.
Evaluation Techniques for Storage Hierarchies

JOHN R. VANDER VEER, Chief, Simulation Applications Section, Data Processing Division, National Aviation Facilities Experimental Center, Federal Aviation Administration, Atlantic City, N.J.
Air Traffic Control System–Digital Simulation Facility

J. S. WALTHER, Hewlett-Packard Company, Palo Alto, Cal.
A Unified Algorithm for Elementary Functions

I. M. WILLERS, Computer Laboratory, University of Cambridge, Cambridge, England
The Automatic Solution of Systems of Ordinary Differential Equations by the Method of Taylor Series

R. V. M. ZAHAR, The Open University, Bletchley, Buckinghamshire, England
The Automatic Solution of Systems of Ordinary Differential Equations by the Method of Taylor Series

Preface

During the past ten years, scientific and technical publications have been increasing at a near exponential rate, and it is safe to predict that this trend will continue. This also applies to conference proceedings, which have become not only more numerous, but more costly.

As a result, busy people who need to know what is being said by leaders in the field of information processing are frustrated by a mounting accumulation of material which they do not have time even to scan, to sort the important from the irrelevant.

Since I too am faced with this personal information processing problem, I have for a long time felt the need for a book containing a collection of significant papers published during the year that would provide an overview of advanced thinking in the information sciences.

This volume fulfills this need. Presented here, selected by experts, are the best papers from seven international organizations in the field of information sciences during 1971. Nearly every major technical society in the English-speaking world is represented between the covers of this book.

You may proceed with confidence. This *is* important reading.

Isaac L. Auerbach
December 1, 1971

PART 1

ASSOCIATION FOR COMPUTING MACHINERY
New York, New York

Two papers that were recipients of the 1971 ACM Annual Programming Systems and Languages Paper Award:

"GEDANKEN–A Simple Typeless Language Based on the Principle of Completeness and the Reference Concept"
by John C. Reynolds

and

"Evaluation Techniques for Storage Hierarchies"
by Richard L. Mattson, Jan Gecsei, Donald R. Slutz, and Irving L. Traiger

1

GEDANKEN—A Simple Typeless Language Based on the Principle of Completeness and the Reference Concept

by *John C. Reynolds*

INTRODUCTION

The recent development of programming languages suggests that the simultaneous achievement of simplicity and generality in language design is a serious unsolved problem. This paper describes an experimental language called GEDANKEN, which was developed to attack the problem.

GEDANKEN is not intended to be a generally useful language, although it could be effective in situations where a fair degree of object program inefficiency is tolerable. Its major purpose (reflected in its name, which is meant as an analogy to gedanken experiments in physics) is to explore the consequences of two basic design principles:

1. *Completeness.* Any value which is permitted in some context of the language is permissible in any other meaningful context. In particular, functions and labels are permitted to be results of functions or values of references (e.g., variables), without imposing restrictions which maintain a stack discipline for run-time storage allocation.

2. *The Reference Concept.* Assignment and indirect addressing are formalized in the following manner: among the possible values that may occur in a program are objects called *references*, which in turn possess other values. The assignment operation always affects the relation between some reference and its value.

Neither of these principles is novel. LISP [1a, 1b] (in its interpretive implementations), ISWIM [2], and PAL [3] all satisfy the principle of completeness, and the reference concept is used in ALGOL 68 [4] and BASEL [5]. But GEDANKEN goes beyond these languages in exploiting the power of these principles, that is, in eliminating other language features which are rendered redundant by completeness and references. Specifically:

The existence of function-returning and reference-returning functions allows all compound data structures to be treated as functions. For example, a one-dimensional ALGOL-like array is treated as a function whose domain is a finite set of consecutive integers and which maps each of these integers into a unique reference. This approach insures that any process which accepts some data structure

Editor's Note: From *Communications of the ACM,* vol. 13, no. 5, May 1970. © 1970 by the Association for Computing Machinery, Inc. Reprinted by permission of the publisher and author.

will accept any logically equivalent structure regardless of its internal representation. More generally, any data structure may be *implicit*; that is, it may be specified by giving an arbitrary algorithm for computing or accessing its components. (Functional data structures have been suggested by Balzer [6], but his realization of the concept is quite different from GEDANKEN.)

The existence of label variables permits the construction of coroutines, quasi-parallel processes, and other unorthodox control mechanisms. This is a direct consequence of not imposing a stack discipline on the program control information.

The main limitation of GEDANKEN is that declarations are not allowed to restrict the value ranges of identifiers, references, or function results. Languages with this property are usually called "typeless," although the types of values may be tested during execution. We do not suggest that type declarations are unimportant or that it is trivial to add them to GEDANKEN without destroying the generality of the language; this is a major theoretical problem.

The originality of GEDANKEN lies primarily in the language features which have been excluded, and the main aim of this paper is to demonstrate that these exclusions (except typelessness) do not impair generality. For this purpose, we include extensive programming examples.

A formal definition of GEDANKEN is given in Reynolds [7]. A complete but extremely inefficient implementation has been produced by translating this formal definition into LISP; this implementation has been used to check all examples given in this paper.

After describing the syntax of the language and the types of values manipulated during program execution, we discuss the applicative part of the language, that is, the evaluation of expressions and the application of functions. Finally, the imperative aspects, such as references, assignment, labels, and jumps, will be introduced.

SYNTAX

Although the importance of GEDANKEN lies in its semantics, a definite syntax must be specified so that programming examples can be given. A GEDANKEN program is a sequence of *tokens* separated by zero or more blanks, with at least one blank used as a separator whenever the juxtaposition would otherwise be ambiguous. The tokens are sequences of characters classified as follows:

constants digit strings (denoting integers), quoted strings
reserved words AND, OR, IF, THEN, ELSE, CASE, OF, IS, ISR
identifiers all other alphanumeric strings beginning with a letter
punctuation tokens λ , = : ( ) ; :=

Certain *predefined* identifiers have standard meanings. These include: TRUE, FALSE, LL, and UL, which denote specific primitive values; ERROR, which denotes a built-in label value causing program termination; and the names of all built-in functions. (These predefined identifiers differ from reserved words in that the programmer can override the standard meanings by declarations.)

The set of token sequences which are well-formed GEDANKEN programs is specified by the context-free grammar (over an infinite vocabulary of tokens) in Table 1-1. The syntactic variables in this grammar are subscripted to distinguish among phrases with a similar semantic role but different levels of precedence. Thus phrases of the classes ⟨exp$_0$⟩, · · ·, ⟨exp$_6$⟩ are all called *expressions,* while phrases of the classes ⟨pform$_0$⟩ and ⟨pform$_1$⟩ are called *parameter forms.* The notation $\{\alpha\}^*$ is used to indicate an arbitrary number (including zero) of occurrences of the string α.

Table 1-1. A Grammar for GEDANKEN

⟨exp$_0$⟩ ::= ⟨constant⟩ | ⟨identifier⟩ | (⟨block⟩)
⟨exp$_1$⟩ ::= ⟨exp$_0$⟩ | ⟨function designator⟩
⟨function designator⟩ ::= ⟨exp$_0$⟩ ⟨exp$_1$⟩
⟨exp$_2$⟩ ::= ⟨exp$_1$⟩ | ⟨exp$_1$⟩ = ⟨exp$_2$⟩
⟨exp$_3$⟩ ::=⟨exp$_2$⟩ | ⟨exp$_2$⟩ AND ⟨exp$_3$⟩
⟨exp$_4$⟩ ::= ⟨exp$_3$⟩ | ⟨exp$_3$⟩ OR ⟨exp$_4$⟩
⟨exp$_5$⟩ ::= ⟨exp$_4$⟩ | ⟨conditional exp⟩ | ⟨lambda exp⟩ | ⟨exp$_4$⟩ := ⟨exp$_5$⟩
⟨conditional exp⟩ ::= IF ⟨exp$_6$⟩ THEN ⟨exp$_6$⟩ ELSE ⟨exp$_5$⟩
⟨lambda exp⟩ ::= λ ⟨pform$_0$⟩ ⟨exp$_5$⟩
⟨exp$_6$⟩ ::= ⟨exp$_5$⟩ | ⟨sequence exp⟩ | ⟨case exp⟩
⟨sequence exp⟩ ::= ⟨empty⟩ | ⟨exp$_5$⟩, ⟨exp$_5$⟩ {, ⟨exp$_5$⟩}*
⟨case exp⟩ ::= CASE ⟨exp$_6$⟩ OF ⟨exp$_5$⟩ {, ⟨exp$_5$⟩}*
⟨pform$_0$⟩ ::= ⟨identifier⟩ | (⟨pform$_1$⟩)
⟨pform$_1$⟩ ::= ⟨pform$_0$⟩ | ⟨sequence pform⟩
⟨sequence pform⟩ ::= ⟨empty⟩ | ⟨pform$_0$⟩, ⟨pform$_0$⟩ {, ⟨pform$_0$⟩}*
⟨decl⟩ ::= ⟨pform$_1$⟩ IS ⟨exp$_6$⟩
⟨recursive decl⟩ ::= ⟨identifier⟩ ISR ⟨lambda exp⟩
⟨label⟩ ::= ⟨identifier⟩ :
⟨statement⟩ ::= {⟨label⟩}* ⟨exp$_6$⟩
⟨block⟩ ::= {⟨decl⟩;}* {⟨recursive decl⟩;}* {⟨statement⟩;}* ⟨statement⟩
⟨program⟩ ::= ⟨block⟩

It should be noted that a block can consist of a single expression; this permits any expression to be parenthesized without changing its semantics.

PRIMITIVE VALUES AND FUNCTIONS

The items of data that are manipulated during the execution of a GEDANKEN program are called *values.* The set of all values is partitioned into seven *types*: *integers, Booleans, characters,* and *atoms* (collectively called *primitive values*), and *functions, references,* and *label values* (collectively called *nonprimitive values*).

(Floating-point numbers are excluded, but their inclusion would not raise any significant problems.) Although the language does not contain type declarations, a complete set of built-in functions is available for testing the type of a value during program execution.

Among the primitive values, only *atoms* are unusual; they are similar to atoms in LISP, except that they lack property lists and print names. More precisely, the atoms are a denumerably infinite set of values which may be tested for equality but which do not possess any ordering or arithmetic operations. Two particular atoms, denoted by the predefined identifiers LL and UL, play a special role in the language. Additional atoms are created by the built-in function ATOM, which returns a distinct atom each time it is applied.

A *function* is a value which may be *applied* to another value, called its *argument.* When so applied, the function will either: (1) return a value called its *result,* (2) transfer control to a label value without returning a result, (3) cause an error stop, or (4) initiate a nonterminating computation. (The application of a function may also alter the state of a computation by producing various *side effects,* which will be discussed later.) The set of arguments for which a function will return a result is called the *domain* of the function. A number of *built-in* functions are provided, which may be used without being defined; additional "user-defined" functions are produced by the evaluation of various expressions.

(Proper procedures, in the sense of ALGOL, are not provided in GEDANKEN since they are equivalent to functions which execute useful side effects but which return an irrelevant result. Functions with multiple arguments are not provided since they are equivalent to functions whose arguments are sequences, as described below.)

The functional approach to data structures is reflected in the absence of a distinct type of value corresponding to the conventional notion of a vector or array; the analogous values in GEDANKEN are functions. Thus we will use the word "vector" to denote those functions which are logically equivalent to conventional vectors.

It is evident that the domain of a GEDANKEN function, which is a vector, must include a finite set of consecutive integers; these integers are the analogue of the subscripts of a conventional vector. But a conventional vector also has the property that its set of subscripts is explicit; that is, there must be some method of testing the vector to determine its least and greatest subscripts. To reflect this property in GEDANKEN, we require that the domain of a vector must include, in addition to the subscript set, the atoms LL and UL, and that the results of applying the vector to LL and UL must be the least and greatest subscripts.

This leads to the following definition. A function F is called a *vector* whenever: (1) its domain includes the atoms LL and UL; (2) the results of applying F to LL and UL are integers such that $F(UL) \geqslant F(LL) - 1$; (3) the domain of F includes all integers i such that $F(LL) \leqslant i \leqslant F(UL)$.

If F is a vector, then the integers F(LL), F(UL), and $F(UL) - F(LL) + 1$ are called the *lower limit, upper limit,* and *length* of F, respectively, and for each integer i such that $F(LL) \leqslant i \leqslant F(UL)$, the result of applying F to i is called the ith *component* of F.

A vector is called a *sequence* if its lower limit is 1.

Although a vector is a kind of function and a sequence is a kind of vector, neither "vector" nor "sequence" is a "type" in the usual sense, since one cannot write a program which will test whether an arbitrary function is a vector or a sequence. Certain operations in GEDANKEN (e.g. evaluation of sequence expressions or application of the built-in function vector) are guaranteed to produce vectors, but equally valid vectors may also be produced by more general mechanisms (e.g. evaluation of lambda expressions). Vectors produced in the latter manner are said to be *implicit.*

(The realization of vectors in GEDANKEN is in contrast to several languages, such as PAL, in which subscript limits are obtained by applying built-in functions to vectors. In the latter approach, vectors are not purely functional since they are amenable to other operations than application. The practical effect is to prohibit implicit vectors.)

The existence of sequences in GEDANKEN justifies the elimination of functions with multiple arguments. The analogue of a conventional function with k arguments, when either $k = 0$ or $k \geqslant 2$, is a function whose single argument is a sequence of length k. For example, the domain of the built-in function ADD is the set of sequences of length two whose components are both integers. (This approach is a direct borrowing from PAL.)

The remaining types of nonprimitive values, *references* and *label values,* will be defined later.

APPLICATIVE SEMANTICS

To describe the semantics of GEDANKEN, we follow Landin [2] and Evans [3] in dividing the language into an applicative part, involving the evaluation of expressions and the application of functions, and an imperative part, involving assignment and control jumps. We first consider the applicative sublanguage, which is obtained by disregarding references, label values, and the operations that manipulate them.

Within this sublanguage, the basic operation is the *evaluation* of expressions. Since the evaluation of an expression will usually involve the evaluation of its subexpressions, the definition of this operation is inherently recursive. Also, when an expression contains free identifiers, its evaluation is only meaningful in the presence of some mapping of these identifiers into values. Such a mapping is called an *environment* and is said to *bind* each identifier to a value.

A complete program is always evaluated in an environment which binds the predefined identifiers into their standard values. Whenever the evaluation of an expression e involves the evaluation of an immediate subexpression e', then, *unless* e is a lambda expression or a block, e' is evaluated in the same environment as e. The evaluation of lambda expressions and blocks (described in detail below) involves the concept of *extension*: if i is an identifier, v is a value, and η and η' are environments such that η' binds i to v and specifies the same binding as η for all other identifiers, then η' is called the *extension* of η formed by binding i to v.

We now describe the evaluation of each nontrivial form of expression. The application of a function to an argument is performed by a *function designator*:

$$\langle\text{function designator}\rangle ::= \underbrace{\langle\text{exp}_0\rangle}_{\substack{\text{function}\\ \text{part}}} \quad \underbrace{\langle\text{exp}_1\rangle}_{\substack{\text{argument}\\ \text{part}}}$$

which is evaluated by first evaluating its function part and its argument part to obtain values v_f (which must be a function) and v_a, and then applying v_f to v_a. (Since the argument part is evaluated before the function is applied, this form of evaluation is similar to call by value in ALGOL, rather than call by name.) Because function designators have a right-associative syntax, the usual composition of functions may be written without parentheses; for example, F(G(X)) may be written as F G X.

Functions may be produced by the evaluation of *lambda expressions*:

$$\langle\text{lambda exp}\rangle ::= \lambda\ \langle\text{pform}_0\rangle\ \underbrace{\langle\text{exp}_5\rangle}_{\text{body}}$$

Basically, the value of a lambda expression is a function which, when it is applied to an argument at some later point during the computation, computes its result by binding the parameter form to its argument and then evaluating the body. More precisely, if f is the function obtained by evaluating $\lambda(p)e$ in the environment η, then the result of applying f to an argument a will be obtained by evaluating e in an environment which is the extension of η formed by binding p to a. (The meaning of binding p to a, when p is not an identifier, will be defined below.)

This binding mechanism is quite conventional (it is called FUNARG binding in LISP and is similar to the mechanism used in ALGOL and in PL/I), but a clear understanding of its implications is vital. There are two separate actions: (1) the evaluation of the lambda expression to produce a function, and (2) the application of this function to its arguments. The body of the lambda expression is not evaluated until (2), but the environment in which the body is evaluated is an extension of the environment used during (1) rather than (2). As a result, when a lambda expression contains free identifiers, its evaluation in different environments will produce different functions. For example, in an environment where Y is bound to an integer k, the evaluation of λ(X) ADD(X, Y) produces a function which increases its argument by k.

Functions which are sequences may also be produced by the evaluation of *sequence expressions*:

$$\langle\text{sequence exp}\rangle ::= \langle\text{empty}\rangle \mid \langle\text{exp}_5\rangle, \langle\text{exp}_5\rangle \{, \langle\text{exp}_5\rangle\}^*$$

Let n be the number of subexpressions. Then the sequence expression is evaluated by first evaluating its subexpressions to obtain values $v_1, \cdots, v_n$ and then producing a sequence of length n whose ith component (for $1 \leqslant i \leqslant n$) is v_i.

Because of their low precedence, sequence expressions are usually parenthesized, but the parentheses themselves do not indicate a sequence expression. Thus the expressions ( ) and (X, Y) both produce sequences, but (X) has the same value as X. There is no sequence expression which produces a sequence of length one, but such sequences can be produced by the built-in function UNITSEQ, which returns a sequence whose only component is the value of its argument.

As noted earlier, a function of n arguments ($n \neq 1$) is treated in GEDANKEN as a function of a sequence of length n. This suggests that when a function produced by a lambda expression expects to receive a sequence as its argument, the parameter form within the lambda expression should be able to bind several different identifiers to the components of the sequence. To provide this capability we extend the notion of a parameter form to include a *sequence parameter form* (which is a rough analogue of a formal parameter list in ALGOL):

⟨sequence pform⟩ ::= ⟨empty⟩ | ⟨pform$_0$⟩, ⟨pform$_0$⟩ {, ⟨pform$_0$⟩}*

The relevant semantics are given by defining (recursively) the *extension* of an environment η formed by binding an arbitrary parameter form p to a value v. This extension is computed as follows:

1. If p is an identifier, then η is extended by binding p to v.
2. If p has the form (p'), then η is extended by binding p' to v.
3. If p is a sequence parameter form, $p_1 . \cdots, p_n$ ($n \neq 1$), then v, which must be a function, is applied to each integer from 1 to n, and η is repeatedly extended by binding each p_i to the result of $v(i)$.

The syntax of sequence expressions and sequence parameter forms preserves conventional notation for functions of several arguments. Thus in the evaluation of (λ(X, Y) *body*) (3,4), X is bound to 3 and Y is bound to 4. However, the sequence argument approach also provides useful unconventional capabilities, for example, (λ(X, Y) *body*) (IF P THEN (3, 4) ELSE (5, 6)). More importantly, the ability to bind a single identifier to an entire sequence provides the equivalent of a function with an indefinite number of arugments, for example, (λX *body*) (IF P THEN (3, 4) ELSE (5, 6, 7)).

GEDANKEN is similar to Euler [8] in treating all types of unlabeled statements as expressions. In particular, a *block* is a form of expression with a meaningful value:

⟨block⟩ ::= {⟨decl⟩;}* {⟨recursive decl⟩;}* {⟨statement⟩;}* ⟨statement⟩

where

⟨decl⟩ ::= ⟨pform$_1$⟩ IS ⟨exp$_6$⟩
⟨recursive decl⟩ ::= ⟨identifier⟩ ISR ⟨lambda exp⟩

Basically, a block is evaluated by first carrying out the bindings indicated by its declarations, recursive declarations, and labels, and then evaluating the statements in order from left to right. The value of the block is the value of the rightmost statement. The values of preceding statements are ignored; in the absence of imperative features, these statements have no effect.

More precisely, a block is evaluated as follows (we include the binding of labels, although it is an imperative aspect of the language):

1. For each declaration (⟨decl⟩), in order from left to right: the right side of the declaration is evaluated, and then the current environment is extended by binding the left side of the declaration to the value of the right side.
2. The current environment is further extended by binding each identifier which occurs on the left of a recursive declaration (⟨recursive decl⟩), or as the label of a statement, to a distinct "dummy" value.
3. The right side of each recursive declaration is evaluated and its value replaces the corresponding dummy value.
4. For each label, an appropriate label value is created and replaces the corresponding dummy value.
5. The statements are evaluated in order from left to right.
6. The value of the block is the value of the rightmost statement.

In steps 2 to 4 the device of binding identifiers to dummy values and then replacing the dummy values allows an environment to be cyclic, that is, to bind an identifier to a value which is produced by evaluating a lambda expression (or label) in the same environment.

The essential difference between (nonrecursive) declarations and recursive declarations is that the right side of a declaration "feels" only the bindings caused by preceding declarations, while the right side of a recursive declaration feels the bindings caused by all declarations in the block, including implicit label declarations. Recursive declarations are needed to define recursive functions conveniently, including families of functions which call one another. (They also permit the definition of functions which jump into the immediately enclosing block.)

Nonrecursive declarations are less essential, but they permit convenient constructions such as X IS ADD(X, 1). More important, their existence allows the right sides of recursive declarations to be limited to lambda expressions, so that meaningless constructions such as X ISR ADD(X, 1) are syntactically illegal.

Conditional expressions have the same meaning as in ALGOL. *Case expressions* have a rather unorthodox meaning (which is convenient for defining implicit sequences): CASE e_0 OF $e_1, \cdots, e_n$ is evaluated by first evaluating e_0 to obtain a value i; then if i is an integer satisfying $1 \leqslant i \leqslant n$, the value of the case expression is obtained by evaluating e_i; if i is LL or UL the value is 1 or n respectively; all other values of i give an error stop.

The remaining forms of expressions are most easily defined as abbreviations. Except for coercion (discussed later), they can be eliminated from a program by applying the following transformations:

$e_1 = e_2 \Rightarrow \text{EQUAL}(e_1, e_2)$
e_1 AND $e_2 \Rightarrow$ (IF e_1 THEN e_2 ELSE FALSE)
e_1 OR $e_2 \Rightarrow$ (IF e_1 THEN TRUE ELSE e_2)
$e_1 := e_2 \Rightarrow \text{SET}(e_1, e_2)$

The built-in function SET will be defined later. EQUAL tests the equality of primitive data, but if either component of its argument is a function or a label value, it will return FALSE. Its action on references will be described later.

Theoretically, nonrecursive declarations, sequence parameter forms, and sequence expressions can also be regarded as abbreviations. Their occurrence in a program can be eliminated by repeated application of the following equivalences:

p IS e; $b \Rightarrow (\lambda(p)(b))(e)$
$\lambda(p_1, \cdots, p_n)\, b$ (when $n \neq 1) \Rightarrow \lambda i(p_1$ IS i 1; $\cdots$; p_n IS $i\, n'$; $b)$
$e_1, \cdots, e_n$ (when $n \neq 1) \Rightarrow$
$\Rightarrow (i_1$ IS e_1 ; $\cdots$; i_n IS e_n ; λi(CASE i OF $i_1, \cdots, i_n$))

where n' is an integer constant whose value is n, and $i, i_1, \cdots, i_n$ are distinct identifiers which do not occur in the program being transformed.

It should be noted that GEDANKEN does not include certain features, such as infix arithmetic operators or *for* statements, which would enhance the conciseness of the language without expanding the range of programs that could be expressed. Such features could be added easily, but they are not germane to the basic purposes of the language.

FUNCTIONAL DATA STRUCTURES

Even the applicative part of GEDANKEN is sufficient to demonstrate the power and flexibility which can be obtained by treating data structures functionally.

As a first example, consider LISP-like list structures. To define analogues of the LISP functions CONS, CAR, and CDR, we treat the two-field list cell produced by CONS as a function whose domain contains two elements (e.g. 1 and 2) and which maps these elements into the values of its CAR and CDR fields. This viewpoint leads directly to the definitions:

```
CONS IS λ(X, Y) λZ IF Z = 1 THEN X ELSE Y;
CAR IS λX X 1;
CDR IS λX X 2;
```

These definitions imply an ability to do list processing without special built-in functions. In a conventional list-processing system (e.g. compiled LISP 1.5 [1a and 1b] or some extensions of ALGOL [4, 9]) user-defined functions are restricted so that storage for the values of their identifiers obeys a stack discipline. Then list structures, which do not obey a stack discipline, must be allocated in a separate storage area, and built-in functions or operations must be provided for accessing this area. But in GEDANKEN, the user may develop list-processing by defining function-returning functions (such as CONS above) which violate a stack discipline. In effect, all storage is potentially list-structured.

Although the above approach is workable and theoretically attractive, it is more convenient to use sequence expressions to create list elements and direct application to obtain their subfields. Thus we write (X, Y) instead of CONS (X, Y), X 1 instead of CAR X, and X 2 instead of CDR X. Following this approach, we introduce lists by first creating an atom to denote the empty list:

```
NIL IS ATOM( );
```

and then defining a list to be either the atom NIL or a sequence of length two whose second component is a list. The following functions will return the length of a list, find the *i*th element of a list, and append one list to another:

```
LISTLENGTH ISR λL IF L = NIL THEN 0
   ELSE INC LISTLENGTH L 2;
LISTELEM ISR λ(I, L) IF L = NIL THEN GOTO ERROR
   ELSE IF I = 1 THEN L 1 ELSE LISTELEM(DEC I, L 2);
APPEND ISR λ(X, Y) IF X = NIL THEN Y
   ELSE (X 1, APPEND(X 2, Y));
```

Hence INC and DEC are built-in functions which increase or decrease an integer by one.

As a second example, consider one-dimensional arrays. We have defined a type of function called a vector which is the analogue of a one-dimensional array, and we have introduced sequence expressions for creating vectors. But a sequence expression can only produce a vector which is a sequence, and it is inconvenient for producing very long vectors. What is needed is a function that will produce a vector from a functional specification of its components, that is, that will accept another function, tabulate its results over a finite range, and return a "lookup" function for the resulting table.

Thus we define a function VECTOR which accepts an argument (L, U, F), where L and U are integers and F is a function. If U < L, VECTOR returns an empty vector V such that V(LL) = L and V(UL) = L − 1. Otherwise, VECTOR evaluates F(I) for each integer I between L and U inclusive, and returns a vector V such that V(LL) = L, V(UL) = U and for L ⩽ I ⩽ U, V(I) is the value of F(I). The basic approach is to recur on the length of the vector, tabulating a single value (bound to T) at each level of recursion.

```
VECTOR ISR λ(L, U, F)
IF GREATER(L, U) THEN
   λ I IF I = LL THEN L ELSE IF I = UL THEN DECL
      ELSE GOTO ERROR
ELSE (V IS VECTOR(L, DEC U, F); T IS F U;
   λ I IF I = UL THEN U ELSE IF I = U THEN T ELSE V I);
```

It is evident that this function, although theoretically correct, will be extremely inefficient in any reasonable implementation. For this reason, a built-in function VECTOR is provided which is defined to be equivalent to the function above (except for coercion).

(This question of efficiency may be clarified by considering implementation mechanisms. In a simple implementation, functions would possess two distinct internal representations: If a function were produced by evaluating a lambda expression, it would be represented by a "lambda record" containing a pointer to code which was compiled from the lambda expression plus values for each free identifier in the lambda expression [i.e. a representation of the environment in which the lambda expression was evaluated]. On the other hand, if a function were created by evaluating a sequence expression or by the application of VECTOR, it would be represented by a "vector record" containing domain limit and indexing information, plus a contiguous array of component values. It is evident that the above definition of VECTOR would yield a vector whose internal representation was a linked list of lambda records, each containing one component value, rather than a contiguous array.)

Using lists and vectors, we may illustrate our assertion that any process which accepts some data structure will accept any logically equivalent structure. Suppose that P is a function which expects a sequence as its argument, and that we wish to give it a sequence whose *i*th component is the *i*th element of a list L. This can be done in a conventional manner by evaluating P VECTOR (1, LISTLENGTH L, λ I LISTELEM(I, L)), which copies the elements of L into a contiguous array. But is is also possible to evaluate P MAKESEQFROMLIST L, where

```
MAKESEQFROMLIST IS λ L
λ I IF I = LL THEN 1 ELSE IF I = UL THEN LISTLENGTH L
   ELSE LISTELEM(I, L);
```

MAKESEQFROMLIST does not copy the components of L; instead, it returns an implicit sequence which will look up the appropriate element of L each time one of its components is accessed.

It is equally possible to produce an implicit list from a sequence:

```
MAKELISTFROMSEQ ISR λ S MLFS1(1, S);
MLFS1 ISR λ(I, S) IF GREATER (I, S UL) THEN NIL
   ELSE λ K (CASE K OF S I, MLFS1(INC I, S));
```

(Here MLFS1 is a subsidiary function which produces an implicit list from the subsequence of S that begins with the *i*th component.)

The data structures shown so far have the limitation that once a structure has been created, its components or elements cannot be altered. To overcome this limitation we must introduce the imperative aspects of GEDANKEN.

REFERENCES

In any programming language that permits assignment, there is a class of objects that are affected by assignment. We will call these objects *references*; other terms commonly used in the literature are "name" and "L-value." At any time during the execution of a program, each reference *possesses* some value. The effect of an assignment operation $r := v$ is to cause the reference denoted by r to possess the value denoted by v.

Within this definitional framework, there are at least three distinct approaches to assignment (see Figure 1-1):

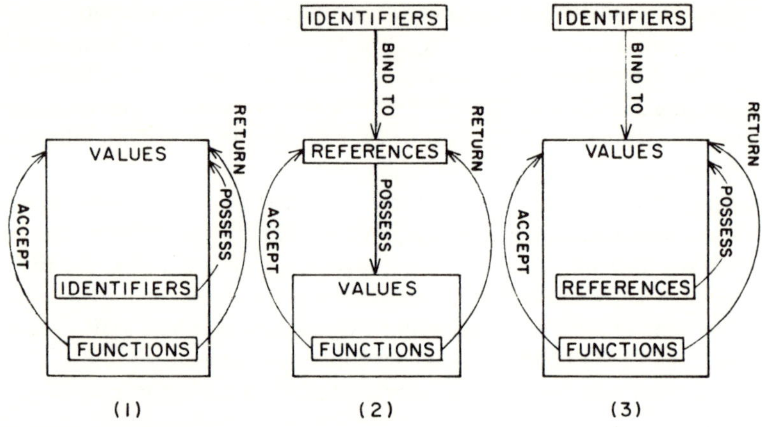

Figure 1-1. Three Approaches to Assignment

(1) Identifiers are used as references. This approach is used in SNOBOL [10], where a form of indirect addressing is achieved by allowing identifiers to occur as values. Unfortunately, the approach does not mesh well with block structure; a discussion of the difficulties is given by Kain [11].

(2) References are distinct from either identifiers or values and are interposed between all other value-denoting entities and their values. Thus the bindings of identifiers, the arguments and results of functions, and the components of vectors are all references, and the values denoted by these entities are actually the values possessed by the references. This approach is used in PAL and to a large extent in FORTRAN and PL/I, except that in the latter languages function results are values and identifiers may be bound directly to functions and label values, but not to primitive values. The approach meshes well with block structure, but is rather inflexible. One moves from the applicative situation, where assignment is impossible, to the opposite extreme, where every value-denoting entity can be affected by assignment.

(3) References are treated as a distinct type of value, so that any value-denoting entity can denote either a conventional value or a reference, which in turn pos-

sesses a value. This approach is used in ALGOL 68 and BASEL. (BASEL also permits a form of assignment which alters identifier binding.) It is compatible with block structure and is more flexible than the previous approach, since the programmer can introduce references in just those contexts where he intends to do assignment. Advantages should accrue in both the optimization of data representations and the checking of erroneous assignment statements.

(The above categorization must be qualified by the fact that FORTRAN, PL/I, ALGOL 68, and BASEL all have type-declaration mechanisms which affect their treatment of assignment. A discussion of this interaction is beyond the scope of this paper.)

In GEDANKEN we have chosen to use the third approach to assignment, thus we introduce a new, denumerably infinite set of values called *references* and stipulate that each reference *possesses* some other value (which may itself be a reference). Three built-in functions are provided to manipulate references: REF, SET, and VAL. REF X returns a distinct reference each time it is applied; this reference is initialized to possess the value X. SET(R, X) (which can be abbreviated R := X) causes R (which must be a reference) to possess the value X, and also returns X; its action on R is an example of a *side effect.* VAL R returns the value possessed by R (which must be a reference).

For example, under the scope of the declaration X IS 3, the identifier X is bound to the integer 3, and this binding cannot be altered by assignment. Evaluation of the expression X := 4 would give an error, since 3 is not a reference. Analogously, under the scope of the declaration X IS REF 3, the identifier X is bound to the reference created by REF, and this binding cannot be changed by assignment. But now evaluation of X := 4 is legitimate and causes the value possessed by the reference bound to X to change from 3 to 4. Thus in the execution of the block

(X IS REF 3; VAL X = 3; X := 4; VAL X = 4)

both equality predicates will be true.

The major difficulty with this approach is the frequent necessity for using the function VAL. For example, under the scope of the declarations X IS REF 3; Y IS REF 4; one would write ADD(VAL X, VAL Y) rather than ADD(X, Y), since ADD acts upon integers rather than references. To alleviate this difficulty, we introduce *coercion* conventions into GEDANKEN; that is, we stipulate that references will be replaced by their values in certain contexts which would otherwise be meaningless.

Specifically, let COERCE be the function

COERCE ISR λ X IF ISREF X THEN COERCE VAL X ELSE X;

(which is available as a built-in function), and define "to coerce X" to mean the replacement of X by COERCE X. Then:

(1) All built-in functions, which would otherwise be meaningless, coerce their argument or the appropriate components of their arguments. For example,

ADD(X, Y) is equivalent to ADD(COERCE X, COERCE Y), but ISREF X is not equivalent to ISREF COERCE X, nor VAL X to VAL COERCE X.

(2) REF X coerces X, SET(R, X) (and therefore R := X) coerces X, and EQUAL(X, Y) (and therefore X = Y) coerces both X and Y. Since these functions would each be meaningful for references without coercion, analogous non-coercing functions, named NCREF, NCSET, and NCEQUAL, are also provided. NCREF and NCSET permit references to possess values which are also references. NCEQUAL can be used to determine whether two values are the same reference.

(3) Conditional and case expressions coerce the values of their leftmost subexpressions.

(4) Expressions involving AND and OR coerce the values of both their subexpressions.

(5) A function designator coerces the value of its function part.

(6) When a sequence parameter form $p_1, \ldots, p_n$ is bound to a value a, each p_i will be bound to (COERCE a) (i).

(7) Vectors created by evaluating sequence expressions or by application of the built-in functions VECTOR or UNITSEQ will coerce their argument.

Despite their ad hoc appearance, most of these coercion rules are instances of the general principle that coercion should occur only in situations which would otherwise give an error termination. The exceptions are rules (2) and (4), which are simply concessions to conventional notation.

DATA STRUCTURES WITH EMBEDDED REFERENCES

The utility of references becomes apparent when reference-returning functions are used to embed references within data structures, yielding structures which can be altered by assignment.

This approach provides precise control over the ways in which data structures can be altered. Thus the GEDANKEN equivalent of an ALGOL-like one-dimensional array is a vector whose components are references, for example,

X IS VECTOR(1, 100, λ I REF 0);

Under the scope of this declaration, assignment can be made to the components of X, for example, X(7) := 10, but not to X itself. In particular, the subscript limits X LL and X UL are fixed by the declaration.

On the other hand, the equivalent of a string variable is provided by a reference whose value is a vector:

S IS REF VECTOR(1, 100, F);

Here assignment can be made to S itself (possibly changing the subscript limits), but not to its components.

A second consequence of the reference concept is the ability to define data structures or sets of data structures which share elements, in the sense that assignment to one element will affect another. Consider a square matrix M. We could define M as a vector of vectors, that is,

```
M IS VECTOR(1, 10, λ I VECTOR(1, 10, λ J REF 0));
```

but this leads to the inconvenience of referring to an element of M by (M I) J. It is more natural to define M as a reference-returning function of pairs of integers:

```
M IS (M1 IS VECTOR(1, 10, λ I VECTOR(1, 10, λ J REF 0));
  λ(I, J) (M1 I) J);
```

so that an element is referred to as M(I, J). Now consider the additional declarations:

```
MT IS λ(I, J) M(J, I); MD IS λ I M(I, I);
```

Here MT and MD denote the transpose and diagonal of M, in the sense that assignment to an element of one matrix affects the corresponding elements of the others.

Elements may also be shared within the same data structure. For example,

```
S IS (S1 IS VECTOR(1, 10, λ I VECTOR(1, I, λ J REF 0));
  λ(I, J) IF NOT GREATER(J, I) THEN (S1 I) J ELSE (S1 J) I);
```

defines a symmetric matrix in which assignment to S(I, J) also alters S(J, I).

The embedding of references in list structures also provides control over the ways in which these structures may be altered. An example is the property list, which is a list of property-value pairs subject to two operations: the value paired with a given property may be looked up, or the value paired with a given property may be changed, adding a new pair to the list if the property is not already present. It is evident that references must occur in the property list at two points; each value must be a reference, so that it can be changed, and the entire list must be a reference, so that new pairs can be added.

The following function manipulates such property lists. Given a property P and *a* (reference to *a*) property list L, PROPVAL(P, L) searches L for an occurrence of P. If P is found, the reference paired with P is returned. Otherwise, a pair consisting of P and a new reference (initialized to zero) is added to L, and the new reference is returned. The argument P is coerced.

```
PROPVAL IS λ(P, L)
  (P IS COERCE P;
  SEARCHL ISR λ X
    IF X = NIL THEN
      (NEWV IS REF 0; L := ((P, NEWV), VAL L); NEWV)
    ELSE IF (X 1) 1 = P THEN (X 1) 2 ELSE SEARCHL X 2;
  SEARCHL VAL L);
```

An application of this function can occur on either side of an assignment operation; on the right side it will act to look up a value, on the left side it will act to alter a value.

A further step can be taken by viewing the property list itself as a reference-returning function which accepts a property and returns a reference to the corresponding value. The following function (of no arguments) returns such *functional* property lists:

```
MAKEPROPLIST IS λ( ) (L IS REF NIL; λ P PROPVAL(P, L));
```

Each application of MAKEPROPLIST returns a new instance of PROPVAL, with L bound to a private "own variable." Since a property can be any primitive value, a functional property list is similar to a reference-valued vector, except that it has an indefinite domain. Indeed, functional property lists can be used to provide an efficient implementation of sparse vectors.

As a final example of the use of references, suppose that READ is a function such that each application of READ produces the next item of data from some input stream, and that we wish to produce an implicit list of the successive items in the stream. The following function (of no arguments) returns such a list:

```
MAKERLIST ISR λ( )
  (B IS REF 0; λ I
    (IF B = O THEN B := (READ( ),MAKERLIST( )) ELSE( );
      B I));
```

The result of MAKERLIST is an implicit list (whose implicit length is infinite), which only applies READ as items of data are actually needed and only stores previously read items which are still accessible.

IMPLICIT REFERENCES

The utility of implicit data structures suggests the introduction of an analogous facility for references. Thus we introduce the concept of an *implicit reference,* that is, a value whose external appearance is the same as a reference, but which may carry out an arbitrary computation each time it is set or evaluated. (Implicit references are related to doublets in POP-2 [12].)

To specify an implicit reference, the programmer must provide two functions: a "setting function" S which will be executed each time a value is assigned to the implicit reference, and an "evaluating function" V which will be executed each time the implicit reference is evaluated. Thus an implicit reference is produced by applying the built-in function IMPREF(S, V), where S and V may be arbitrary functions of one and zero arguments, respectively. Each application of IMPREF produces a distinct implicit reference, and these implicit references satisfy the predicate ISREF and are coerced in the same manner as conventional references. But the effect of SET or VAL on an implicit reference is to execute S or V. Specifically, if R is the result of IMPREF(S, V), then

```
NCSET(R, X) = (S X; X)
SET(R, X) = (X IS COERCE X; S X; X)
VAL R = V ( )
```

To illustrate the use of implicit references, consider the problem of protecting a reference-valued vector. Suppose that P is a function which accepts a vector whose components are references. We wish to apply P to such a vector V, but to protect the components of V from being affected by P; i.e. we want these components to revert to their original values after the application of P is finished. The simplest approach is to copy V by executing P VECTOR(V LL, V UL, λ I REF V I), but this will be inefficient if V is large and only a few components are reset by P. An alternative approach is to maintain a "change list" of the components of V which have been altered by P. This may be done by executing P PSEUDOCOPY V, where

```
PSEUDOCOPY IS λ V
  (CL IS REF NIL;
  SEARCHCL ISR λ(X, I, F, G) IF X = NIL THEN G( )
    ELSE IF (X 1) 1 = I THEN F (X 1) 2
    ELSE SEARCHCL(X 2, I, F, G);
  λ I (I IS COERCE I;
    IF I = LL THEN V LL ELSE IF I = UL THEN V UL
    ELSE IF NOT ISINTEGER I OR GREATER(V LL, I)
      OR GREATER(I, V UL)
      THEN GOTO ERROR
    ELSE IMPREF(
      λ X SEARCHCL(VAL CL, I, λ R NCSET(R, X),
        λ( ) (CL := ((I, NCREF X), VAL CL)),
      λ( ) SEARCHCL(VAL CL, I, VAL, λ( ) VAL V I))));
```

The result of PSEUDOCOPY is an implicit vector whose components are implicit references. Internally, CL is a reference to the change list, which is a list of pairs, each containing an integer argument of some altered component and a reference to the current value of that component. SEARCHCL is a subsidiary function which searches a change list X for a pair beginning with the integer I. If such a pair is found, SEARCHCL returns the result of F applied to the reference paired with I; otherwise SEARCHCL returns the result of G, which is a function of no arguments. (The noncoercing functions NCSET and NCREF are used to allow the values possessed by the components of V to be references.)

LABEL VALUES

The final type of value used in GEDANKEN is the *label value.* These values are created during execution of a block containing labeled statements and are used as arguments to the built-in function GOTO, which never returns but instead causes a transfer of control to the computational state represented by the label value.

A more precise description requires introducing a model of the interpretation of GEDANKEN by an abstract machine. A complete description of such a model (given in [7]) is beyond the scope of this paper, but the following aspects are relevant to an understanding of the label and GOTO mechanisms:

During the execution of a program (at any instant when a statement is about to be evaluated) the *state* of the abstract interpreter will include the following entities:

1. A *control,* which gives a list of the statements remaining to be evaluated in the current block.
2. An *environment,* which gives the identifier bindings to be used in the current block.
3. A *dump,* which specifies the computations to be performed after the current block is completed. The dump is a pushdown stack containing an entry for each block and lambda-expression body whose evaluation is incomplete; each entry contains a control and an environment (plus additional information which is needed to describe partially evaluated compound expressions).
4. A *memory,* which specifies the mapping of references into their values.

A label value consists of a control, an environment, and a dump. During the evaluation of a block, immediately before the first statement is evaluated, a label value is created for each label in the block; each label value contains a list of the statements between the corresponding label and the block end, plus the current environment (including the bindings of the labels themselves) and dump.

When the built-in function GOTO is applied to a label value, the current control, environment, and dump are replaced by the constituents of the label value, and execution continues with the first statement of the new control. The memory is not altered.

This mechanism permits jumps within the same block (which leave the environment and dump unchanged) or to higher level blocks, with the same effect as in ALGOL. But the fact that label values can be possessed by references or returned by functions also provides the ability to jump back into a block after it has been exited from. It is this capability that allows the construction of coroutines.

COROUTINES

A coroutine is a procedure which can relinquish control to its calling program and later be reactivated to continue computation. The simplest situation is that of two procedures, each of which treats the other as a subroutine.

As an example, suppose that COMPILE is a procedure which produces a succession of data items called instructions, outputting each instruction by applying a function OUT, and that ASSEMBLE is a procedure which accepts a succession of instructions, inputting each instruction by applying a function IN. If OUT and IN are arguments to COMPILE and ASSEMBLE, respectively, we have

```
COMPILE ISR λ OUT (· · · OUT X · · ·);
ASSEMBLE ISR λ IN (· · · X := IN( ) · · ·);
```

We now want to couple these procedures so that ASSEMBLE receives the output of COMPILE. Specifically, we want to run ASSEMBLE until it requests input, then run COMPILE until it produces the required output, then run ASSEMBLE again, etc. The necessary program can be written by using label-valued references that are global to both IN and OUT:

```
(LC IS REF 0; LA IS REF 0; INST IS REF 0;
LC := LC1;ASSEMBLE(λ( ) (LA := LA1; GOTO LC;
  LA1: VAL INST)); GOTO DONE;
LC1: COMPILE(λ X (LC := LC2, INST := X;
  LC2:)); GOTO ERROR;
DONE:);
```

Here LA and LC are label-valued references saving the current states of ASSEMBLE and COMPILE, and INST is a third reference used to hold the instruction being transmitted from COMPILE to ASSEMBLE. If COMPILE finishes while ASSEMBLE is still waiting for another instruction, an error stop occurs.

NONDETERMINISTIC ALGORITHMS

Label values in GEDANKEN are closely related to "processes" in simulation languages such as SIMULA [13a and 13b]. Both are mechanisms which allow the state of a suspended computation to be saved as an item of data. The essential difference is that further execution of a computation which was saved as a process causes the process to be updated, while further execution of a computation saved as a label value leaves the label value unchanged. Thus label values can be used to repeatedly initiate execution from the same state.

This capability can be used to program a mode of execution for nondeterministic algorithms [14] in which alternative paths are pursued concurrently. A simple example is nondeterministic parsing. It is fairly straightforward to convert a context-free grammar into a recursive parsing function. Unfortunately, for many grammars this function will contain nondeterministic branches, that is, points at which a conditional branch must be performed, although the current state of the parse is insufficient to determine this branch.

When such nondeterminism exists, parsing can be accomplished by simulating a finite set of independent parsers, all accepting the same input string and obeying the same program but with different control states. When a parser encounters a nondeterministic branch, it expands into two separate parsers; when a parser reads an input character that is inconsistent with its control state, it is deleted.

Specifically, we assume that PARSE(IN, AMB, FAIL) is a function which accepts two functions IN and AMB, and a label value FAIL, and returns some representation of a successful parse. The function IN, of no arguments, is applied by PARSE to read each character of the input string. The function AMB, whose argument is a label value, is applied to execute a nondeterministic branch; one side of the branch returns from AMB while the other jumps to the label-valued argument. PARSE jumps to the label value FAIL when it encounters an inconsistent character. We assume that PARSE does not set any references, or at least that it does not expect the value of any reference to be preserved across an application of IN or AMB.

The following program carries out the concurrent execution of PARSE, synchronizing the independent parsers by their reading of characters:

```
(C IS REF NIL; W IS REF NIL; R IS REF NIL;
   CHAR IS REF NIL;
 C := (PARSE(λ( ) (W := (L1, VAL W); GOTO CONT;
      L1: VAL CHAR),
   λ L2 (R := (L2, VAL R)), CONT),
 VAL C);
 CONT: IF R = NIL AND W = NIL THEN GOTO DONE
      ELSE IF R = NIL
        THEN (CHAR := READCHAR( ); R := W;W := NIL)
      ELSE ( );
   (L IS R 1; R := R 2; GOTO L);
DONE: VAL C)
```

Each independent parser is represented by a label value if it has not completed its parse or by its result if it has completed its parse. The finite set of parsers is maintained by the values of the references C, W, and R. C gives a list of the results of completed parses, W gives a list of label values representing the parsers waiting for the next character, and R gives a similar list for the parsers ready for execution before reading the next character. The reference CHAR keeps track of the current character and is updated by the built-in function READ-CHAR. The label CONT is reached whenever execution is to be switched from one parser to another. The final value of the block is the list of completed parses; the input string is ill formed, well formed, or ambiguous, depending on whether this list has zero, one, or more than one element.

(This approach to parsing is basically the same as that used in the COGENT programming system [15a and 15b]. It is presented here as an illustration of the generality of GEDANKEN, but it does not represent a significant advance in the field of parsing techniques. Although it is reasonably efficient for a large class of unambiguous grammars—at least, if the function PARSE is carefully constructed —some ambiguous grammars will cause an exponential growth in the number of parsers and are better treated by other methods, such as that of Earley [16].)

LIMITATIONS AND POSSIBLE EXTENSIONS

The goal of applying the basic principles of GEDANKEN to the design of an efficient general purpose programming language raises several interesting research problems:

1. *Addition of Type Declarations.* The most natural approach is probably

an extension of Hoare's concept of record classes [9]. The programmer would be able to declare an arbitrary number of disjoint function, reference, and label classes, and would specify the range of each identifier, function result, and reference value to be some union of such classes (and/or predefined classes of primitive values). All functions in the same class would have the same domain-range relation and all references in the same class would have the same set of possible values.

However, the functional approach to data structures will require unusual flexibility in the specification of the domain-range relations of functions. If an inhomogeneous data structure such as a record is to be treated as a function, then it must be possible to specify that the range of such a function depends on its argument. For example, the set of lists of integers would be the union of the set {NIL} with a class of functions with domain (1, 2) which map 1 into an integer but map 2 into a list of integers.

An elaboration of this approach to type, limited to a purely applicative language, is described in [17].

2. *Open Functions.* Efficient implementation of functional data structures will require that certain functions be compiled into open code, that is, that function designators should be replaced by modified copies of the corresponding lambda-expression body and that these copies should then be simplified to take advantage of constant arguments. This capability could be provided by a macro-definitional facility. A second approach, more in keeping with the spirit of GEDANKEN, would be to permit certain lambda expressions to be given an OPEN attribute.

This raises the question of whether a compiler could determine automatically when a designator of a lambda-defined function should be replaced by a copy of the function body. One might conjecture that such an expansion could be performed for any function which was defined by a nonrecursive declaration. Unfortunately, this conjecture is disproved by the existence of a nonrecursive *fixed-point function*:

Y IS λG (U IS λV G(λX (V V) X); U U);

which can be used to convert any simply recursive function (i.e. a function which calls itself directly but not indirectly via other functions) into an equivalent nonrecursive function [18].

Thus suppose a recursive function F is defined by F ISR *b*, where F is the only identifier which occurs free in *b*. Let F1 be the nonrecursive function defined by F1 IS λF (*b*). Then the function (Y F1) can be shown to be equivalent to F, with the same domain of termination. Moreover, the expansion of a function designator such as (Y F1) X by repeated substitution of the definitions of Y and F1 will never terminate.

3. *Storage Allocation.* A serious drawback of the principle of completeness is the elimination of any run-time stack discipline, so that all data storage must be recovered by garbage collection. This problem might be alleviated by adding language facilities for indicating contexts where a stack discipline is applicable.

Even without such facilities, it may be possible to determine by program analysis, particularly with appropriate type declarations, situations where storage can be recovered without garbage collection.

4. *Side Effects.* In the applicative subset of GEDANKEN, the immediate subexpressions of a function designator or a sequence expression can be evaluated in any order, or the steps of their evaluation can be intermixed, without affecting the result or termination of any program. This property, which is obviously desirable for code optimization or multiprocessing, is destroyed by the introduction of assignment, since subexpressions can execute interfering side effects.

The situation is exacerbated by the introduction of label values, since the order of evaluation can then affect the number of times a subexpression is executed. The program

```
(X IS REF 0; (X := INC X, GOTO L); L:  VAL X)
```

produces one with left-to-right evaluation of the sequence expression, but produces zero with right-to-left evaluation. Label-valued references lead to more paradoxical programs, such as

```
(X IS REF 0; L IS REF 0; M IS REF 0; L := L1;
  (X := INC X, (M := M1; M1:  GOTO L));
  L1: L := L2; GOTO M; L2:  VAL X)
```

which produces one with left-to-right evaluation, zero with right-to-left evaluation, and possibly two with intermixed evaluation.

This problem is common to a wide variety of languages. One either imposes a fixed order of evaluation, as in ALGOL 60 or GEDANKEN, or he permits a significant class of well-formed programs to have indeterminate interpretations, as in ALGOL 68 or PL/I. But a more flexible approach might be possible, for example, a limited form of imperative features that could be added to an applicative language without destroying order-of-evaluation independence.

5. *Other Label-Value Problems.* Label-valued references can easily cause the preservation of data which will no longer be accessed by a computation. If L is a label-valued reference, then GOTO L will cause execution to proceed from the computational state denoted by L. But the unchanged state must also be saved in case GOTO L is executed again before the value of L is changed. If in fact such a repeated jump cannot occur, then information will be saved unnecessarily unless the programmer goes to the trouble of resetting L immediately after the original jump. (As an example, the program for linking the coroutines COMPILE and ASSEMBLE will preserve the states of these routines unnecessarily.)

Presumably, it would be better to force the programmer to extra trouble in order to preserve, rather than discard, a reactivated computational state. This might be accomplished by adapting the concept of "process" used in simulation languages and by providing a basic function for copying processes. However, it is not clear how to combine the process concept with an ALGOL-like use of label values in a clean manner which does not violate the principle of completeness.

A further difficulty is the inability of a label value to preserve the values of references (i.e. the memory). In the nondeterministic parser described earlier, the restriction on the use of references in the function PARSE arises from this problem.

6. *Secondary Storage and File Management.* Even with open functions and sophisticated code optimization, it may be intolerably inefficient to impose a purely functional approach on all data structures. But the functional approach still holds considerable promise for the treatment of large structures which require secondary storage. A stated, but usually unmet, goal of most data management systems is the complete separation of the logical properties of a file from its physical representation. A natural approach to this goal would be to equate a logical file with a collection of functions for accessing the file, and to permit these functions to be implicit.

ACKNOWLEDGMENTS

The author wishes to thank Dr. M. D. MacLaren of Argonne National Laboratory and Professor Arthur Evans, Jr. of Massachusetts Institute of Technology for their stimulating discussions and helpful suggestions.

REFERENCES

1a. McCarthy, J. Recursive functions of symbolic expressions and their computation by machine, Pt. I. *Comm. ACM 3,* 4 (Apr. 1960), 184-195.

1b. ——, et al. LISP 1.5 programmers manual. MIT Press, Cambridge, Mass., 1962.

2. Landin, P. J. The next 700 programming languages. *Comm. ACM 9,* 3 (Mar. 1966), 157-166.

3. Evans, A. PAL–A language designed for teaching programming linguistics. Proc. ACM 23rd Nat. Conf. 1968, Brandon/Systems Press, Princeton, N.J., pp. 395-403.

4. van Wijngaarden, A. (Ed.), Mailloux, B. J., Peck, J. E. L., and Koster, C. H. A. Report on the algorithmic language ALGOL 68. MR 101, Mathematisch Centrum, Amsterdam, Feb. 1969.

5. Cheatham, T. E., Jr., Fischer, A., and Jorrand, P. On basis for ELF–An extensible language facility. Proc. AFIPS 1968 Fall Joint Comput. Conf., Vol. 33 Pt. 2, MDI Publications, Wayne, Pa., pp. 937-948.

6. Balzer, R. M. Dataless programming. Proc. AFIPS 1967 Fall Joint Comput. Conf. Vol. 31, MDI Publications, Wayne, Pa., pp. 535-544.

7. Reynolds, J. C. GEDANKEN–A simple typeless language which permits functional data structures and coroutines. ANL-7621, Argonne Nat. Lab., Argonne, Ill., Sept. 1969.

8. Wirth, N., and Weber, H. EULER–A generalization of ALGOL and its formal definition: Pt. 1, Pt. II. *Comm. ACM 9,* 1 and 2 (Jan., Feb. 1966), 13-25, 89-99.

9. Wirth, N., and Hoare, C. A. R. A contribution to the development of ALGOL. *Comm. ACM 9,* 6 (June 1966), 413-432.
10. Farber, D. J., Griswold, R. E., and Polonsky, I. P. The SNOBOL3 programming language. *Bell Syst. Tech. J. 45* (July-Aug. 1966), 895-944.
11. Kain, R. Y. Block structures, indirect addressing, and garbage collection. *Comm. ACM 12,* 7 (July 1969), 395-398.
12. Burstall, R. M., and Popplestone, R. J. POP-2 reference manual. In *Machine Intelligence 2,* E. Dale and D. Michie (Eds.), American Elsevier, New York, 1968, pp. 205-246.
13a. Dahl, O. J., and Nygaard, K. SIMULA–An ALGOL-based simulation language. *Comm. ACM 9,* 9 (Sept. 1966), 671-678.
13b. ——, Myhrhaug, B., and Nygaard, K. SIMULA 67 common base language. Publ. No. S-2, Norwegian Computing Center, Oslo, May 1968.
14. Floyd, R. W. Nondeterministic algorithms. *J. ACM 14,* 3 (Oct. 1967), 636-644.
15a. Reynolds, J. C. An introduction to the COGENT programming system. Proc. ACM 20th Natl. Conf., 1965, pp. 422-436.
15b. ——, COGENT programming manual. ANL-7022, Argonne Nat. Lab., Argonne, Ill., Mar. 1965.
16. Earley, J. An efficient context-free parsing algorithm. *Com. ACM 13:* 2 (Feb. 1970), 94-102.
17. Reynolds, J. C. A set-theoretic approach to the concept of type. Working paper, NATO Conf. on Techniques in Software Engineering, Rome, Oct. 1969.
18a. Evans, A. Private communication.
18b. Morris, J. H. Lambda-calculus models of programming languages. MAC-TR-57, Project MAC, MIT, Cambridge, Mass., Dec. 1968.

2
Evaluation Techniques for Storage Hierarchies

by *R. L. Mattson, J. Gecsei, D. R. Slutz, and I. L. Traiger*

Increasing speed and size demands on computer systems have resulted in corresponding demands on storage systems. Since it has been generally recognized that the speed and capacity requirements of storage systems cannot be fulfilled at an acceptable cost-performance level within any single technology, storage hierarchies that use a variety of technologies have been investigated.

Several papers describe the general concepts of hierarchy design [1-3] and evalution [4-6], whereas others deal with specific hierarchy systems, such as the core-drum combination on the ICT Atlas computer [7-9] and the cache-core combination on the IBM System/360, Model 85 [10, 11].

This paper introduces an efficient technique called "stack processing" that can be used in the cost-performance evaluation of a large class of storage hierarchies. The technique depends on a classification of page replacement algorithms as "stack algorithms" for which various properties are derived. These properties may be of use in the general areas of program modeling and system analysis, as well as in the evaluation of storage hierarchies. For a better understanding of storage hierarchies, we briefly review some basic concepts of their design.

Hierarchy Concepts

The purpose of a storage system is to hold information and to associate the information with a logical address space known to the remainder of the computer system. For example, the Central Processing Unit (CPU) may present a logical address to the storage system with instructions to either retrieve or modify the information associated with that address. If the storage system consists of a single device, then the logical address space corresponds directly to the physical address space of the device. Alternatively, a storage system with the same address space can be realized by a hierarchy of storage devices ranging from fast but expensive to slower but relatively inexpensive devices. In such storage hierarchies, the logical address space is often partitioned into equal-size pages (or unequal-size segments) that represent the blocks of information being moved between devices in the hierarchy.

Editor's Note: From *IBM Systems Journal,* vol. 9, no. 2, 1970. Reprinted by permission of the publisher, International Business Machines Corporation, and the authors.

A hierarchy management facility is included to control the movement of pages and to effect the (generally dynamic) association between the logical address space and the physical address space of the hierarchy. When the CPU references a logical address, the hierarchy management facility first determines the physical location of the corresponding logical page and may then move the page to a fast storage device where the reference is effected. Since these actions are "transparent" to the remainder of the computer system (except for timing), the logical operation of the hierarchy is indistinguishable from that of a single-device system.

The goal of the hierarchy management facility is to maximize the number of times logical information is in the faster devices when being referenced. As this goal is approached, most references are directed to the fast, small stores, whereas most of the logical address space is distributed over the slower, large stores. The storage system then acquires the approximate speed of the fast stores while maintaining the approximate cost-per-bit of the slower and less expensive stores. This increase in cost-performance is the primary justification for storage hierarchies.

Clearly, many factors can affect the cost-performance of a storage hierarchy. On the performance side, one must consider the capacity and characteristics of each storage device, the physical structure of the hierarchy, the way in which information is moved by the hierarchy management facility, and the expected pattern of storage references. On the cost side, the hardware and/or software required to find and move logical information must be considered, as well as the cost-per-bit and capacity of each device. Because of these factors, it is quite difficult to design an "optimal" hierarchy.

The typical approach to hierarchy evaluation employed by computer designers has been to simulate as many hierarchy systems as possible, at various levels of detail [9-12]. During the first stages of design, a large number of relatively simple simulations may be run with fixed, standard address traces. These traces are assumed to be "typical sequences of storage references obtained from existing computer systems; they are used to approximate the reference behavior of future systems. The purpose of these simulations is to measure such statistics as data flow and frequency of access to each device in order to estimate the overall performance of an actual system. The resulting performance estimates can then be used to narrow the field of possible designs, which then receive more detailed examination.

Alternatively, one may try to develop analytical techniques that avoid point-by-point simulation but still yield accurate statistics for data flow and access frequencies. Several papers deal with such techniques for hierarchy evaluation [4-6]. In general, the approach here is to run a relatively small number of simulations and extrapolate the measured statistics to a larger class of hierarchies. The difficulty with this approach is the need for various assumptions about the statistical properties of address traces and data flows required to formulate the analytical equations. Moreover, it is difficult to include a quantitative dependence on such factors as data path structure, page replacement algorithm [13], and address mapping scheme [3], so that many simulations may still be necessary.

Objectives of the Paper

This paper presents a technique that can be used to circumvent much of the simulation effort required in hierarchy evaluation. Specifically, we present an efficient procedure that determines, for a given address trace, the exact frequency of access to each level of a hierarchy as a function of page size, replacement algorithm, number of levels, and capacity at each level. In the following we consider a class of multilevel, demand-paging hierarchies [14] with the same replacement algorithm at every level. The procedures developed here are applicable to a large class of well-known replacement algorithms having certain inclusion properties defined later. These algorithms—which we call stack algorithms—include "least frequently used," "least recently used," "optimal," and a "random" replacement algorithm.

THE SYSTEM MODEL

Basic Model Concepts

An H-level paged storage hierarchy consists of a collection of storage devices, $M_1, M_2, \cdots, M_H$, a network of data paths connecting the devices, and a hierarchy management facility. Each device is partitioned into physical blocks called *page frames*. For convenience, the highest-level store M_1 is called the *local store* and the lowest-level store M_H is the *backing store*, as shown in Figure 2-1. The hierarchy management facility controls page movement between the devices and associates each logical page with a physical page frame. Special storage and processing hardware may be required, but they are not included in our model.

References to the storage hierarchy are presented by a single device called the *generator* and are sequentially serviced in the order in which they are presented. References from the generator may represent the requests of several devices, such as the CPU and the channel, in an actual system. The time sequence of logical-address references $X = x_1, x_2, \cdots, x_L$ is called an *address trace*, where each address consists of n bits as shown in Figure 2-2. The set of 2^n possible addresses is partitioned into 2^k pages of 2^{n-k} logical addresses each. The high-order k bits of each address represent the number of the page containing the address, and the low-order $n - k$ bits represent the location or displacement of the address within the page. Since information movement on the hierarchy is accomplished by transferring pages between levels, we can analyze space allocation and data movement for a trace X by considering a corresponding *page trace* $X^k = x_1^k, x_2^k, \cdots, x_L^k$—where each x_t^k is the number of the page containing address x_t. When we consider a given fixed-page size, we omit the superscript k and denote pages by x_t.

A reference from the generator can be serviced only from the local store M_1. Thus if the desired page resides in a lower level device M_i, i.e. where $i > 1$, the hierarchy management facility must bring that page up to M_1 for servicing. The

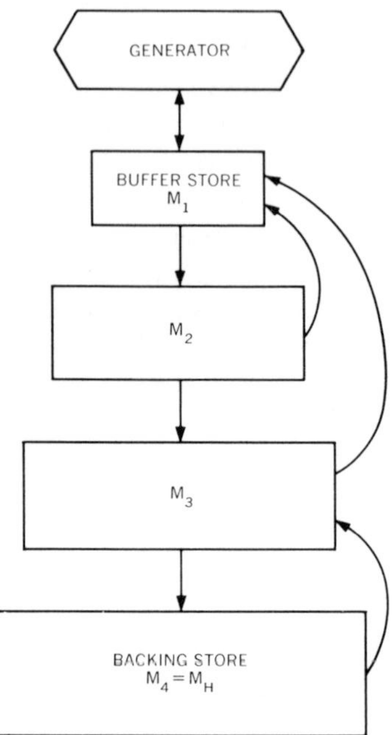

Figure 2-1. Linear Storage Hierarchy

hierarchy provides a path for bringing pages up to M_1, which may or may not require staging through intermediate levels. Any temporary storage required for bringing a page up to M_1 is included in the hierarchy management hardware, and is therefore not represented in our model. In this paper we restrict our attention to *linear storage hierarchies* in which the only paths for moving pages down the hierarchy are direct ones from each level M_i to level M_{i+1}, where $i = 1, 2, \cdots, H - 1$. The reasons for this restriction are discussed later in this paper. Note that the four-level hierarchy in Figure 2-1 is a linear hierarchy.

The capacity of the backing store is assumed to be at least 2^k page frames, and all logical pages initially reside in the backing store. At any time, each logical page resides in exactly one page frame of the hierarchy. A *mapping function* is associated with each hierarchical level, and it specifies for each logical page the page frames it may occupy in that level. The mapping function is further defined as:

- *Unconstrained* if any page can occupy any page frame of the storage device.
- *Fully constrained* if each page can occupy only a single page frame.
- *Partially constrained* in all other cases.

In a later section we define a technique called "congruence mapping," which generates a whole spectrum of mapping functions.

For simplicity in developing techniques for analyzing storage hierarchies, we first consider a two-level, demand-paged hierarchy with unconstrained mapping.

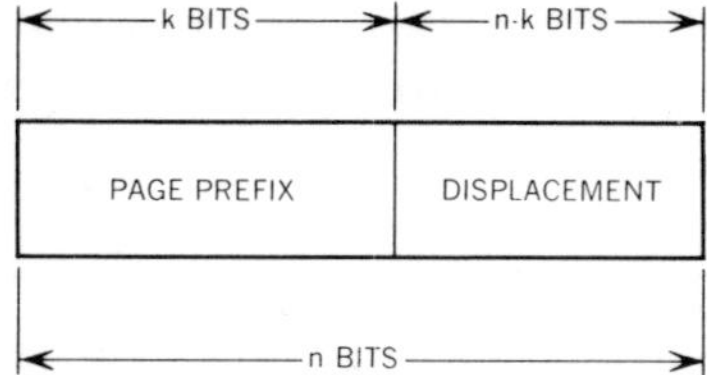

Figure 2-2. Logical Address

Later our results are extended to certain classes of multilevel linear hierarchies employing the three types of mapping functions. The local store, or buffer, has a capacity of C pages and is directly connected to the backing store, as shown in Figure 2-3. At time t the generator presents a request for page x_t to the hierarchy. Under *demand paging*, if x_t is in the buffer, the reference proceeds and no page movement occurs. Otherwise, x_t is brought to the buffer from the backing store. If the buffer is already full, x_t replaces some page y_t in the buffer. The selection of the particular page y_t is performed by the buffer *replacement algorithm.* This operation is a key element of storage management.

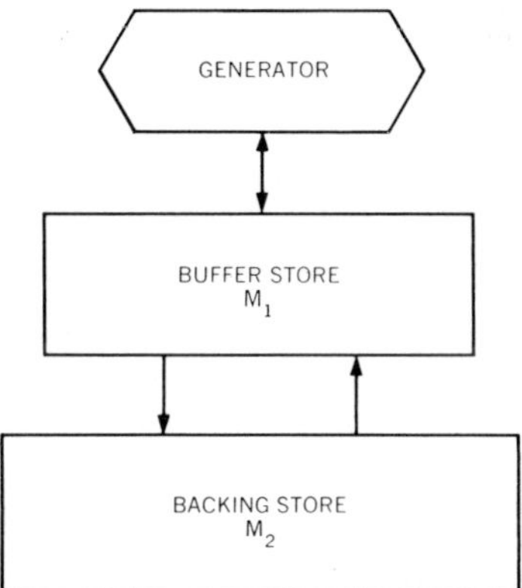

Figure 2-3. Two-Level Hierarchy

In the two-level hierarchy shown in Figure 2-3, a reference to a page residing at either level M_1 or M_2 is called an access to that level.

For a given hierarchy and page trace, we define the *access frequencies* F_1 and F_2 where F_i is the relative number of accesses to level M_i during the processing of the trace. Thus, if N_1 accesses are made to level M_1, and $N_2 = L - N_1$ accesses are made to level M_2, we obtain $F_1 = N_1/L$ and $F_2 = N_2/L$.

Some important measures of storage hierarchy performance can be obtained from these access frequencies. For example, one can combine access frequencies with a set of effective access times $\{T_i\}$ to obtain an effective (or average) hierarchy access time

$$\bar{T} = F_1 T_1 + F_2 T_2$$

In general, access times depend on the access paths, device access times, and characteristics of the hierarchy management facility. The access frequencies depend only on the page trace, capacity of the buffer, and replacement algorithm.

For a two-level hierarchy, accesses to the buffer are called *successes*; the relative frequency of success as a function of capacity is given by the *success function* $F(C)$. For a given capacity C, page trace $X = x_1, x_2, \cdots x_L$, replacement algorithm, and arbitrary time t (where $1 \leqslant t \leqslant L$), the set of pages in the buffer just after the completed reference to x_t is denoted by $B_t(C)$. The initial buffer contents is represented by $B_0(C)$. By convention

$$B_0(C) = \phi$$

for all C where ϕ is the empty set. The set of distinct pages references in $x_1, x_2, \cdots, x_t$ is denoted by Γ_t, and the number of pages in Γ_t is denoted by

$$\gamma_t = |\Gamma_t|$$

Demand paging in the two-level hierarchy is formally defined by the following requirements, wherein the operator "+" denotes the union of disjoint sets:

1. If $x_t \in B_{t-1}(C)$ then $B_t(C) = B_{t-1}(C)$
2. If $x_t \notin B_{t-1}(C)$ and $|B_{t-1}(C)| < C$ then $B_t(C) = B_{t-1}(C) + \{x_t\}$
3. If $x_t \notin B_{t-1}(C)$ and $|B_{t-1}(C)| = C$ then $B_t(C) = B_{t-1}(C) - \{y_t\} + \{x_t\}$

where $y_t \in B_{t-1}(C)$ is determined by the replacement algorithm. Under demand paging, a buffer of capacity C simply fills as required by 1 and 2, while the first C distinct pages are referenced. Subsequently, referenced pages are swapped in, as required by 1 and 3.

LEAST RECENTLY USED REPLACEMENT

We now consider a particular replacement algorithm called "least recently used" (LRU) and show that the entire success function can be obtained by stack processing in a single pass of the address trace. Briefly, the single-pass technique requires the maintaining of a list of pages, called an LRU stack, and measuring a distance on this stack for every page reference. Frequencies of these stack distances are used to calculate the success function. The existence of the LRU stack follows from an inclusion property satisfied by LRU replacement, whereas the use of distance frequencies hinges on the related concept of critical capacity.

Success Function

Under LRU the page selected for replacement is the one that has not been referenced for the longest time (i.e., the least recently used page). One way to obtain the success function for a given trace is to simulate the two-level hierarchy system for each buffer capacity. Such a simulation determines the buffer contents at every time t, and counts the number of times the current reference x_t is found in the buffer. In Figure 2-4 we show an example of this simulation procedure for a given page trace and buffer capacities $C = 1, 2, 3, 4$. Pages are denoted by lower-case letters, and page successes are marked by asterisks.

A greatly simplified method for obtaining the success function under LRU replacement can be derived from certain properties of that replacement algorithm. For any page trace and buffer capacity C, the buffer is initially empty, and in, say, τ time units, it fills up with the first C distinct pages referenced by the trace. At time τ, the buffer contains the C pages most recently referenced through time τ. When a new page is referenced at a later time ($t > \tau$), this page replaces the last recently used page in the buffer. Thus at time t, the buffer still contains the C most recently referenced pages. It is easy to see that under LRU the buffer contains the C most recently referenced pages for all subsequent times, and that

TIME	1	2	3	4	5	6	7	8	9	10
PAGE TRACE	a	b	b	c	b	a	d	c	a	a
SIMULATIONS										
C=1 F(1)=0.20	a	b	b *	c	b	a	d	c	a	a *
C=2 F(2)=0.30	a	a b	a b *	c b	c b *	a b	a d	c d	c a	c a *
C=3 F(3)=0.50	a	a b	a b *	a b c	a b c *	a b c *	a b d	a c d	a c d *	a c d *
C=4 F(4)=0.60	a	a	a b *	a b c	a b c *	a b c *	a b c d	a b c d *	a b c d *	a b c d *

Figure 2-4. Determining Success Function by Buffer Simulation

this property holds for all page traces and buffer capacities. One can generate the buffer contents $B_t(C)$ for any time t on a trace and any capacity by scanning backward from point t and collecting the first C distinct pages encountered.

Since the set of C most recently referenced pages is always contained in the set of $C + 1$ most recently referenced pages, the buffer contents $B_t(C)$ at any time must be a subset of $B_t(C + 1)$. In fact, $B_t(C)$ is a proper subset of $B_t(C + 1)$ if at least $C + 1$ distinct pages have been referenced through time t, More formally, under LRU replacement, the buffer contents for any page trace $X = x_1, x_2, \cdots, x_L$ and any time t (where $1 \leqslant t \leqslant L$) satisfy the following *inclusion property*:

$$B_t(1) \subset B_t(2) \subset \cdots \subset B_t(\gamma_t) = B_t(\gamma_t + 1) = \cdots \qquad (1)$$

where

$$|B_t(C)| = C \qquad \text{for } 1 \leqslant C \leqslant \gamma_t$$

and

$$|B_t(C)| = \gamma_t \qquad \text{for } C \geqslant \gamma_t$$

The inclusion property can be observed in Figure 2-4 where at time $t = 5$, for example

$$B_t(1) = \{b\}$$

$$B_t(2) = \{c, b\}$$

$$B_t(3) = \{a, b, c\}$$

and

$$B_t(4) = \{a, b, c\}$$

Because of the inclusion property the buffer contents at any time and for all capacities can be represented in the following compact and useful way. We order the set of pages Γ_t into a list $S_t = s_t(1), s_t(2), \cdots s_t(\gamma_t)$, where

$$s_t(i) = B_t(i) - B_t(i-1) \qquad \text{for } i = 1, 2, \cdots, \gamma_t \qquad (2)$$

Hence

$$B_t(C) = \begin{cases} \{s_t(1), s_t(2), \cdots, s_t(C)\} & \text{for } C \leqslant \gamma_t \\ \{s_t(1), s_t(2), \cdots, s_t(\gamma_t)\} & \text{for } C \geqslant \gamma_t \end{cases} \qquad (3)$$

The list S_t is referred to as the *LRU stack*, with $s_t(1)$ as the top entry and $s_t(\gamma_t)$ as the bottom entry. As an example, the LRU stack for $t = 5$ in Figure 2-4 is

$$S_5 = [b, c, a]$$

The stack S_0 at time $t = 0$ has no entries and is therefore called a null stack, that is, one with no entries. The entire sequence of LRU stacks corresponding to Figure 2-4 is included in Figure 2-5.

TIME	1	2	3	4	5	6	7	8	9	10
PAGE TRACE	a	b	b	c	b	a	d	c	a	a
LRU STACK	a	b	b	c	b	a	d	c	a	a
		a	a	b	c	b	a	d	c	c
				a	a	c	b	a	d	d
							c	b	b	b
STACK DISTANCE	∞	∞	1	∞	2	3	∞	4	3	1
DISTANCE COUNTERS n(\)										
1	0	0	1	1	1	1	1	1	1	(2)
2	0	0	0	0	1	1	1	1	1	(1)
3	0	0	0	0	0	1	1	1	2	(2)
4	0	0	0	0	0	0	0	1	1	(1)
∞	1	2	2	3	3	3	4	4	4	(4)

Figure 2-5. Sequence of LRU Stacks

Besides representing the buffer contents for all capacities, the LRU stack can be used to efficiently determine the success function $F(C)$. Let us suppose that at time t, page x_t has been previously referenced and thus is a member of at least one set $B_{t-1}(C)$, where $1 \leqslant C \leqslant \gamma_{t-1}$. Let C_t denote the least buffer capacity such that

$$x_t \in B_{t-1}(C)$$

We call C_t the *critical capacity* since, from the inclusion property given in Equation 1, $x_t \in B_{t-1}(C)$ if and only if $C \geqslant C_t$. If x_t has not been previously referenced, we set $C_t = \infty$ because x_t is not contained in a buffer of any finite capacity.

From the definition of LRU stacks in Equation 2, it may be seen that C_t is simply the position of page x_t in the stack S_{t-1}, so that

$$x_t = s_{t-1}(C_t)$$

We call this page position the *stack distance* Δ_t, since Δ_t is essentially the "distance" from the top of the stack to

$$x_t = s_{t-1}(\Delta_t)$$

(Note that here $\Delta_t = C_t$. When constrained mapping functions are considered, the stack distance may not always equal the critical capacity.) If x_t has not been previously referenced, then Δ_t is set to infinity. The sequence of stack distances for our example is included in Figure 2-5.

The significance of stack distances is that they lead directly to the success function. To see this, let $n(\Delta)$ be the number of times the stack distance Δ is observed in processing a trace. Since the stack distance equals the critical capacity, the number of times that the referenced page is found in the buffer is

$$N(C) = \sum_{\Delta=1}^{C} n(\Delta) \tag{4}$$

and the success function is given by the expression

$$F(C) = N(C)/L \tag{5}$$

In practice the set $\{n(\Delta)\}$ can be determined from a set of distance counters, as shown in Figure 2-5. All counters are set initially to zero, and the counter for each distance Δ is incremented whenever that distance occurs. For k-bit page numbers, we need at most $2^k + 1$ counters, corresponding to $1 \leqslant \Delta \leqslant 2^k$ and $\Delta = \infty$. At the conclusion of a page trace, the final values of the distance counters are the values $\{n(\Delta)\}$, and $F(C)$ is obtained from Equations 4 and 5.

Numerical Example

We now calculate the value of the success function in a numerical example. For Δ's of 1, 2, 3, 4, and ∞, the corresponding final counter values in Figure 2-5 are

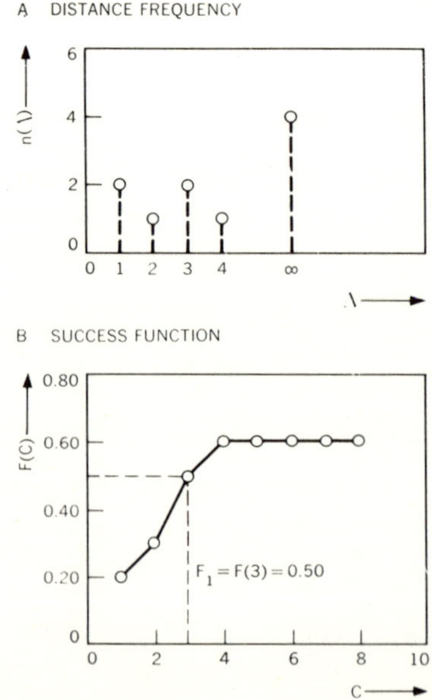

Figure 2-6. Obtaining Success Function from Distance Frequencies

2, 1, 2, 1, and 4. This distribution is shown in Figure 2-6(A). Dividing by L equals 10 in Figure 2-5, and summing cumulatively, we obtain the success function shown in Figure 2-6(B). One can verify that the $F(C)$ values for the curve in Figure 2-6(B) agree with those obtained in the simulations of Figure 2-4.

To find the access frequencies F_1 and F_2, for a given buffer capacity C, we take $F_1 = F(C_1)$ and $F_2 = 1 - F_1$. As an example, for $C = 3$ pages, $F_1 = F(3) = 0.50$ as indicated in Figure 2-6(B), $F_2 = 1 - 0.50 = 0.50$, and the average access time $\overline{T}$ of the hierarchy is $0.50T_1 + 0.50T_2$.

Note that $F(C)$ is always a monotonic, nondecreasing function of C for LRU replacement, since $F(C)$ is obtained by cumulative summation as shown in Equation 4. Also, $F(C)$ never exceeds $(L - \gamma_L)/L$ for any capacity, because all pages initially reside in the backing store.

To avoid constructing each LRU stack separately, we now give an iterative construction of S_t from S_{t-1} and x_t. Observe that at every time t, the stack S_t is simply the list of pages in Γ_t, according to their most recent reference. The most recently referenced page is $s_t(1)$ since $s_t(1) = x_t$. The second most recently referenced page is $s_t(2)$, and $s_t(\gamma_t)$ is the least recently referenced page in Γ_t.

Let us suppose that page x_t has been previously referenced and appears at position Δ on stack S_{t-1}. For time t, we know that x_t must be the top entry in S_t, because it is the most recently referenced page. Consider now a page b at some position j on S_{t-1} where $1 \leqslant j \leqslant \Delta$. At time $t - 1$, page b is the jth most recently referenced page, and the intervening pages do not include x_t. At time t, page x_t is added to this set so that page b must now be at position $j + 1$ on stack S_t. If j is greater than Δ, page b must remain at position j at time t, since the set of more recently referenced pages is unchanged from time $t - 1$.

The net effect of this page motion is shown in Figure 2-7(A). Page x_t is moved to the top of the stack, pages previously above x_t are down-shifted one position, and all other pages retain the same position. If x_t were not previously referenced, x_t would be placed on the top and all other pages would be down-shifted one position as shown in Figure 2-7(B).

This iterative procedure can be used to generate the sequence of stacks in Figure 2-5. In an actual evaluation, it is not necessary to store the entire sequence of stacks. Rather, only the current stack must be maintained as the trace is scanned. When a page reference occurs, that page is put on the top of the stack, and entries in the stack are down-shifted one-by-one, starting from the top. If page x_t is encountered, its distance Δ_t is recorded and x_t is erased because it has already been placed on top. The position vacated by x_t is filled by the page downshifted from position $\Delta_t - 1$. If x_t is not encountered, the downshifting proceeds to the bottom of the stack, and distance $\Delta_t = \infty$ is recorded.

STACK ALGORITHMS

We now examine the general class of replacement algorithms that satisfy the inclusion property. Such algorithms are called *stack algorithms*. It is shown that

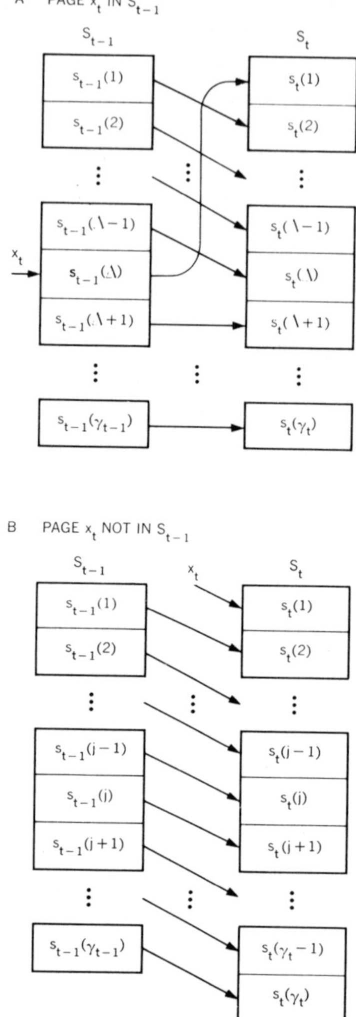

Figure 2-7. Constructing LRU Stacks

stacks can be iteratively maintained for any stack algorithm and that stack distance frequencies for a given trace can be used to obtain the corresponding success function. The main problems considered are (1) to efficiently generate stacks $\{S_t\}$ for an arbitrary stack algorithm, and (2) to identify those algorithms that are stack algorithms. Several examples of stack algorithms are described, along with one replacement algorithm that is not a stack algorithm.

A replacement algorithm is called a *stack algorithm* if the buffer contents in a demand-paged, two-level hierarchy satisfy the inclusion property given in Equation 1 for every page trace and every point in time. As shown for LRU replacement, a stack can be defined according to Equation 2 in such a way that the buffer contents for all capacities are given by Equation 3. Furthermore, since the stack distance Δ_t is a critical capacity, the success function for any page trace can be obtained by summing the stack distance frequencies $\{n(\Delta)\}$ according to Equation 4. This summation implies that the success function is a monotonic and nondecreasing function of the capacity C for every stack algorithm.

Stack Generation

Let us now consider a replacement algorithm R as a collection of mappings

$$R_C : B_{t-1}(C) \to y_t(C) \qquad \text{where} \qquad y_t(C) \in B_{t-1}(C)$$

is the page replaced by x_t in a buffer of capacity C. From the constraints of demand paging, we know that R is applied only when the following conditions are true: $x_t \notin B_{t-1}(C)$ and $|B_{t-1}(C)| = C$. If the inclusion property is satisfied up to and including time $t - 1$, then R must satisfy certain restrictions at time t to maintain the inclusion property. Specifically, if a replacement is required for some capacity $C + 1$ (and therefore for C), then $y_t(C + 1)$ must be either $y_t(C)$ or $s_{t-1}(C + 1)$. To prove this, let us assume the following:

$$B_{t-1}(C) \subset B_{t-1}(C + 1)$$

$$|B_{t-1}(C)| = C$$

$$|B_{t-1}(C + 1)| = C + 1$$

and

$$x_t \notin B_{t-1}(C + 1)$$

Note that from Equation 2, page $s_{t-1}(C + 1)$ is contained in $B_{t-1}(C + 1)$ but not in $B_{t-1}(C)$. If page $y_t(C + 1)$ is neither $s_{t-1}(C + 1)$ nor $y_t(C)$, then $y_t(C + 1)$ is some other page $z \in B_{t-1}(C)$. However, page z is included in $B_t(C)$, but not in $B_t(C + 1)$, which would violate the inclusion property.

We have given a necessary condition for stack algorithms. The same condition is also sufficient, because if $y_t(C + 1)$ is either $y_t(C)$ or $s_{t-1}(C + 1)$, then $B_t(C)$ is a subset of $B_t(C + 1)$. Therefore we conclude that a replacement algorithm is a stack algorithm if and only if for every time t

$$y_t(C + 1) = s_{t-1}(C + 1) \qquad \text{or} \qquad y_t(C+1) = y_t(C) \tag{6}$$

for

$$1 \leqslant C < \gamma_{t-1} \qquad \text{and} \qquad C + 1 < \Delta_t$$

Stack Algorithm Identification

Important replacement algorithms that satisfy Equation 6 are those that induce a total ordering on all previously referenced pages and use this ordering to make replacement decisions. The ordering can be represented in the form of a *priority list*

$$P_t = p_t(1), p_t(2), \cdots, p_t(\gamma_{t-1})$$

where $p_t(i)$ has a higher priority than $p_t(i+1)$ for $1 \leqslant i < \gamma_{t-1}$. The algorithm then selects for replacement the page in $B_{t-1}(C)$ that has the lowest priority.

A convenient notation for working with priorities is $\min(A)$, where A is an arbitrary set of pages in Γ_{t-1}, and $\min(A)$ is the unique page in A having lowest priority on the list P_t. If $B_{t-1}(C) \subset B_{t-1}(C+1)$ and $x_t \notin B_{t-1}(C+1)$, we can express the replaced pages $y_t(C)$ and $y_t(C+1)$ as follows:

$$y_t(C) = \min\ [B_{t-1}(C)] \tag{7}$$

and

$$y_t(C+1) = \min\ [B_{t-1}(C+1)] \tag{8}$$

$$= \min\ [B_{t-1}(C), s_{t-1}(C+1)] \tag{9}$$

$$= \min\{\min\ [B_{t-1}(C)], s_{t-1}(C+1)\} \tag{10}$$

$$= \min\ [y_t(C), s_{t-1}(C+1)] \tag{11}$$

Equations 7 to 9 are based on the definition of the replacement algorithm, whereas Equation 10 is based on the properties of minimization.

We conclude from Equation 11 that any replacement algorithm that induces a priority list P_t for every time t satisfies Equation 6 and is therefore a stack algorithm. For example, the priority list for LRU is just the ordering of pages in Γ_{t-1} by most recent reference. The priority list for least frequently used (LRU) replacement is the ordering of referenced pages by most frequent reference, together with a scheme to break ties.

Stack Updating

Before describing other examples of stack algorithms, let us develop a stack updating procedure for algorithms inducing a priority list. For any page trace $X = x_1, x_2, \cdots, x_L$ and any time t, where $1 \leqslant t \leqslant L$, suppose that stack S_{t-1} is available. Also, for any two pages $a, b \in \Gamma_{t-1}$, let max (a, b) denote the page having higher priority. If x_t has been previously referenced and appears at position Δ_t on stack S_{t-1}, the stack at time t is given by

$$s_t(1) = x_t \tag{12}$$

$$s_t(i) = \max\ [y_t(i-1), s_{t-1}(i)] \quad \text{for} \quad 2 \leqslant i < \Delta_t \tag{13}$$

$$s_t(\Delta_t) = y_t(\Delta_t - 1) \tag{14}$$

$$s_t(i) = s_{t-1}(i) \qquad \text{for } \Delta_t < i \leqslant \gamma_{t-1} \tag{15}$$

Equations 12, 14, and 15 are based on the constraints of demand paging, whereas Equation 13 is derived from Equation 11.

If x_t has not been previously referenced, the defining equations for stack S_t are the following:

$$s_t(1) = x_t \tag{16}$$

$$s_t(i) = \max\,[y_t(i-1), s_{t-1}(i)] \quad \text{for } 2 \leqslant i \leqslant \gamma_{t-1} \tag{17}$$

$$s_t(\gamma_t) = y_t(\gamma_{t-1}) \tag{18}$$

In this case, Equations 16 and 17 express the fact that replacements are required for all buffer capacities in the range $1 \leqslant C \leqslant \gamma_{t-1}$. Equation 18 corresponds to the new page x_t being added to the stack, with the result that a buffer of capacity

$$\gamma_t = \gamma_{t-1} + 1$$

is now full.

Figure 2-8 illustrates the stack updating procedure as given in Equations 12 to 18. The top entry $s_t(1)$ is always x_t, and the first page replaced is

$$y_t(1) = s_{t-1}(1) \qquad \text{for } \Delta_t > 1$$

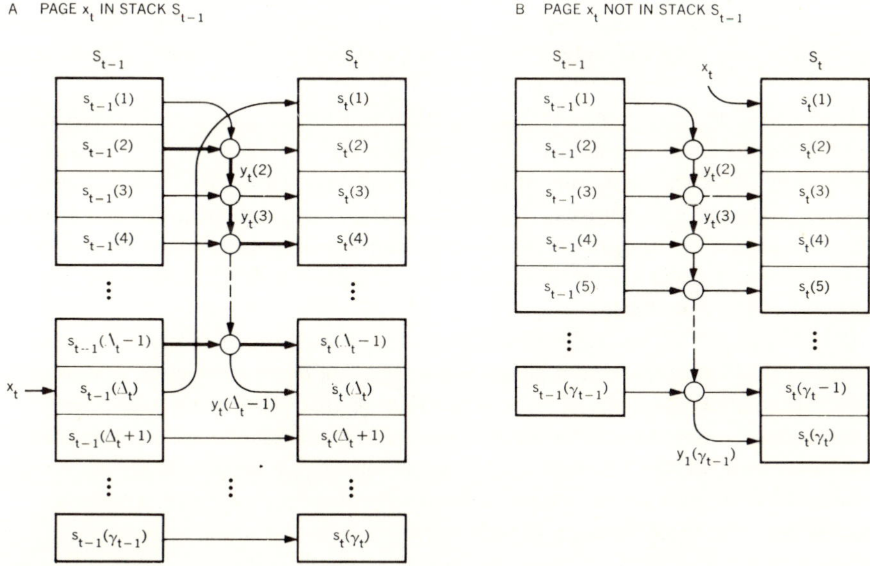

Figure 2-8. Stack Updating

Each subsequent entry $s_t(i)$ is then determined iteratively from $s_{t-1}(i)$ and $y_t(i-1)$ according to Equation 13 or 17. If x_t is found on stack S_{t-1} as shown in Figure 2-8(A), we use Equation 14 to determine $s_t(\Delta_t)$. All lower entries are unchanged from time $t-1$. If x_t is not found on stack S_{t-1}, as shown in Figure 2-8(B), then $\Delta_t = \infty$ and we use Equation 18. In either case, the replacement algorithm does not have to be applied to all the pages for stack updating. Only a sequence of pairwise decisions between pages $s_{t-1}(i)$ and $y_t(i-1)$ is required.

Comparing our stack updating procedure with the one for LRU shown in Figure 2-7, we see that page $y_t(C)$ under LRU is always $s_{t-1}(C)$. In fact, the priority list P_t is exactly equal to stack S_{t-1}, since both lists give the order of pages in Γ_{t-1} by most recent reference. Thus

$$y_t(C) = s_{t-1}(C)$$

and Equations 13 and 17 then reduce to

$$\begin{aligned} s_t(i) &= \max\,[s_{t-1}(i-1), s_{t-1}(i)] \\ &= s_{t-1}(i-1) \end{aligned}$$

For an arbitrary stack algorithm, the stack updating is more complex than for LRU, and the order of stack elements at time $t-1$ may be very different from that at time t.

Examples of Stack Algorithms

Let us now examine several examples of stack algorithms. In general, any replacement algorithm that bases its decisions on some page usage quantity, whether measured or predicted, naturally induces a priority list and is therefore a stack algorithm. One example, of course, is LRU, and another example, previously mentioned, is least frequently used (LFU) replacement.

Under LFU the page replaced from a buffer at time t is that page that has been referenced the fewest number of times over the interval $1 \leqslant \tau \leqslant t$, or perhaps over some "backward window" interval $t-h \leqslant \tau \leqslant t$, where $0 < h \leqslant t$. If two or more pages are tied for least frequency of use, then some arbitrary rule is used to break the tie. As long as the rule is consistent for all pages and all capacities (e.g., if the tied pages are numerically ordered) a priority list P_t is induced, and LFU is a stack algorithm.

Other examples of stack algorithms may arise in analytical studies of program behavior. If an address trace is generated from some random process, it may be desirable to study the behavior of replacement algorithms that base their decisions on the parameters of the random process. One such process is a time-invariant, first-order Markov chain [15, 16], where any page c is referenced immediately after page b with a fixed transition probability π_{bc}. The process is completely described by the matrix $\Pi = \{\pi_{bc}\}$, (where b and c range over all referenced pages) and by the page referenced at time $t = 1$.

One possible replacement algorithm is to remove the page least likely to be referenced next. We call this strategy "least transition probability" (LTP) since, for page x_t equal to page b, the page c chosen for removal is the one that minimizes π_{bc} over those pages in the buffer. Supplying an appropriate rule for breaking ties, we see that LTP induces a priority list and is a stack algorithm.

Another replacement algorithm is to remove the page with the largest expected time until next reference. We call this strategy LNR for "longest next reference."

The expected times until next reference can be obtained from the Π-matrix by standard techniques [17]. As with LTP, LNR induces a priority list if we supply an appropriate tie-breaking rule.

To analyze an actual program trace under LTP or LNR (perhaps for testing a Markov model of the program), page reference statistics may be used to estimate the matrix Π. For example, the observed transition frequencies over some interval $t - h$ to t can be used to generate a time-varying estimator matrix $\hat{\Pi}_t$. A priority list P_t can then be constructed for each time t according to the probabilities in $\hat{\Pi}_t$, with the result that the overall strategy for replacement remains a stack algorithm.

Other stack algorithms may base their decisions on information from the programmer or compiler, or on properties of the computer system. For example, the programmer or compiler may supply to the system [14] special "program directives" that indicate which pages should be given high priorities in the immediate future. Another case is where the operating system assigns priorities to program pages in a multiprogrammed system, based perhaps on the position of the program in the task queue. If all the pages in the address space can be ordered in a priority list P_t for each time t, the resulting replacement algorithm is a stack algorithm.

First-In/First-Out

In the examples given, we see that priority lists can arise in a variety of ways. We now consider a replacement algorithm called "first-in/first-out" (FIFO) that is not a stack algorithm. Under FIFO, the page that has remained in the buffer for the longest (continuous) time up to time t is removed.

A peculiarity of FIFO is illustrated by the following page trace

$$X = a\ b\ c\ d\ a\ b\ e\ a\ b\ c\ d\ e$$

As shown in Reference 18, the success function for this trace is not monotonic, and takes the form shown in Figure 2-9. Since stack algorithms have monotonic success functions, we conclude that FIFO is not a stack algorithm and does not induce a priority list P_t at every time t. In amplifying this conclusion, we note that the relative priorities between pages in Γ_{t-1} may depend on the buffer capacity C. Thus in the example, one can verify that page d has the lowest priority of all pages in $B_6(3)$ in the sense that d has been in the buffer longest. However, page d has highest priority in $B_6(4)$, since it was brought into the buffer latest.

Whenever the priorities among pages depend on the capacity of the buffer, we cannot define a single priority list that applies to every capacity. One instance of this is when priorities depend on the frequency of reference to pages after their entering the buffer. Another case is when priorities depend on total time spent in the buffer.

As long as priorities are independent of capacity and as long as one can order

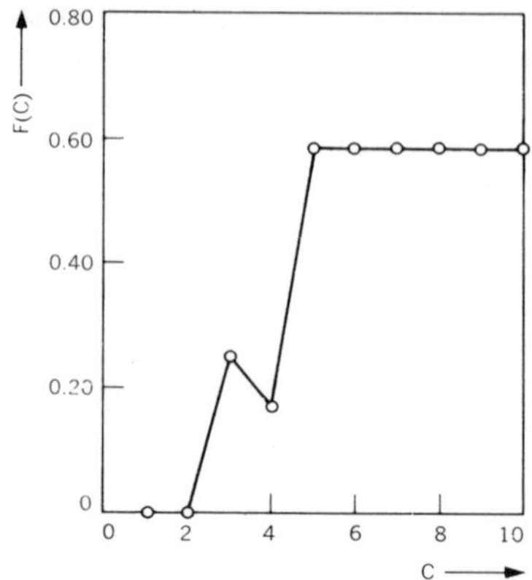

Figure 2-9. Success Function for FIFO Replacement

the referenced pages to reflect these priorities, then stack-processing techniques can be used to find the success function.

AN OPTIMUM REPLACEMENT ALGORITHM

We now discuss a replacement algorithm that yields the maximum value for the success frequency over the space of all replacement algorithms—for every page trace and every buffer capacity. Such an algorithm is said to be an *optimum replacement algorithm*. Belady [13] describes an optimum replacement algorithm called MIN and shows how to evaluate the success frequency for a given page trace and a given buffer capacity. In the following discussion, we describe a stack algorithm called OPT and prove that it is also an optimum replacement algorithm. Using certain properties of LRU and OPT, we can determine the entire success function for OPT in two passes of a page trace.

OPT

The replacement algorithm OPT has the following characteristics. Whenever a page must be pushed from the buffer, the chosen page is the one whose next reference is farthest in the future. If a tie results because two or more buffer pages are never referenced again, the tie is broken by an arbitrary rule Ω that pushes the page with the latest alphabetical or numerical order. An example of OPT replacement is shown in Figure 2-10, for the buffer capacity $C = 3$. As an illustration, notice that at time $t = 5$ page c is pushed from the buffer, since the other buffer pages a and b are referenced sooner. At time $t = 9$, page b is pushed from the buffer, because page d is referenced again (at time $t = 10$), and page a has priority over page b by our rule Ω.

A formal proof that OPT is an optimal replacement algorithm is given in the appendix of this chapter. We note here that OPT is not realizable in an actual

TIME	1	2	3	4	5	6	7	8	9	10
PAGE TRACE	a	b	c	a	d	b	a	d	c	d
BUFFER CONTENTS FOR C = 3	a	a	a	a	a	a	a	a	a	a
		b	b	b	b	b	b	b	c	c
			c	c	d	d	d	d	d	d
				*		*	*	*		*

Figure 2-10. Example of OPT Replacement

computer system because it requires knowledge of future page references. However, OPT does serve as a useful benchmark for any replacement algorithm, including stack-type algorithms. To show that OPT is a stack algorithm, observe that a priority list P_t can be constructed for OPT at each time t. Specifically, P_t is the list of the pages referenced again, ordered by their time of next reference, followed by the list of the pages not referenced again, as ordered by the tie-breaking rule Ω.

Stack Processing Example

The stack processing technique for OPT is illustrated in Figure 2-11. Priority lists are ordered as described above, and curly brackets denote the pages ordered under the rule Ω. For example, at time $t = 8$ the priority list is $P_8 = c, d, a, b,$

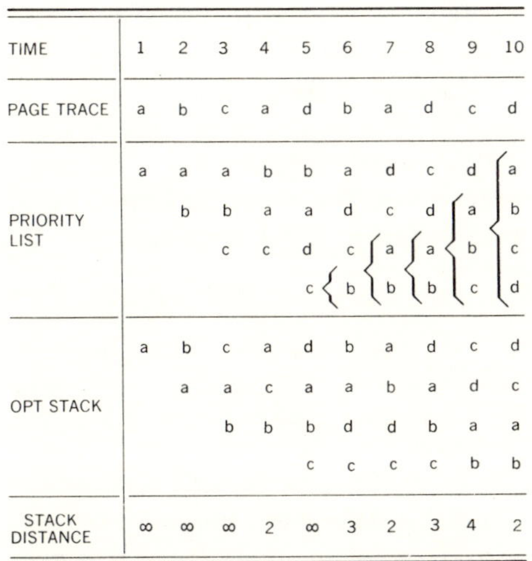

TIME	1	2	3	4	5	6	7	8	9	10
PAGE TRACE	a	b	c	a	d	b	a	d	c	d
PRIORITY LIST	a	a	a	b	b	a	d	c	d	a
		b	b	a	a	d	c	d	a	b
			c	c	d	c	a	a	b	c
					c	b	b	b	c	d
OPT STACK	a	b	c	a	d	b	a	d	c	d
		a	a	c	a	a	b	a	d	c
			b	b	b	d	d	b	a	a
					c	c	c	c	b	b
STACK DISTANCE	∞	∞	∞	2	∞	3	2	3	4	2

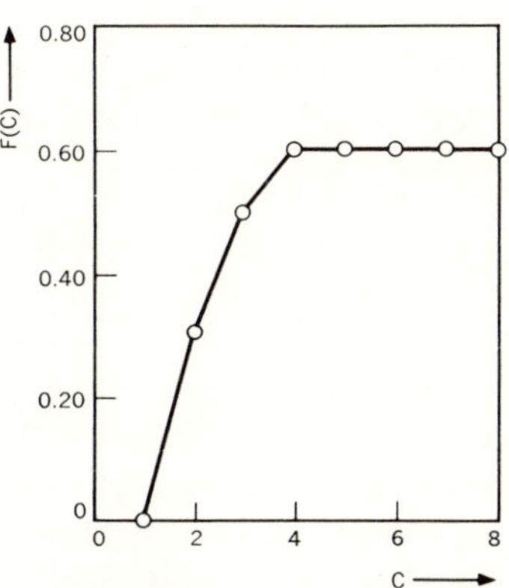

Figure 2-11. Stack Processing and Success Function for OPT Replacement

because c is the next page referenced (at $t = 9$), and d is the second page referenced (at $t = 10$). Pages a and b are not referenced again, and thus are ordered according to rule Ω. The sequence of OPT stacks is constructed using the priority lists, and the success function is obtained from the stack distance frequencies. A major difficulty with the technique is the amount of forward scanning required to construct the priority lists.

Forward Distance

Fortunately, a more efficient procedure exists for obtaining the priority lists. For a given page trace X, we define the *forward distance* $w_t(a)$ to a page a at time t as the number of distinct pages referenced in $x_{t+1}, \cdots, x_{t'}$, (where $x_{t'}$ is the first reference to page a after time t). If page a is not referenced again, the forward distance is defined as infinity. Note that the priority list under OPT is a listing of the pages in Γ_{t-1} according to their increasing forward distances. An illustrative example of forward distance determination is given in Figure 2-12.

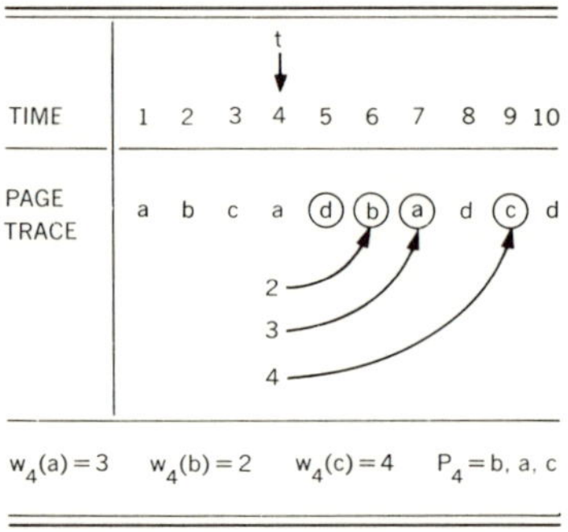

Figure 2-12. Determination of Forward Distances at Time t = 4

If the forward distances to all pages in Γ_{t-1} are known at time $t-1$, the new forward distances at time t can be determined iteratively from the single forward distance $w_t(x_t)$. Specifically, for page $a \neq x_t$ and $w_t \triangleq w_t(x_t)$, we have

$$w_t(a) = \begin{cases} w_{t-1}(a) - 1 & \text{for} \quad w_{t-1}(a) \leqslant w_t \quad \text{and} \quad w_{t-1}(a) \neq \infty \\ w_{t-1}(a) & \text{for} \quad w_{t-1}(a) > w_t \quad \text{or} \quad w_{t-1}(a) = \infty \end{cases} \tag{19}$$

To determine the sequence of forward distances $\{w_t\}$ for a page trace X, consider the *reverse trace* $X^R = x_L, x_{L-1}, \cdots, x_2, x_1$. Suppose that X^R is analyzed according to LRU replacement and that x_i and x_j denote two successive references to page a in the reverse trace. Thus $X^R = x_L, \cdots, x_i = a, \cdots, x_j = a, \cdots, x_1$. At time j, the stack distance Δ_j is the number of distinct pages referenced in $x_i, \cdots, x_{j+1}$. (Note that x_{j+1} precedes x_j in X^R.) However, this number of distinct pages is precisely the forward distance w_j for page trace X. Thus the sequence of LRU stack distances for trace X^R, namely, $\Delta_L, \Delta_{L=1}, \cdots, \Delta_2, \Delta_1$, is the reverse of the sequence of forward distances $w_1, w_2, \cdots, w_{L=1}, w_L$ for trace X.

Maximum Success Function

These results form the basis of a two-pass stack processing technique for determining the success function for OPT replacement. The technique is illustrated by Figure 2-13. The first pass is a backward scan of the page trace X using LRU replacement, denoted by the left-pointing arrow. The LRU stack distances are stored, in reverse order, on a "distance tape." The second pass is a forward scan using OPT replacement, as shown by the right-pointing arrow. Forward distances read from the distance tape are used to maintain the OPT priority lists according to Equation 19.

The LRU stack distances gathered from the reverse page trace yield important information about the forward page trace. Specifically, we claim that the success function for the reverse trace X^R under LRU replacement is equal to the success function for the forward trace X under LRU replacement. Thus one can use the backward scan of X, not only to generate the distance tape for OPT, but also to generate the success function for LRU.

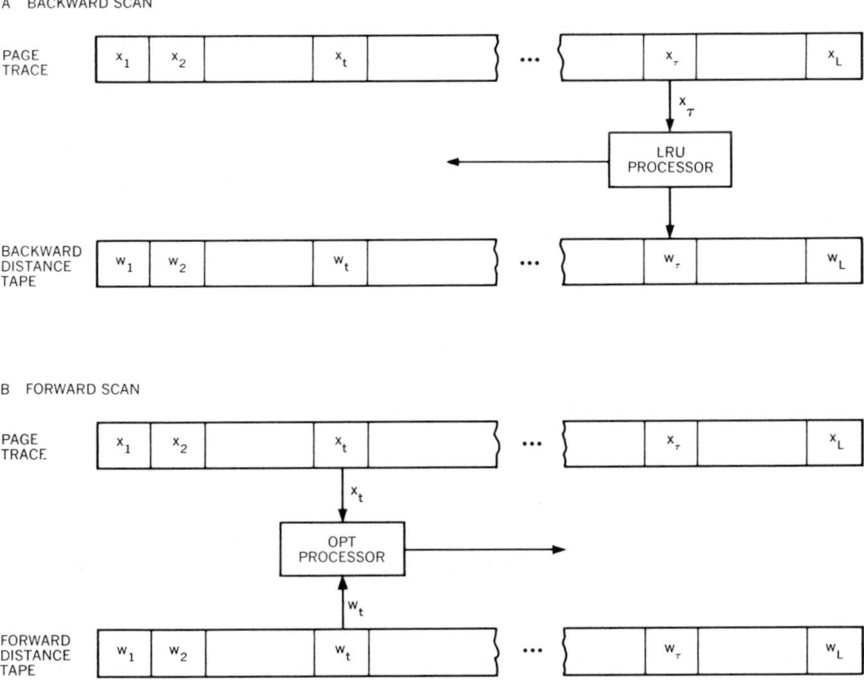

Figure 2-13. Two-Pass Technique for LRU and OPT Replacement

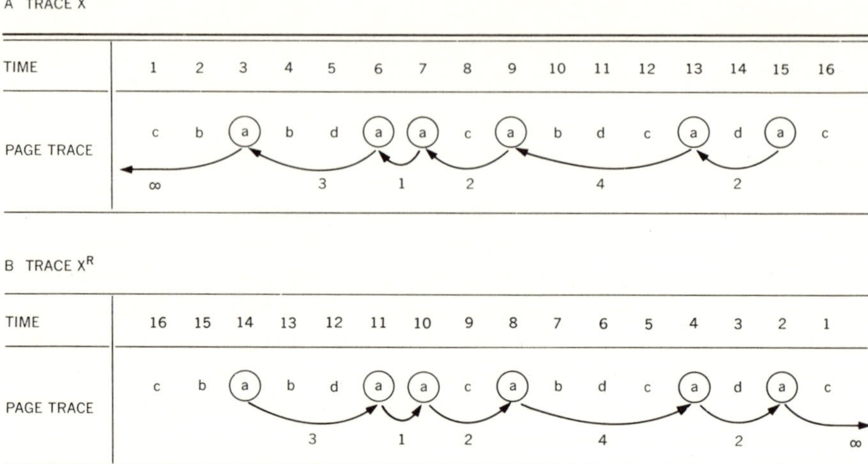

Figure 2-14. Sequence of LRU Distances for Page *a*

To prove this result, let $F_{\mathrm{LRU}}(C, X)$ denote the LRU success function for trace X, and consider the set of LRU stack distances measured for a given page a in X and X^R. As the example in Figure 2-14 illustrates, these sets are always identical. Since this holds for every distinct page in the trace, the distance frequencies for X and X^R are identical, so that the success functions $F_{\mathrm{LRU}}(C, X^R)$ and $F_{\mathrm{LRU}}(C, X)$ are equal.

Another result, which is proved in the appendix, is that $F_{\mathrm{OPT}}(C, X)$ is equal to $F_{\mathrm{OPT}}(C, X^R)$, where $F_{\mathrm{OPT}}(C, X)$ is the OPT success function for trace X. Thus our two-pass technique can be implemented with forward-backward scans as well as with backward-forward scans. During the first scan, the success function for LRU is obtained and the distance tape generated. During the second scan, the success function for OPT is obtained.

RANDOM REPLACEMENT

In the stack algorithms considered thus far, a unique success function is associated with each trace. We now extend stack-processing techniques to cover a "random replacement" algorithm (RAND) that does not always yield a unique success function. With RAND, if the buffer has a capacity of C, any given page is chosen for replacement with a probability of $1/C$. In analyzing RAND, one might perform a Monte Carlo simulation for each buffer capacity to obtain a RAND success function. Repeating these simulations would yield a set of sample success functions to characterize RAND. The sample success functions could then be used to estimate an "average" success function.

A question that arises is whether stack processing can be used to generate a sample success function for RAND or any other algorithm that bases a replacement choice on the value of some random variable. We observe that RAND is not a stack algorithm, because there certainly exists a trace and a time t for which the inclusion property fails to hold with a nonzero probability.

Our approach is to define a replacement algorithm RR, which is a stack algorithm having the same statistical properties as RAND for each capacity C. The algorithm RR is defined as follows: at each time t, the priority list P_t is obtained by randomly ordering the set of pages in Γ_{t-1} (each of the $\gamma_{t-1}!$ possible orderings is equally likely to be chosen). Observe that RR is a stack algorithm, since it induces a priority list.

To establish that RR is statistically equivalent to RAND, assume that a replacement is necessary in a buffer of capacity C at time t. Since $y_t(C) = \min\,[B_{t-1}(C)]$, and P_t is randomly chosen, the probability that any given page is $y_t(C)$ is $1/C$—the same as for RAND.

One difficulty in implementing RR is the generation of the random priority list P_t. Fortunately, it is possible to update the stack without actually constructing the entire priority list. Assuming that $\Delta_t > j$, let $q_j(t)$ denote the probability that page $s_{t-1}(j)$ has priority over page $y_t(j-1)$ at time t. If $s_{t-1}(j)$ does not have priority over $y_t(j-1)$, we know that $s_{t-1}(j) = \min\,[B_{t-1}(j)]$. Since this occurs with probability $1/j$, we obtain

$$1 - q_j(t) = 1/j$$

or

$$q_j(t) = (j-1)/j \tag{20}$$

Using Equation 20, the stack can be updated at time t for RR replacement by choosing page $s_t(j) = s_{t-1}(j)$ with probability $(j-1)/j$, for $2 \leqslant j < \Delta_t$ and $j < \gamma_{t-1}$. As a check, let us compute the probability Q that an arbitrary page b is pushed from a buffer of capacity C at time t. Assuming that page b occurs at some position k on stack S_{t-1} where $1 \leqslant k \leqslant C$, then Q is given by the following expression:

$$\begin{aligned} Q &= P_r\{y_t(C) = b\} \\ &= P_r\{s_t(k) = y_t(k-1),\, s_t(k+1) = s_{t-1}(k+1), \\ &\qquad s_t(k+2) = s_{t-1}(k+2), \cdots, s_t(C) = s_{t-1}(C)\} \end{aligned} \tag{21}$$

The events in the joint probability in Equation 21 are independent, so that we obtain

$$\begin{aligned} Q &= P_r\{s_t(k) = y_t(k-1)\} \cdot P_r\{s_t(k+1) = s_{t-1}(k+1)\} \\ &\quad \cdot P_r\{s_t(k+2) = s_{t-1}(k+2)\} \cdot \cdots \cdot P_r\{s_t(C) = s_{t-1}(C)\} \\ &= \left(\frac{1}{k}\right)\left(\frac{k}{k+1}\right)\left(\frac{k+1}{k+2}\right)\cdots\left(\frac{C-1}{C}\right) \\ &= \frac{1}{C} \end{aligned}$$

Since $Q = 1/C$ holds for any page b and capacity C, we have verified that the stack updating for RR can be accomplished using Equation 20, and that RR has the same statistical properties as RAND for each buffer capacity. Note that although a particular value of a point on the success function, for example $F(4) = 0.3$, is equally likely to occur under both RAND and RR, the occurrence of a particular success function is not equally likely.

As the example with RR illustrates, stack-processing techniques can be extended to cover probabilistic replacement algorithms. In fact, a replacement algorithm can have a mixture of probabilistic and nonprobabilistic aspects. For instance, the arbitrary rule used to break ties in LFU and other algorithms may choose a page at random. Another possibility is for a replacement algorithm to favor some pages probabilistically in the construction of the priority list, thereby realizing a "biased replacement" algorithm [12]. In any case, the only requirement is that the priority list be constructed to reflect the probabilistic properties of the desired replacement algorithm for every capacity C.

CONGRUENCE MAPPING

Up to now, we have restricted our attention to two-level storage hierarchies with unconstrained mapping at the first level. Under this type of mapping, any page in the buffer may be replaced by the referenced page. The advantages of unconstrained mapping are that all available page frames in the buffer can be used and that seldom used pages cannot become "locked" into the buffer by mapping constraints. A disadvantage with unconstrained mapping is that extensive associative searches may be necessary to locate pages in the buffer. Moreover, the implementation overhead of the replacement algorithm may be excessive, since relative priority information must be maintained for all pages in the buffer. To offset these disadvantages, a contrained mapping scheme can be employed whereby each page is restricted to occupy a member of only a subset of the buffer page frames.

One such mapping technique is called *congruence mapping*, by which the 2^k distinct pages in the address space are partitioned into 2^α disjoint *congruence classes*, where $0 \leqslant \alpha \leqslant k$, and each class contains $2^{k-\alpha}$ pages. The classes are numbered consecutively from 0 to $2^\alpha - 1$, and class membership is determined from the α low-order bits of the page number. In this case, the α low-order bits constitute the *class number* $[x]$ of a page, and the remaining $k - \alpha$ bits are called the *page prefix* as shown in Figure 2-15. The quantity α is called the *class length*. For a class length equal to zero, we set $[x] = 0$ for all pages.

In a two-level hierarchy with congruence mapping, every congruence class is assigned an equal number of page frames in the buffer—to be used exclusively by members of that class. This number is called the *class capacity* and is denoted by D. (The total capacity of the buffer in pages is thus $C = 2^\alpha \cdot D$.) When a page x is referenced, it may appear in any of the D page frames reserved for class $[x]$. If the reference page is not in the buffer, and if the D page frames are all occupied by other members of class $[x]$, a replacement algorithm selects one of these

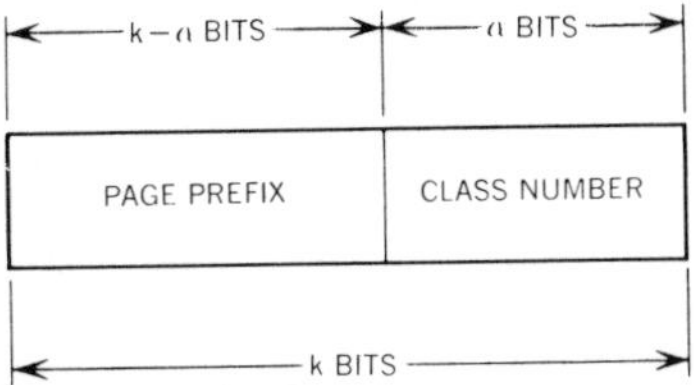

Figure 2-15. Page Number

pages for removal. We assume that the same replacement algorithm is used separately for each of the classes.

Note that when the class length α is zero, all pages are in the same class and the mapping is unconstrained. When the buffer capacity C is a power of 2, and when $C = 2^\alpha$, only one page is allocated to each class, and the mapping function is fully constrained. Thus for a fixed buffer capacity $C = 2^h$, where $0 \leqslant h \leqslant k$, we can vary the mapping function from unconstrained to partially and fully constrained simply by varying the value of α from 0 to h.

Since the congruence classes are disjoint, and since the same number of buffer page frames are allocated to each class, it is possible to treat a buffer as a collection of 2^α distinct buffers—one for each class $[x]$. If we also view the backing store as 2^α individual backing stores, as shown in Figure 2-16, the two-level hierarchy partitions into a collection of 2^α distinct subhierarchies, each with a buffer capacity of D page frames. When the replacement algorithm is a stack algorithm, these subhierarchies can be evaluated separately using stack-processing techniques. In practice, 2^α stacks (one for each subhierarchy) can be maintained as the trace is processed. Each page reference x causes only the stack for class $[x]$ to be updated, and a stack distance Δ to be determined from that stack.

In congruence mapping, to calculate the success function for a given trace and given class length α, the stack distances must be carefully interpreted. Whenever a stack distance Δ is measured, the corresponding critical capacity of the entire buffer is $2^\alpha \cdot \Delta$, since this is the minimum buffer capacity necessary to contain the referenced page. Therefore, the success function $F^\alpha(C)$ for the set of capacities $C = 2^\alpha \cdot D$ where $D = 1, 2, \cdots$, is given by

$$F^\alpha(C) = F^\alpha(2^\alpha \cdot D) = \sum_{\Delta=1}^{D} \frac{n(\Delta)}{L}$$

where $n(\Delta)$ is the total number of times the distance Δ occurs for any of the stacks.

Generally, stack-processing techniques must be used separately for each value of the class length α. However, for LRU replacement, only a single stack need be maintained in order to determine the success functions for all values of α in the interval $0 \leqslant \alpha \leqslant k$. Recall that under LRU, the stack S_{t-1} is the list of all the pages in Γ_{t-1} ordered according to most recent reference. To form the stack

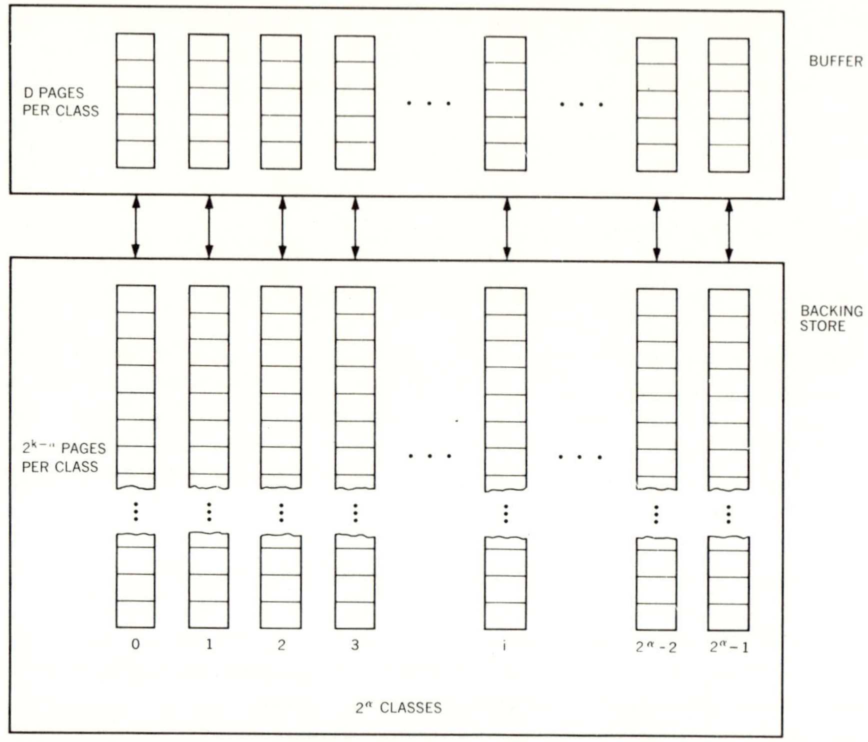

Figure 2-16. Two-Level Hierarchy with Congruence Mapping

$S_{t-1}(i, \alpha)$ corresponding to congruence class i and class length α, one would list the pages in class i according to their most recent reference. However, this ordering is preserved in the stack S_{t-1} for any i and any α. Therefore, $S_{t-1}(i, \alpha)$ can be determined by listing in order all the stack entries of S_{t-1} belonging to class i. In practice, it is not necessary to actually construct each stack $S_{t-1}([x_t], \alpha)$ in order to find the distance Δ_t^α. One can determine all the stack distances $\{\Delta_t^\alpha\}$ in one scan of the LRU stack S_{t-1}. To do this, we first define the *right match function* $RM(x, y)$ for the two page numbers x and y as the number of consecutive low-order bits that match. For example, RM(01101,00101) = 3, and RM(0000,0001) = 0. Note that the class numbers of two pages are equal ($[x] = [y]$) if and only if the class length satisfies the inequality $\alpha \leqslant RM(x, y)$. Now suppose that the current reference is to page x, and consider the jth entry on stack S_{t-1}, which is $y = s_{t-1}(j)$. The occurrence of page y on the stack will contribute to the distance Δ_t^α if and only if $RM(x, y) \geqslant \alpha$. Therefore, Δ_t^α can be determined by counting the number of stack entries y above (and including) page x that satisfy $RM(x, y) \geqslant \alpha$.

A simple procedure for determining Δ_t^α for all α is to scan down the stack and maintain a set of right match frequency counters $\{\mu(r)\}$ for $0 \leqslant r \leqslant k$. Counter

$\mu(r)$ is incremented whenever $RM(x, y)$ is equal to r. If page x has been previously referenced, we eventually find $RM(x, y) = k$ (corresponding to $x = y$), and each distance Δ_t^α is given by

$$\Delta_t^\alpha = \sum_{r=\alpha}^{k} \mu(r) \qquad \text{where} \qquad 0 \leqslant \alpha \leqslant k \tag{23}$$

However, if page x has not been previously referenced, the bottom of stack S_{t-1} is reached and Δ_t^α is set equal to infinity for all class lengths α. In either case, each distance Δ_t^α is used to increment the appropriate distance counter for class length α.

An example of this procedure is indicated in Figure 2-17. In Figure 2-17(A), the right match functions are found by scanning down the stack. In Figure 2-17(B), the right match frequencies $\{\mu(r)\}$ are plotted in reverse order as a

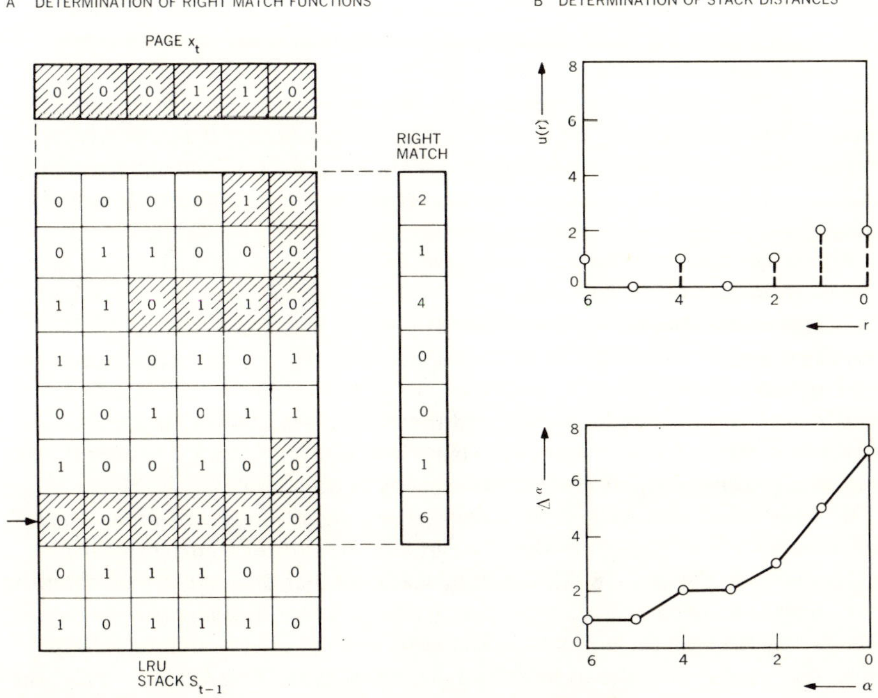

Figure 2-17. Right Match Function for LRU Replacement

function of r. Cumulative summation, according to Equation 23, then yields the desired LRU stack distances $\{\Delta_t^\alpha\}$. Note that the stack distance for class length zero is the same stack distance Δ as obtained for LRU replacement with unconstrained mapping.

MULTILEVEL HIERARCHIES

In previous sections of this paper, stack-processing techniques are developed to obtain the success function for a two-level hierarchy. For each buffer capacity, this success function represents the relative number of accesses to the buffer for a given page trace.

We now show that the same success function can be used to find the access frequencies for all levels of a multilevel, linear hierarchy for any number of levels and any capacity at each level. Recall that in a linear hierarchy, the only downward data path from each level M_i is to the next level M_{i+1}, for $1 \leqslant i < H$. Also a path or sequence of paths is available from each level M_i, for $1 < i \leqslant H$, to the local store. Furthermore, no replacement decisions are required when a page moves upward through intermediate levels. We now assume that the same replacement algorithm is used at all levels and that the mapping function is unconstrained at every level. (Hierarchies with constrained mapping functions are considered later in this paper.) At time $t = 0$, the backing store contains all pages, and these pages are moved to the local store M_1 on demand. When M_1 is full, pages replaced in M_1 are pushed down to the next lower level in the hierarchy, M_2 . As each successively lower level M_i fills, the pages replaced in M_i are pushed to the next level M_{i+1}. At level M_1, the replacement algorithm is applied to the set of pages already present, thereby making room for the currently referenced page x_t. At the intermediate levels M_i, for $2 \leqslant i < H$, the replacement algorithm is applied to the set of pages in M_i and to the page pushed from level M_{i+1}.

When page x_t is accessed from some level M_i (for $2 \leqslant i \leqslant H - 1$), a page is replaced from each of the levels $M_1, M_2, \cdots, M_{i-1}$. The page replaced from level M_{i-1} is guaranteed to find space at level M_i, since a page frame was vacated by x_t. When page x_t is accessed from the backing store M_H, a page is displaced from each of the levels $M_1, M_2, \cdots$, until a vacant page frame is found. Note that positions of pages in the hierarchy—and therefore the access frequencies—do not depend on the structure of upward data paths to the local store, but depend only on the replacement algorithm and the capacity at each level.

We have shown that when a stack replacement algorithm is used for a two-level hierarchy, the top C_1 pages of the stack are the contents of a buffer of capacity C_1 as shown in Figure 2-18(A). Let us now assume that the replacement algorithm for a multilevel hierarchy induces a priority list at every time and that this list determines the replacement decisions at every level of the hierarchy. If this is true, then for any number of levels and any set of capacities $C_1, C_2, \cdots, C_H$, the contents of each level at any time can be determined from the stack for this replacement algorithm. More precisely, let $B_t^i(C_i)$ denote the contents of level M_i at time t, and let σ_i denote the sum $C_1 + C_2 + \cdots + C_i$. We then claim that

$$B_t^i(C_i) = B_t(\sigma_i) - B_t(\sigma_{i-1}) \qquad \text{for } i = 1, 2, \cdots, H - 1 \tag{24}$$

A TWO-LEVEL HIERARCHY

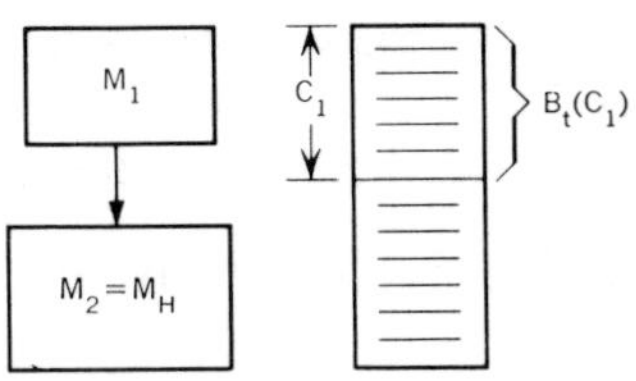

B MULTILEVEL HIERARCHY

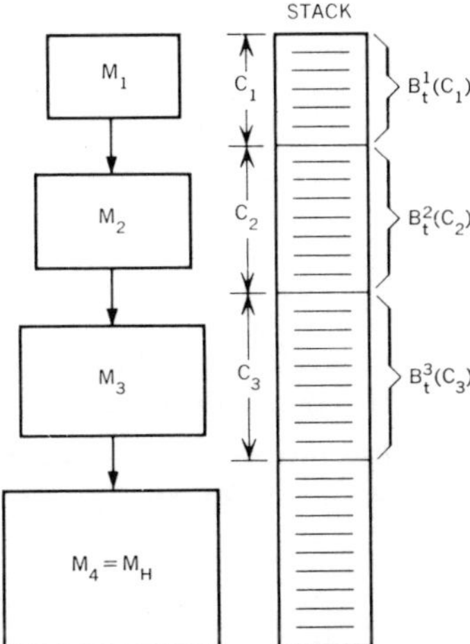

Figure 2-18. Relationship Between Stack and Hierarchy Levels

or equivalently that $B_t^1(C_1)$ can be identified as the first C_1 entries of stack S_t, and B_t^2 can be identified as the next C_2 entries, etc. This result is illustrated for a four-level hierarchy in Figure 2-18(B).

The main elements of the proof of this result are as follows. Assume that Equation 24 is satisfied at time $t - 1$, and that page $x_t = s_{t-1}(\Delta_t)$ is an element of $B_{t-1}^g(C_g)$ (i.e., level M_g is accessed.) As stack S_{t-1} is updated to stack S_t, page $y_t(C_1)$ is removed from the top C_1 elements of S_{t-1}, with the result that pages $s_t(1), \cdots, s_t(C_1)$ represent $B_t^1(C_1)$. Now observe that page $y_t(C_1 + C_2)$ is removed from the top $C_1 + C_2$ elements of S_{t-1}. In terms of the hierarchy, we know that $y_t(C_1)$ is pushed to the next lower level M_2, since the hierarchy is a linear one. The replacement algorithm then selects a page from $y_t(C_1) + B_{t-1}^2(C_2)$ for removal from M_2. Since page $y_t(C_1)$ has lowest priority in $B_{t-1}^1(C_1)$, the page selected for removal has lowest priority in $B_{t-1}^1(C_1) + B_{t-1}^2(C_2)$.

But this page is $y_t(C_1 + C_2)$, so that $s_t(1), \cdots, s_t(C_1 + C_2)$ represent $B_t^1(C_1) + B_t^2(C_2)$, and thus $s_t(C_1 + 1), \cdots, s_t(C_1 + C_2)$ represent $B_t^2(C_2)$.

A similar argument applies to subsequent levels M_i where $2 < i \leqslant g - 1$. Page $y_t(\sigma_{i-1})$ is pushed from level M_{i-1} of the hierarchy and competes with the pages in $B_{t-1}^i(C_i)$. The replacement algorithm selects for replacement the page

$$\min\,[y_t(\sigma_{i-1}), B_{t-1}^i(C_i)] = \min\,[B_{t-1}(\sigma_i)] = y_t(\sigma_i)$$

with the result that

$$B_t(\sigma_i) = B_t^1(C_1) + B_t^2(C_2) + \cdots + B_t^i(C_i)$$

and

$$B_t^i(C_i) = B_t(\sigma_i) - B_t(\sigma_{i-1})$$

At level M_g, the page $y_t(\sigma_{g-1})$ that has been pushed from M_{g-1} finds a vacant page frame, and all lower levels remain unchanged. Then

$$B_t^g(C_g) = B_{t-1}^g(C_g) + y_t(\sigma_{g-1}) - x_t = B_t(\sigma_g) - B_t(\sigma_{g-1})$$

and

$$B_t^j(C_j) = B_{t-1}^j(C_j) = B_t(\sigma_j) - B_t(\sigma_{j-1}) \qquad \text{for } j > g$$

Thus we have shown that Equation 24 is satisfied at time t.

The significance of this result is that a stack distance Δ, where $C_1 + \cdots + C_{g-1} < \Delta \leqslant C_1 + \cdots + C_g$, corresponds to an access to hierarchy level M_g, and the relative number of such Δ's is simply the access frequency F_g to that level. Thus

$$F_g = \sum_{\Delta=\sigma_{g-1}+1}^{\sigma_g} \frac{n(\Delta)}{L} = F(\sigma_g) - F(\sigma_{g-1}) \qquad \text{for} \qquad 1 \leqslant g \leqslant H - 1 \quad (25)$$

As with two-level hierarchies, all other accesses are directed to the backing store so that

$$F_H = 1 - \sum_{i=1}^{H-1} F_i$$

The determination of access frequencies for a four-level hierarchy is illustrated graphically in Figure 2-19. Note that the technique illustrated in the figure cannot be used for an arbitrary hierarchy or success function. However, the technique can be used for any linear hierarchy as long as the replacement algorithm always induces a single priority list for all hierarchy levels.

Our treatment of multilevel linear hierarchies can be extended to include hierarchies with congruence mapping functions. We assume that the same class length α is used for every level and that D_i page frames are allocated to each congruence class at level M_i. The total capacity of level M_i is then

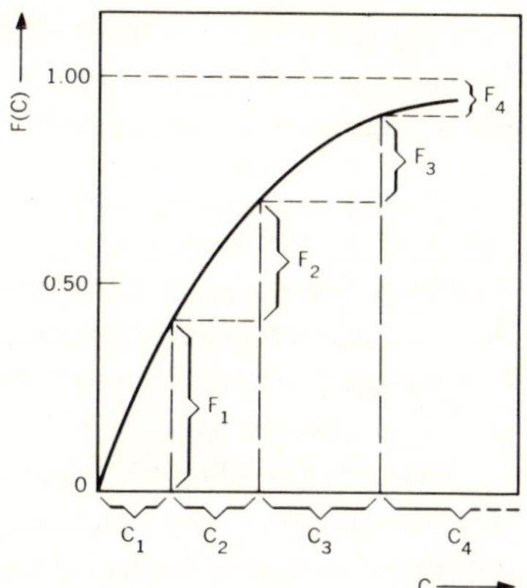

Figure 2-19. Obtaining Access Frequencies from Success Function

$$C_i = 2^{\alpha} \cdot D_i \quad \text{where} \quad 1 \leqslant i \leqslant H. \tag{26}$$

Using the success function $F^{\alpha}(C)$ and Equations 25 and 26, we obtain the access frequency F_i^{α} for each level as follows:

$$F_i^{\alpha} = \begin{cases} F^{\alpha}(\sigma_i) - F^{\alpha}(\sigma_{i-1}) & \text{for} \quad 1 \leqslant i \leqslant H-1 \\ 1 - \sum_{i=1}^{H-1} F_i^{\alpha} & \text{for} \quad i = H \end{cases} \tag{27}$$

When using Equation 27 or the graphic technique shown in Figure 2-19, it is important to remember that the success function for multilevel hierarchies with congruence mapping is defined only when the storage capacity is a multiple of 2^{α}.

POSSIBLE EXTENSIONS

It is possible to extend stack-processing techniques to account for various changes in the hierarchy model. For example, with appropriate encoding of the n-bit address, systems with page sizes that are not a power of 2 can be evaluated. Similarly, other encodings of the n-bit address can be used to evaluate systems with congruence mapping functions for any number of congruence classes with equal or unequal class sizes. Indicative of other changes of the hierarchy model that can be handled by stack processing techniques are the following:

- Pre-loading program pages into the buffer for starting execution
- Loading a working set [19] of pages into the buffer when resuming program execution
- Returning all pages to the backing store upon program interruption
- Maintaining copies of pages in several levels of the storage hierarchy
- Bringing pages to the local store only for fetch operations

- Returning pages to the backing store for references such as stores from an I/O channel
- Moving unequal size pages or segments between levels

To illustrate how stack-processing techniques can be adapted to these variations in hierarchy design, we describe two extensions in some detail. In our original model, the generator does not distinguish fetch operations from store operations. In some computer systems, however, pages are brought to the local store only for fetch operations, and usage statistics for page replacement algorithms refer only to references for fetches. Stores to pages in lower levels of the hierarchy are broadcast to these levels by the hierarchy management facility, and no pages are moved. The justification for fetch-store hierarchies is that fetches or additional stores usually do not immediately follow stores to a page.

The evaluation of fetch-store hierarchies requires that the generator tag each reference as either a fetch or a store. For fetches, the priority list and the stack are updated, and a fetch distance Δ^f is recorded. For stores, neither the priority list nor the stack is updated, but a store distance Δ^s is recorded. The distributions $\{n^f(\Delta^f)\}$ and $\{n^s(\Delta^s)\}$ can then be used to determine the fetch and store access frequencies to each level of the hierarchy. It should be clear that this technique also works if congruence mapping is included. We can also consider a modified fetch-store design where the page usage statistics are updated for a store operation even though no page motion occurs. This change is incorporated by updating the priority list for both fetches and stores. Thus, for modified fetch-stores, the net change in our model is that the stack is not updated for store operations.

Besides distinguishing fetches from stores, a computer system may also distinguish the various sources of store requests. For example, a "call-back" feature can be used by which a page in the buffer is moved to the backing store if the page is stored into by an I/O device. The motivation here is to free the buffer of pages not needed by the CPU, and to service all I/O stores from the backing store.

For a call-back hierarchy, the generator must specify at least two kinds of references—CPU references, and stores from the I/O channel. Stack-processing techniques can then be modified as follows. When a CPU store or fetch occurs, the stack is updated in the normal way (except for special entries to be described later), and a distance counter $n^{CPU}(\Delta)$ is incremented. When an I/O store occurs, say at time t, a counter $n^{I/O}(\Delta)$ is incremented. If page x_t does not occur on stack S_{t-1}, then S_t is equal to S_{t-1}. If page x_t does occur on stack S_{t-1}, then $S_t = S_{t-1}$ except that x_t is replaced by the special entry "#." This entry, counted for all stack distance measurements, represents the empty page frame caused by page x_t returning to the backing store. To ensure that empty page frames are filled as soon as possible, all #-entries are assigned the lowest priority in replacement decisions.

The call-back feature can be used in conjunction with the fetch-store or modified fetch-store schemes. In all cases, the correctness of the modified stack-processing techniques can be established.

Since stack processing allows a large sample of "typical" address tapes to be analyzed, for many hierarchy models, the efficiency gained at the early stages of hierarchy design may be great enough to impact the whole design process. More of these traces can be processed in a given time, and more hierarchy designs can be evaluated for a given number of traces. The availability of this data may help justify the "typical"-trace approach to design or help in the development of other models for system requirements. As an example, program models can be more deeply investigated by evaluating both a program and its model under a very large number of address traces. Improvement in program modeling, in turn, may enhance the success of analytical disciplines that use these models, such as storage interference studies for multiprogrammed systems.

CONCLUDING REMARKS

The concepts presented in this paper have been used to develop a variety of stack-processing techniques that are useful in the evaluation of storage hierarchies. Using the inclusion property, we define a class of page replacement algorithms, called stack algorithms, and show that replacement algorithms that induce priority lists–such as least recently used, least frequently used, and random replacement–belong to this class.

For any stack algorithm, the frequency of stack distances can be obtained from an address trace by stack processing and used to calculate the success functions. The success function can then be used to determine the relative frequency of access to all levels of a multilevel, linear storage hierarchy, with any number of levels and any capacity at each level.

For least recently used replacement (LRU), the access frequencies of hierarchies with congruence mapping functions can be determined in a single pass of the address trace–for any number of congruence classes, any number of levels and any capacity per class at each level.

Some special results are presented concerning an optimal replacement algorithm (OPT). It is shown that OPT is a stack algorithm and that OPT minimizes the number of page swaps for any address trace and buffer capacity. Also, both OPT and LRU can be evaluated with a forward pass of the address trace followed by a backward pass of the same address trace.

We conclude that stack-processing techniques can eliminate much of the simulation effort required in storage hierarchy evaluation. Furthermore, we believe that the classification of stack algorithms and the various extensions to stack processing techniques may provide insight into the areas of program modeling, system analysis, and computer design.

ACKNOWLEDGMENT

The authors wish to acknowledge J. H. Eaton for his helpful comments and criticism, and T. W. MacDowell for his help in the proof of Theorem 4.

Appendix

Two results mentioned in the paper concerning the OPT replacement algorithm are proved here. To do this, it is first shown that given any trace and replacement algorithm (not necessarily using demand paging) another replacement algorithm exists which uses demand paging and causes the same or a fewer total number of pages to be loaded into the buffer. This result is used to show that OPT is an optimal replacement algorithm and, in fact, that OPT causes the minimum total number of pages to be loaded into the buffer. Finally, it is shown that the success function under OPT for any trace is identical to the success function under OPT for the reverse of the trace.

Definition

- $|S|$ denotes the number of elements in a set S.
- $|a|_X$ denotes the number of occurrences of a symbol a in a sequence X.
- $A = \{a, b, \cdots\}$ is a finite set of N *page addresses* or *pages*.
- $X = x_1, x_2, \cdots, x_L$ is a finite sequence of L elements from A, and is called a *trace*.
- $B_t(C) \subseteq A$ denotes the contents of a buffer of capacity C at time t, and is called a *state*.

Throughout this appendix, we consider a two-level storage hierarchy with fixed buffer capacity C. Consequently, we use B_t instead of $B_t(C)$. The term B_t denotes the contents of the buffer immediately after reference x_t is made; B_0 is called the *initial buffer* state; and ϕ, the empty set, denotes an empty buffer state.

Definition

- $P = p_1, p_2, \cdots, p_L$ is a finite sequence of L sets, $p_t \subseteq A$, called an *O-policy*.
- $Q = q_1, q_2, \cdots, q_L$ is a finite sequence of L sets, $q_t \subseteq A$, called an *I-policy*.

A policy is a particular realization of a replacement algorithm for a given trace. For such a trace and initial buffer state B_0, an *I*-policy and an *O*-policy together determine the sequence of buffer states that will occur during the trace. An *I*-policy gives the set of pages loaded into the buffer, and an *O*-policy gives the set removed. If $p_t = \phi$, no page is removed, and if $q_t = \phi$, no page is loaded in. Note that only certain pairs of *O*- and *I*-policies are meaningful. For example, a page cannot be removed if it is not in the buffer. We consider only meaningful policies, where $q_{t+1} \not\subseteq B_t$ and $p_{t+1} \subseteq B_t + q_{t+1}$, for $0 \leqslant t \leqslant L-1$. In this case, B_{t+1} is obtained from B_t by

$$B_{t+1} = [B_t + q_{t+1}] - p_{t+1}$$

Definition

Let X be a trace and B_0 (where $|B_0| \leqslant C$) an initial state. A sequence of states $B = B_0, B_1, \cdots, B_L$ is a *valid sequence* if $x_t \in B_t$, for $1 \leqslant t \leqslant L$. A policy pair P and Q is a *valid pair* for X and B_0 if application of the pair results in a valid sequence.

Note that valid policy pairs are quite general in that any number of pages may be moved into or out of the buffer. However, most of our attention is directed toward *demand paging* where

$$\left.\begin{array}{lll} \cdot\ |p_t| \leqslant 1 & \text{and} & |q_t| \leqslant 1 \\ \cdot\ x_t \in B_{t-1} \Rightarrow p_t = q_t = \phi & & \\ \cdot\ p_t \neq \phi \Rightarrow q_t \neq \phi & \text{and} & |B_{t-1}| = C \end{array}\right\} \quad \text{(A1)}$$

for all t, $1 \leqslant t \leqslant L$.

Under demand paging, single pages are loaded when necessary until the buffer fills; subsequently, page swaps occur only when necessary.

One measure of goodness for a policy pair P and Q is the total number of pages loaded into the buffer $\Sigma_{t=1}^{L} |q_t|$ under the policy pair. The following theorem supports the usefulness of demand paging.

Theorem 1

Let P and Q be a valid policy pair for X and B_0. There exists a valid demand policy pair P^D and Q^D for X and B_0 such that

$$\sum_{t=1}^{L} |q_t^D| \leqslant \sum_{t=1}^{L} |q_t|$$

Proof. P^D and Q^D will be constructed by forming a sequence of valid policy pairs (P^0, Q^0), (P^1, Q^1), (P^2, Q^2), $\cdots$, (P^K, Q^K), where $P^0 = P$, $Q^0 = Q$, $P^K = P^D$, $Q^K = Q^D$, and $\Sigma_{t=1}^{L} |q_t^j| \leqslant \Sigma_{t=1}^{L} |q_t^{j-1}|$ for $1 \leqslant j \leqslant K$. Informally, P^j and Q^j are constructed from P^{j-1} and Q^{j-1} by altering p_t^{j-1} and q_t^{j-1} to satisfy the demand paging constraints where p_t^{j-1} and/or q_t^{j-1} are the first occurrences of nondemand paging in P^{j-1} and Q^{j-1}. This is done by "sliding" offending elements of p_t^{j-1} and/or q_t^{j-1} to a later time in P^j and Q^j. If $a \in p_t^j$ and $a \in q_t^j$ ever occurs then we trivially remove page a from both p_t^j and q_t^j. Clearly, this does not disturb the validity of P^j and Q^j and only decreases the value of $\Sigma_{t=1}^{L} |q_t^j|$.

To construct P^j and Q^j from P^{j-1} and Q^{j-1}, $1 \leqslant j \leqslant K$, let t be the smallest time such that p_t^{j-1} and/or q_t^{j-1} do not satisfy Equation A1. Set $P^j = P^{j-1}$ and $Q^j = Q^{j-1}$, except as noted below. Suppose that $x_t = a$ and that q_t^{j-1}, for $t < L$, does not satisfy Equation A1. If $a \notin q_t^{j-1}$, then set $q_t^j = \phi$ and $q_{t+1}^j = q_{t+1}^{j-1} + q_t^{j-1}$. (Note that "+" is defined here since $q_t^{j-1} \cap p_t^{j-1} = \phi$). If $a \in q_t^{j-1}$, then set $q_t^j = a$, and $q_{t+1}^j = q_{t+1}^{j-1} + [q_t^{j-1} - a]$. If $t = L$, then set $q_L^j = \phi$ if $a \notin q_L^{j-1}$, or $q_L^j = a$ if $a \in$

q_L^{j-1}. In all cases, note that Q^j is valid, since $q_t^j \notin B_{t-1}^j$ for $1 \leq t \leq L$, and that $\Sigma_{t=1}^L |q_t^j| \leq \Sigma_{t=1}^L |q_t^{j-1}|$.

Now suppose that p_t^{j-1} for $t < L$, does not satisfy Equation A1. We observe first that $|q_t^j| \leq 1$ and $q_t^j = a$, if $a \notin B_{t-1}^{j-1}$. If $q_t^j = \phi$ or $|B_{t-1}^{j-1}| < C$, then set $p_t^j = \phi$ and $p_{t+1}^j = p_{t+1}^{j-1} + p_t^{j-1}$. If $q_t^j = a$ and $|B_{t-1}^{j-1}| = C$, set $p_t^j = b$ for some $b \in p_t^{j-1}$ and $p_{t+1}^j = p_{t+1}^{j-1} + [p_t^{j-1} - b]$. (Note that $p_t^{j-1} \neq \phi$, since $|B_{t-1}^{j-1}| = C$ and $q_t^{j-1} \neq \phi$.) For $t = L$, set $p_L^j = b \in p_L^{j-1}$ if $q_L^j = a$ and $|B_{L-1}^{j-1}| = C$, or $p_L^j = \phi$ otherwise. In all cases, we observe that P^j is valid, since $p_t^j \subseteq B_{t-1}^j$ for $1 \leq t \leq L$. Since P^j and Q^j satisfy demand paging at least up through time t, the desired demand policies must eventually be obtained. Thus the theorem is proved.

Before considering an optimum replacement algorithm we make two observations. First, under demand paging, a valid policy pair P and Q can be completely represented by specifying just the O-policy P. This follows from Equation A1 because $q_t \neq \phi$ can only occur when $x_t = a$ and $a \notin B_{t-1}$ (in which case we know that $q_t = a$). Second, for demand policies P and Q, we can use $|\phi|_P$ as an alternative criterion of goodness. To see this let u be the smallest integer such that $|B_t| = C, t \geq u$. Then $|\phi|_P$ is given by the following expression:

$$|\phi|_P = u + (L - u) - \sum_{t=u+1}^{L} |q_t| \tag{A2}$$

Since u in Equation A2 is not a function of the policies, $\Sigma_{t=1}^u |q_t|$ is a constant and

$$|\phi|_P = \left(L + \sum_{t=1}^{u} |q_t|\right) - \sum_{t=1}^{L} |q_t| = \text{constant} - \sum_{t=1}^{L} |q_t| \tag{A3}$$

OPTIMUM REPLACEMENT ALGORITHM

For a given trace X and initial state B_0 let us define an optimum policy pair P and Q as a pair that is valid and minimizes $\Sigma_{t=1}^L |q_t|$ over the class of valid policies. From Theorem 1 there always exists an optimum policy pair which is also a demand policy pair. Since (A3) holds for all demand policies we can find an optimum demand policy pair if we can find a demand policy P^D such that $|\phi|_{P^D} \geq |\phi|_P$ where P is any demand policy.

Definition

Let X be a trace, and let $a \in A$ be a page. The *forward distance* $d(a, x_t)$ to page a from page x_t is the number of distinct pages occurring in $x_{t+1}, \cdots, x_e$, where e is the smallest integer satisfying $e > t$ and $x_e = a$. If no such e exists then $d(a, x_t) = \infty$.

Definition

Let X be a trace and B_0 an initial state. A valid demand policy P^o, called an OPT *policy*, for X and B_0 is defined as follows. For $t = 1, 2, \cdots, L$, whenever $p_t \neq \phi$ is required then $p_t = a$ where

$$(\forall b \in B_{t-1})(d(a, x_t) \geqslant d(b, x_t))$$

The forward distance to a page is just the number of distinct pages referenced before that page is referenced again. An OPT policy requires that the page removed from the buffer be one with the greatest forward distance. Note that an OPT policy is a particular realization of the OPT replacement algorithm discussed in the paper. We observe that, at time t, all pages with finite forward distances have distinct forward distances. However, more than one page may have an infinite forward distance. This means that there may exist more than one OPT policy for a given X and B_0. It should be clear that all such policies P^o have the same value of $|\phi|_{P^o}$.

To show that any P^o maximizes $|\phi|_{P^o}$ over the class of demand policies we use the following lemma.

Lemma 1

Let X be a trace and B_0 and B_0' initial states where

$$\left.\begin{aligned} B_0' &= T_0 + \{a\} \\ B_0 &= T_0 + \{b\} \end{aligned}\right\}' \quad \text{for } T_0 \subseteq A \quad \text{and} \quad a, b, \notin T_0 \tag{A4}$$

and $d(a, x_1) \leqslant d(b, x_1)$. For any demand policy P, corresponding to X and B_0, there exists a demand policy P', corresponding to X and B_0', such that

$$|\phi|_{P'} \geqslant |\phi|_P$$

Proof. Given P, we construct P'. Suppose page a first occurs in X at x_{i_a} and b at x_{i_b}. Thus, $i_a < i_b \leqslant L$ is assumed. If either b or a does not occur in X, then set i_b or i_a equal to $L + 1$. We consider three cases.

Case 1. $p_j = b$ where p_j is the first occurrence of b in P, and $1 \leqslant j < i_a$. Here we set $p_k' = p_k$, $1 \leqslant k \leqslant L$ and $k \neq j$, and $p_j' = a$. This results in $B_t = T_t + \{b\}$ and $B_t' = T_t + \{a\}$, $0 \leqslant t \leqslant j - 1$ and $B_t = B_t'$, $j \leqslant t \leqslant L$. Since pages a and b are both not referenced up to time j, it should be clear that P' is a valid demand policy (because P is) and that $|\phi|_{P'} = |\phi|_P$.

Case 2. $p_{i_a} = b$ where p_{i_a} is the first occurrence of b in P. In this case we set $p_k' = p_k$, $1 \leqslant k \leqslant L$ and $k \neq j$, and $p_{i_a}' = \phi$. As in Case 1, P' is a valid demand policy and $|\phi|_{P'} = |\phi|_P + 1 \geqslant |\phi|_P$.

Case 3. $p_j \neq b$, $1 \leqslant j \leqslant i_a$. Here we must consider two subcases.

Case 3A. $p_{i_a} = c$. At time $t = i_a$ the states of the buffer are given by

$$B'_{i_a} = T_{i_a} + \{a\}$$

$$B_{i_a} = T_{i_a} + \{b\} + \{a\} - \{c\} \qquad \text{for } c \in T_{i_a}$$

which can also be written as follows:

$$B'_{i_a} = [T_{i_a} + \{a\} - \{c\}] + \{c\}$$

$$B_{i_a} = [T_{i_a} + \{a\} - \{c\}] + \{b\}$$

Note that this is the same form as Equation A4 with T_0 replaced by $[T_{i_a} + \{a\} - \{c\}]$ and a replaced by c. If $d(c, x_{i_a+1}) \leqslant d(b, x_{i_a+1})$ then we have a situation identical to that in the statement of Lemma 1 where X is now $x_{i_a+1}, \cdots, x_L$. Setting $p'_k = p_k$ for $1 \leqslant k \leqslant i_a - 1$ and $p'_{i_a} = \phi$, we again consider Cases 1, 2, and 3. Since the "new" X is strictly shorter than the original X, this situation can only occur a finite number of times. Note that P' is valid as far as it is specified and that $p'_1, \cdots, p'_{i_a}$ contains one more $p_1, \cdots, p_{i_a}$.

If $d(c, x_{i_a+1}) > d(b, x_{i_a+1})$, we set $p'_k = p_k$ for $1 \leqslant k \leqslant i_a - 1$ and $p'_{i_a} = \phi$, and consider two more cases. First, if $p_l = b$, where p_l is the first occurrence of b in X and $l < i_b$, we set $p'_k = p_k$, for $i_a + 1 \leqslant k \leqslant L$, and $k \neq l$ and $p'_l = c$. Here $B'_t = B_t$ for $l \leqslant t \leqslant L$, and as in Case 1, we see that $|\phi|_{P'} \geqslant |\phi|_P$ still holds. Second, if $p_l \neq b$, for $l < i_b$, we set $p'_k = p_k$, $i_a + 1 \leqslant k \leqslant L$, and $k \neq i_b$ and $p'_{i_b} = c$. Again we have $B'_t = B_t$ for $i_b \leqslant t \leqslant L$, but we note that $p_{i_b} = \phi$, whereas $p'_{i_b} = c \neq \phi$. However, since $p_{i_a} \neq \phi$ and $p'_{i_a} = \phi$, the relation $|\phi|_{P'} \geqslant |\phi|_P$ still holds.

Case 3B. $p_{i_a} = \phi$. Since $q_{i_a} = a$ we observe that $|B_{i_a-1}| < C$. Let l be the smallest integer such that $p_l \neq \phi$. If no such integer exists, then let $l = L + 1$. We set $p'_k = p_k$ for $1 \leqslant k \leqslant i_a$ and consider two cases. First, if $i_b < l$ then we set $p'_k = p_k$ for $i_a + 1 \leqslant k \leqslant L$. Note that $Q' = Q$ except at times i_a and i_b. Since $|B'_t| = |B_t|$ for $i_b \leqslant t \leqslant L$, we see that P' is valid, and $|\phi|_{P'} = |\phi|_P$, since $P' = P$. Second, for the case $i_b > l$, note that $x_l = c$, where $c \neq a$ and $c \neq b$. We set $p'_k = p_k$ for $i_a + 1 \leqslant k \leqslant L$ and $k \neq l$, and $p'_l = \phi$. If $p_l = b$, then $|B'_t| = |B_t|$ for $l \leqslant t \leqslant L$, and $|\phi|_{P'} = |\phi|_P + 1 \geqslant |\phi|_P$. If $p_l = a$, then the buffer states at times $l - 1$ and l are:

$$B'_{l-1} = T_{l-1} + \{a\} \qquad B'_l = T_{l-1} + \{a\} + \{c\}$$

$$B_{l-1} = T_{l-1} + \{a\} + \{b\} \qquad B_l = T_{l-1} + \{b\} + \{c\}$$

Rewriting the buffer states at time l as

$$B'_l = [T_{l-1} + \{c\}] + \{a\}$$

$$B_l = [T_{l-1} + \{c\}] + \{b\}$$

we arrive at a case similar to Case 3A. As in Case 3A, P' contains one more ϕ than P in the interval $t = 1, \cdots, l$. Therefore we treat this case in the same way, with the result $|\phi|_{P'} \geqslant |\phi|_P$. Finally, if $p_l = d$ where $d \neq a$ and $d \neq b$ the buffer states at time l can be written as

$$B_l' = [T_{l-1} + \{a\} + \{c\} - \{d\}] + \{d\}$$

$$B_l = [T_{l-1} + \{a\} + \{c\} - \{d\}] + \{b\}$$

which again can be treated as in Case 3A.

Note that the situation where $i_b = l$ cannot arise in Case 3B, since $b \in B_{i_b-1}$. We have therefore successfully exhausted the possible cases, and Lemma 1 is proved.

OPT IS AN OPTIMAL REPLACEMENT ALGORITHM

Theorem 2

Let X be a trace, B_0 an initial state, and P a valid demand policy for X and B_0. If P^o is any valid OPT policy for X and B_0, then $|\phi|_{P^o} \geqslant |\phi|_P$.

Proof. We recall first that every OPT policy for X and B_0 has exactly the same number of ϕ's. To prove the theorem, we need only find any OPT policy P^o such that $|\phi|_{P^o} \geqslant |\phi|_P$. To do this we will construct a finite sequence of policies $P^1, P^2, \cdots, P^j$, where P^j is an OPT policy and $|\phi|_P \leqslant |\phi|_{P^1} \leqslant \cdots \leqslant |\phi|_{P^j}$.

P^1 is constructed as follows. Let i be the smallest integer such that $p_i \neq p_i^o$, where p_i^o is an element of an OPT policy. Suppose that $p_i = a$ and $p_i^o = b$. (Neither p_i nor p_i^o can be ϕ, since both are demand policies.) We observe that

$$\left.\begin{aligned} B_i &= T_i + \{b\} \\ B_i^o &= T_i + \{a\} \end{aligned}\right\} \quad \text{for} \quad a, b \notin T_i$$

where $d(a, x_i) \leqslant d(b, x_i)$. Since $x_i \neq a$ and $x_i \neq b$, it follows that $d(a, x_{i+1}) \leqslant d(b, x_{i+1})$. Treating B_i as B_0, B_i^o as B_0', and $x_{i+1}, \cdots, x_L$ as X, we can use Lemma 1 to find a policy $p_{i+1}', \cdots, p_L'$ that contains as least as many ϕ's as $p_{i+1}, \cdots, p_L$. We then define $P^1 = p_L^1, \cdots, p_L^1$ as

$$p_k^1 \begin{cases} p_k, & 1 \leqslant k \leqslant i-1 \\ b, & k = i \\ p_k', & i+1 \leqslant k \leqslant L \end{cases}$$

Note that P^1 is valid and that $|\phi|_P \leqslant |\phi|_{P^1}$. Furthermore, $p_k^1 = p_k^o$, $1 \leqslant k \leqslant l_1$ for some $l_1 \geqslant i$.

Policy P^2 is constructed from P^1 in a similar manner with the results that $p_k^2 = p_k^o$, $1 \leqslant k \leqslant l_2$ where $l_2 > l_1$ and $|\phi|_{P^1} \leqslant |\phi|_{P^2}$. Since X is finite, construction of $P^1, P^2, \cdots$ must result in P^j, for finite j, where $p_k^j = p_k^o$, $1 \leqslant k \leqslant L$. It follows from $|\phi|_P \leqslant |\phi|_{P^1} \leqslant \cdots \leqslant |\phi|_{P^j}$ that $|\phi|_P \leqslant |\phi|_{P^j}$ where P^j is an OPT policy and the theorem is proved.

Combining the relation in Equation A3 for demand paging with Theorems 1 and 2, we have the following theorem.

OPT MINIMIZES PAGE LOADING

Theorem 3

Let X be a trace, B_0 an initial state, and P^o a valid OPT policy. (Also, let Q^o be the corresponding I-policy.) For any valid policy pair P and Q,

$$\sum_{t=1}^{L} |q_t| \geqslant \sum_{t=1}^{L} |q_t^o|$$

Thus we see that an OPT policy results in a minimum number of pages being loaded into the buffer over the class of all valid policies. After giving preliminary Lemmas 2 and 3, we present a final theorem concerning OPT policies.

Lemma 2

For a trace X, let the set B_C represent the first C distinct pages referenced in X. For a buffer of capacity C, if P is a valid demand policy for X and some $B_0' \subseteq B_C$, then P is a valid demand policy for X and any $B_0' \subseteq B_C$.

Proof. Let i be the smallest integer such that $x_1, \cdots, x_i$ contains C distinct pages. If $B_0 \subseteq B_C$ then, for any valid demand policy P, we have $B_i = B_C$, since $p_1 = p_2 = \cdots = p_i = \phi$. For $B_0' \subseteq B_C$ this also holds, so P is a valid demand policy for X and B_0'. (Note that for different initial states, $B_0 \subseteq B_C$, the Q policies will not be the same.)

Lemma 3

For a trace X, let the set E_C represent the last C distinct pages referenced in X. For a buffer of capacity C, if P is a valid demand policy for X and B_0, there exists a valid demand policy P' with a state sequence $B_0, B_1', B_2', \cdots, B_L'$ such that $B_L' = E_C$ and $|\phi|_{P'} \geqslant |\phi|_P$.

Proof. Let i be the smallest integer such that $x_i, \cdots, x_L$ contains C distinct pages. Suppose, under policy P, that B_{i-1} contains n elements of E_C, that is, $|B_{i-1} \cap E_C| = n$. It follows that at least $C - n$ pages will be loaded into the buffer following time $i - 1$. Setting $p_k' = p_k$ for $1 \leqslant k \leqslant i - 1$, we will specify the remainder of P' in such a way that exactly $C - n$ pages are loaded into the buffer following time $t - 1$. We observe that, since at most C distinct pages are referenced following time $i - 1$, we never need remove a page b from the buffer where $b \in E_C$. Thus, if a page must be removed at time l for $i \leqslant l \leqslant L$, there always exists a page c, where $c \notin E_C$, in the buffer and we set $p_l' = c$. If P' is constructed in this manner,

$$\sum_{t=1}^{L} |q_t'| \leqslant \sum_{t=1}^{L} |q_t|$$

and from Equation A3 we have $|\phi|_{P'} \geqslant |\phi|_P$. Furthermore, since no page in E_C is ever removed from the buffer following time $t = i$ and $|E_C| = C$, we see that $B'_L = E_C$.

FORWARD/BACKWARD OPT

Theorem 4

Let $x = x_1, \cdots, x_L$ be a trace and ${}^rX = x_L, \cdots, x_1$ its *reverse*. If P^o is an OPT policy for X and $B_0 = \phi$, and ${}^rP^o$ is an OPT policy for ${}^rX$ and ${}^rB_0 = \phi$, then $|\phi|_{P^o} = |\phi|_{{}^rP^o}$.

Proof. Let us assume that the theorem does not hold. Thus, without loss of generality, suppose that $|\phi|_{{}^rP^o} = |\phi|_{P^o} + k$ where k is an integer and $k > 0$. If D distinct pages are referenced in X (and in ${}^rX$) and if $D \leqslant C$, the buffer capacity, then we have an immediate contradiction, since $|\phi|_{P^o} = |\phi|_{{}^rP^o} = L$. We therefore assume $D > C$.

Let us denote the state sequence under P^o as $B_0, B_1, \cdots, B_L$. From Lemma 2 we can set $B_0 = B_C$ without disturbing the validity of P^o. From Lemma 3 we can alter P^o such that $B_L = E_C$. Note that the altered policy contains the same number of ϕ's as P^o, since P^o is an OPT policy. (We subsequently refer to the altered policy as P^o.) Similarly, if ${}^rB_0, {}^rB_1, \cdots, {}^rB_L$ is the state sequence under ${}^rP^o$ we can assume that ${}^rB_0 = {}^rB_C$ and ${}^rB_L = {}^rE_C$.

Consider now the state sequence ${}^rB_L, {}^rB_L, {}^rB_{L-1}, \cdots, {}^rB_2, {}^rB_1$. Since $x_L \in {}^rB_1, x_{L-1} \in {}^rB_2, \cdots, x_2 \in {}^rB_{L-1}, x_1 \in {}^rB_L$, we see that this sequence is a valid (not necessarily demand) sequence for the trace X. Let us denote the corresponding valid policy pair as P' and Q'. We observe first that, since ${}^rE_C = B_C$, we have ${}^rB_L = B_C = B_0$. Thus P' and Q' (as well as P^o) are valid policies for X and B_0. Next we observe that ${}^rB_L = {}^rB_{L-1} + \{{}^rq_L^o\} - \{{}^rp_L^o\}$ can be written as ${}^rB_{L-1} = {}^rB_L + \{{}^rp_L^o\} - \{{}^rq_L^o\}$. But we also have ${}^rB_{L-1} = {}^rB_L + \{q'_2\} - \{p'_2\}$, which yields $q'_2 = {}^rp_L^o$ and $p'_2 = {}^rq_L^o$, since ${}^rp_L^o \cap {}^rq_L^o = \phi$. Similarly, since ${}^rB_{L-1} = {}^rB_{L-2} + \{{}^rq_{L-1}^o\} - \{{}^rp_{L-1}^o\}$, we have $q'_3 = {}^rp_{L-1}^o$ and $p'_3 = {}^rq_{L-1}^o$. Continuing in this manner we can show that

$$\left.\begin{aligned} q'_t &= {}^rp^o_{L+2-t} \\ p'_t &= {}^rq^o_{L+2-t} \end{aligned}\right\} \quad \text{for} \quad 2 \leqslant t \leqslant L \tag{A5}$$

Now, since $x_L \in {}^rB_0$ (recall that ${}^rB_0 = {}^rB_C$), it follows that ${}^rp_1^o = {}^rq_1^o = \phi$. Similarly, since $x_1 \in B_0$ (recall that $B_0 = B_C$), it follows that $p'_1 = q'_1 = \phi$. We can then trivially assume that $p'_1 = {}^rq_1^o$ and $q'_1 = {}^rp_1^o$. The significance of this is that, using Equation A5, we have established a one-to-one correspondence between P' and ${}^rQ^o$, and between Q' and ${}^rP^o$. In particular, $|\phi|_{P'} = |\phi|_{{}^rQ^o}$ and $|\phi|_{Q'} = |\phi|_{{}^rP^o}$. We now observe that $|\phi|_{{}^rQ^o} = |\phi|_{{}^rP^o}$, since $|{}^rB_0| = |{}^rB_1| = \cdots = |{}^rB_L| = C$. In other words, ${}^rp_t^o = \phi$ if and only if ${}^rq_t^o = \phi$, since the buffer is always full. We thus have shown that $|\phi|_{P'} = |\phi|_{{}^rQ^o} = |\phi|_{{}^rP^o}$.

Recall that P' and Q' are not necessarily demand policies. From Theorem 1 we can find a demand policy pair P'' and Q'' such that

$$\sum_{t=1}^{L} |q_t''| \leqslant \sum_{t=1}^{L} |q_t'|$$

From Equation A5 and the discussion that follows, we know that

$$|p_t'| = |q_t'| \qquad \text{for } 1 \leqslant t \leqslant L.$$

Since P'' and Q'' are demand policies, and since $|B_0| = |B_1''| = \cdots = |B_L''| = C$, we have $|p_t''| = |q_t''|$ for $1 \leqslant t \leqslant L$. Combining these results yields

$$\sum_{t=1}^{L} |p_t''| \leqslant \sum_{t=1}^{L} |p_t'| \qquad \text{or} \qquad |\phi|_{P''} \geqslant |\phi|_{P'}$$

But then we have $|\phi|_{p''} \geqslant |\phi|_{P'} = |\phi|_{rPo} = |\phi|_{Po} + k$. Since P^o was given as an OPT policy, we have from Theorem 2 a contradiction with $|\phi|_{p''} > |\phi|_{Po}$ for the demand policy P''. Thus our original assumption is false, and it must be the case that $|\phi|_{rPo} = |\phi|_{Po}$.

REFERENCES

1. A. Opler, "Dynamic flow of programs and data through hierarchical storage," *Information Processing 1965, Proceedings of IFIP Congress* **1**, 273-276 (1965).
2. E. Morenoff and J. B. McLean, "Application of level changing to a multi-level storage organization," *Communications of the Association for Computing Machinery* **10**, 3, 149-154 (1967).
3. C. J. Conti, "Concepts for buffer storage," *IEEE Computer Group News* **2**, 8, 9-13 (1969).
4. W. Anacker and C. P. Wang, "Performance evaluation of computing systems with memory hierarchies," *IEEE Transactions on Electronic Computers* **EC-16**, 6, 764-773 (1967).
5. R. L. Mattson and J. P. Jacob, "Optimization studies for computer systems with virtual memory," *Information Processing 1968, IFIP Congress Booklet I,* 47-54 (1968).
6. J. E. Shemer and G. A. Shippey, "Statistical analysis of paged and segmented computer systems," *IEEE Transactions on Electronic Computers* **EC-15**, 6, 855-863 (1966).
7. J. Fotheringham, "Dynamic storage allocation in the ATLAS computer, including an automatic use of a backing store," *Communications of the Association for Computing Machinery* **4**, 10, 435-436 (1961).
8. T. Kilburn, D. B. G. Edwards, M. J. Lanigan, and F. H. Sumner, "One-level storage system," *IEEE Transactions on Electronic Computers* **EC-11**, 2, 223-235 (1962).

9. M. H. J. Baylis, D. G. Fletcher, and D. J. Howarth, "Paging studies made on the I.C.T. ATLAS computer," *Information Processing 1968, IFIP Congress Booklet D,* 113-118 (1968).
10. D. H. Gibson, "Considerations in block-oriented systems design," *AFIPS Conference Proceedings, Spring Joint Computer Conference* **30**, Academic Press, New York, New York, 75-80 (1967).
11. S. J. Liptay, "Structural aspects of the System/360 Model 85: II The cache," *IBM Systems Journal* 7, 1, 15-21 (1968).
12. R. W. O'Neill, "Experience using a time-sharing multiprogramming system with dynamic address relocation hardware," *AFIPS Conference Proceedings, Spring Joint Computer Conference* **30**, Academic Press, New York, New York, 611-621 (1967).
13. L. A. Belady, "A study of replacement algorithms for a virtual-storage computer, *IBM Systems Journal* **5**, 2, 78-101 (1966).
14. C. J. Kuehner and B. Randell, "Demand paging in perspective," *AFIPS Conference Proceedings, Fall Joint Computer Conference* **33**, 1011-1018 (1968).
15. C. V. Ramamoorthy, "The analytic design of a dynamic look ahead and program segmenting system for multiprogrammed computers," *Proceedings of the 21st National Conference of the Association for Computing Machinery,* Thompson Book Company, Washington, D. C., 229-239 (1966).
16. J. Kral, "One way of estimating frequencies of jumps in a program," *Communications of the Association for Computing Machinery* **11**, 7, 475-480 (1968).
17. J. G. Kemeny and J. L. Snell, *Finite Markov Chains,* D. Van Nostrand Company, Inc., Princeton, New Jersey (1960).
18. L. A. Belady, R. A. Nelson, and G. S. Shedler, "An anomaly in spare-time characteristics of certain programs running in a paging machine," *Communications of the Association for Computing Machinery* **12**, 6, 349-353 (1969).
19. P. J. Denning, "The working set model for programming behavior," *Communications of the Association for Computing Machinery* **11**, 5, 323-333 (1968).

PART 2

AMERICAN FEDERATION OF INFORMATION PROCESSING SOCIETIES, INC.

Montvale, New Jersey

Two papers that were recipients of the AFIPS Outstanding Paper Award:

"A Unified Algorithm for Elementary Functions"
by John S. Walther
1971 Spring Joint Computer Conference

and

"Optimum Test Patterns for Parity Networks"
by D. C. Bossen, Daniel L. Ostapko, and A. M. Patel
1970 Fall Joint Computer Conference

3

A Unified Algorithm for Elementary Functions

by *J. S. Walther*

SUMMARY

This paper describes a single unified algorithm for the calculation of elementary functions, including multiplication, division, sin, cos, tan, arctan, sinh, cosh, tanh, arctanh, ln, exp, and square root. The basis for the algorithm is coordinate rotation in a linear, circular, or hyperbolic coordinate system, depending on which function is to be calculated. The only operations required are shifting, adding, subtracting, and the recall of prestored constants. The limited domain of convergence of the algorithm is calculated, leading to a discussion of the modifications required to extend the domain for floating point calculations.

A hardware floating point processor using the algorithm was built at Hewlett-Packard Laboratories. The block diagram of the processor, the microprogram control used for the algorithm, and measures of actual performance are shown.

INTRODUCTION

The use of coordinate rotation to calculate elementary functions is not new. In 1956 Volder developed a class of algorithms for the calculation of trigonometric and hyperbolic functions, including exponential and logarithm. In 1959 he described a COordinate Rotation DIgital Computer (CORDIC) for the calculation of trigonometric functions, multiplication, division, and conversion between binary and mixed radix number systems. Daggett in 1959 discussed the use of the CORDIC for decimal-binary conversions. In 1968 Liccardo did a master's thesis on the class of CORDIC algorithms.

It is not generally realized that many of these algorithms can be merged into one unified algorithm.

COORDINATE SYSTEMS

Let us consider coordinate systems parameterized by m in which the radius R and angle A of the vector $P = (x, y)$ shown in Figure 3-1 are defined as

Editor's Note: From *Spring Joint Computer Conference, 1971.* Reprinted by permission of the publisher, American Federation of Information Processing Societies, Inc., and the author.

$$R = [x^2 + my^2]^{1/2}$$

$$A = m^{-1/2} \tan^{-1}[m^{1/2}y/x]$$

It can be shown that R is the distance from the origin to the intersection of the curve of constant radius with the x axis, while A is twice the area enclosed by the vector, the x axis, and the curve of constant radius, divided by the radius squared. The curves of constant radius for the circular $(m = 1)$, linear $(m = 0)$, and hyperbolic $(m = -1)$ coordinate systems are shown in Figure 3-1.

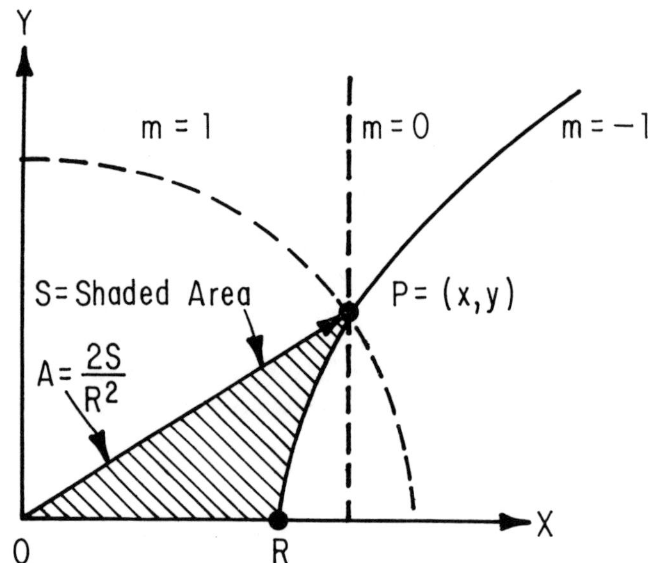

Figure 3-1. Angle A and Radius R of the Vector $P = (x, y)$

ITERATION EQUATIONS

Let a new vector $P_{i+1} = (x_{i+1}, y_{i+1})$ be obtained from $P_i = (x_i, y_i)$ according to

$$x_{i+1} = x_i + my_i\delta_i \tag{3}$$

$$y_{i+1} = y_i - x_i\delta_i \tag{4}$$

where m is the parameter for the coordinate system and δ_i is an arbitrary value. The angle and radius of the new vector in terms of the old are given by

$$A_{i+1} = A_i - \alpha_i \tag{5}$$

$$R_{i+1} = R_i{*}K_i \tag{6}$$

where

$$\alpha_i = m^{-1/2} \tan^{-1}[m^{1/2} \delta_i] \tag{7}$$

$$K_i = [1 + m\delta_i^2]^{1/2} \tag{8}$$

The angle and radius are modified by quantities which are independent of the coordinate values. Table 3-1 gives the equations for α_i after applying identities $A2$ and $A5$ from the appendix.

Table 3-1. Angles and Radius Factors

Coordinate System m	*Angle* α_i	*Radius Factor* K_i
1	$\tan^{-1}\delta_i$	$(1 + \delta_i^2)^{1/2}$
0	δ_i	1
−1	$\tanh^{-1}\delta_i$	$(1 - \delta_i^2)^{1/2}$

For n iterations we find

$$A_n = A_0 - \alpha \tag{9}$$

$$R_n = R_0^* K \tag{10}$$

where

$$\alpha = \sum_{i=0}^{n-1} \alpha_i \tag{11}$$

$$K = \prod_{i=0}^{n-1} K_i \tag{12}$$

The total change in angle is merely the sum of the incremental changes, while the total change in radius is the product of the incremental changes.

If a third variable z is provided for the accumulation of the angle variations

$$z_{i+1} = z_i + \alpha_i \tag{13}$$

and the set of difference equations (3), (4), and (13) is solved for n iterations, we find

$$x_n = K\{x_0 \cos(\alpha m^{1/2}) + y_0 m^{1/2} \sin(\alpha m^{1/2})\} \tag{14}$$

$$y_n = K\{y_0 \cos(\alpha m^{1/2}) - x_0 m^{-1/2} \sin(\alpha m^{1/2})\} \tag{15}$$

$$z_n = z_0 + \alpha \tag{16}$$

where α and K are as in equations (11) and (12). These relations are summarized in Figure 3-2 for $m = 1$, $m = 0$, *and* $m = -1$ for the following special cases.

1. A is forced to zero: $y_n = 0$.

2. z is forced to zero: $z_n = 0$.

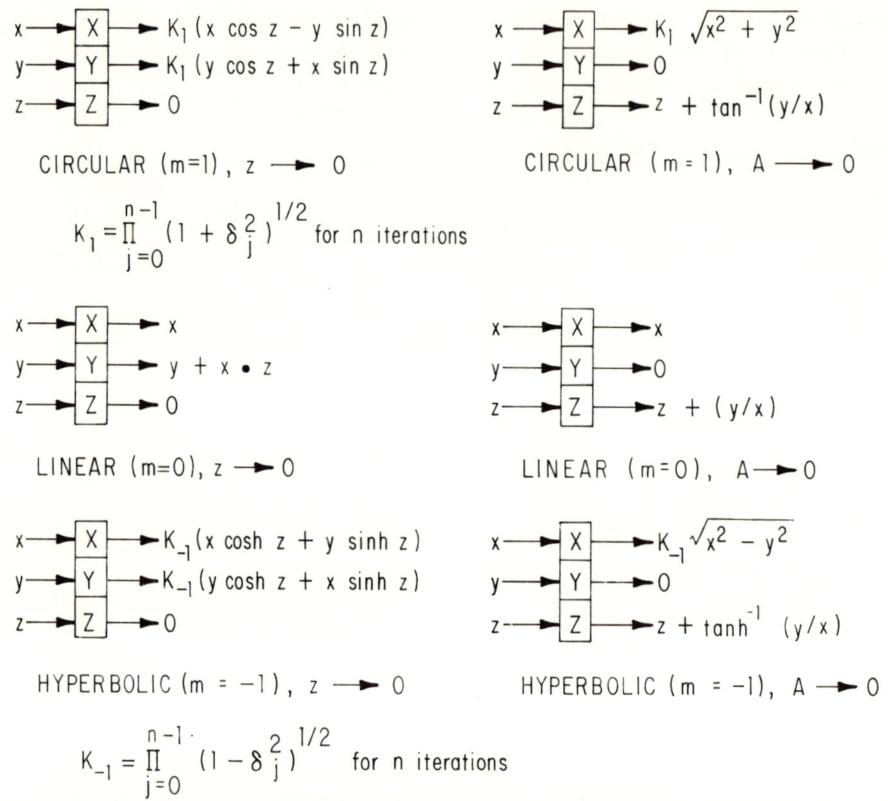

Figure 3-2. Input-Output Functions for CORDIC Modes

The initial values x_0, y_0, z_0 are shown on the left of each block in the figure, while the final values x_n, y_n, z_n are shown on the right. The identities given in the appendix were used to simplify these results. By the proper choice of the initial values the functions $x\,z$, y/x, $\sin z$, $\cos z$, $\tan^{-1} y$, $\sinh z$, $\cosh z$, and $\tanh^{-1} y$ may be obtained. In addition, the following functions may be generated:

$$\tan z = \sin z / \cos z \tag{17}$$

$$\tanh z = \sinh z / \cosh z \tag{18}$$

$$\exp z = \sinh z + \cosh z \tag{19}$$

$$\ln w = 2 \tanh^{-1} [y/x] \text{ where } x = w + 1 \text{ and } y = w - 1 \tag{20}$$

$$(w)^{1/2} = (x^2 - y^2)^{1/2} \text{ where } x = w + \tfrac{1}{4} \text{ and } y = w - \tfrac{1}{4} \tag{21}$$

CONVERGENCE SCHEME

The angle A of the vector P may be forced to zero by a converging sequence of rotations α_i which at each step brings the vector closer to the positive x axis. The magnitude of each element of the sequence may be predetermined, but the direction of rotation must be determined at each step such that

$$|A_{i+1}| = ||A_i| - \alpha_i| \tag{22}$$

The sum of the remaining rotations must at each step be sufficient to bring the angle to at least within α_{n-1} of zero, even in the extreme case where $A_i = 0$, $|A_{i+1}| = \alpha_i$. Thus,

$$\alpha_i - \sum_{j=i+1}^{n-1} \alpha_j < \alpha_{n-1} \tag{23}$$

The domain of convergence is limited by the sum of the rotations.

$$|A_0| - \sum_{j=0}^{n-1} \alpha_j < \alpha_{n-1} \tag{24}$$

$$\max |A_0| = \alpha_{n-1} + \sum_{j=0}^{n-1} \alpha_j \tag{25}$$

To show that A converges to within α_{n-1} of zero within n steps, we first prove the following theorem.

Theorem

$$|A_i| < \alpha_{n-1} + \sum_{j=i}^{n-1} \alpha_j \tag{26}$$

holds for $i \geqslant 0$.

Proof

We proceed by induction on i. The hypothesis (26) holds for $i = 0$ by (24). We now show that if the hypothesis is true for i then it is also true for $i + 1$. Subtracting α_i from (26) and applying (23) at the left side yields

$$-\left[\alpha_{n-1} + \sum_{j=i+1}^{n-1} \alpha_j\right] < -\alpha_i \, |A_i| - \alpha_i < \left[\alpha_{n-1} + \sum_{j=i+1}^{n-1} \alpha_j\right] \tag{27}$$

Application of (22) then yields

$$|A_{i+1}| < \alpha_{n-1} + \sum_{j=i+1}^{n-1} \alpha_j \tag{28}$$

as was to be shown. Therefore, by induction, the hypothesis holds for all $i \geqslant 0$. In particular, the theorem is true for $i = n$ so that

$$|A_n| < \alpha_{n-1} \tag{29}$$

The same scheme may be used to force the angle in z to zero. The proof of convergence proceeds exactly as before, except that A is replaced by z in equations (22) through (29). By equation (25) z has the same domain of convergence as A.

$$\max |z_0| = \max |A_0|. \tag{30}$$

Note that since K is a function of δ_i^2, where $\delta_i = m^{-1/2} \tan[m^{1/2}\alpha_i]$, K is independent of the sequence of signs chosen for the α_i. Thus for a fixed sequence of α_i magnitudes, the constant $1/K$ may be used as an initial value to counteract the factor K present in the final values.

USE OF SHIFTERS

The practical use of the algorithm is based on the use of shifters to effect the multiplication by δ_i. If ρ is the radix of the number system and F_i is an array of integers, where $i \geqslant 0$, then a multiplication of x by

$$\delta_i = \rho^{-F_i} \tag{31}$$

is simply a shift of x by F_i places to the right. The integers F_i must be chosen such that the angles

$$\alpha_{m,F_i} = m^{-1/2} \tan^{-1} (m^{1/2} \rho^{-F_i}) \tag{32}$$

satisfy the convergence criterion (23). The domain of convergence is then given by (25).

Table 3-2 shows some F sequences, convergence domains, and radius factors for a binary code.

Table 3-2. Shift Sequences for a Binary Code

radix ρ	*coordinate system* m	*shift sequence* F_{mi}, $i \geqslant 0$	*domain of convergence* *max* $\vert A_0 \vert$	*radius factor* K
2	1	0, 1, 2, 3, 4, i, . . .	~1.74	~1.65
2	0	1, 2, 3, 4, 5, $i+1$, . . .	1.0	1.0
2	−1	1, 2, 3, 4, 4, 5, ... *	~1.13	~0.80

*for $m = -1$ the following intergers are repeated: $\{4, 13, 40, 121, \ldots, k, 3k+1, \ldots\}$

The hyperbolic mode $(m = -1)$is somewhat complicated by the fact that for $\alpha_i = \tanh^{-1}(2^{-i})$ the convergence criterion (23) is not satisfied. However, it can be shown that

$$\alpha_i - \left(\sum_{j=i+1}^{n-1} \alpha_j \right) \alpha_{3i+1} < \alpha_{n-1} \tag{33}$$

and that therefore if the integers $\{4, 13, 40, 121, \ldots, k, 3k+1, \ldots\}$ in the F_i sequence are repeated then (23) becomes true.

EXTENDING THE DOMAIN

The limited domain imposed by the convergence criterion (25) may be extended by means of the prescaling identities shown in Table 3-3. For example, to calculate the sine of a large argument, we first divide the argument by $\pi/2$ obtaining a quotient Q and a remainder D where $|D| < \pi/2$. The table shows that only $\sin D$ or $\cos D$ need be calculated and that $\pi/2$ is within the domain of convergence. Note that the sine and cosine can be generated simultaneously by the CORDIC algorithm and that the answer may then be chosen as plus or minus one of these according to Q mod 4. As a second example, to calculate the logarithm of a large argument we first shift the argument's binary point E places until it is just to the left of the most significant non-zero bit. The fraction M then satisfies $0.5 \leqslant M < 1.0$, and, as shown in the table, therefore falls within the domain of convergence. The answer is calculated as $\log_e M + E \log_e 2$.

ACCURACY

The accuracy at the nth step is determined in theory by the size of the last of the converging sequence of rotations α_i, and for large n is approximately equal in digits to F_{n-1}. The accuracy in digits may conveniently be made equal to L, the length of storage used for each variable, by choosing n such that $F_{n-1} = L$.

In practice the accuracy is limited by the finite length of storage. The truncation of input arguments performed to make them fit within the storage length gives rise to unavoidable error, the size of which depends on the sensitivity of the calculated function to small changes in the input argument. In a binary code, the truncation of intermediate results after each of L iterations gives rise to a total of at most $\log_2 L$ bits of error. This latter error can be rendered harmless by using $L + \log_2 L$ bits for the storage of intermediate results.

In a normalized floating point number system it is desirable that all L bits of the result be accurate, independent of the absolute size of the argument. To accomplish this for very small arguments it is necessary to keep each storage register in a normalized form; i.e., in a form where there are no leading zeroes. It is possible to do this by transforming the iteration equations (3), (4), (13) to a normalized form according to the following substitutions:

Table 3-3. Prescaling Identities

Identity	*Domain*	*Domain Convergence*
$\sin\left(Q\frac{\pi}{2}+D\right)=\begin{cases}\sin D \text{ if } Q \bmod 4 = 0\\ \cos D \text{ if } Q \bmod 4 = 1\\ -\sin D \text{ if } Q \bmod 4 = 2\\ -\cos D \text{ if } Q \bmod 4 = 3\end{cases}$	$\lvert D\rvert < \frac{\pi}{2} = 1.57$	1.74
$\cos\left(Q\frac{\pi}{2}+D\right)=\begin{cases}\cos D \text{ if } Q \bmod 4 = 0\\ -\sin D \text{ if } Q \bmod 4 = 1\\ -\cos D \text{ if } Q \bmod 4 = 2\\ \sin D \text{ if } Q \bmod 4 = 3\end{cases}$	$\lvert D\rvert < \frac{\pi}{2} = 1.57$	1.74
$\tan\left(Q\frac{\pi}{2}+D\right)=\sin\left(Q\frac{\pi}{2}+D\right)\Big/\cos\left(Q\frac{\pi}{2}D\right)$	$\lvert D\rvert < \frac{\pi}{2} = 1.57$	1.74
$\tan^{-1}\left(\frac{1}{y}\right)=\frac{\pi}{2}-\tan^{-1}(y)$	$\lvert y\rvert < 1.0$	∞
$\sinh(Q\log_e 2+D)=$ $\frac{2^Q}{2}[\cosh D+\sinh D-2^{-2Q}(\cosh D-\sinh D)]$	$\lvert D\rvert < \log_e 2 = 0.69$	1.13
$\cosh(Q\log_e 2+D)=$ $\frac{2^Q}{2}[\cosh D+\sinh D+2^{-2Q}(\cosh D-\sinh D)]$	$\lvert D\rvert < \log_e 2 = 0.69$	1.13
$\tanh(Q\log_e 2+D)=$ $\sinh(Q\log_e 2+D)/\cosh(Q\log_e 2+D)$	$\lvert D\rvert < \log_e 2 = 0.69$	1.13
$\tanh^{-1}(1-M2^{-E})=\tanh^{-1}(T)+(E/2)\log_e 2$	$0.17 < T < 0.75$	$(-0.81, 0.81)$
where $T=(2-M-M2^{-E})/(2+M-M2^{-E})$	for $0.5 \leqslant M < 1, E \geqslant 1$	
$\exp(Q\log_e 2+D)=2^Q(\cosh D+\sinh D)$	$\lvert D\rvert < \log_e 2 = 0.69$	1.13
$\log_e(M2^E)=\log_e M+E\log_e 2$	$0.5 \leqslant M < 1.0$	$(0.10, 9.58)$
$\mathrm{sqrt}(M2^E)=\begin{cases}2^{E/2}\,\mathrm{sqrt}(M) & \text{if } E \bmod 2 = 0\\ 2^{(E+1)/2}\,\mathrm{sqrt}(M/2) & \text{if } E \bmod 2 = 1\end{cases}$	$\begin{cases}0.5 \leqslant M < 1.10\\ 0.25 \leqslant M/2 < 0.5\end{cases}$	$(0.03, 2.42)$
$(M_x 2^{E_x})(M_z 2^{E_z})=(M_x M_z)2^{E_x+E_z}$	$0.5 \leqslant \lvert M_z\rvert < 1.0$	$(-1.0, 1.0)$
$(M_y 2^{E_y})/(M_x 2^{E_x})=(M_y/2M_x)2^{E_y-E_z+1}$	$0.25 \leqslant \lvert M_y/2M_x\rvert < 1.0$	$(-1.0, 1.0)$

$$x \text{ becomes } x' \tag{34}$$

$$y \text{ becomes } y'\,2^{-E} \tag{35}$$

$$z \text{ becomes } z'\,2^{-E} \tag{36}$$

$$\alpha_F \text{ becomes } \alpha_F'\,2^{-F} \tag{37}$$

where E, a positive integer, is chosen such that the initial argument, placed into either the y or z register, is normalized.

The result of the substitutions is

$$x' \leftarrow x' + my'2^{-(F+E)} \tag{38}$$

$$y' \leftarrow y' - x'2^{-(F-E)} \tag{39}$$

$$z' \leftarrow z' + \alpha_F'2^{-(F-E)} \tag{40}$$

For simplicity the subscripts i and $i + 1$ have been dropped. Instead, α has been expressed as a function of F as in equation (32), and the replacement operator ($\leftarrow$) has been used. i may be initialized to a value such that $F_i = E$:

$$i_{\text{initial}} \leftarrow \{i \mid F_i = E\}, \tag{41}$$

and n may be chosen such that L significant bits are obtained:

$$n \leftarrow \{n \mid F_{n-1} - E = L\}. \tag{42}$$

Note that $n - i_{\text{initial}} \approx L$ and that therefore providing $L + \log_2 L$ bits for the storage of intermediate results is still adequate.

The radius factor K is now a function of $i = i_{\text{initial}}$ as well as m.

$$K_{m,i} = \prod_{j=i}^{n-1} (1 + m2^{-2F_j})^{1/2} \tag{43}$$

Fortunately, not all the reciprocal constants $1/K_{m,i}$ need to be stored since for large values of i

$$\frac{1}{K_{m,i}} \approx 1 - m(^2/_3)2^{-2i}, \tag{44}$$

and therefore all the constants having $i > L/2$ are identical to within L significant bits. Therefore, only $L/2$ constants need to be stored for $m = +1$ and also for $m = -1$. For $m = 0$ no constants need to be stored since $K_{0,i} = 1$ for $i \geqslant 1$.

A similar savings in storage can be made for the angle constants $\alpha_{m,F}$ since for large values of F

$$\alpha'_{m,F} \equiv \alpha_{m,F}\, 2^F \approx 1 - m(^1/_3)2^{-2F} \tag{45}$$

and thus, as for the K constants, only $L/2$ constants need to be stored for $m = +1$ and also for $m = -1$. For $m = 0$ no constants need to be stored since $\alpha'_{0,F} = 1$ for $F \geqslant 1$.

HARDWARE IMPLEMENTATION

A hardware floating point processor based on the CORDIC algorithm has been built at Hewlett-Packard Laboratories. Figure 3-3 shows a block diagram of the processor which consists of three identical arithmetic units operated in parallel. Each arithmetic unit contains a 64-bit register, an 8-bit parallel adder/subtracter, and an 8-out-of-48 multiplex shifter. The assembly of arithmetic units is controlled by a microprogram stored in a read-only memory (ROM),

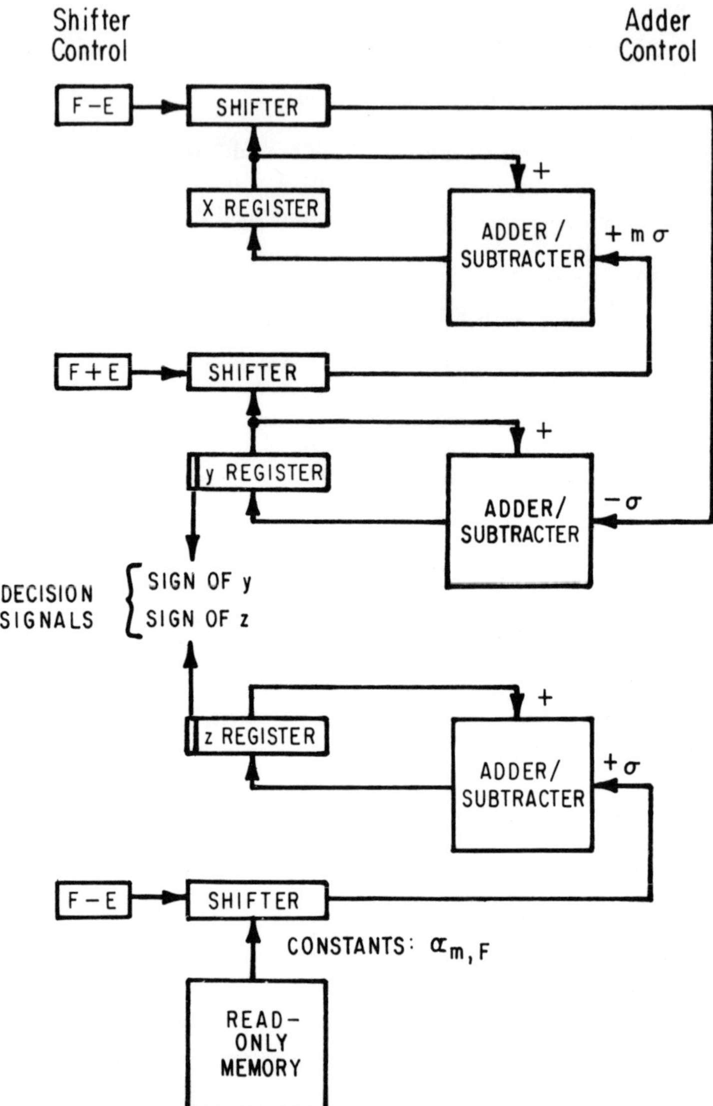

Figure 3-3. Hardware Block Diagram

which also contains the angle and radius-correction constants. The ROM contains 512 words of 48 bits each and operates on a cycle time of 200 nanoseconds.

The processor accepts three data types: 48-bit floating point, 32-bit floating point, and 32-bit integer. All the functions are calculated to 40 bits of precision (approximately 12 decimal digits), and the accuracy is limited only by the truncation of input arguments.

The essential aspects of the microprogram used to execute the CORDIC algorithm are shown in Figure 3-4. The initial argument and correction constants are loaded into the three registers and m is set to one of the three values $1, 0, -1$. If the initial argument is small, it is normalized and E is set to minus the binary exponent of the result; otherwise, E is set to zero. Next, i is initialized to a value such that $F_{m,i} = E$. A loop is then entered and is repeated until $F_{m,i} - E = L$. In this loop the direction of rotation necessary to force either of the angles A or z to zero is chosen; the binary variable σ, used to control the three

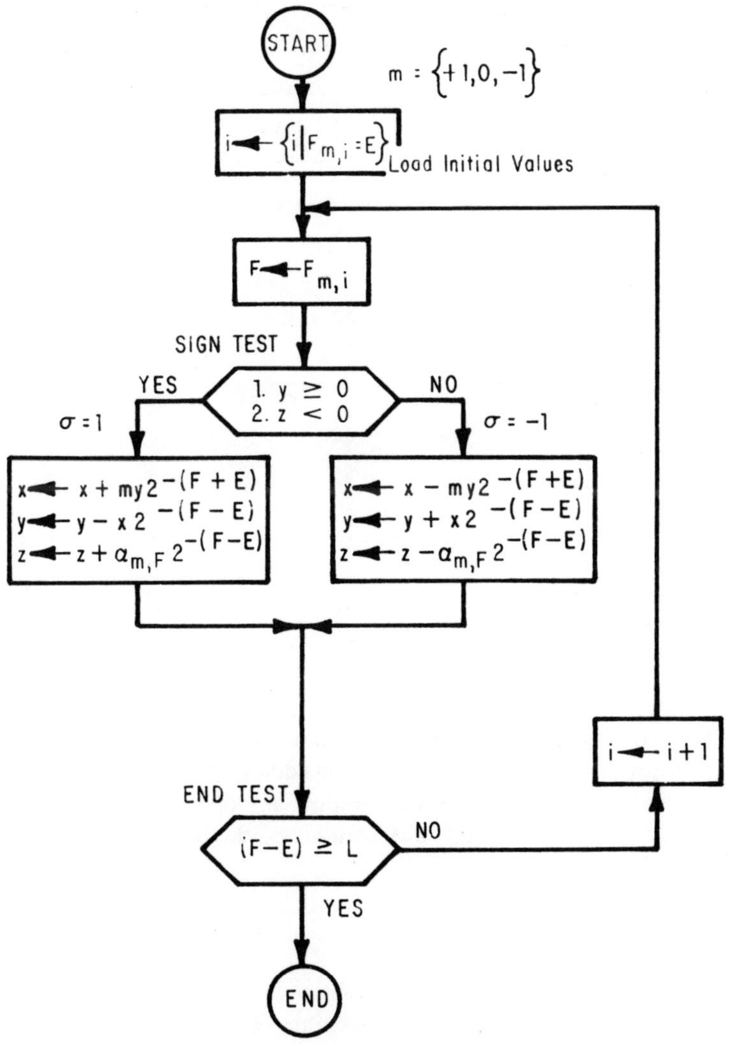

Figure 3-4. Flowchart of the Microprogram Control

adder/subtracters, is set to either +1 or −1, and the iteration equations are executed.

Table 3-4 gives a breakdown of the maximum execution times for the most important functions. The figures in the column marked "data transfers from computer" are the times for operand and operation code transfers between the processor and an HP-2116 computer.

Table 3-4. Maximum Execution Times

ROUTINE	CORDIC EXECUTION μsec	PRESCALE, NORMALIZE, misc. μsec	DATA TRANSFERS from COMPUTER μsec	TOTAL μsec
LOAD	0	5	25	30
STORE	0	0	15	15
ADD	0	15	25	40
SUBTRACT	0	25	25	50
MULTIPLY	60	15	25	100
DIVIDE	60	15	25	100
SIN	70	85	5	160
COS	70	85	5	160
TAN	130	85	5	220
ATAN	70	15	5	90
SINH	70	55	5	130
COSH	70	55	5	130
TANH	130	55	5	190
ATANH	70	45	5	120
EXPONENTIAL	70	55	5	130
LOGARITHM	70	45	5	120
SQUARE ROOT	70	25	5	100

The processor retains the result of each executed function. Thus add, subtract, multiply, and divide require only one additional operand to be supplied, and the one operand functions do not require any operand transfers. The first operand is loaded via the LOAD instruction, and the final result is retrieved via the STORE instruction.

CONCLUSION

The unified CORDIC algorithm is attractive for the calculation of elementary functions because of its simplicity, its accuracy, and its capability for high speed execution via parallel processing. Its applications include desktop calculators, as in the HP-9100 series; air navigation computers, as described in Volder's original work; and floating point processors, as illustrated in this paper.

ACKNOWLEDGMENT

The author wishes to thank the many people at Hewlett-Packard Laboratories and Cupertino Division for their contributions and support.

REFERENCES

1. D. H. Daggert. *Decimal-binary conversion in Cordic.* IRE Transactions on Electronic Computers, Vol. EC-8, No. 3, pp. 355-339, September, 1959.
2. M. A. Liccardo. *An interconnect processor with emphasis on Cordic mode operation.* Masters Thesis EE Dept. University of California at Berkeley, September, 1968.
3. J. E. Volder. *Binary computation algorithms for coordinate rotation and function generation.* Convair Report IAR-1, 148 Aeroelectronics Group, June 1956.
4. J. E. Volder. *The Cordic trigonometric computing technique.* IRE Transactions on Electronic Computers, Vol. EC-8, No. 3, pp. 330–334, September, 1959.

APPENDIX

Mathematical identities

Let $i = (-1)^{1/2}$

$$z \equiv \lim_{m \to 0} m^{-1/2} \sin(zm^{1/2}) \tag{A1}$$

$$z \equiv \lim_{m \to 0} m^{-1/2} \tan^{-1}(zm^{1/2}) \tag{A2}$$

$$\sinh z \equiv -i \sin(iz) \tag{A3}$$

$$\cosh z \equiv \cos(iz) \tag{A4}$$

$$\tanh^{-1} z \equiv -i \tan^{-1}(iz) \tag{A5}$$

4
Optimum Test Patterns for Parity Networks

by *D. C. Bossen, D. L. Ostapko, and A. M. Patel*

INTRODUCTION

The logic related to the error detecting and/or correcting circuitry of digital computers often contains portions which calculate the parity of a collection of bits. A tree structure composed of Exclusive-OR gates is used to perform this calculation. Similar to any other circuitry, the operation of this parity tree is subject to malfunctions. A procedure for testing malfunctions in a parity tree is presented in this report.

Two important assumptions are maintained throughout this paper. First, it is assumed that the parity tree is realized as an interconnection of Exclusive-OR gates whose internal structure is unknown or may differ. This requires that each gate in the network receive a complete functional test. Second, it is assumed that detection of single gate failures is desired.

Since each gate must be functionally tested, an m-input Exclusive-OR gate must receive 2^m input patterns. It will be shown that 2^m test patterns are also sufficient to test the network of any size, if m is the maximum number of input lines to any Exclusive-OR gate. Hence the procedure yields the minimum number of test patterns necessary to completely test the network for any single Exclusive-OR gate failure. It will also be shown, by example, that the procedure is fast and easy to apply even for parity trees having a large number of inputs.

GATE AND NETWORK TESTABILITY

Since the approach is to test the network by testing every gate in the network, it is primarily necessary to discuss what constitutes a test for an individual Exclusive-OR gate. Although it is assumed that the parity trees are realized as a network of Exclusive-OR gates, no internal realization is assumed for the Exclusive-OR gates. Hence it will be presumed that all 2^k input patterns are necessary to diagnose a single k-input Exclusive-OR gate. Each gate, therefore, is given a complete functional test so that single error detection means that any error in one Exclusive-OR gate can be detected. Following is the definition of a gate test.

Editor's Note: From *Fall Joint Computer Conference, 1970.* Reprinted by permission of the publisher, American Federation of Information Processing Societies, Inc., and the authors.

Definition 1

A test for a k-input Exclusive-OR gate is the set of 2^k distinct input patterns of length k. Figure 4-1 shows a three-input Exclusive-OR gate, the $2^3 = 8$ input test patterns, and the output sequence which must result if a complete functional test is to be performed.

Figure 4-1. Three Input Exclusive-OR Gate with Test Patterns

If the output sequence and the sequences applied to each input are considered separately, each will be a vector of length 2^k. Thus the Exclusive-OR gate can be considered to operate on input vectors while producing an output vector. Figure 4-2 shows a three-input Exclusive-OR gate when it is considered as a vector processor. In terms of vectors, a test is defined as follows.

WHERE $\underline{a}$ = 00010111, $\underline{b}$ = 00101011, $\underline{c}$ = 01001101, $\underline{d}$ = 01110001

Figure 4-2. Three Input Exclusive-OR Gate as a Vector Processor

Definition 2

A test for a k-input Exclusive-OR gate is a set of k vectors of length 2^k which, when considered as k sequences of length 2^k, presents all 2^k distinct test patterns to the gate inputs.

Theorem 1

If K is a test for a k-input Exclusive-OR gate, then any set $M, M \subset K$, having $m, 2 \leqslant m \leqslant k - 1$, elements forms 2^{k-m} tests for an m-input Exclusive-OR gate.

Proof

Consider the k vectors in K as sequences. Arrange the sequences as a k by 2^k matrix in which the last m rows are the sequences in M. Code each column as a binary number with the highest order bit at the top. Since the columns are all distinct according to definition 1, each of the numbers 0 through $2^k - 1$ must appear exactly once. Considering just the bottom m rows, it follows that each of the binary numbers 0 through $2^m - 1$ must appear exactly 2^{k-m} times. Since each of the possible sequences of m bits appears 2^{k-m} times, definition 1 implies that the set M forms 2^{k-m} tests for an m-input Exclusive-OR gate.

Network Testability

Two conditions are necessary for a network of Exclusive-OR gates to be completely tested. First, each gate must receive a set of input vectors that forms a test. Second, any one gate error must be detectable at the network output. For the first condition it is necessary that the set of vectors from which the tests are taken be closed under the operation performed by the k-input Exclusive-OR gates. The second condition requires that any erroneous output vector produce an erroneous network output vector. The structure of this set of vectors and their generation will be discussed in the following sections.

AN EXAMPLE

The test pattern generation procedure is so simple and easy to apply that it will be presented by way of an example before the theoretical properties of the desired sequences are discussed. The algorithm proceeds by selecting an arbitrary output sequence and then successively determining input sequences which test each gate to produce the desired output.

Figure 4-3 presents the seven sequences and the associated addition table that will be used in the example. Figure 4-4 illustrates the gate-labeling procedure that will be used to determine the inputs when the output is specified. Figure 4-5 shows the parity tree with 57 inputs and 30 Exclusive-OR gates of two and three inputs arranged in a four-level tree. The procedure generates eight test patterns which will completely test all 30 gates of the tree.

W_0	=	1 0 1 1 1 0 0
W_1	=	0 1 0 1 1 1 0
W_2	=	0 0 1 0 1 1 1
W_3	=	1 0 0 1 0 1 1
W_4	=	1 1 0 0 1 0 1
W_5	=	1 1 1 0 0 1 0
W_6	=	0 1 1 1 0 0 1

	W_0	W_1	W_2	W_3	W_4	W_5	W_6
W_0	0	W_5	W_3	W_2	W_6	W_1	W_4
W_1		0	W_6	W_4	W_3	W_0	W_2
W_2			0	W_0	W_5	W_4	W_1
W_3				0	W_1	W_6	W_5
W_4					0	W_2	W_0
W_5						0	W_3
W_6							0

Figure 4-3. Test Sequences and Their Addition Table

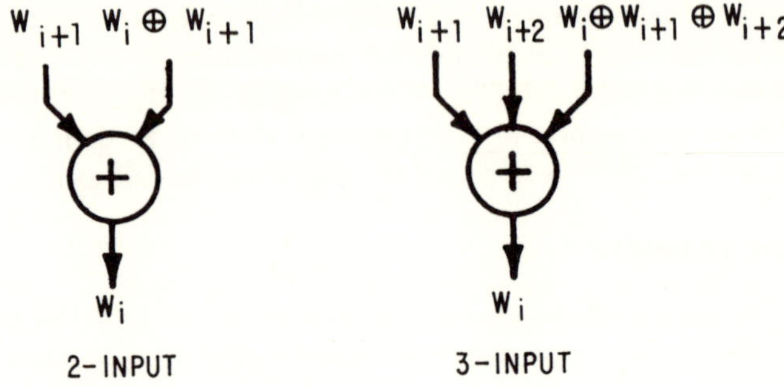

W i+1 Wi ⊕ Wi+1
Wi
2-INPUT
Wi+1 Wi+2 Wi⊕Wi+1 ⊕Wi+2
Wi
3-INPUT

NOTE: $W_i \equiv W_i \pmod 7$

Figure 4-4. Gate Labeling Procedures

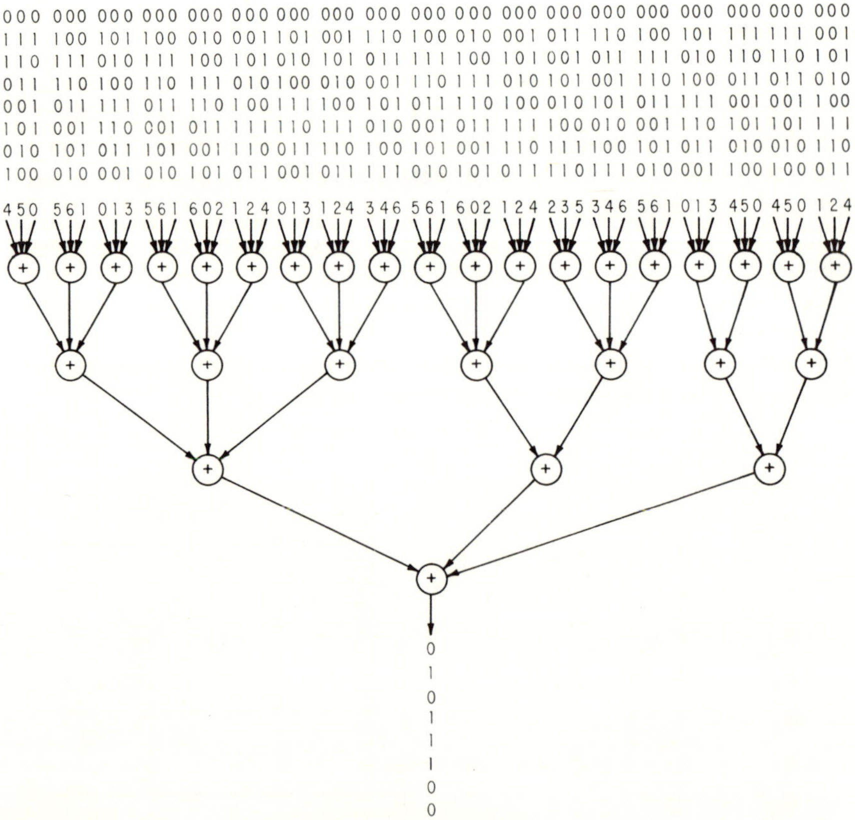

000 000 000 000 000 000 000 000 000 000 000 000 000 000 000 000 000 000 000
111 100 101 100 010 001 101 001 110 100 010 001 011 110 100 101 111 111 001
110 111 010 111 100 101 010 101 011 111 100 101 001 011 111 010 110 110 101
011 110 100 110 111 010 100 010 001 110 111 010 101 001 110 100 011 011 010
001 011 111 011 110 100 111 100 101 011 110 100 010 101 011 111 001 001 100
101 001 110 001 011 111 110 111 010 001 011 111 100 010 001 110 101 101 111
010 101 011 101 001 110 011 110 100 101 001 110 111 100 101 011 010 010 110
100 010 001 010 101 011 001 011 111 010 101 011 110 111 010 001 100 100 011
450 561 013 561 602 124 013 124 346 561 602 124 235 346 561 013 450 450 124
0
1
0
1
1
1
0
0

Figure 4-5. Four-Level Parity Tree with Test Patterns

The procedure is initiated by assigning an arbitrary sequence to the output of the tree. In the example, W_0 is selected as the final output sequence. Employing the three-input gate-labeling procedures shown in Figure 4-4, the inputs are determined to be W_1, W_2, and W_4. With these three sequences, the gate is completely tested. These inputs are then traced back to the three gates in the third level. Using the gate-labeling procedure again, the inputs for the gates from left to right are W_2, W_3, W_5; W_3, W_0; and W_5, W_2. The sequences assigned to the inputs can be determined quickly and easily by making use of tracing and labeling. Under proper operation, each gate is completely tested and a single gate failure will produce an incorrect sequence at the output. Above each input the required sequence is listed, and the correct output is the sequence W_0. The test patterns are obtained by reading across the sequences and noting the correct output. The test is completed by adding the all-zero test pattern. This should produce a zero output.

THEORETICAL PRELIMINARIES

Consider the set of vectors generated by taking all mod-2 linear combinations of the k vectors of a given test set K. This set is obviously closed under mod-2 vector addition. In a parity check tree network an input of any subset of vectors from this set will produce vectors in the set at all input-output nodes of the Exclusive-OR gates. Some further insight can be gained by viewing the above set as a binary group code. The generator matrix G of this code, whose rows are k vectors from K, contains all possible k-tuples as columns. If we delete the column of all 0's in G, the resulting code is known as a MacDonald [1] code in which the vector length n is $2^k - 1$ and the minimum distance d is 2^{k-1}. The cyclic form of the MacDonald code is the code generated by a maximum length shift register [2].

Theorem 2

Any independent set of k vectors from the Maximum Length Shift Register Code of length $2^k - 1$ forms a test set for a k-input Exclusive-OR gate, excepting the pattern of all 0's.

Proof

Any independent set of k-vectors from the code forms a generator of the code. In the Maximum Length Shift Register Code, as well as in the MacDonald Code, $2d - n = 1$. This implies* [3] that any generator matrix of the code contains one column of each non-zero type. By definition 2, this forms the test for a k-input Ex-OR gate excepting the test pattern of all 0's.

*In Reference 3 it is shown that in a group code with $2d - n = t > 0$, there are t columns of each type.

Corollary

For an m-input gate, $m \leqslant k$, any set of m-vectors from a MLSRC of length $2^k - 1$ forms a sufficient test.

The proof follows from Theorems 1 and 2.

The maximum length shift register sequences can be generated [2] by using a primitive polynomial $p(X)$ of degree k in GF (2). Let $g(X) = (X^n - 1)/p(X)$ where $n = 2^k - 1$. Then the first vector W_0 of the MLSRC is the binary vector obtained by concatenating $k - 1$ zeros to the sequence of the coefficients of $g(X)$. The vectors $W_1, W_3 \ldots W_{2^k-2}$ are then obtained by shifting W_1 cyclically to the right by one digit for $2^k - 2$ times. The method is illustrated for $k = 3$. A primitive polynomial of degree 3 in GF (2) can be obtained from tables [2], e.g., $X^3 + X + 1$ is primitive.

$$g(X) = (X^7 - 1)/(X_3 + X + 1) = X^4 + X^2 + X + 1.$$

Then W_0 is obtained from $g(X)$ as

$$W_0 = 1\ 0\ 1\ 1\ 1\ 0\ 0$$

The sequences $W_1, W_2 \ldots W_6$ are obtained by shifting W_0 cyclically as,

$$W_1 = 0\ 1\ 0\ 1\ 1\ 1\ 0$$

$$W_2 = 0\ 0\ 1\ 0\ 1\ 1\ 1$$

$$W_3 = 1\ 0\ 0\ 1\ 0\ 1\ 1$$

$$W_4 = 1\ 1\ 0\ 0\ 1\ 0\ 1$$

$$W_5 = 1\ 1\ 1\ 0\ 0\ 1\ 0$$

$$W_6 = 0\ 1\ 1\ 1\ 0\ 0\ 1$$

Note that when W_{2^k-2} is shifted cyclically to the right by 1 digit, the resulting vector is W_0. For the purpose of uniformity of relationship among the vectors, we introduce the notation: $W_i \equiv W_{i(\mathrm{mod}\ 2^k-1)}$. Now the following theorem gives a method of selecting independent vectors from a MLSRC.

Theorem 3

The vectors $W_i, W_{i+1}, \ldots, W_{i+k-1}$ in a MLSRC of length $2^k - 1$ form an independent set.

Proof

Suppose $g(X)$ is given by $g(X) = g_r X^r + g_{r-1} X^{r-1} + \ldots + g_1 X + g_0$, where $r = (2^k - 1) - k$. Then the set of vector $W_0, W_1, \ldots, W_{k-1}$ are given by

$$
\begin{array}{l}
W_0 = g_r\ g_{r-1}\ \cdot\ \ \cdot\ \cdot\ \cdot\ g_0\ 0\ 0\ 0\ \cdot\ \cdot\ 0 \\
W_1 = 0\ g_r\ \ g_{r-1}\ \cdot\ \cdot\ \cdot\ \cdot\ g_0\ 0\ 0\ \cdot\ \cdot\ 0 \\
W_2 = 0\ 0\ \ g_r\ \ \cdot\ \cdot\ \cdot\ \cdot\ \cdot\ g_0\ 0\ \cdot\ \cdot\ 0 \\
\cdot \\
\cdot \\
\cdot \\
W_{k-1} = 0\ 0\ \ 0\ \ 0\ \cdot\ \cdot\ \cdot\ g_r\ \cdot\ \cdot\ \cdot\ \cdot\ g_0
\end{array}
$$

Clearly they are linearly independent. Because of the cyclic relationship, this implies that $W_i, W_{i+1}, \ldots, W_{i+k-1}$ are independent.

Corollary

The vectors $W_{i+1}, W_{i+2}, \ldots, W_{i+m-1}$, and $W_i \oplus W_{i+1} \oplus \cdots \oplus W_{i+m-1}$, $(m \leqslant k)$, form an independent set. With this as a test to an m-input Ex-OR gate, the correct output vector is W_i.

As a direct consequence of the above theorems we have the following algorithm for the test pattern generation for a given Exclusive-OR network.

Algorithm for Test Pattern Generation

It is assumed that the Exclusive-OR network is constructed in the form of a tree by connecting m-input Ex-OR gates where m may be any number such that $m \leqslant k$.

1. Select any vector W_i from a MLSRC of length $2^k - 1$ as the output of the network.
2. Label the inputs to the last Ex-OR as $W_{i+1}, W_{i+2}, \ldots, W_{i+m-1}$, and $W_i \oplus W_{i+1} \oplus \ldots \oplus W_{i+m-1}$.
3. Trace each of the above inputs back to the driving gate with the same vector. Repeat steps (2) and (3) to determine the proper inputs to the corresponding gates.
4. The vectors at the input lines to the Ex-OR tree are then the test input vectors with the correct output as W_i.
5. An additional all-0 pattern as input to the network with 0 as correct output completes the test.

It is easy to see that the test patterns generated by the above algorithm provide a complete test for each Ex-OR gate in the parity check tree. Furthermore, any single gate failure will generate an erroneous word which *will* propagate to the output. This is due to the linearity of an Ex-OR gate. Suppose one of its inputs is the sequence W_i with a corresponding correct output sequence W_j. If the input W_i is changed by an error vector to $W_i + e$, then the corresponding output is $W_j + e$. Clearly the error will appear superimposed on the observed network output.

TEST MECHANIZATION

We have shown that the necessary test patterns for a parity tree can be determined by a simple procedure using a set of k independent vectors or code words $W_0, W_1, \ldots, W_{k-1}$ from a MLSRC as the input to each gate of k inputs. The result of applying this procedure to a network is an input sequence W_i for each network input and each network output. Testing is accomplished by applying the determined sequences simultaneously to each input and then comparing the expected network outputs with the observed network outputs.

Let the gate having the greatest number of inputs in the network show k inputs. The entire test can be mechanized using a single $(2^k - 1)$-stage feedback shift register. To do this, a unique property of the MLSR codes is used. From this property it follows that the entire set of non-zero code words is given by the $2^k - 2$ cyclic shifts of any non-zero code word, together with the code word itself.

If a $(2^k - 1)$-stage shift register is loaded with a particular code word W_0 as in Figure 4-6, then the sequence of bits observed at position 1 during $2^k - 1$ shifts of the register is the code word W_0. Similarly for every other position i, a different code word W_{i-1} is observed, so that the entire set of $2^k - 1$ sequences is available. Since the correct output of the network is one of the code words, it is also available at one of the stage outputs for comparison. The general test configuration is given by Figure 4-7.

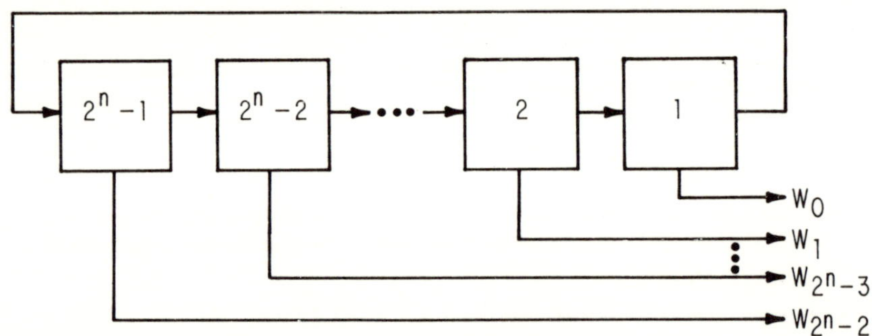

Figure 4-6. Shift Register for Generating Test Patterns

SELF-CHECKING PARITY TREE

Let us suppose that the test sequences and the shift register connections for a parity network have been determined as in Figure 4-7. A modification of this mechanization can be used to produce a self-testing parity network under its normal operation. The key idea is to monitor the normal randomly (assumed) occurring inputs to the network and to compare them with the present outputs of the shift register. When and only when a match occurs, the comparison of the outputs of the parity networks with the appropriate code words is used to indicate either correct or incorrect operation, and the shift register is shifted once.

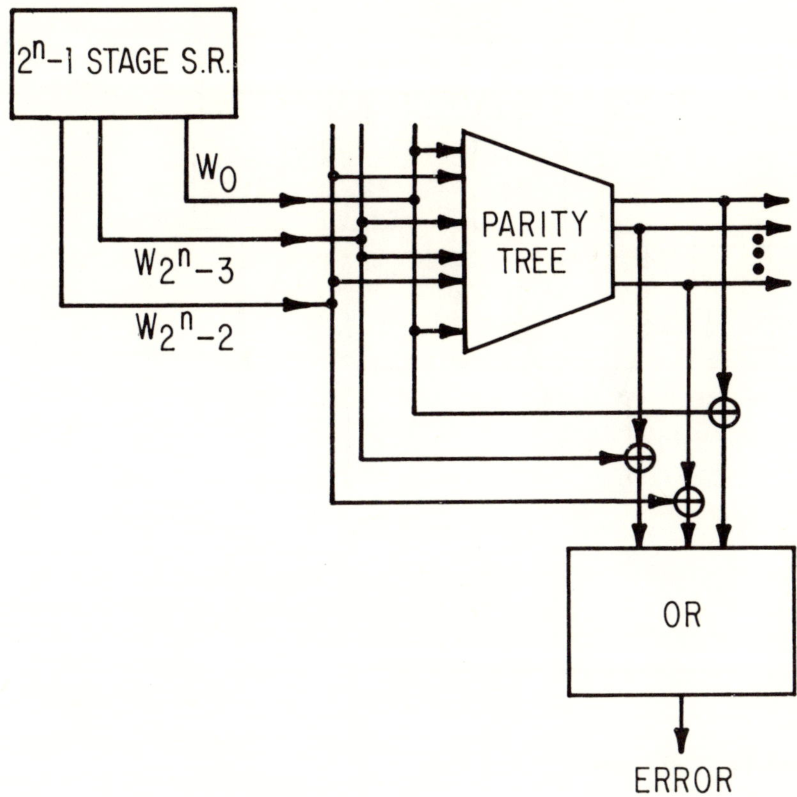

Figure 4-7. General Testing Scheme

This brings a new test pattern for comparison with the normal inputs. Every $2^k - 1$ shifts of the register means that a complete test for all single failures has been performed on the network.

The mechanization of the self-checking parity tree is shown in Figure 4-8. The inputs to the AND gate $A^1_{w_i}$ are the set of input lines of the parity tree which receive the test sequence W_i. The inputs to the AND gates $A^0_{w_i}$ are the inverse of the input lines of the parity tree which receive the test sequence W_i.

An alternate approach to self-checking is to use the testing circuit of Figure 4-7 as a permanent part of the parity tree. The testing is performed on a time-sharing or periodic basis while the circuit is not used in its normal mode. This is easily accomplished by having the clock, which controls the shift register, gated by a signal which indicates the parity tree is not being used. This could be a major portion of the memory cycle when the parity tree under consideration is used for memory ECC.

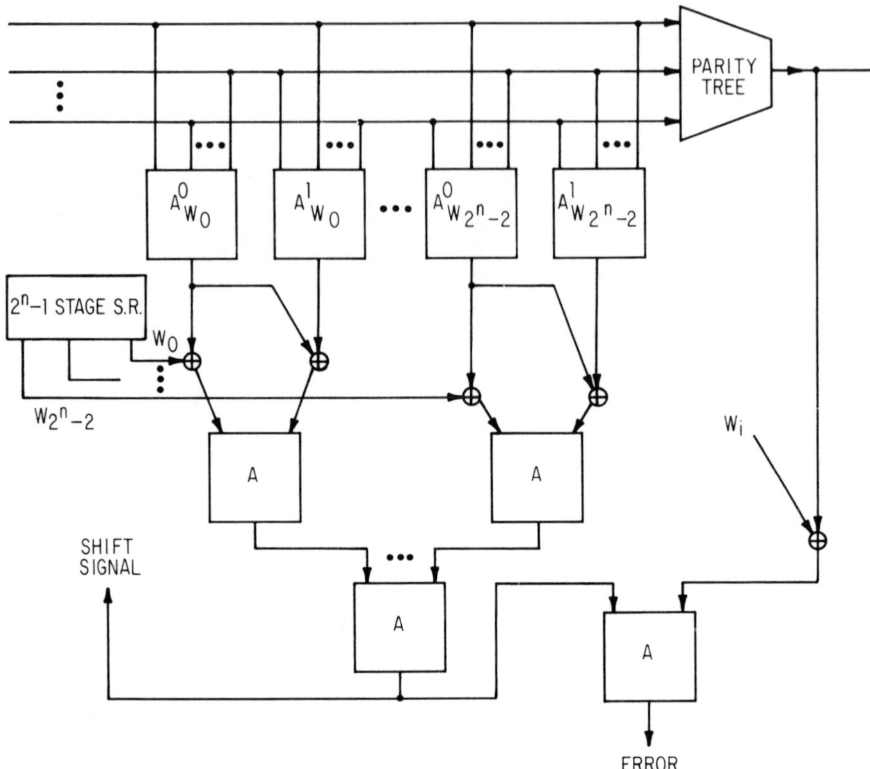

Figure 4-8. Self-Checking Parity Tree

CONCLUSION

We have shown that a very low and predictable number of test patterns are necessary and sufficient for the complete testing of a parity tree under the single failure assumption. The required tests are easily and rapidly determined by an algorithm which is presented. (An application of this technique is also given for a self-checking parity tree.) Since the effect of the input test patterns is a complete functional test of each gate, the tests are independent of any particular failure mode.

REFERENCES

1. J. E. MacDonald. *Design methods for maximum minimum-distance error correcting codes.* IBM J of R & D, Vol. 4, pp. 43-47, 1960.
2. W. W. Peterson. *Error-correcting codes.* MIT Press, Cambridge, Massachusetts 1961.
3. A. M. Patel. *Maximal group codes with specified minimum distance.* IBM J of R & D, Vol. 14, pp. 434-443, 1970.

PART 3

INTERNATIONAL FEDERATION FOR INFORMATION PROCESSING

Vienna, Austria

Two papers from the *Proceedings IFIP Congress 71 at Ljubljana* selected by an independent panel:

"Theory of Program Schemata"
by A. P. Ershov

and

"Shape Grammars and the Generative Specification of Painting and Sculpture"
by George Stiny and James Gips

5
Theory of Program Schemata

by *A. P. Ershov*

INTRODUCTION

The mathematical theory of computation and programming has always been of concern to IFIP. The well-known contribution of John McCarthy [41] has actually encouraged a new trend in the theory of programming, and many interesting and important investigations have resulted.

In this paper we shall consider another trend in the theory of programming initiated by Yu.I. Yanov in his classical paper [53] in which he investigated equivalent formal transformations of program schemata. We shall discuss this trend here, not because the author is concerned with this subject personally nor because Soviet mathematicians have made an essential contribution to it. In the first place, this trend will be dealt with because, in the author's opinion, in its depths there develops a solution to some fundamental problems of the theory of programming which will extend our knowledge of the nature of things and, through creating a new formal algorithmic language, will influence directly the technology of designing programming systems; besides, it will provide programmers with aids to programming new generations of computers–multiprocessor computer systems. To make this situation obvious and to attract attention to it is my purpose here. Those who work on the theory of programming might be interested to compare this paper with the review paper of 1967 [11]. Though this paper, to some extent, follows the above-mentioned review, the comparison will show only how many changes have taken place during the last four years.

METATHEORY

At present, the theory of programming has developed a diversified mathematical discipline with about 200 publications and its own internal structure. We shall begin our review with the metatheory of programming.

Editor's Note: From *IFIP Congress 71,* August 1971. Reprinted by permission of the publisher, North Holland Publishing Co.

Programs

The definition of a program begins with the description of some constructive objects representing the program. Such constructive objects are usually words (texts), labelled graphs, and some finite sets and systems of sets. It is usual to introduce a language for the program description; this way of constructing objects representing programs is called a syntax for program description.

Execution

An inherent part of the formal definition of programs is the concept of program execution. This concept is introduced by specifying a universal algorithm applied to any program. The process of applying this algorithm to some program is called program execution.

The process of program execution can have free parameters. Some of these free parameters relate to the program being executed. Usually these parameters are program arguments specifying its input data. Thus execution of some fixed program becomes a function of its input data. Sometimes the universal algorithm itself can have free parameters. In this case a fixed program, even with its fixed arguments, yields a whole set of executions corresponding to variations of the parameters of the universal algorithm. This approach is typical for certain problems in the theory of parallel programming.

Program execution is regarded as a process developing in time. The process is a sequence of events. The events are usually assumed to take place instantaneously at the bounds of time intervals. There is always a terminal event whose advent stops program execution. There are resulting events accompanying the terminal event. They allow us to declare some object to be a result of program execution. Thus, some function can be connected with a program, this function being called to be computed or realized by the program. The arguments of this function are the program's input data. The result of the function for a given argument is the result of program execution corresponding to this argument.

Let us examine some common features of definitions of programs and their execution. Program execution is a sequence of information transformations. So the concept of a program usually consists of two parts—operational and informational. These parts are not necessarily distinguishable at the syntactical level (e.g., in the computer memory there is no difference between instructions and processed information), but at the level of program execution there is always considered to be some unit of action which processes some units of information. The objects specifying units of action are called instructions or statements. The ability of the program to store information is provided by its memory. The program memory usually has some structure which allows the statements to act upon certain of the memory components (called locations or variables) rather than on the memory as a whole. An essential role in program formalism belongs to the means of identification of the memory components.

Statement execution in the general case consists of the processing of the information stored in the memory locations and in the definition of its successor (the statement which is executed after the given one). Thus between the statements there are two types of binary relation (statement B is an immediate successor of the statement A; statement B takes as arguments the results of statement A). An important generalization of these relations in control and information transfer is their "transitive closures" (statement B can be executed after statement A; the arguments of statement B are functionally dependent on the results of statement A). The splitting of a program into statements acting on the memory and the analysis of control and informational relations between the statements are perhaps the most general and typical features of the existing formalisms in the theory of programming.

Figure 5-1 is an example of a concrete program. Program statements form a so-called control flow graph. There are entry and exit vertices in the graph. They may contain input and output statements of the program. Each vertex, except the exit one, has one or two successors and is called, following Kaluzhnin [23], a transformer or a recognizer, respectively. Any kind of assignment statement which is constructed over some basic system of elementary operations can be a transformer. The recognizer is a predicate logic function having the form of a condition or an if-clause (in languages such as ALGOL and FORTRAN). The arguments and results of the statements are attached with variables—memory locations storing results of computations and implementing informational connections between statements.

Equivalence

The third essential part of the formalism of the program concept is the notion of the equivalence of programs. When a program calculates some function (as is usually the case), there is a natural and most general definition of equivalence: two programs which have a common set of arguments are functionally equivalent if their functions are the same.

However, an unavoidable obstacle in developing a general theory is the following negative result in the theory of algorithms. Some property of a program is said to be internal if it takes place for all programs functionally equivalent to it. Rice [46] has proved that for any internal property of a program there is no algorithm which would recognize those programs which possess the given property (naturally, the class of programs should be reasonably meaningful, for instance, it should compute any recursive functions).

The principal way of narrowing the concept of the equivalence of programs is to compare not only the values of the functions evaluated by programs, but also some history of computation during the execution. Formally, the concept of history is introduced as follows. In addition to the universal algorithm of the program execution another algorithm is introduced (it will be called a tracing algorithm) which, in accordance with the program and a set of its input

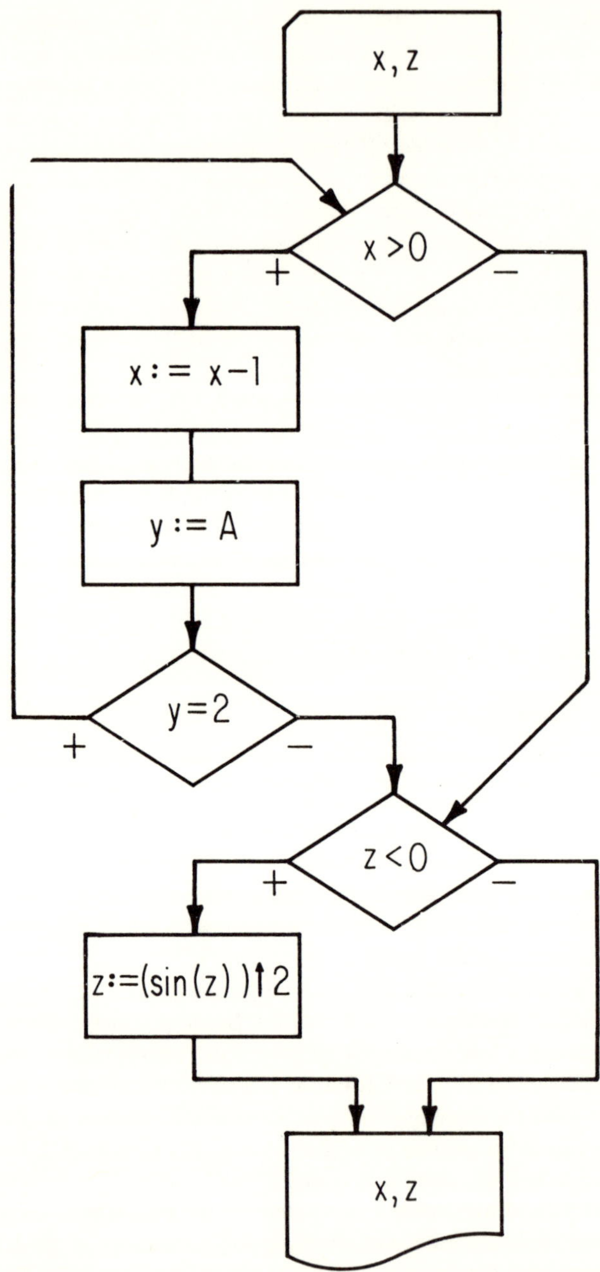

Figure 5-1. A Program

data, constructs some object. The latter is called the history of the program realization and contains some information about its execution. The history may comprise any number of details, but the result of the program execution has to be recovered by it in a single-valued way. Hence programs with coincident histories automatically have coincident results. A special case of a history is the program itself (an identical tracing algorithm). This history, naturally, is a most detailed one because we can get from the program any information by applying to it the universal algorithm of execution. The equivalence based on this history appears to be narrowest: the program is equivalent only to itself. In between the two poles there are a variety of definitions of equivalence differing in details of the considered program histories.

Below we shall outline the main types of program history considered in the theory.

(i) *Operational program history.* This consists of the sequence of transformers passed during program execution. Sometimes this sequence is accompanied by a sequence of memory states after execution of every statement from the history.

(ii) *Operational-logic program history.* Additional to (i), this includes all recognizers passed during execution of the program.

(iii) *An information flow graph of the program realization.* Transformers form the vertices of the graph. The vertex A is connected to the vertex B by an arc if B uses the result of A as one of its arguments.

(iv) *An information-logic graph of the program realization.* The vertices of the recognizers passed are added to the information graph. Their arguments are connected to the corresponding results by information flow arcs. Besides, each recognizer is connected by a special relation with each vertex of the information-logic graph, the passing or non-passing of which directly depends on the execution of the given recognizer.

(v) *The termal value of resulting variables.* It is obvious that the information flow graph is a graph which does not contain any cycles. This makes it possible, for each argument a of any vertex v of the graph, to construct a tree which involves all the vertices reachable from v in moving backwards the arcs of information flow. In this case, if some vertex is reachable in two ways, it is split into two. Then the argument a becomes a root of the resulting tree. This tree, which can be written algebraically as an expression or a term, is called, following Itkin, a termal value of the argument a. Moving "down" the information flow graph we finally obtain termal values of the resulting variables.

(vi) *Logic-termal history of realization.* This is achieved by adding to the termal value of the resulting variables the chain of the passed recognizers, together with the termal values of their arguments. The logic-termal history of realization is constructed from the information-logic graph.

Figure 5-2 shows examples of the above histories for some realization of the program in Figure 5-1. We can see that these histories are grouped in pairs. Each pair contains less information about realization than the previous pair. The second history in each pair contains some additional information about the execution of recognizers. For the evaluation of results as functions of the initial

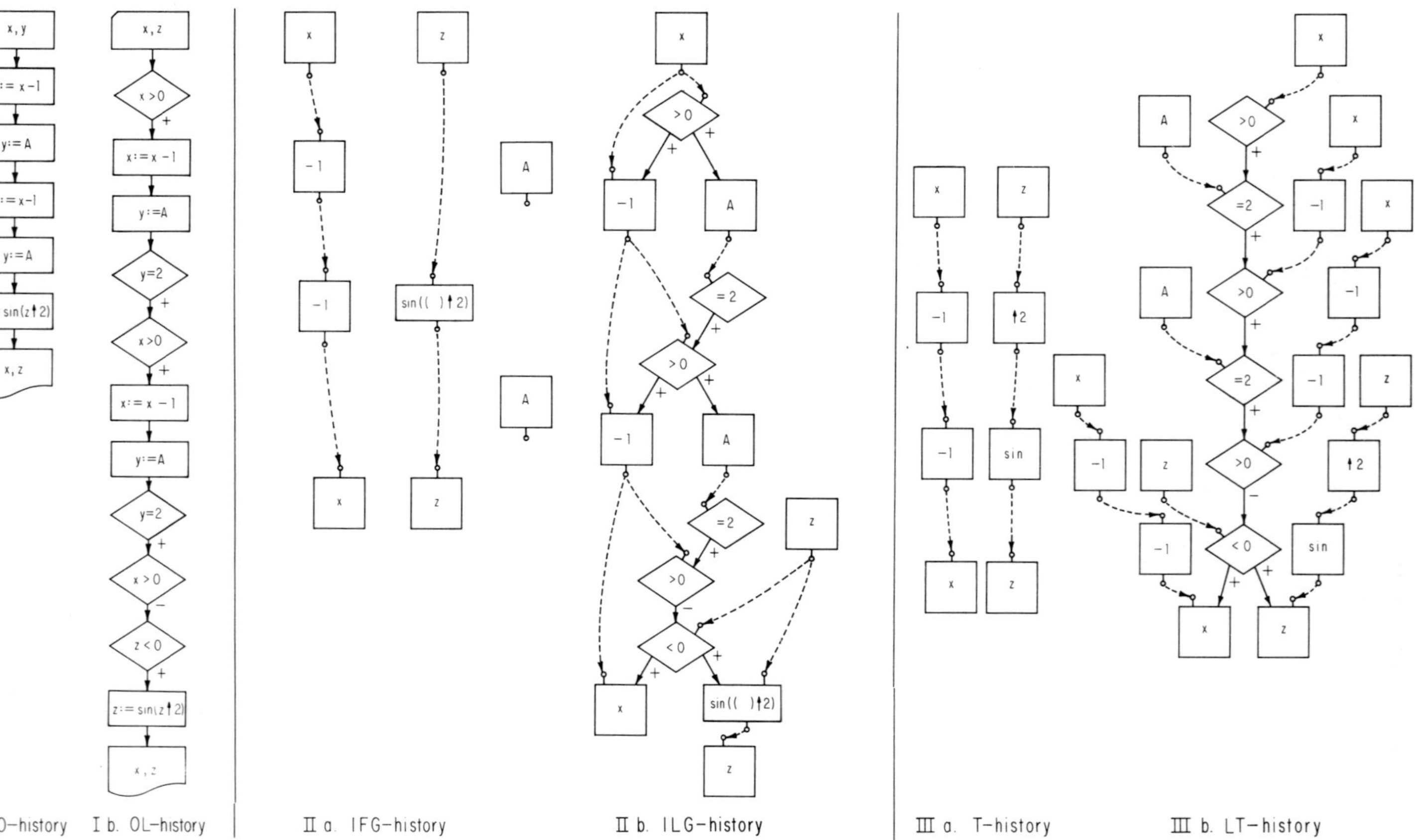

Figure 5-2. Examples of Histories

data, the information history alone is sufficient. However, it follows from numerous results, which are discussed below, that an attempt to deal with the information history only (even a most detailed one) yields algorithmically unsolvable equivalence. Moreover, in some cases the order of execution of recognizers is an essential characteristic of the program realization.

Figure 5-3 shows examples of the equivalent programs for different definitions of history.

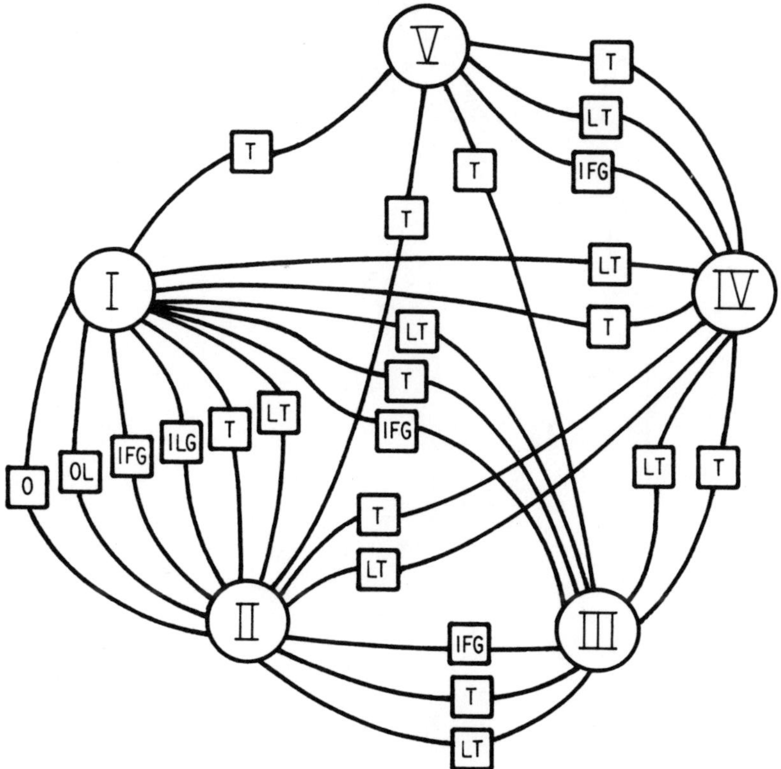

Figure 5-3. Examples of Equivalent Programs

Program Schemata

Consideration of a more detailed history of computation is in itself insufficient for developing effective methods of recognition of equivalence and of formal transformations of programs. The above mentioned results make us draw more restrictive conclusions: it is possible to construct a real class of programs such that none of the known non-trivial equivalences will be recognizable algorithmically. Therefore in order to obtain more constructive and concrete results one must sacrifice the concept of a program in spite of its universality and consider simpler and more abstract objects. Among such

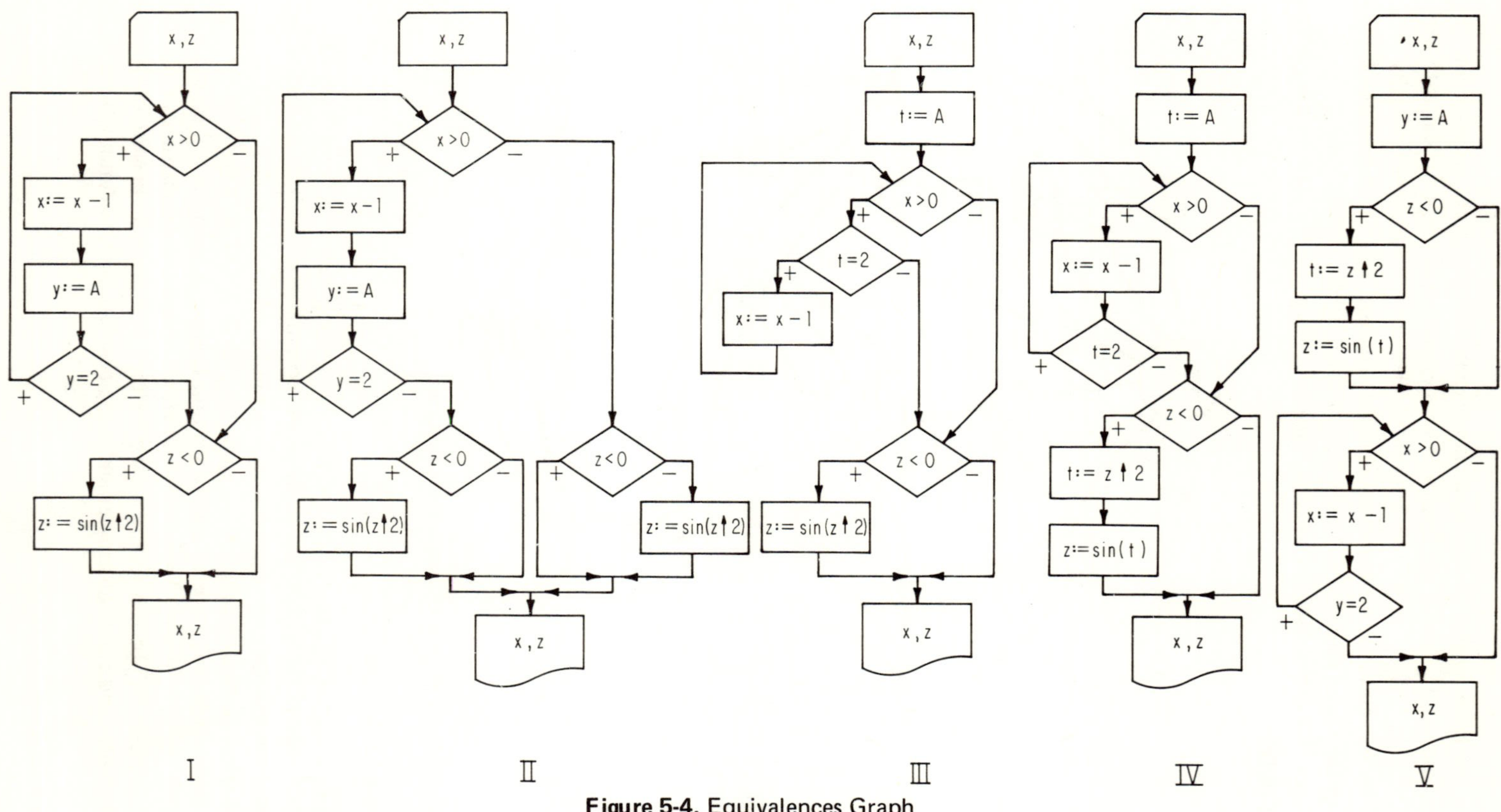

Figure 5-4. Equivalences Graph

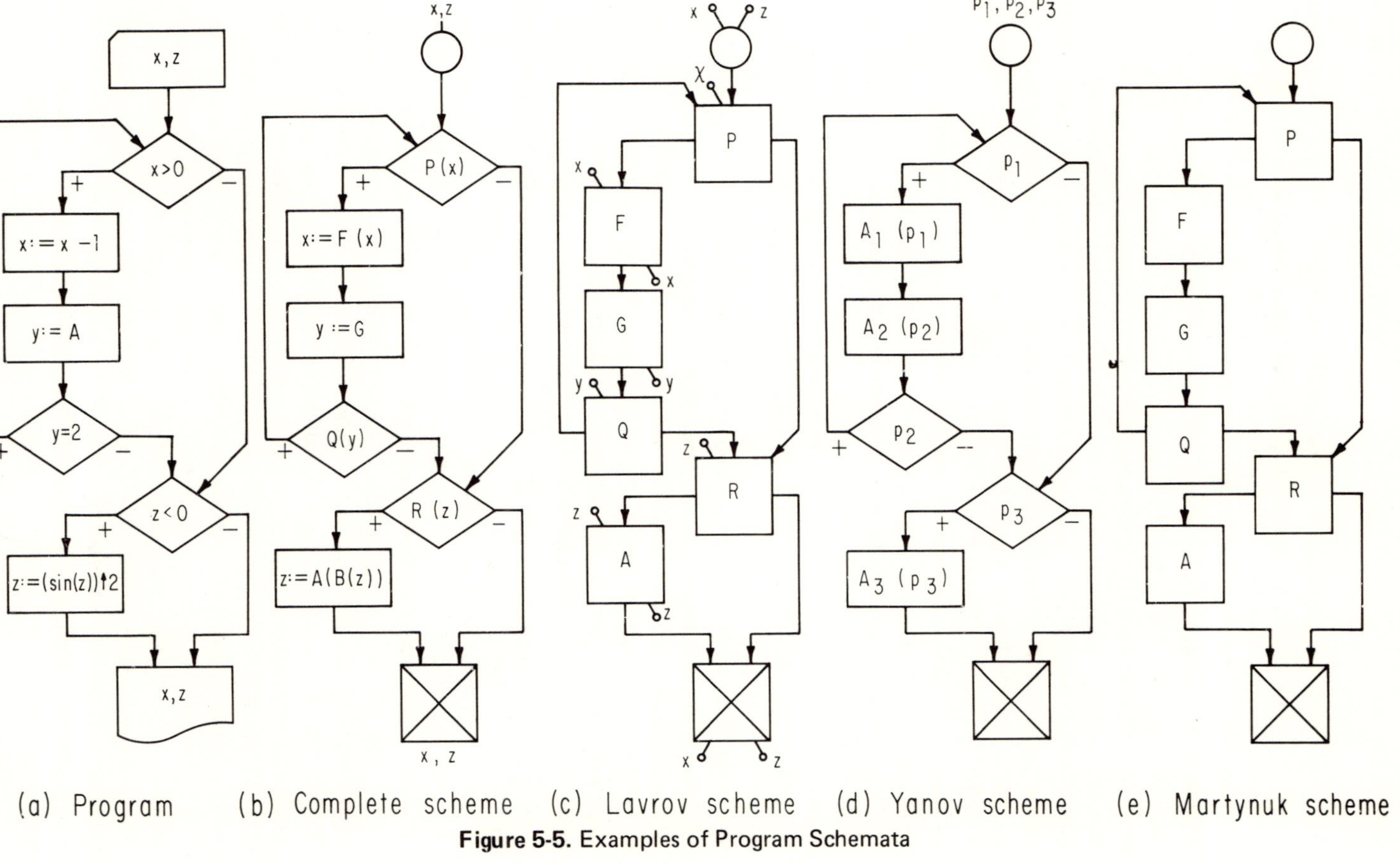

Figure 5-5. Examples of Program Schemata

objects are program schemata or abstract programs. They retain many structural properties of programs, in particular, the splitting into statements with indications of the information and control flow between them. This makes it possible for program schemata to construct many of the characteristics typical of concrete programs, for example, histories of program execution. In program schemata variables, operations and predicates are represented by formal symbols without any internal properties. These formal objects keep only the information needed for constructing histories of their realizations; for example, for formal operations the number of formal arguments and the names of formal variables substituted for them is indicated. For a formal statement of control transfer those statements to which control may be transferred are labelled and so on. Figure 5-5 gives examples of program schemata from Figure 5-1.

Concrete programs are obtained from schemata by means of interpretation, which consists of bringing some concrete variables and operations into correspondence with formal variables and operations. Very important is the concept of the set I of all interpretations of program schemata. The theory is developed in such a way that a fact ascertained for some scheme should be true for any interpreting program. In particular, in this way the notion of equivalence of two program schemata is introduced: two program schemata, S_1 and S_2, are equivalent in the sense of history H if for any interpretation $i \in I$ concrete programs $S_1(i)$ and $S_2(i)$ are equivalent in the sense of this same history.

In order to emphasize the depth of the approach to definition of equivalence as an invariant for any interpretation of schemata, Figure 5-6 illustrates two examples of four pairs of program schemata in which schemata (b) are equivalent in any interpretation, and schemata (a) are equivalent only in some interpretations. The same figure gives examples of interpretations in which even functional equivalence is broken.

Another approach to the definition of equivalence is as follows. The concept of execution and evaluation of functions is not introduced in the scheme. Instead of the universal algorithm of execution and the tracing algorithm, there are introduced "covering" generating processes which generate a set of histories containing in itself a set of histories of any interpretation for the given scheme. The fact that instead of the algorithm of execution there is considered a non-deterministic generating process in which at every step of its application there takes place a free choice of one of the alternatives without regard for the past history of the process development, has the following result. The set of histories generated by the scheme becomes simpler, i.e., it allows the mass problems connected with this set to be effectively solved. Since the set of histories of the program scheme S involves any history of the respective interpretation $S(i)$, this guarantees that a certain fact ascertained for S will automatically take place for $S(i)$. This refers, first of all, to ascertaining the fact of equivalence for program schemata.

Following are the main characteristics of program schemata:

(i) The set of statements constituting a program scheme is explicitly represented in the scheme.

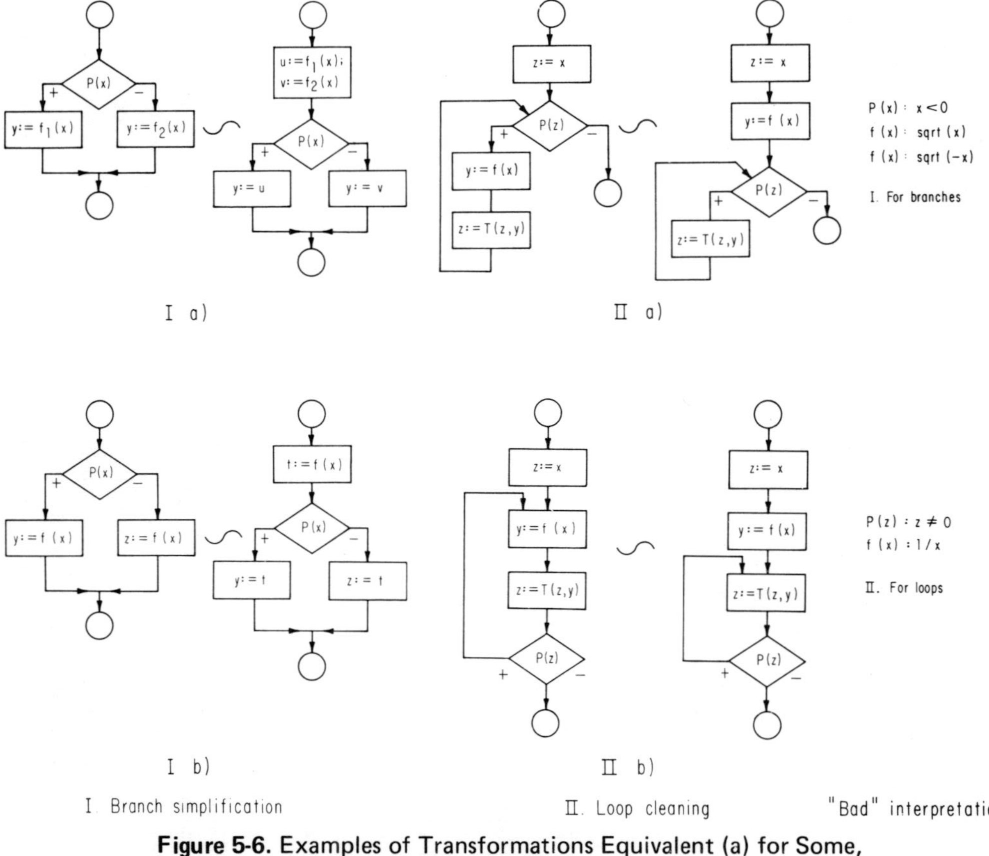

Figure 5-6. Examples of Transformations Equivalent (a) for Some, (b) for All Interpretations

(ii) In constructing realizations, one of the successors of a statement is usually chosen arbitrarily without regard to the history of the movement towards the given statement.

(iii) In considering some variable "evaluated" by some statement, it is treated as an independent variable (i.e., it is assumed to take any value after "execution" of the given statement regardless of the past history).

The need for the two different approaches to definition of equivalence of program schemata is due to some methodological reasons: the first approach is the more straightforward way toward practical applications, while the second allows creation of a "purer" theory which does not employ the concept of interpretation. For some classes of program schemata, these two approaches actually provide one and the same definition of equivalence. But for other classes the definition of equivalence, through a set of all interpretations, again leads to algorithmically undecidable problems. In this case the theory is constructed in such a way that equivalence over a set of histories, formed by the generating process, should be a sufficient condition of equivalence defined by means of interpretations. It will be noted that the requirement of such consistency presumes some additional conditions for the choice of the history by which one can judge program equivalence, because it is impossible to construct a proper generating process for any history which would provide decidability of equivalence and a sufficient condition for the equivalence defined through interpretations.

REVIEW

Below we give a review of the basic results in the theory of programming. This review is not complete and is perhaps subjective in character. In order to distinguish between different types of program schemata, they will be identified here as "somebody's schemata," where "somebody" is the author's name in whose work this class of schemata was considered for the first time.

Martynuk schemata appeared in the literature in 1961 [37]. They do not contain any information about a program except a control flow graph. An identity relation can be introduced between vertices of the control flow graph. For Martynuk schemata it is natural to introduce the generating process of constructing chains (paths in the control flow graph from the entry to the exit vertices). Two Martynuk schemata are regarded as equivalent if they generate one and the same set of chains. The problem of recognition of equivalence is decidable here; this was proved by Tuzov [49], but in principle it had been known earlier in the theory of automata, as the set of chains of an oriented graph with specified entry and exit vertices is a regular event.

The complete system of transformations for Martynuk schemata is rather simple; it was constructed by Itkin. Some forms of transformation of schemata, mainly, splitting of vertices, were used by Cooper [4] and Cocke and Miller [3] for regularization of the structure of the control flow graph.

For Martynuk schemata one important methodical problem was studied and almost completely solved. The theory of these program schemata becomes essentially simpler if any chain in it is permissible, i.e., there exists an interpretation which realizes this chain. At the same time, in practice there are more often programs in which not all sequences of instructions, prescribed by the control flow graph, are realized. Therefore the following problem arises: let the restrictions on the set of a scheme's chains be described by some means, external with respect to the topology of the scheme G. It is required to construct another scheme G' whose total set of chains is the same as that of the scheme G subject to these restrictions. There arises here the problem of finding the most general language for the description of the restrictions on the chains, as well as the methods of construction of the scheme G'. First steps toward the solution of this problem of reduction were made by Smirnov [48], then a rather general result was obtained by Martynuk [39].

Martynuk schemata proved to be a convenient model for the description of a number of algorithms for the construction of some sets of schemata vertices (of so-called transitive closures of binary relations between vertices) [38] and their decompositions into subschemata [50]. These algorithms are of great importance in program optimization.

Yanov schemata were introduced in the literature by Lyapunov and Yanov in 1956 [36]. A complete presentation of results was issued in 1958 [53]. The latter became a classical work owing to its completeness: all the basic components of the theory of program transformations were explicitly formulated and, within the constructed system of concepts, were completely studied. Among these components are the formalization of the concepts of program schemata, the assignment of the equivalence relation, the determination of the algorithm recognizing schemata equivalence, and finally, the construction of the system of transformations, which is complete in the sense that any pair of equivalent programs can be transformed into each other by successive applications of these transformations retaining equivalence. In order to prove the completeness of the transformations, Yanov successfully used the apparatus of the theory of logic calculus in which the rule of transformation is treated as an axiom postulating conservation of equivalence during transformation.

According to Yanov a scheme is a linear sequence of statements $A_1, ..., A_n$ and of recognizers having the form of arbitrary Boolean functions of the variables $p_1, ..., p_k$. The statements and conditions can be labelled. A so-called shift distribution for the scheme is defined, which consists of bringing the shift—that is, some subset of variables $p_1, ..., p_k$—to correspond to any statement of the scheme. The variables occurring in the shift of some statement are interpreted as its results.

A sequence of statements executed during a movement through the scheme from the entry point to the exit is assumed to be a scheme's realization. A set of realizations is given by the following generating process. An arbitrary set Δ of values of the variables $p_1, ..., p_k$ is taken and control is transferred to the entry point of the scheme. The construction is made by induction. If with the value Δ we pass to the recognizer *a*, then, if $a(\Delta)$ is true, control is transferred to the label indicated in the recognizer; if $a(\Delta)$ is false, control is transferred to the statement or the recognizer following *a*. If with the value Δ we pass to the statement $A(T)$, where T is the shift of A, then the statement A is put in the realization and Δ may be arbitrarily transformed into the value Δ' differing from Δ by no more than the values of the variables occurring in T. The process of constructing the realization terminates when the exit point has been reached or if it enters a loop consisting of several recognizers.

Two schemata are said to be equivalent if their sets of realizations are the same. Yanov found an algorithm for the recognition of equivalence of any two schemata and constructed a complete system of transformations containing 14 axioms and 3 rules of inference.

In paper [8] the Yanov theory of schemata was translated into the language of graph-schemata.

Figure 5-7 illustrates the relation between the old and the new methods of definition. The new definition appears to be more adequate to the problem under consideration. It was reflected, first of all, in the simplification of axiomatics of transformations: only 6 axioms in [8] corresponded to 14 axioms in [53]. Moreover, the new technique made it possible to effect the rule of inference which uses the concept of logical subordination. Some recognizer *a* is subordinated to a Boolean function f if the evaluation of *a* during the "execution" of the scheme is made only for those values of the Boolean variables on which f is true. The function F_a such that $F \to F_a$ ($\to$ is the implication symbol) for any f, subordinating *a*, is said to be a complete condition of the execution of *a*. The application of the inference rule for logical subordination allows *a* to be substituted by $a \wedge f$ for any f, including F_a. The inefficiency of this rule was in that the checking of the logical subordination was made in [53] by a complicated algorithm of scheme transformation by means which are beyond the scope of axiomatics.

Instead of this algorithm 4, axioms were introduced in [8] which specify some reversible transformation of the Yanov scheme, which consists of the labelling of arcs of the control flow graph by Boolean functions. A free application of these axioms eventually develops in the scheme a so-called stationary labelling, the coming of which for each vertex being revealed by the checking of some identical relations between the functions labelling the ingoing and outgoing arcs of the vertex. If labelling is stationary $Fa = f_1 \vee f_2$, where f_1 and f_2 are functions which label the output arcs of the recognizer *a*. Hence the considered rule of inference has a principally simpler condition for its applicability. Figure 5-8 illustrates a system of transformations of Yanov schemata.

Simpler axiomatics allowed investigation of some more profound properties of the rules of transformation. Yanov [54] explored which meaningful properties of his schemata were responsible for the necessity to have non-local rules of transformation. It appeared that the assumption of unessential (never exe-

$$p_1\ p_2\ p_3\ \rfloor_1\ p_1\ \lfloor_3\ A_1\ \ A_2\ p_2\ \lfloor_3\ \underline{\text{false}}\ \lfloor_1\ p_3\ \lfloor_4\ A_3\ \ \underline{\text{true}}\ \rfloor_4$$

$$A_1 \longleftrightarrow \{p_1\} \quad A_2 \longleftrightarrow \{p_2\} \quad A_3 \longleftrightarrow \{p_3\}$$

(a) linear scheme

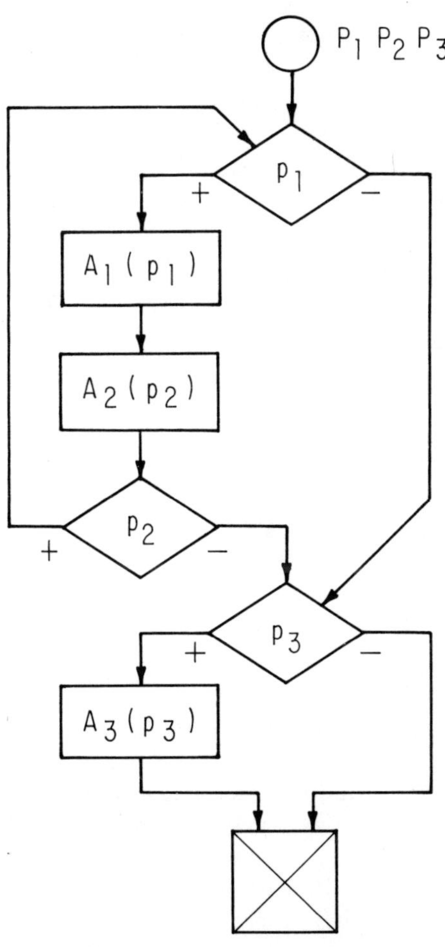

(b) graph – scheme

Figure 5-7. Yanov Scheme in Linear and Graph Forms

cuted) statements and the presence of non-trivial shift distributions are such properties. It was found that only for the schemata without non-essential statements

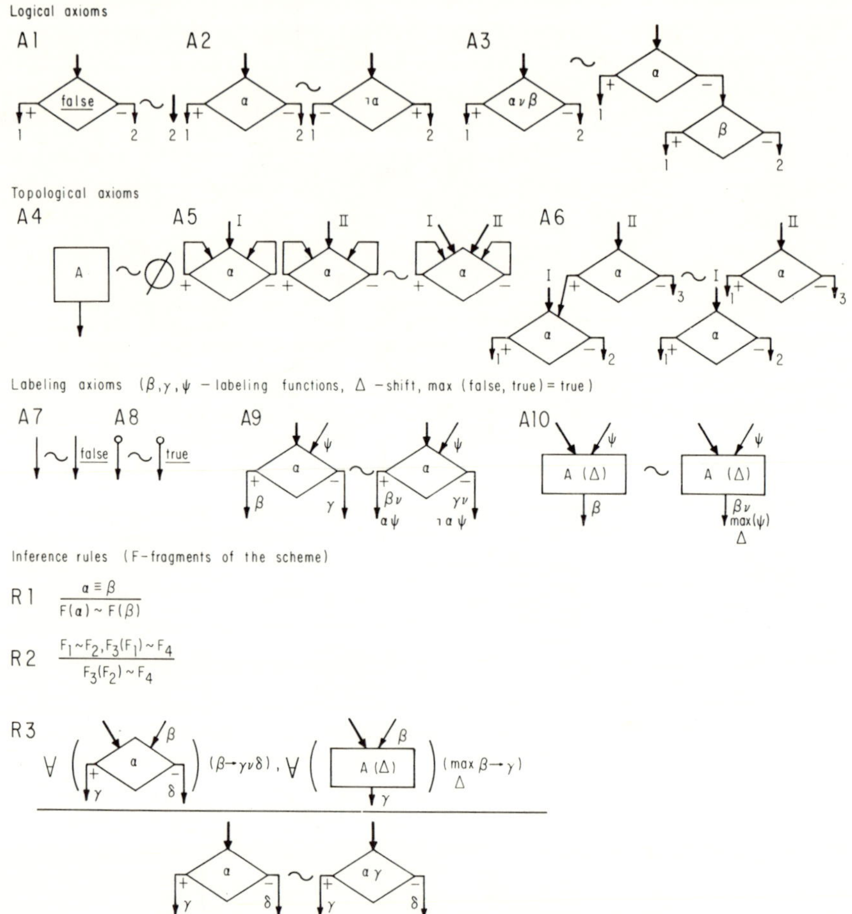

Figure 5-8. Transformation System for Yanov Schemata

and with universal shift distribution (each statement may change all Boolean variables of schemata), there is a complete system of purely local transformations; it was also possible to find a general criterion of locality of transformation rules of Yanov schemata (Sabelfeld [47]).

Papers [53] and [8] set a definite style in the approach to the problems of the theory of transformations which can be traced in a number of the works that followed.

Gorel [14] proved logical independence of the transformations from [8]. Itkin constructed a complete system of transformations for Yanov schemata allowing identity relation between statements [18]; he also found a system of transformations for a simple extension of Yanov schemata onto parallel programs [19]. Gorel constructed a system of transformations for Yanov schemata in which equivalence is considered only on finite sequences of statements [15].

All the above works used essentially labelling methods in the construction of systems of transformations; they proved to be convenient for the formalization of such transformations which require for their application a preliminary collection of information about the scheme as a whole. Valkovsky [52] considered the methods of arc labelling of Yanov schemata by Boolean functions from a general viewpoint and described a class of information which can be obtained by applying different labellings.

The problems of Yanov schemata are not yet exhausted. The following are the most pressing problems, the solution of which will help to extend the applicability of the theory:

(i) It is necessary to change the definition of Yanov schemata so that one can compare systems containing different Boolean variables and a different number of them. Besides, the present need to consider any recognizer as a function of all Boolean variables is already too burdensome. In other words, it is necessary to describe in more detail the information relations between statements, producing values of Boolean variables, and recognizers using them.

(ii) Now schemata are regarded as equivalent if the corresponding sequences of statements in the compared schemata are precisely the same, with, perhaps, regard for the identity relation between statements. It is very interesting to admit the existence of commutativity relations between statements and to compare statements sequences transformable each to the other by permutations of commutative statements.

The solution of this problem is of great importance because it will largely bring to a logical completion the branch of research started by Yanov, since statement permutations and identifications are the main techniques of program transformations. Tuzov [51] solved the problem of the recognition of the equivalence of Yanov schemata with commutative statements, but only by making some rather artificial assumptions. Letichevsky [34] also solved a similar problem with regard to commutativity in a particular case of schemata within the framework of his research of semigroup equivalence (see below).

Lavrov schemata appeared in the literature in 1961 [31] in connection with the memory economization problem. They are now the most often used models for some applied problems of programming theory—program optimization algorithms. In Lavrov schemata the information flow is considered under the assumption that the logical structure of a program is fixed. Formally, Lavrov schemata are introduced in the following way: a Martynuk scheme is taken where every statement has some non-negative number of information inputs and outputs (it is enough to assume no more than one output). An arbitrary symbol of a variable, or memory location is attached to every input and output.

It is strange that until now there has existed no general theory of Lavrov schemata (in the sense of finding a most general but recognizable equivalence or of constructing a canonical form and complete transformation system). All concrete studies are based on some assumptions or restrictions which play the role of sufficient conditions providing equivalence. It seems that the most general approach was used by Kotov in his work on parallel programming [26]. In fact, an information logic graph is considered as a history in Lavrov schemata. There is another, in some sense conjugate, approach to the definition of Lavrov schemata invariants. An information flow graph is the collection of all the information connections which are realized by an operational logic history. Sometimes it is a reasonable alternative to consider, for a given information connection between statements A and B, the set of all paths from A to B in the scheme which realize this connection. These paths are called the routes of the information connection. The set of all routes of all information connections of a Lavrov scheme is, however, a stricter invariant than the set of information logic graphs.

Let us mention the main results obtained for Lavrov schemata. Lavrov [31] and Ershov [6] solved the problem of minimizing the number of variables in a Lavrov scheme. This problem in a more general form was also considered by Nikitin [43]; Martynuk [40] found a sufficient and, seemingly, necessary condition of the "transportability" of a statement from one position in a scheme to another for equivalence over the information logic graph using the identity relation between statements. Pottosin [45] considered this problem with respect to "loop cleaning" in compilers. There is a series of works originating in a group centered around Dr. J. Cooke (USA) in which the information and control flow is studied for optimization purposes (the elimination of common subexpressions, register optimization, and so on): Cocke [2], Allen [1], Kennedy [25], Kotov [26] considered a series of Lavrov schemata transformations (variable renaming, splitting and transposition of statements) that allow the transformation of a given scheme into another possissing more internal parallelism.

Ershov [9] considered a version of Lavrov schemata in which information connections between statement inputs and outputs, instead of variable names, are specified explicitly in the form of a collection of direct binary relations forming a scheme information flow graph (not to be mixed with a realization information flow graph). It allows the development of a theory which is independent of variants of memory allocation. This approach has proved useful in program optimization problems and in parallel programming. It was discovered that information flow graphs exist which, having been added to a control flow graph, cannot be realized by any Lavrov scheme. Itkin [21] found a criterion for the realizability of a given information flow graph by a Lavrov scheme.

Semigroup Equivalence

Let us return to a discussion of the various kinds of realization histories that have been considered in the metatheory section. We can note that all histories appear from the operational history which for program schemata looks like a word:

$$s_{i_1} s_{i_2} \dots s_{i_k}$$

in the alphabet $S = \{s_1, ..., s_n\}$, where $s_1, ..., s_n$ are statement symbols. The difference between less detailed histories and the operational history can be explained as the result of applications of some relations between scheme statements. The result of these applications is that instead of the requirement of literal identity of the operational histories, we allow the compared histories to be different but within the limits of prescribed relations between statements. Let us consider several examples:

(i) Two operational histories coincide except for those statements between which identity relations are introduced

$$s_i = s_j$$

(ii) Two operational histories have a common information flow graph. It can be expressed in terms of commutatively relations in the form

$$s_i s_j = s_j s_i$$

These relations are used in such a way that statements which are connected with a path in the information flow graph are non-commutative but disconnected statements are commutative. Figure 5-9 presents a variety of operational histories with a common information flow graph, differing only within the limits of commutativity relations.

(iii) If a composite statement, for example,

$$y := x + z \uparrow 2$$

is reducible to a series of simpler statements, in this case:

$$t := z \uparrow 2 \qquad\qquad y := x + t$$

then this can be taken into account by introducing defining relations of the following kind:

$$s_i = s_k s_l$$

Thus any kind of equivalence can be described in a form of a collection G of defining relations

$$\left.\begin{array}{l} w_1 = w_2^1 \\ w_2 = w_2^1 \\ \dots\dots\dots \\ w_n = w_n^1 \end{array}\right\} G$$

where w and w^1 are concrete words from the set W of words in the alphabet S.

We will say that two words from W are equal over G if one of them can be transferred into the other by successive applications of relations from G considered as rules of replacement in which an occurrence of a word that appears on one side of a rule is replaced by the corresponding word from the other side. Then the set W partitioned into a set of classes of equal words is called a semigroup $P(G,S)$ over alphabet S, specified by defining relations G.

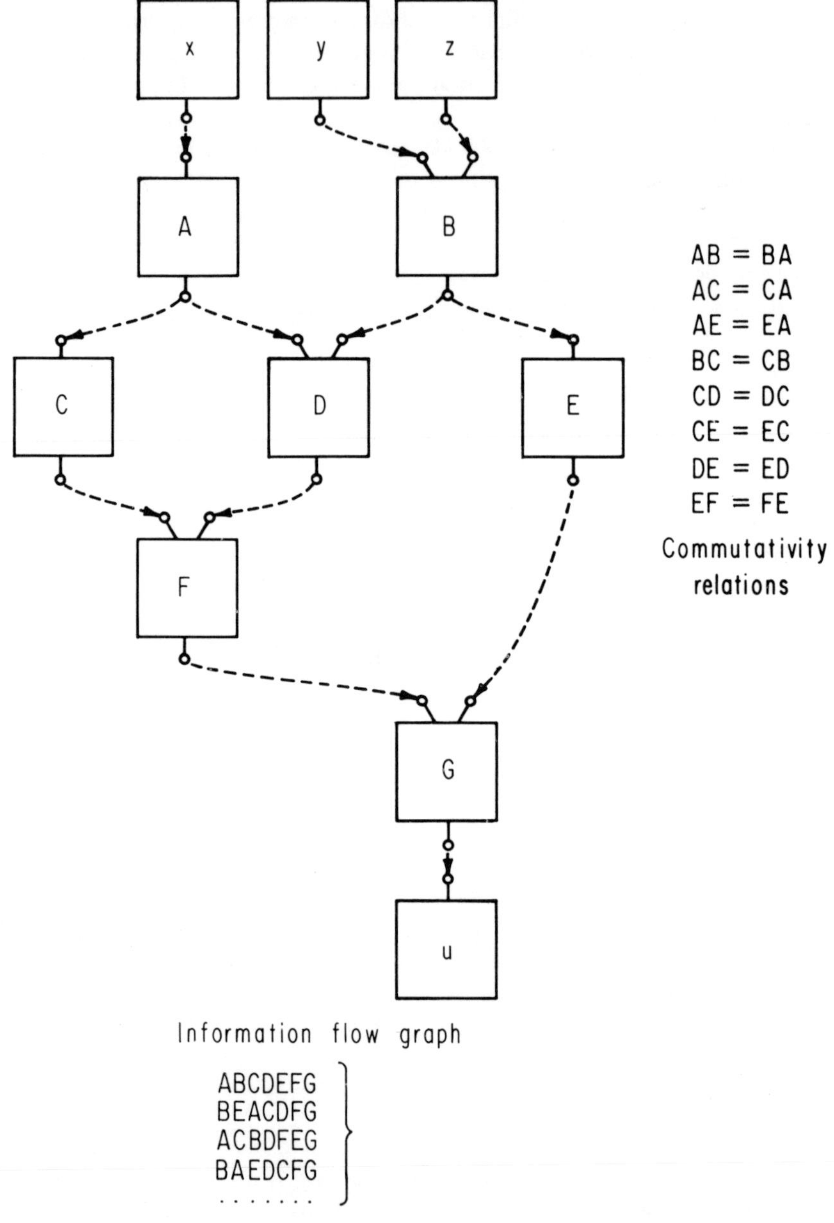

Figure 5-9. Variety of Operational Histories for an Information Flow Graph

The equivalence thus introduced is called a semigroup equivalence over the semigroup $P(G,S)$. Two schemata, A_1 and A_2, are equivalent in this sense if:

(i) for any operational history h_1 of the scheme A_1, the scheme A_2 contains a history h_2 which is equal to h_1 over G, and vice versa;

or

(ii) for any interpretation i, any history of the program $A_1(i)$ is equal over G to the corresponding history of the program $A_2(i)$, and vice versa. The difference between the two equivalence definitions is just whether or not an interpretation is used in the equivalence consideration.

Figure 5-10 shows an example of two schemata for which the defining relations corresponding to equivalence with respect to termal value are given.

Such a unified approach to the equivalence definition allows us to put a general problem: What should the semigroup $P(G,S)$ be in order to provide a decidable semigroup equivalence?

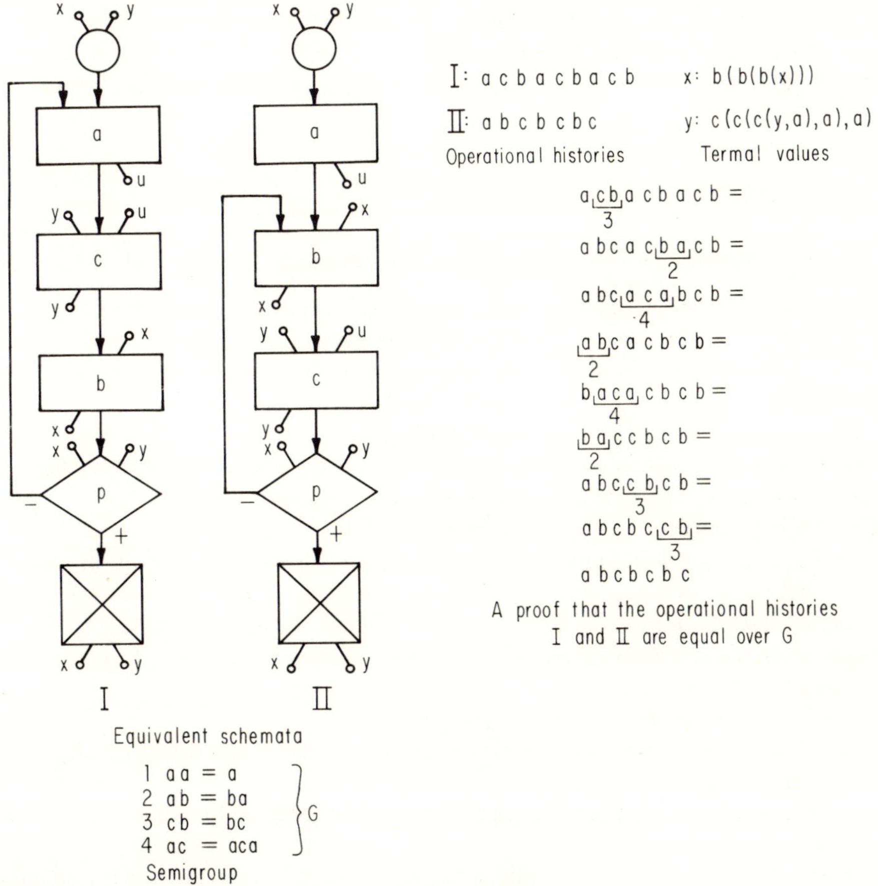

Figure 5-10. Examples of Semigroup T-Equivalences

The semigroup equivalence concept was introduced by Letichevsky, who obtained strong and rather general results in this direction [34]. Readers acquainted with the semigroup theory will be interested in the formulation of a general result obtained by Letichevsky:

For the decidability of a semigroup equivalence, it is sufficient that the semigroup:

(i) should not contain a decomposable unit,

(ii) should satisfy the rule of left contraction.

These interesting results were obtained within the framework of a research initiated by Acad. V.M. Glushkor and connected with the application of methods of algebraic automata theory to theoretical programming problems (see the general problem formulation and review of results in Glushkov and Letichevsky [13]).

Nevertheless, it has to be mentioned that direct use of the results obtained is still difficult because the semigroup equivalence technique does not easily take into account the logical structure of a scheme. Some progress, but not yet enough, was made by Nepomnyashchy [42] with respect to Yanov schemata. The limits of this paper prevent us from going deeper into this important point.

THE PROBLEMATICS

The Fundamental Problem of Theoretical Programming

The author believes this problem to be the problem of the development of a complete program schemata theory, where the control flow analysis made for Yanov schemata and the information flow analysis made for Lavrov schemata are combined.

The complete theory is understood as follows:

(i) finding an algorithm for the recognition of program schemata equivalence;

(ii) constructing a complete system of equivalent transformations;

(iii) finding a canonical form of program schemata;

(iv) constructing a working transformation system for use in optimization problems.

Let us describe in more detail the class of program schemata for which this problem statement makes sense. There are the following symbols and expressions:

variables: *x, y, z,* etc.,

operations of a certain "arity": *f, f*( ), *f*(,), etc.,

terms: expressions which are constructed from variables and operations by ordinary rules,

predicate symbols of a certain "arity": *true, false* (identical predicates), *p*( ), *p*(,), etc.,

predicate terms—predicate symbols, the arguments of which are terms, and also arbitrary Boolean functions of these elementary predicate terms.

A transformer is considered to be an assignment statement of the form:

$$y := T$$

where y is a variable and T is a term.

There is considered a specific kind of assignment, namely the transfer statement, which has the form:

$$y := x$$

where x is a variable.

A recognizer is considered to be an arbitrary predicate term.

Let us consider now a definition of the equivalence of such program schemata.

The situation is such that until now it has been impossible to give a precise equivalence definition in the framework of which the fundamental problem should be attacked. The corresponding history must be much more detailed than merely the termal values of resulting variables, but it may, seemingly, be a little weaker than the logic-termal history. A search for a weaker history is necessary, at least in order to provide parallel programs with an appropriate logic-termal history, where every result has to have its own series of predicates which it depends on and where the predicates themselves, it seems, should be structured as a tree instead of as a sequence. There is an example of such a history in Figure 5-11, wherein the history is compared with an ordinary logic-termal history. Moreover, it is necessary to be able to ignore, in a logic-termal history, dependencies on such predicates which, although they occur in the chain of statements, nevertheless do not influence the result evaluation.

Figure 5-12 demonstrates a trivial example of this kind.

Now we shall summarize what has been done in the direction of the solution of the fundamental problem.

It is not generally known that the first attack on this problem was made by Krinitsky in 1959 almost immediately after the Yanov work. This was known only to a limited number of people through Krinitsky's dissertation [28]. Some fragments of the research appeared four years later [30], only recently has a full account of his work been published [29]. The work appears to be rather obsolete now, but nevertheless, the problem was completely solved for a class of program schemata without loops. It is, indeed, a very particular case, but it cannot diminish the quality and value of this work.

The functional equivalence was, in fact, considered in this work; that is, two schemata are equivalent if corresponding functions are equal in any interpretation. An equivalence recognition algorithm, a canonical form, and a complete system of equivalent transformations were found and described.

Several years later, similar results were obtained by Igarashi. They also were described first in a dissertation dated 1964 [16], but were later published in a modified form [17].

From the other side, the fundamental problem has suffered from a series of negative results establishing the undecidability of the equivalence for a variety

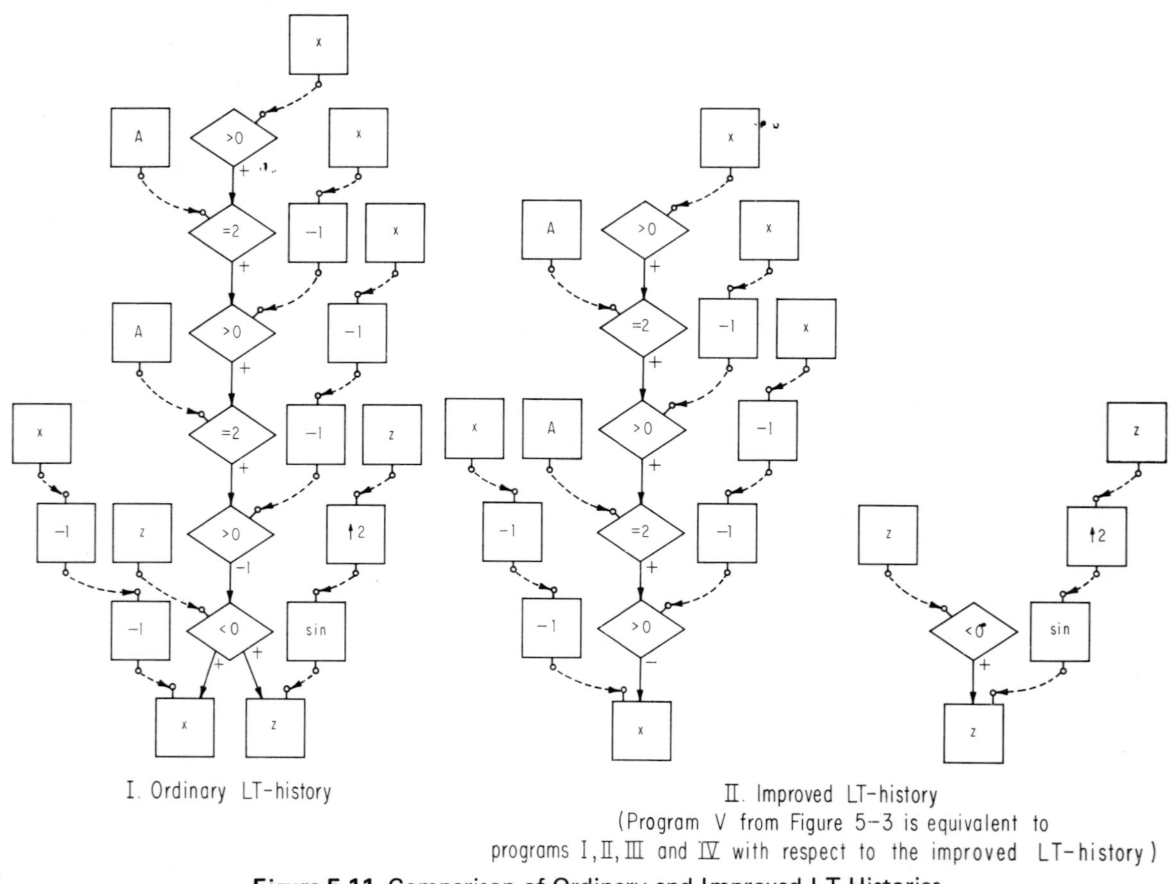

Figure 5-11. Comparison of Ordinary and Improved LT-Histories

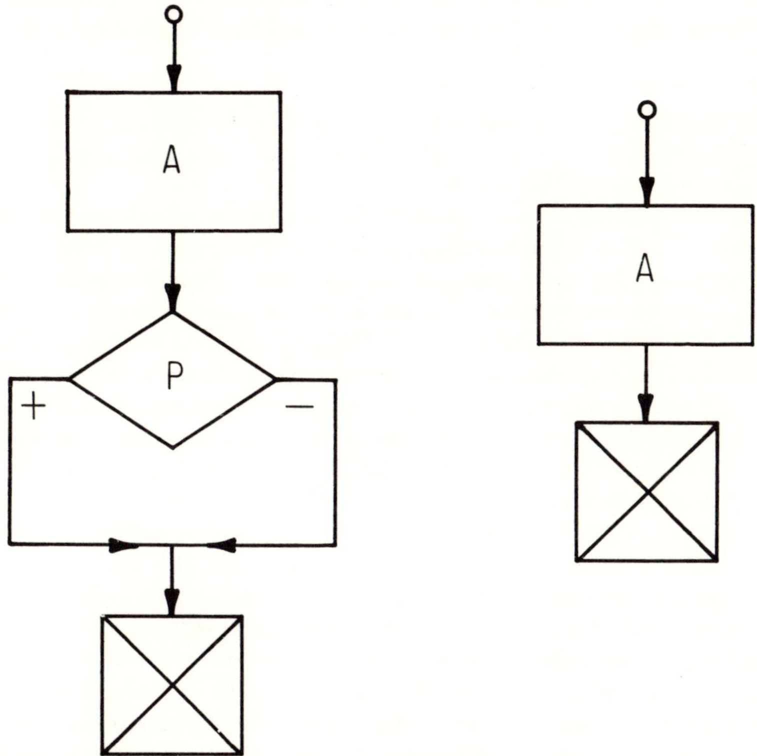

Figure 5-12. These Schemata Are Not LT-Equivalent

of histories. A little later, Paterson, independently of Letichevsky, proved the undecidability of the recognition of the functional equivalence. The full exposition of this important result appeared in a reverse sequence in 1969 (Letichevsky [34]) and 1970 (Luckham, Park, and Paterson [35]). Besides this, Letichevsky has shown that, for program schemata, equivalence over termal values is the same as functional equivalence.

Some particular classes of schemata with decidable functional equivalence were described in these papers. One of these classes is particularly interesting, a class of schemata in which all information flow can be implemented only through one memory location.

Paterson's and Letichevsky's work was greatly strengthened by Itkin and Zwienogrodsky [22] who have shown that any "reasonable" equivalence definition based on the set of all interpretations and applicable to any program schemata implies an algorithmic undecidability. The "reasonability" of an equivalence definition is expressed in the following terms:

(i) An equivalence relation is said to be essentially interpretive if the non-equivalence of two schemata S_1 and S_2 implies that there exists an interpretation i in which for some initial data the operational logic history of the realization of the program $S_1(i)$ differs from the corresponding operational logic history of $S_2(i)$.

(ii) An equivalence relation is said to be nonsingular if the existence of a statement which, in some interpretation i, would be essential for one program $S_1(i)$ and inessential for other program $S_2(i)$ is a sufficient condition for the non-equivalence of schemata S_1 and S_2.

Itkin's and Zwienogrodsky's theorem states that if an equivalence relation being considered for all program schemata is essentially interpretive and non-singular, then the recognition of the equivalence is algorithmically undecidable. This theorem may be considered as a formalization and proof of Paterson's thesis [44, p. 30] formulated by him in 1968; "Indeed, we can at one stroke prove the undecidability of any relation lying between the general and weak equivalences."

The theorem mentioned above implies that any equivalence that is based on the set of only those scheme statements sequences that are realized in at least one interpretation, leads to the undecidability. In means that the only possible non-trivial and effective theories of equivalence are those which consider sets of histories generated by some non-deterministic and simplified generating process. In connection with this, a new result obtained by Itkin [20] is important. He considered program schemata similar to those introduced in this section subjected to the condition that in recognizer positions elementary predicate terms are allowed, but not their Boolean functions. The equivalence notion is considered over sets of logic-termal histories. These histories are deduced from logic-operational histories, those histories in their turn being generated by a generating process similar to that of the Yanov and Lavrov schemata. This kind of equivalence has been proved by Itkin to be decidable for any pair of schemata. The result allows us to express some optimism in respect of the solution of the fundamental problem as a whole.

Algebra of Programming

Let us consider possible future contributions to programming that can give a solution of the fundamental problem. At this point we leave the concrete mathematical content of the paper and enter into the field of assumption, hypothesis, and even speculation. Nevertheless, it seems reasonable to estimate some perspectives that can be opened with possible solution of this problem.

First, the fundamental problem solution will provide an integration of the many existing but scattered methods of language and compiler implementation. The author has some experience in programming system development and has a profound belief that most of the so-called universal optimization methods are applied within the limits of the formalism established by the fundamental problem.

A transformation system that preserves logic-termal history can be a common mathematical basis for such compilation algorithms as:

—expression and conditional statement decomposition;
—dedicated register and scratch-pad memory optimization;
—economy of common parts of computation;
—static memory economy;
—procedure optimization;
—all kinds of optimization connected with transposition statements with a program;
—many kinds of loop optimization.

Such an integration of techniques and such an accurate proof of compilation algorithms is of a special importance for universal programming processors that are directed by language descriptions. It is caused by the necessity of having some general model of a program in order to provide the preservation of the semantic correctness of any program in any source language during the compilation. It is also caused by the necessity of having powerful optimizing algorithms that can overcome the inherent inefficiency of a decomposed source program, for only optimizing capabilities can make universal compilers competitive with compilers tailored to a specific language.

Second, the fundamental problem solution, in our opinion, is the only way to develop a constructive theory of parallel programming. Sequencial programs, written in current algorithmic languages, reflect an economic way of human thinking and thus may often be executed in the same form as they were written. In principle, it is not the case with parallel programming. The reason is not only that human intuition and its algorithmic way of reasoning fail when it has to control a large number of cooperating parallel processes; the generation of a parallel program for tens or even hundreds of processing elements in a large computer system is a complicated procedure which has to be performed dynamically and at high speed. A precise and complete program schemata theory is the only basis for the development of algorithms for parallel program generation and for job-planning for many processors. The theory of parallel programming is a proper subject for a separate paper and so it is barely touched on here. We will only say that the two most important (in our opinion) works on parallel programming (Karp and Miller [24], Kotov and Narinyani [27], are fully based on some fragment of program schemata theory.

Finally, the fundamental problem solution is not bound to the possibility of constructing new or of proving existing mechanical compilation procedures. Any success in the solution of this problem will lead us to the construction of an ALGEBRA OF PROGRAMMING—a universal symbolism which will enable us to manipulate processes and algorithms in a way similar to that in which mathematical symbolism enables us to manipulate functions and other traditional mathematical objects. The author is, obviously, not the first to draw attention to this broad scientific problem; it is enough to refer once more to well-known works by McCarthy [41] and Glushkov [12]. We want to stress, however, that only the fundamental problem solution will give the first adequate material for an algebra of programming.

Internal Language

A bridge is usually constructed from both sides. It is true for connections between theory and technology of programming, too. A program schemata is an abstract model of real constructions in programming. Some time ago the author investigated the question of connections between program schemata and algorithmic languages and computer instruction sets [5]. Doubtless, many others have also studied this question. In the ALPHA compiler [7] there exists a special pass where a program under compilation is converted into a Lavrov scheme and subjected to an information flow analysis for global memory economy purposes. The experience has shown that a direct application of the algorithms of analysis or transformation to real programs is often not very easy. It is necessary to introduce into compiler writing technology, specific forms of program representation which would be adequate for theoretical constructions.

The author believes that a variety of problems in the application of theoretical proofs and algorithms to programming technology is focused on the problem of the construction of an internal, or intermediate, algorithmic language. This would be one more universal algorithmic language destined not for the writing of programs by human beings but mainly for use as an internal representation of a program at some intermediate level or levels.

It has to be said that the concept of an internal language is already a useful concept in programming. There are a variety of programming systems that use this concept explicitly. In such systems the internal language performs one or several functions from the following list:

- —a logical stage in a multipass compilation scheme
- —a semantic language for compilers directed by a language description
- —an aid to representing decomposed programs
- —an intermediate language for multilanguage programming systems
- —an intermediate language for programming systems with a variety of object computers
- —a level of analysis and optimization of a compiled program.

Internal languages in these systems, however, either are too special or have suffered from too narrow or too non-rigorous an approach. There seems to be great interest in the crystallization of the internal language at a level that would be independent on any particular project and in giving to it features that allow its direct use in most of the applications listed above. Some considerations in the form of design specifications of such an universal approach can be found in [10].

CONCLUSION

The author's enthusiasm for program schemata theory should not imply that this field covers all the actual problematics of programming. Many distinguished papers will be presented to the [IFIP] Congress and they will extend considerably our understanding of the current state and perspectives of programming.

But it is important to stress that program schemata theory for the first time is leaving the suburbs of peripheral and private exercises in the formalization of programming concepts and is coming into the marketplace. The growth point is here. Scientific groups in Stanford, Berkeley, Cambridge (MIT), New York, Kiev, Novosibirsk, and some other places, previously scattered, are now entering into a period of intensive scientific competition which will result in rapid changes in the theory of programming.

An important role in this belongs to the *Journal of Computer and System Sciences* and the *Kibernetika* magazine, where the majority of recent publications in the field has appeared. The author strongly believes that in 5 to 10 years, program schemata theory will become a standard university course and that a new generation of programmers possessing this and other new knowledge will overcome the current methodological difficulties of our profession.

The author expresses his deep gratitude to Mr. V.E. Itkin (Novosibirsk Computing Center) and Dr. J.S. Rohl (Manchester University) for their kind assistance in the preparation of this paper.

REFERENCES

[1] F. Allen, A basis for program optimization, presented to IFIP Congress 71 (Ljublana, August 23-28, 1971).

[2] J. Cocke, Global common subexpression elimination, Proc. Symp. on compiler optimization, Sigplan Notices 5, 7 (1970).

[3] J. Cocke and R. Miller, Some analysis techniques for optimizing computer programs, Proc. Second Intern. Conf. of Systems Sci., Hawaii (Jan. 1969).

[4] D. C. Cooper, Computer programs and graph transformations (Carnegie Institute of Technology, Pittsburgh, Sept. 19, 1966).

[5] A. P. Ershov, A description of basic constructions of programming, Cybernetics problems 8 (Fizmatgiz, Moscow, 1962).

[6] A. P. Ershov, Reduction of the problem of the memory economy during program writing to the problem of colouring graph vertices, DAN SSSR 142, 4 (1962).

[7] A. P. Ershov, Editor, ALPHA – an automatic programming system (Nauka, Novosibirsk, 1967).

[8] A. P. Ershov, On Yanov program schemata, Cybernetics problems 20 (Nauka, Moscow, 1967).

[9] A. P. Ershov, On program schemata over common and distributed memory, Kibernetika (Kiev) 4 (1968).

[10] A. P. Ershov, A multilanguage programming system oriented to languages description and universal optimization algorithms, Proc. IFIP working conf., Algol 68 implementation (Munich, July 20-24, 1970).

[11] A. P. Ershov and A. A. Lyapunov, On formalization of the program concept, Kibernetika (Kiev) 5 (1967).

[12] V. M. Glushkov, Some problems in automata theory and artificial intelligence, Kibernetika (Kiev) 2 (1970).

[13] V. M. Glushkov and A.A. Letichevsky, Theory of algorithms and discrete processors, Advances in information and system science, Vol. 1 (Plenum Press, New York, 1969).
[14] E. L. Gorel, Logical independence of the axiomatics of Yanov program schemata, Proc. 1st All-union conf. on program. Part A (Kiev, November 1968).
[15] E. L. Gorel, On Yanov schemata with the finite equivalence relation, Kibernetika (Kiev) (1972) (in press).
[16] S. Igarashi, An axiomatic approach to the equivalence problems of algorithms with applications, Rep. Comp. Centre Univ. Tokyo, 1, 1 (1968).
[17] S. Igarashi, On the equivalence of programs represented by Algol-like statements. Rep. Comp. Centre Univ. Tokyo, 1, 1 (1968).
[18] V. E. Itkin, Yanov program schemata with identical statements. Proc. 1st All-union conf. on program. Part A (Kiev, November 1968).
[19] V. E. Itkin, Parallel program schemata, Kibernetika (Kiev) 1 (1971).
[20] V. E. Itkin, Logic-termal equivalence of program schemata. Kibernetika (Kiev) (1971) (in press).
[21] V. E. Itkin, A criterium of the realizability of program schemata over distributed memory, Kibernetika (Kiev) (1972) (in press).
[22] V. E. Itkin and Z. Zwienogrodsky, On equivalence of program schemata, J. Comp. Syst. Sci. 5 (1971) (in press).
[23] L. A. Kaluzhnin, On algorithmization of mathematical problems, Cybernetics problems 2 (Fizmatgiz, Moscow, 1959).
[24] R. M. Karp and R. E. Miller, Parallel program schemata, J. Comp. Syst. Sci. 3 (1969).
[25] K. Kennedy, Informal paper, Courant Institute, NYU (1970).
[26] V. E. Kotov, Transformation of program schemata into asynchronous programs, Dissertation autoreferate (Comp. Center Siberian Divn. Ac. Sci., Novosibirsk, 1970).
[27] V. E. Kotov and A. S. Narinyani, On transformation of sequential programs into asynchronous parallel programs, Information Processing 68 (North-Holland, Amsterdam, 1969).
[28] N. A. Krinitsky, Equipower transformations of logical schemata. Dissertation autoreferate (Moscow State University, 1959).
[29] N. A. Krinitsky, Equipower algorithm transformations and programming (Soviet Radio, Moscow, 1970).
[30] N. A. Krinitsky, G. A. Mironov and G. D. Frolov, Programming (Nauka, Moscow, 1966).
[31] S. S. Lavrov, On memory economy in closed program schemata, Journ. comp. math. and math. Phys. 1, 4 (1961).
[32] A. A. Letichevsky, The functional equivalence of automata with a terminal state, DAN SSSR 185, 1 (1969).
[33] A. A. Letichevsky, Functional equivalence of discrete processors I, Kibernetika (Kiev) 2 (1969).

[34] A. A. Letichevsky, Functional equivalence of discrete processors II, Kibernetika (Kiev) 2 (1970).
[35] D. C. Luckam, D. M. R. Park and M. S. Paterson, On formalised computer programs, J. Comp. Syst. Sci. 4, 3 (1970).
[36] A. A. Lyapunov and Yu. I. Yanov, On logical program schemata, Proc. Conf. "Perspectives of the development of the Soviet Mathematical Machinery" (Moscow, March 12-17, 1956) Part III.
[37] V. V. Martynuk, Path finding in an algorithm scheme, J. comp. math. and math. phys. 1, 1 (1961).
[38] V. V. Martynuk, An economical construction of the transitive closure of a binary relation, Journ. comp. math. and math. phys. 2, 3 (1962).
[39] V. V. Martynuk, On an analysis of the control-flow graph for a program scheme, Journ. comp. math, and math. phys. 5, 2 (1965).
[40] V. V. Martynuk, On a change in the order of the execution of a statement in a program scheme, Digital computing machinery and programming 2 (Soviet Radio, Moscow, 1967).
[41] J. McCarthy, Towards a mathematical science of computation, Proceedings of the IFIP congress, Munich, 1962 (North-Holland, Amsterdam, 1963) 21-28.
[42] V. A. Nepomnyashchy, On one method of equivalence recognition for program schemata and discrete transformers, Proc. 2nd All-union conf. on program. Part K (Novosibirsk, Febr. 3-6, 1970).
[43] A. S. Nikitin, On a class of equivalent transformations of program schemata, Kibernetika (Kiev) 5 (1966).
[44] M. S. Paterson, Program schemata, Machine intelligence 3 (Edinburgh Univ. Press, 1968).
[45] I. V. Pottosin, To the problem of loop cleaning, Digital computing machinery and programming 2 (Soviet Radio, Moscow, 1967).
[46] H. G. Rice, Classes of recursively enumerable sets and their decision problems, Trans. Amer. Math. Soc. 74, 2 (1953).
[47] V. K. Sabelfeld, A locality criterium for program schemata transformations, Kibernetika (Kiev) (1971) (in press).
[48] Yu. I. Smirnov, On a program scheme transformation, Journ. comp. math. and math. phys. 3, 3 (1963).
[49]. V. A. Tuzov, On graph-schemata-minimization, J. comp. math. and math. phys. 8, 3 (1968).
[50] V. A. Tuzov, On transformations of program graph-schemata, Proc. 1st All-union conf. on program. Part G (Kiev, November, 1968).
[51] V. A. Tuzov, Decision problems for graph-schemata with commutative statements, Proc. 2nd All-union conf. on program. Part K (Novosibirsk, February 3-6, 1970).
[52] V. A. Valkovsky, Some results on properties of Yanov scheme configurations, Kibernetika (Kiev) (1971) (in press).

[53] Yu. I. Yanov, On logical algorithm schemata, Cybernetics problems 1 (Fizmatgiz, Moscow, 1958).
[54] Yu. I. Yanov, On local transformations of algorithm schemata, Cybernetics problems 20 (Nauka, Moscow, 1967).

6
Shape Grammars and the Generative Specification of Painting and Sculpture

by *George Stiny and James Gips*

A method of shape generation using shape grammars which take shape as primitive and have shape specific rules is presented. A formalism for the complete, generative specification of a class of non-representational, geometric paintings or sculptures is defined, which has shape grammars as its primary structural component. Paintings are material representations of two-dimensional shapes generated by shape grammars, sculptures of three-dimensional shapes. Implications for aesthetics and design theory in the visual arts are discussed. Aesthetics is considered in terms of specificational simplicity and visual complexity. In design based on generative specifications, the artist chooses structural and material relationships and then determines algorithmically the resulting art objects.

We present a formalism for the complete specification of families of non-representational, geometric paintings and sculptures. Formally defining the specification of an art object independently of the object itself provides a framework in which theories of design and aesthetics can be developed. The specifications introduced are algorithmic and made in terms of recursive schemata having shape grammars as their basic formal component. This represents a departure from previous mathematical approaches to the visual arts [1], [2] which have been informal rather than effective and, except for Focillon [3], paradigmatic rather than generative. The painting and sculpture discussed are material representations of shapes generated by shape grammars. Our underlying aim is to use formal, generative techniques to produce good art objects and to develop understanding of what makes good art objects.

The class of paintings shown in Figure 6-1 is used as an explanatory example. Over fifty classes of paintings and sculptures have been defined using generative specifications and produced using traditional artistic techniques.

PAINTING

Informally, the specification of painting consists of the definition of a language of two-dimensional shapes, the selection of a shape in that language for

Editor's Note: From *IFIP Congress 71,* August 1971. Reprinted by permission of the publisher, North Holland Publishing Co., and the authors.

painting, the specification of a schema for painting the areas contained in the shape, and the determination of the location and scale of the shape on a canvas of given size and shape.

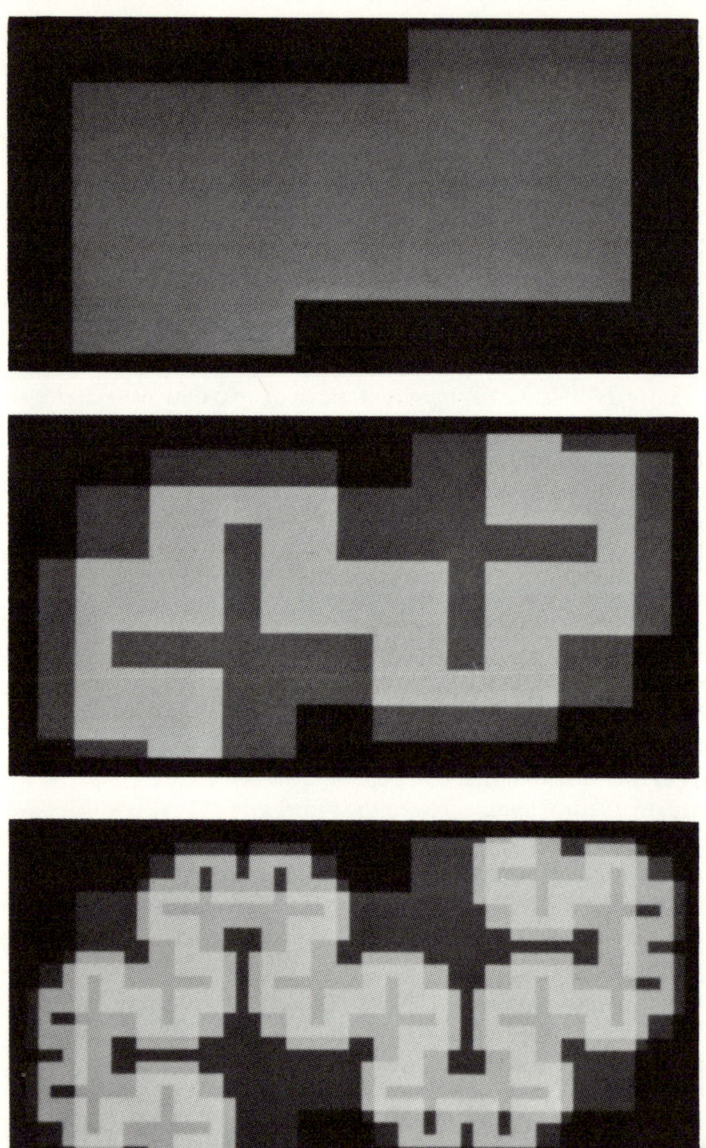

Figure 6-1. *Urform I, II, and III* (Stiny, 1970. Acrylics on canvas, each canvas 30 ins. x 57 ins.) Colors are: darkest–blue, second darkest–red, second lightest–orange, lightest–yellow.

A *class of paintings* is defined by the double (S,M). S is a specification of a class of shapes and consists of a shape grammar, defining a language of two-dimensional shapes, and a selection rule. M is a specification of material representations for the shapes defined by S and consists of a finite list of painting rules and a canvas shape (limiting shape). Figure 6-2 shows the complete, generative specification of the class of paintings shown in Figure 6-1.

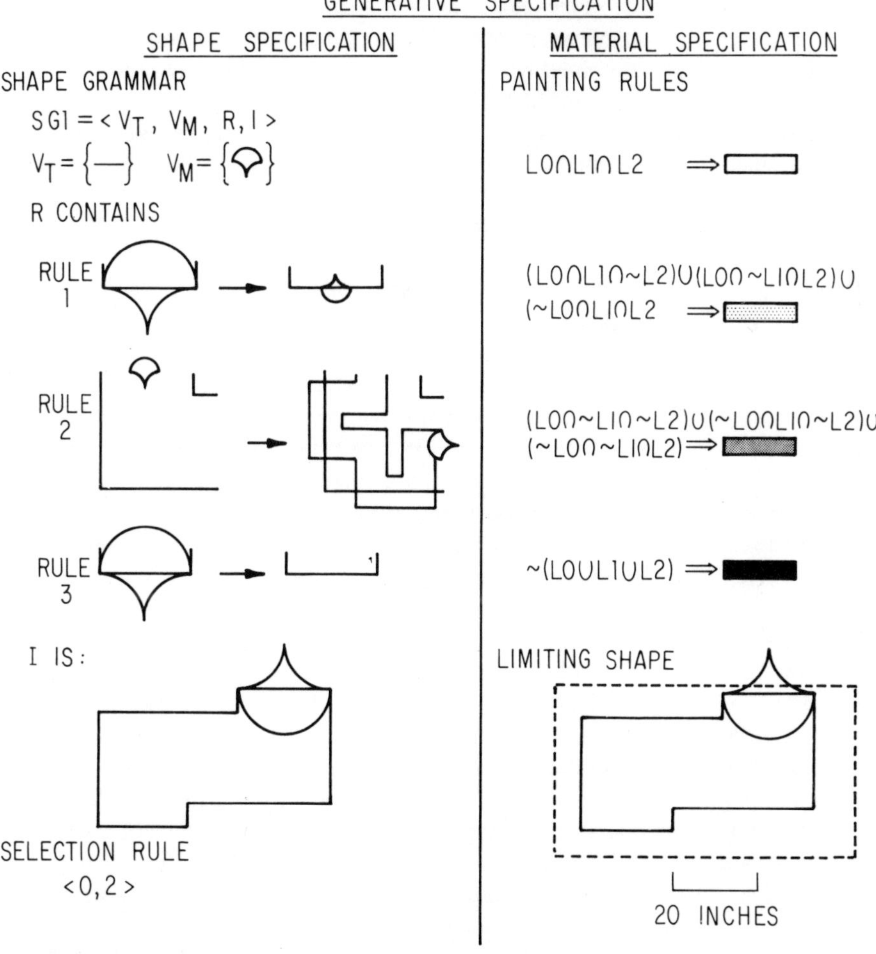

Figure 6-2. Complete, generative specification of the class of paintings containing *Urform I, II, and III.*

Shape Grammars

Shape grammars are similar to phrase structure grammars, which were introduced by Chomsky [4] in linguistics. Where phrase structure grammars are defined over an alphabet of symbols and generate one-dimensional strings of symbols, shape grammars are defined over an alphabet of shapes and generate *n*-dimensional shapes. The definition of shape grammars follows the standard definition of phrase structure grammars [5].

Definition. A *shape grammar* (SG) is a 4-tuple: SG = (V_T, V_M, R, I) where

1. V_T is a finite set of shapes.
2. V_M is a finite set of shapes such that $V_T^* \cap V_M = \phi$.
3. R is a finite set of ordered pairs (u,v) such that *u* is a shape consisting of an element of V_T^* combined with an element of V_M and *v* is a shape consisting of (A) the element of V_T^* contained in *u* or (B) the element of V_T^* contained in *u* combined with an element of V_M or (C) the element of V_T^* contained in *u* combined with an additional element of V_T^* and an element of V_M.
4. I is a shape consisting of elements of V_T^* and V_M.

Elements of the set V_T^* are formed by the finite arrangement of an element or elements of V_T in which any element of V_T may be used a multiple number of times with any scale or orientation. Elements of V_T^* appearing in some (*u*,*v*) of R or in I are called terminal shape elements (or *terminals*). Elements of V_M are called non-terminal shape elements (or *markers*). Elements (*u*,*v*) of R are called *shape rules* and are written u → v. I is called the *initial shape* and normally contains a *u* such that there is a (*u*,*v*) which is an element of R.

A shape is generated from a shape grammar by beginning with the initial shape and recursively applying the shape rules. The result of applying a shape rule to a given shape is another shape consisting of the given shape with the right side of the rule substituted in the shape for an occurrence of the left side of the rule. Rule application to a shape proceeds as follows: (1) find part of the shape that is geometrically similar to the left side of a rule in terms of both non-terminal and terminal elements; (2) find the geometric transformations (scale, translation, rotation, mirror image) which make the left side of the rule identical to the corresponding part in the shape; and (3) apply those transformations to the right side of the rule and substitute the right side of the rule for the corresponding part of the shape. Because the terminal element in the left side of a shape rule is present identically in the right side of the rule, once a terminal is added to a shape it cannot be erased. The generation process is terminated when no rule in the grammar can be applied.

The *language* defined by a shape grammar (L(SG)) is the set of shapes generated by the grammar that do not contain any elements of V_M. The language of a shape grammar is a potentially infinite set of finite shapes.

Example. In SG1, shown in Figure 6-2, V_T contains a straight line; terminals consist of finite arrangements of straight lines. V_M consists of a single element.

R contains three rules—one of each type allowed by the definition. The initial shape contains one marker.

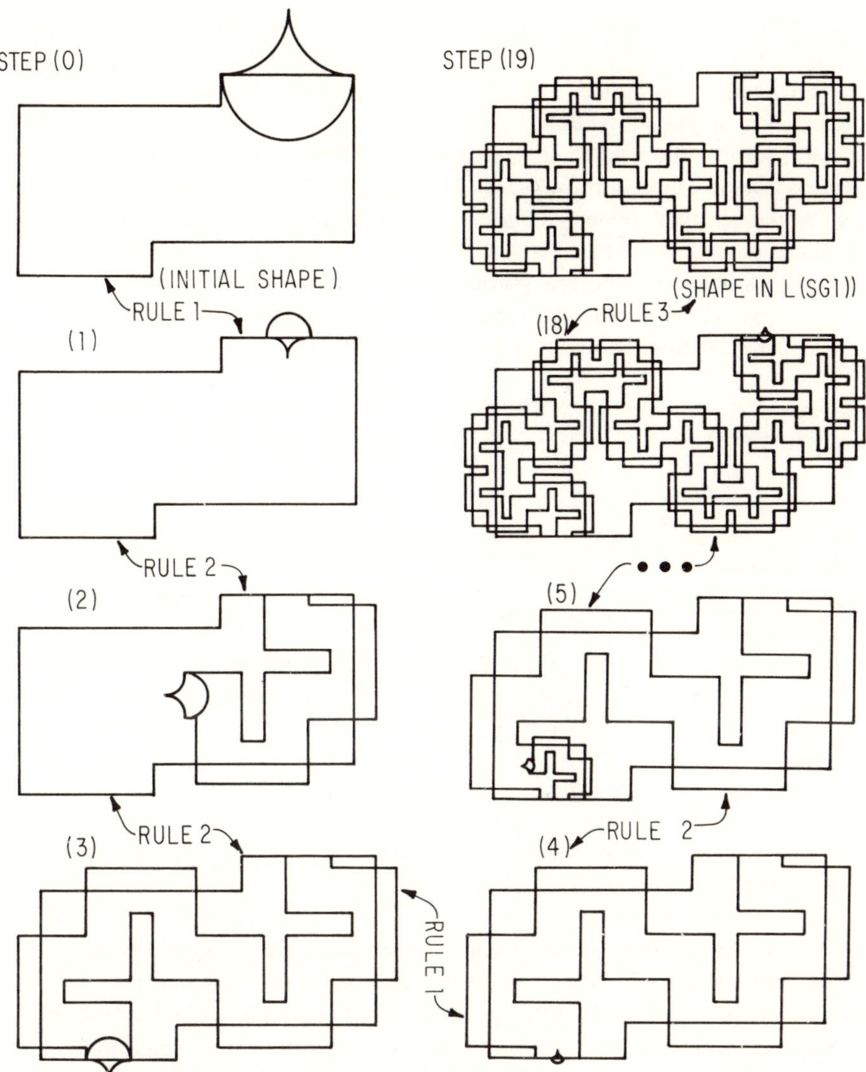

Figure 6-3. Generation of a shape using SG1.

The generation of a shape in the language, L(SG1), defined by SG1 is shown in Figure 6-3. Step 0 shows the initial shape. Recall that a rule can be applied to a shape only if its left side can be made identical to some part of the shape, with respect to both marker and terminal. Either rule 1 or rule 3 is applicable to the shapes indicated in steps 0, 3, and 18. Application of rule 3 results in the removal of the marker, the termination of the generation process (as no rules are now applicable), and a shape in L(SG1). Application of rule 1 reverses the direction of the marker, reduces it in size by one-third, and forces the continuation of the generation process. Markers restrict rule application to a specific part of the shape and indicate the relationship in scale between the rule applied and the shape to which it is applied. Rule 2 is the only rule applicable to the shape indicated in steps 1, 2, and 4-17. Application of rule 2 adds a terminal to the shape, advances the marker, and forces the continuation of the generation process. Shape generation using SG1 may be regarded in this way: the initial shape contains two connected “⅂L” ’s, and additional shapes are formed by the recursive placement of seven smaller “⅂L” ’s on each “⅂L” such that all “⅂L” ’s of the same size are connected. Notice that the shape produced in this way can be expanded outward indefinitely but is contained within a finite area. The language defined by SG1 is shown in Figure 6-4.

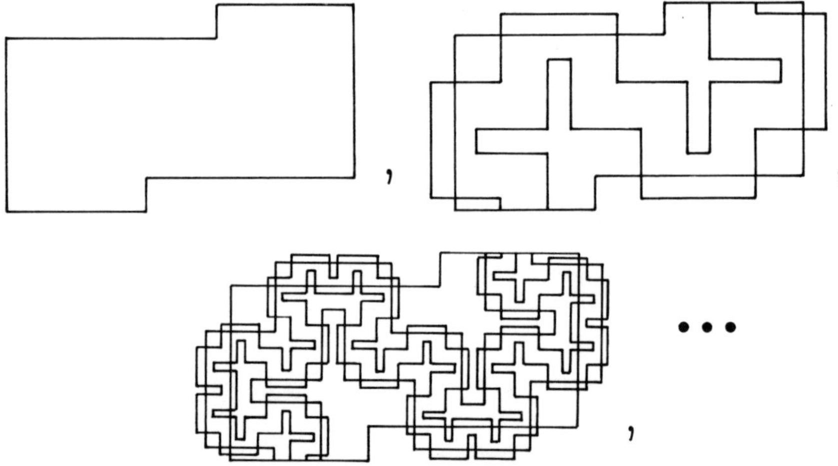

Figure 6-4. The language defined by SG1, L(SG1).

Discussion. SG1 defines a language containing rectilinear shapes of two dimensions. Grammars can be written to define languages containing shapes with demensions greater than two and can define curved as well as rectilinear shapes.

In shape grammars, shape is assumed to be primitive, that is, definitions are made ultimately in terms of shape. These grammars use rules that are shape rather than property specific. The definition of shape grammars allows rules of three types. Where rule type B is logically redundant in the system, it was included because it was found useful in defining painting and sculpture formalisms. Different rule types consistent with the idea of shape grammars are possible and can define classes of grammars analogous to the different classes of phrase structure grammars [5].

Where we use shape grammars exclusively to generate shapes for painting and sculpture, they can also be used to simulate Turing machines and to generate musical scores, structural descriptions of chemical compounds, and the sentences—and their tree structures—in languages defined by phrase structure grammars. Grammar-grammars, where the sentences generated are themselves shape grammars, are possible. While no parsing algorithms have been developed, shape grammars seem applicable to the analysis, as well as the generation, of shapes.

Selection Rules

Painting requires a small class of shapes, which are not beyond its techniques for representation. Because a shape grammar can define a language containing a potentially infinite number of shapes ranging from the simple to the very (infinitely) complex, a mechanism (selection rule) is required to select shapes in the language for painting. The concept of level provides the basis for this mechanism and also for the painting rules discussed in the next section.

The *level* of a terminal in a shape is analogous to the depth of a constituent in a sentence defined by a context freephrase structure grammar. Level assignments are made to terminals during the generation of a shape using these rules:

1. The terminals in the initial shape are assigned level 0.
2. If a shape rule is applied, and the highest level assigned to any part of the terminal corresponding to the left side of the rule is N, then
   (a) If the rule is of type A, any part of the terminal enclosed by the marker in the left side of the rule is assigned N.
   (b) If the rule is of type B, any part of the terminal enclosed by the marker in the left side of the rule is assigned N and any part of the terminal enclosed by the marker in the right side of the rule is assigned N + 1.
   (c) If the rule is of type C, the terminal added is assigned N + 1.
3. No other level assignments are made.

Parts of terminals may be assigned multiple levels. The marker must be a closed shape in order for rules 2a and 2b to apply. Rules 1 and 2c are central to level assignment; rules 2a and 2b are necessary for boundary conditions. The terminals belonging to each of the three levels defined by level assignment in the example are shown individually in Figure 6-5.

A *selection rule* is a double (m,n) where m and n are integers. m is the minimum level required and n is the maximum level allowed in a shape generated by a shape grammar for it to be a member of the class defined by S. Because the terminals added to a shape during the generation process cannot be erased and level assignments are permanent, the selection rule is used as a halting algorithm for shape generation. Where a single painting is to be considered uniquely, as is traditional, the class can be defined to contain only one element.

Where several paintings are to be considered serially or together to show the repeated use or expansion of a motif, as has become popular [6], the class can be defined to contain multiple elements.

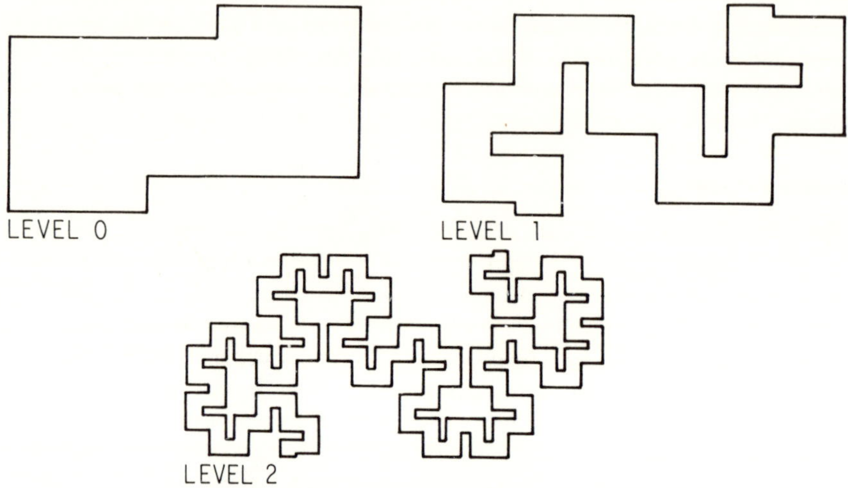

Figure 6-5. The terminals that form the boundaries of the first three levels of shapes generated by SG1.

The class of shapes containing just the three shapes in Figure 6-4 is specified by the double (SG1,(0,2)). The minimum level required is 0 (all shapes in L(SG1) satisfy this requirement) and the maximum level allowed is 2 (only three shapes in L(SG1) satisfy this requirement). (SG1,(2,2)) specifies the class containing only the most complex shape in Figure 6-4.

Painting Rules

Painting rules define a schema for painting the areas contained in a shape. Structurally equivalent areas can be painted identically by specifying these areas in terms of the level assignments to the terminals which form their boundaries.

Painting rules indicate how the areas contained in a shape are painted by considering the shape as a Venn diagram as in naive set theory. The terminals of each level in a shape are taken as the outline of a set in the Venn diagram. As parts of terminals may be assigned multiple levels, sets may have common boundaries. Levels 0, 1, 2, . . . *n* are said to define sets L0, L1, L2, . . . Ln respectively, where *n* is given in the selection rule.

A *painting rule* has two sides separated by a double arrow (⇒). The left side of a painting rule defines a set using the sets determined by level assignment and the usual set operators, for example, union (∪), intersection (∩), complementation (~), and exclusive or (⊗). The sets defined by the left sides of the painting rules of M must partition the universal set. The right side of a painting rule is a rectangle painted in the manner the set defined by the left side of the rule is to be painted. The rectangle gives implicitly medium, color, texture, edge definition, etc. Because the left sides of painting rules form a partition, every area of the shape is painted in exactly one way. Any level in a shape may be ignored by excluding the corresponding set from the left sides of the rules.

Using the set notation, all possible overlap configurations in a shape can be specified independently of their shape. The effect of the painting rules in the example is to count set overlaps. Areas with three overlaps are painted lightest, two overlaps second lightest, one overlap second darkest, and zero overlaps darkest.

The Limiting Shape

The *limiting shape* defines the size and shape of the canvas on which a shape is painted. Traditionally the limiting shape is a single rectangle, but this need not be the case. For example, the limiting shape can be the same as the outline of the shape painted or it can be divided into several parts. The limiting shape is designated by broken lines, and its size is indicated by an explicit notation of scale. The initial shape of the shape grammar in the same scale is located with respect to the limiting shape. The initial shape need not be located within the limiting shape. Informally, the limiting shape acts as a camera viewfinder. The limiting shape determines what part of the painted shape is represented on a canvas and in what scale.

SCULPTURE

Sculpture is the material representation of three-dimensional shapes and is defined analogously to painting. A *class of sculptures* is defined by the double (S,M). S is a specification of a class of shapes and consists of a shape grammar, defining a language of three-dimensional shapes and a selection rule. M is a specification of material representations and consists of a finite list of sculpting rules and a limiting shape. Sculpting rules take the same form as painting rules with medium, surface, edge, etc., given implicitly in a rectangular solid. The limiting shape is three-dimensional.

AESTHETICS

Generative specifications of painting and sculpture have wide implications in aesthetic theory, a theory that regards the art object as a coherent, structured whole. In this context, aesthetics proceeds by the analysis of that whole into its determinate parts toward a definition of the relationship of part to part and part to whole in terms of "unified variety" [7], "order" and "complexity" [8],

[9], "a series of planned harmonies", "an internal organizing logic", "the play of hidden rules" [3], etc. The relationship between the wealth of visual information presented in an art object and the parsimony of structural and material information required to determine that object seems central to this aesthetics. Wealth of visual information may be associated with "variety" and "complexity" and is taken to mean *visual complexity.* Parsimony of structural and material information may be associated with "order" and "an internal organizing logic" and is taken to mean *specificational simplicity.* Visual complexity and specificational simplicity have been studied independently in other contexts [10], [11]. With a generative specification of art objects, investigations such as these can be used as the starting point for the development of a formal, mathematical aesthetics. We believe that painting and sculpture that have a high visual complexity which does not totally obscure an underlying specificational simplicity make for good art objects. The use of the words "beautiful" and "elegant" to describe computer programs, mathematical theorems, or physical laws is in the spirit of this aesthetics–parsimonious specification supporting complex phenomena.

DESIGN

The formalism defined for the specification of painting and sculpture gives a complete description of a class of paintings or sculptures which is independent of the members of the class and is made in terms of a generative schema. For design theory in the visual arts, this means that the definition and solution of design problems can be based on the specification of an art object instead of the object itself. Generative specifications provide a well-defined means of expressing the artist's decisions about shapes and their organization and representation, in the design of non-representational, geometric art. Once the decisions are made as to the relationships that are to underly a class of paintings or sculptures, a generative specification is defined and the structural and material consequences of the relationships are determined algorithmically. This enables the artist to obtain art objects with specificational simplicity and visual complexity which are faithful to these relationships and which would be difficult to design by other means.

REFERENCES

[1] E. Panofsky, The History of the Theory of Human Proportions as a Reflection of the History of Styles, in Meaning in the Visual Arts (Doubleday Anchor Books, Garden City, New York, 1955).

[2] A. Hill (ed.), Directions in Art, Theory and Aesthetics (New York Graphic Society Ltd., Greenwich, Conn., 1968).

[3] H. Focillon, The Life of Forms in Art (Wittenborn, Schultz, Inc., New York, 1948).

[4] N. Chomsky, Syntactic Structures (Mouton and Co., The Hague, 1957).
[5] S. Ginsberg, The Mathematical Theory of Context-Free Languages (McGraw-Hill, New York, 1966).
[6] J. Coplans, Serial Imagery (New York Graphic Society Ltd., Greenwich, Conn., 1968).
[7] G. T. Fechner, Vorschule der Aesthetik (Breitkopf Hartel, Leipzig, 1897).
[8] G. D. Birkhoff, Aesthetic Measure (Harvard University Press, Cambridge, Mass., 1932).
[9] H. J. Eysenck, The Empirical Determination of an Aesthetic Formula, Psychological Review 48 (1941) pp. 83-92.
[10] F. Attneave, Physical Determinants of the Judged Complexity of Shapes, Journal of Experimental Psychology 53 (1957) pp. 221-227.
[11] J. Feldman, J. Gips, J. Horning and S. Reder, Grammatical Complexity and Inference, Stanford Artificial Intelligence Project Memo 89 (June 1969).

PART 4

THE BRITISH COMPUTER SOCIETY

London, England

Two best papers submitted to the British Computer Society during 1971, as announced by the Selection Panel of the Publications Committee of the British Computer Society:

"A System for Stereo Viewing"
by A. Ortony

and

"The Automatic Solution of Systems of Ordinary Differential Equations
by the Method of Taylor Series"
by David Barton, I. M. Willers, and R. V. M. Zahar

7
A System for Stereo Viewing*

by *A. Ortony*

INTRODUCTION

For most computer applications involving the display of three-dimensional objects, a two-dimensional representation is adequate. However, there are times when the material to be displayed is such that intelligibility can be greatly increased if the objects can be viewed stereoscopically, e.g. in the case of pipework (Strauss and Poley, 1968; Barry *et al.,* 1969). This applies particularly in the case of objects which are relatively unfamiliar, for in such cases comprehension requires more visual cues (Gregory, 1970). Our interest in a stereo viewing facility was prompted by the desire to couple it with a hidden line removal program (Jones, 1970) and also by the desire to display molecular models, which at least for those of us who are chemically naïve, are frequently very difficult to interpret in their two-dimensional representations. The initial aim, therefore, was to design and produce a viable stereoscopic 3D viewing system quickly and cheaply. It appears that any inexpensive split-screen method suffers from two disadvantages. First, it is only suitable for solo-viewing, and second, it halves the effective screen resolution (Ophir, Shepherd, and Spinard, 1969). The technique described in this paper overcomes the first of these problems.

OPTICAL DESIGN

The principle underlying what we call the transmission/reflection method is illustrated in Figure 7-1. The software supplies two images. These images, the stereo pair, are derived by computing projections corresponding to views for each eye. The factors influencing the choice of views are discussed later. They appear on the CRT screen, one above the other, the upper one being inverted. The lower image, Pv, is transmitted through a sheet of vertically polarizing polaroid on the lower half of the screen; the upper image, Ph, is transmitted through a sheet of horizontally polarizing polaroid on the upper half of the screen. The lower image is then transmitted through, and the upper image reflected off, a transmitting/reflecting surface (T/R), the upper being, in consequence, reinverted

*British Patent Application Number: 13844/70.

Editor's Note: From *The Computer Journal,* vol. 14, no. 2. Reprinted by permission of the publisher, The British Computer Society, and the author.

to restore it to its correct orientation. Thus the transmitting/reflecting surface, the mirror, overlays the two images when viewed from a suitable range of angles from above and the images are then discriminated using orthogonally polarized spectacles. It is worth noting here that it is essential that the reflected image be horizontally polarized and the transmitted one vertically polarized. This is be-

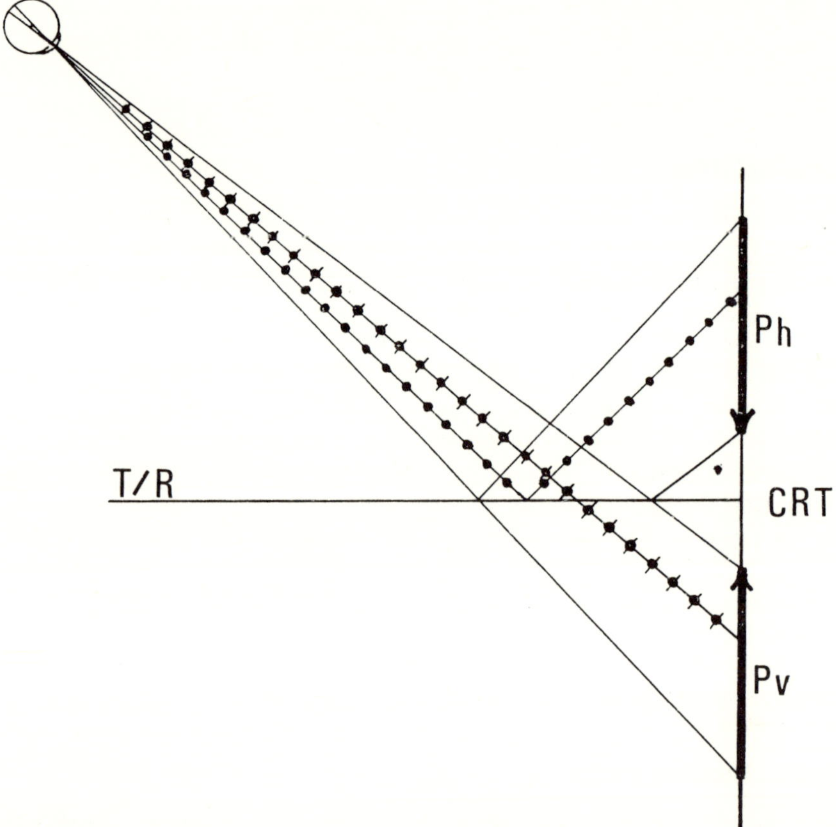

Figure 7-1.

cause light reflected from a specular surface is partially polarized in a plane perpendicular to the plane of incidence. The extent to which this partial polarization takes place depends on the angle of incidence and the refractive index, it being a maximum for glass at what is known as Brewster's angle (approximately equal to 57°), and a minimum (zero, in fact) if the light strikes the surface at a normal (Jenkins and White, 1957). This means that the light reflected off the surface of the mirror would be already partially horizontally polarized (and the transmitted light partially vertically polarized) even in the absence of any polarizing material.

Clearly the polaroid must not be used in a way which conflicts with the natural polarizing tendency.

One of the advantages of this method is that under good viewing conditions, it is impossible for the eyes to see the wrong image. Thus, if the head is kept upright, the polaroid filters in the spectacles will cut out the image which is polarized at right angles to the filters. Of course, improved cut-out has to be achieved at the expense of increased light loss, but the image intensity was sufficient to enable us to achieve virtual extinction through one filter while retaining an acceptable intensity through the other.

The inverted image on the upper half of the screen is always directly visible by the eye viewing through the horizontally polarizing filter. However, this image can be obscured by arranging a mask in the appropriate position, thus eliminating the only distracting optical feature.

PROTOTYPE PERFORMANCE

In terms of efficiency the first piece of apparatus built fell short of the optimum that can be achieved using the transmission/reflection method.

The use of a sheet of perspex to act as a partially reflecting surface carried serious problems in its wake, this in spite of the fact that neutral density was used, which not only helps to match the intensity of the images but also minimizes the secondary reflections off its lower surface. One problem was that the perspex, lacking rigidity, tended to bend and warp very readily and in consequence it proved tedious to align the images so that the horizontal lines coincided. In the absence of such vertical alignment, perception of depth becomes impossible. The extent to which the eyes can compensate for vertical non-alignment is so small, of the order of ½° or so, that the condition becomes very stringent.

A semi-silvered mirror in place of the perspex might at first sight seem to provide the solution in that it is much more rigid and has the additional advantage of causing less light loss. However, the cost of a suitably sized semi-silvered mirror is not inconsiderable and there are severe problems connected with cleaning.

An improved version with a considerably reinforced frame carrying a gray plate glass reflecting/transmitting surface has solved the problem. The glass has a 48-percent transmission factor and is ¼ inch thick. It is thus free from problems of bending as well as being much flatter than perspex. In addition, the intensities of the stereo images are matched over a greater range of viewing angles. In practice, however, even with the prototype model, users can, having once adjusted the apparatus, make very satisfactory use of it.

With the prototype model attached to the console of a DEC Type 340 display, the user may view from up to about 1½ meters from the screen before the images become difficult to perceive. Walking around the screen, the viewer can achieve 3D perception through about 80°. This is illustrated in Figure 7-2.

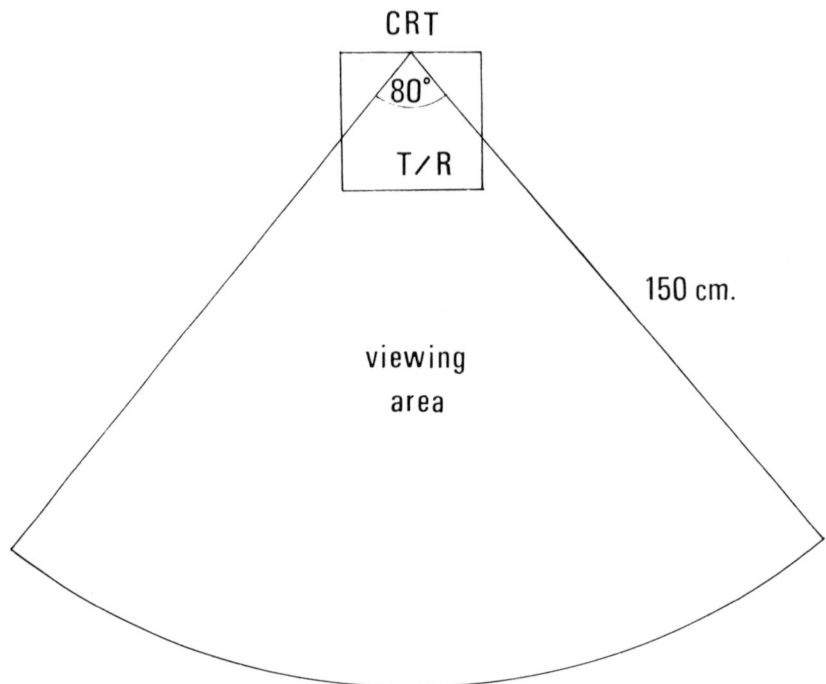

Figure 7-2.

The most satisfactory angle of elevation to the mirror from which to view is about 30°, but good results can be obtained between 20° and 40°, through which range the image intensities are always adequately matched.

There are, of course, better and worse positions from which to view insofar as distortion is concerned. Indeed, the limitations on angles around the screen over which successful viewing can be achieved are largely due to distortion. Distortion also occurs with backward and forward movement in that retreating from the screen gives rise to an apparent increase in depth due to the fact that there is no change in stereo image disparity with the change in distance (Gregory, 1966). However, short of monitoring head movements, no stereo system can cope with this; work in this area is understood to be in progress in the Computer Science Department at the University of Utah.

The only type of projection that can present the same appearance to the eyes as the object from which it is taken is a perspective projection which, furthermore, requires that viewing take place from the unique viewpoint assumed in the projection. In practice there is considerable tolerance on the closeness of the eyes to the correct viewpoint before distortion becomes apparent.

The accuracy of the view given by an orthogonal or oblique-type projection, which is free of perspective, increases with the distance that the object is assumed to be from the eyes and in the limiting case (i.e. when the object is at infinity) such a projection is indistinguishable from a perspective projection. But when these projections are used to create stereo pairs, the stereo effect is improved if the object is close to the eyes. Thus a balance has to be struck between the effectiveness of the stereo effect and the degree of correspondence between the object and its appearance.

To optimize the stereo effect the apparent average position of the object along the Z-axis must be as close to the plane of the display screen as possible, since the eyes accommodate (focus) according to convergence on the screen. Thus an effort should be made in writing the software to arrange for a minimal mean disparity to ease initial fusion and for a range of disparities which, while still giving adequate depth information, minimizes the eye strain due to focus/convergence conflict. It may be necessary to use software tricks to bring the object within the vicinity of the screen, and possibly, in the case of a very deep object, to scale it down along the Z-axis (i.e. the depth axis).

Procedures of this kind will, of course, cause distortion to varying degrees, but if one regards the primary purpose of a stereo facility to be the provision of relative depth information with the absolute information held in core, these distortions are of little consequence.

One objection to the device is that having once decided on a view, it is not then possible to photograph the images and have them immediately viewable through a conventional stereoscope, because the pairs are one above the other, the upper one being inverted. While it is true that the pairs displayed on the screen are of little use for the purpose mentioned, there is no reason why standard stereo pairs should not be produced for photography by software. A further disadvantage in this connection is the need to remove the apparatus before taking photographs; this might prove inconvenient if a long series of photographs were required. Again, however, software could be used to store and subsequently output the series with the pairs in the standard orientation.

Here it is worth mentioning that the loss of resolution mentioned at the outset need not necessarily extend to photographs of stereo pairs. If the pair members are output successively, they can obviously employ the whole screen area, even though this might be a less convenient arrangement.

ADVANTAGES OF THE SYSTEM

It was considered useful to compare the T/R method with the more obvious alternatives, namely viewing stereoscopic pairs with a Wheatstone mirror stereoscope and with optical prisms. The Medical Research Council's Mill Hill laboratory was using the mirror stereoscope for viewing stereo pairs of molecules, and if properly adjusted, 3D views were easy to achieve (White, Perkins *et al.,* 1970). The system uses two pairs of mirrors, each pair routing its image to the eye, thus enabling fusion to take place while the eyes converge normally. The result of the set-up at Mill Hill was most impressive.

The effect of prisms is to shift the apparent position of a viewed object laterally, thus, as illustrated in Figures 7-3 and 7-4, well-separated stereo pairs can appear to originate from the same place. Tests were carried out using a pair of strong (10°) acromatic prisms mounted in goggles. Some users found looking through the prisms rather unpleasant and that their prolonged use caused headaches. This was presumably due to the fact that the goggles were worn continuously, even when not required to assist fusion of pairs, consequently, the user suffered from "seeing double." In fact, the prisms used were too strong, but if several people wished to view the display at the same time they would need to have prisms of graded strengths according to their distance from the screen and so viewers near the screen would, in fact, need quite strong prisms. If one is to use prisms as a way of stereo viewing, the prisms should almost certainly be in a fixed position so that they are looked through but not worn. This would be an unsatisfactory viewing arrangement

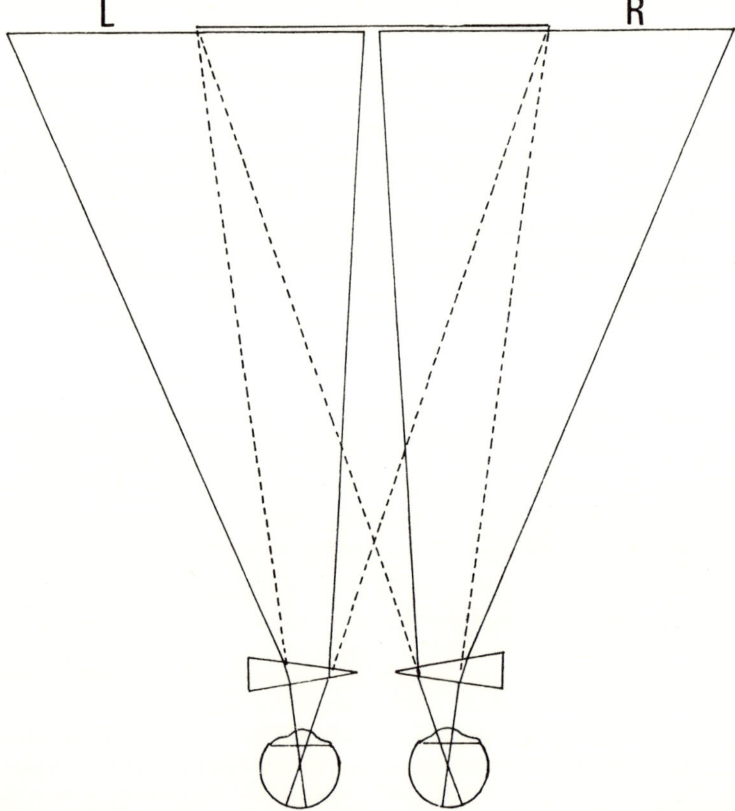

Figure 7-3.

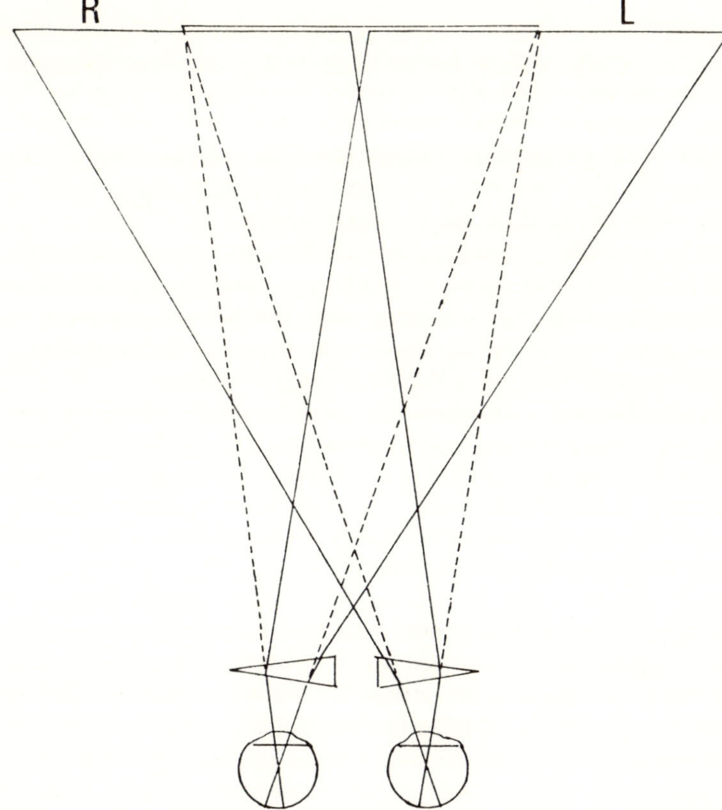

Figure 7-4.

since it does not permit simultaneous viewing and involves moving into a special fixed position in order to view the display.

The latter objection is also the main objection to the mirror stereoscope, another minor objection being that a different adjustment of angle may be required for different users, which entails adjustment before use. On the other hand, there is absolutely no doubt that both alternatives are far superior optically to the transmission/reflection method. Both suffer from almost negligible light loss and deterioration in image quality, while the transmission method involves a considerable light loss, since there are two filters between the screen and the eye. This light loss has been of no importance in our tests, the intensity and quality being at all times more than adequate for working purposes.

The most important advantage that the T/R method has over its comparable rivals such as the mirror stereoscope or fusion by prisms is based on the way in which the images are discriminated. Since the images are already overlaid, image-routing is a question of isolation by filters rather than by geometry.

This means that the isolation is position-independent, and this in turn allows freedom of movement without loss of depth perception. From the point of view of an individual viewer this freedom of movement has great ergonomic advantages. In addition, multiple viewing is a simple and cheap matter involving only additional pairs of polaroid filters for the eyes. Sets of mirror stereoscopes or prisms would be costly and cumbersome and yet still require that they be fixed for satisfactory viewing.

Further, as a means of viewing, polaroid filters have an imperceptible effect when viewing ordinary scenes and there is therefore a minimal disturbing effect resulting from their continued use when the user is looking away from the screen. Thus, if one has to view the screen through something, polaroid filters seem the least objectionable way of doing so.

Finally, an advantage some people gain is that polaroid filters are easy to place over standard spectacles, which means that in most cases of people who wear spectacles, there is no difficulty in viewing. The exception to this is rather alarming in that if the lenses of the spectacles are made of plastic, the effect of the polaroid can be destroyed. However, fortunately, none of our viewers has yet had this experience.

Graphical interaction may be encouraged in this system by displaying two appropriately positioned marker spots, one in each image. These would be perceived as a point in the 3D space occupied by the objects being viewed. The point would be movable by software so that any part of the displayed object could be picked out. The input control could come from any convenient physical device, which provides for the varying of the three coordinates, such as a "joystick" having three translational degrees of freedom.

In any event, a satisfactory stereo display together with interactive facilities is of great assistance in making progress with some of the more complex tasks involved in manipulating three-dimensional shapes.

POSTSCRIPT

Since this paper was submitted we have acquired a semi-aluminized mirror to replace the neutral density glass. Performance has improved, there being less light loss and better intensity matching. However, our suspicions about cleaning the mirror proved correct; the solution of this problem would considerably increase the cost of the mirror.

ACKNOWLEDGMENTS

I wish to thank my colleague and co-inventor, Mr. C. B. Jones, whose collaboration made this work possible.

My thanks are also due for advice and encouragement to Professor R. L. Gregory of the University of Bristol, and Mr. G. Coulouris of Imperial College.

I would like to thank Imperial College Civil Engineering Department for the photographs. The work described was carried out under SRC Contract B/SR/2071, "Computer Processing of Three-Dimensional Shapes."

REFERENCES

Barry, C. D., Ellis, R. A., Graesser, S. M., and Marshall, G. R. (1969). Display and manipulation in three dimensions, in *Pertinent Concepts in Computer Graphics,* ed. Fairmaer and Nievergelt, University of Illinois Conference.

Gregory, R. L. (1966). *Eye and Brain,* Weidenfeld & Nicholson, London, p. 57.

Gregory, R. L. (1970). *The Intelligent Eye,* Weidenfeld & Nicholson, London, p. 69.

Jenkins, F. A., and White, H. E. (1957). *Fundamentals of Optics,* 3rd Edition, McGraw-Hill, New York, pp. 488-492.

Jones, C. B. (1971). A New Approach to the 'Hidden Line' Problem, *The Computer Journal,* Vol. 14 (in press).

Ophir, D., Shepherd, B. J., and Spinard, R. J. (1969). Three-Dimensional Computer Display, *Comm. A.C.M.,* Vol. 12, No. 6, June, pp. 309-310.

Strauss, C. M., and Poley, S. (1968). 3DPDP, a Three-Dimensional Piping Design Program, IFIP Congress.

White, J., Perkins, J., Franklin, D. A., Piper, E., and Tattam, F. G. (1970). Interactive Computer-generated Stereoscopic Displays for Biomedical Research, Computer Graphics 70, Brunel University.

8

The Automatic Solution of Systems of Ordinary Differential Equations by the Method of Taylor Series

by *D. Barton, I. M. Willers, and R. V. M. Zahar*

The Taylor series method for the solution of a system of ordinary differential equations is well known. However, the difficulty of implementing a general-purpose algorithm that will enable an arbitrary differential system to be solved by this method is so great that the procedure has been largely neglected in the literature in favor of computationally more simple techniques. Briefly, the method is to replace each variable present in the differential system by a Taylor series centered at a certain origin. With the exception of the constant terms, the coefficients in each series are regarded as unknown quantities. The differential equations of the system may be used to obtain a set of recurrence relations from which these unknowns can be calculated. Thus a formal power series solution to an initial value problem may be determined, and the series will be convergent in some region about the origin. The truncated formal series are then evaluated at some point within the region and hence a new set of initial values obtained. The recurrence relations then yield a second series solution valid in a region about the new origin; consequently, the differential equations may be solved by a numerical version of the technique of analytic continuation into a finite region. We are not concerned here with the numerical techniques that are available for choosing the new origin, as this has been discussed by Barton, Willers, and Zahar (1970), but here confine ourselves to the automatic derivation of the recurrence relations and their efficient encoding.

There is a systematic approach to the problem that is frequently employed by hand. The equations of the differential system are first reduced to a certain canonical form from which the recurrence relations may be easily deduced. These relations are then written down explicity, and finally an efficient integration procedure is constructed which employs the recurrence relations. The procedure of reduction to canonical form and the derivation of the recurrence relations is best illustrated by an example. Consider the differential system

$$y' = y^2 + z$$
$$z' = z^2 \qquad (1)$$

Editor's Note: From *The Computer Journal,* vol. 14, no. 3. Reprinted by permission of the publisher, The British Computer Society, and the authors.

where

$$y = z = 1 \quad \text{when} \quad t = 0$$

Introducing new variables a, b, c, we obtain the canonical form for system (1)

$$\begin{aligned} a &= y^2 \\ b &= a + z \\ c &= z^2 \\ y' &= b \\ z' &= c \end{aligned} \tag{2}$$

where

$$y = z = 1 \quad \text{when} \quad t = 0$$

To obtain a formal series solution to system (2) about the point $t = t_0$ we write

$$y = \sum_{i=0}^{\infty} y_0^{(i)} (t - t_0)^i$$

together with similar expansions for the variables z, a, b, and c. Then from the equations of system (2) we obtain the recurrence relations

$$\begin{aligned} a_0^{(N)} &= \sum_{j=0}^{N} y_0^{(N-j)} y_0^{(j)} \\ b_0^{(N)} &= a_0^{(N)} + z_0^{(N)} \\ c_0^{(N)} &= \sum_{j=0}^{N} z_0^{(N-j)} z_0^{(j)} \\ y_0^{(N+1)} &= b_0^{(N)}/(N+1) \\ z_0^{(N+1)} &= c_0^{(N)}/(N+1) \end{aligned} \tag{3}$$

while the initial conditions of system (2) yield $y_0^{(0)} = z_0^{(0)} = 1, t_0 = 0$.

A complication arises when the original differential system contains non-rational functions for example sin (x) or cos (x). It is possible to deal with these functions in two different ways and we illustrate both techniques by reference to the example of the system

$$y' = 1 + \sin(y) \tag{4}$$

where

$$y = 1 \quad \text{when} \quad t = 0.$$

It is known (for example, see Moore, 1966) that the Taylor coefficients of sin (y) may be determined by a recurrence relation when those of y are known. With this result in mind, a suitable canonical reduction of system (4) is given by (5) on introducing new variables a, b.

$$a = \sin\ (y)$$

$$b = 1 + a$$

$$y' = b \tag{5}$$

where

$$y = 1 \quad \text{when} \quad t = 0.$$

The appropriate recurrence relations may now be directly written down.

To illustrate the second technique let us assume that the recurrence relation for the Taylor coefficients of sin (y) in terms of those of y was not known. In this case we introduce the new variables a and b and augment system (4) by the differential equations defining sin and cos. Hence we obtain

$$y' = 1 + a$$

$$a' = by'$$

$$b' = -ay'$$

where

$$y = 1, a = \sin\ (1), b = \cos\ (1) \text{ when } t = 0.$$

Introducing new variables c, d, e, f, and g, we obtain from system (6) the canonical system

$$c = 1 + a$$

$$d = bc$$

$$e = ac$$

$$f = -e$$

$$y' = c$$

$$a' = d$$

$$b' = f \tag{7}$$

where

$$y = 1, a = \sin\ (1), b = \cos\ (1) \quad \text{when} \quad t = 0.$$

We see therefore that non-rational functions may be treated either by the use of a recurrence relation, when this is available, or alternatively by the use of the defining differential equations. However, the latter technique complicates the problem to some extent and, of course, raises the order of the differential system.

The general procedure for the solution of an initial value problem, described above, is clearly a tedious and error-prone task for even a moderately complicated set of equations. A number of programming systems have been produced, which automate parts of the general method, but for all of the programs it is necessary to present the differential system in canonical form. For equations presented in this form Gibbon (1960) describes an implementation that treats non-rational functions by both of the techniques described above, while Moore (1966) describes two systems that treat non-rational functions by the two methods separately.

In this paper we show that an initial value problem, stated in a formal but natural manner, may be considered as a sentence of a simple language. The syntactic analysis of this sentence yields a tree structure from which the canonical form of the differential equations of the problem may be obtained. Further, we show that an optimized form of the canonical representation may be deduced from the initial representation and finally that a program, in any suitable target language, corresponding to the equivalent recurrence relations (cf. equation (7)) used in an appropriate order may be obtained. The entire process is analogous to the generation of code from a sentence written in a programming language, and the program that carries it out will be referred to as a compiler. The compiled program may then be called by a numerical system for the integration of the differential equations. The complete system has been implemented on the Atlas 2 computer in Cambridge. The Atlas implementation is an interactive program and Figure 8-1 is a sample protocol for the solution of an initial value problem that is self-explanatory.

THE AUTOMATIC REDUCTION OF A DIFFERENTIAL SYSTEM TO STANDARD FORM

In our discussion of the syntactic analysis and compilation of an initial value problem we omit any description of the statements controlling the output of numerical values during the integration procedure and accordingly assume that the PRINT statement in the example, Figure 8-1, is replaced by the word END. The general form of presentation of an initial value problem to the system is therefore

INTEGRATE

$$y_i^{(n_i)} = f_i(t, y_1, \ldots, y_1^{(k_1)}, \ldots, y_m, \ldots y_m^{(k_m)}, r_1, \ldots r_p) \qquad 1 \leqslant i \leqslant m$$

$$r_i = g_i(t, y_1, \ldots, y_1^{(l_1)}, \ldots, y_m, \ldots, y_m^{(l_m)}, r_1, \ldots r_{i-1}, r_{i+1}, \ldots, r_p)$$

$$1 \leqslant i \leqslant p$$

WITH INITIAL CONDITIONS

$$y_i^{(j)} = h_i^j(y_1, \ldots, y_1^{(n_1-1)}, \ldots, y_m, \ldots, y_m^{(n_m-1)})$$

$$1 \leqq i \leqq m \text{ and } 0 \leqq j < n_i - 1$$

$t = t_0$

END

```
INTEGRATE
Y'' =Y + SIN(2Y)
WITH INITIAL CONDITIONS
Y=1
Y'=0
FOR T=0:.5:4.5 PRINT T,Y
```

T	Y
+0	+1.0000000000
+5.0000000000E-1	+1.2386711772
+1.0000000000	+1.9263729413
+1.5000000000	+2.9718800676
+2.0000000000	+4.7283440467
+2.5000000000	+7.7188005083
+3.0000000000	+1.2680794661E1
+3.5000000000	+2.0878615426E1
+4.0000000000	+3.4404689117E1
+4.5000000000	+5.6712871112E1

Figure 8-1.

where k_j and l_j are positive integers and in the equation for $y_i^{(ni)}$ we have $k_i < n_i$.

Further, t is the independent variable. It must be understood that for the purpose of input to the computer each equation defines the variable on the left-hand side explicitly and that for our implementation distinct variables y_i and r_i are written using different letters of the alphabet. Further, we write

$$y_i^{(j)} = \frac{d^j y_i}{dt^j}$$

as a letter followed by a sequence of j primes. Finally, we call the equation defining $y_i^{(n_i)}$ a differential equation and that defining r_i an identity.

Consider now the language composed of the following basic symbols where composite symbols are underlined:

+ − * / ↑ ′ = =∫ nl ( ) neg sin cos
INTEGRATE WITH INITIAL CONDITIONS END

and defined by the grammar

⟨initial value problem⟩ → INTEGRATE nl ⟨differential system⟩ WITH
INITIAL CONDITIONS nl ⟨initial point⟩ END
⟨differential system⟩ → ⟨equation⟩ | ⟨equation⟩ ⟨differential system⟩
⟨equation⟩ → ⟨name⟩ = ⟨expression⟩ nl | ⟨name⟩ =∫ ⟨expression⟩ nl
| ⟨name⟩ =∫ ⟨equation⟩
⟨initial point⟩ → ⟨value⟩ | ⟨value⟩ ⟨initial point⟩
⟨value⟩ → ⟨name⟩ = ⟨expression⟩ nl

Here the operator =∫ is diadic and y =∫ ⟨expression⟩ means integrate the expression, assign the result to y and yield the result y. A ⟨name⟩ is the address of a portion of space allocated to a certain variable appearing in the differential system and a ⟨numerical constant⟩ is a suitably marked address of the location of the value of that constant. Finally, an ⟨expression⟩ is an arithmetic expression composed of ⟨names⟩ and ⟨numerical constants⟩ with the usual operators + − * / ↑ neg sin cos etc., together with the parentheses ( ) in the usual way, except that we allow the operator ′(prime) as well. The operator ′ denotes differentiation with respect to t.

This language plays a central role in the compilation that proceeds, in four stages, to reduce the source text of an initial value problem to a program in target language (e.g. machine code or FORTRAN). This program will solve the problem by the method of Taylor series. It should be mentioned that this grammar will accept ill-defined as well as well-defined initial value problems and the detection of badly posed problems is left until the code generation stage of compilation. The four distinct stages of compilation are as follows:

1. Lexical analysis
2. Formal syntax analysis and reduction to matrix form
3. Optimization of the matrix form
4. Code generation

These will be described, in turn, with reference to the example

```
      INTEGRATE
      Y'' = 2R + SIN (Y + 1) + 1 + Y
      R = (1 + Y) ↑ 2
      WITH INITIAL CONDITIONS
      Y = Y'
      Y' = 1
      T = 0
END
```

Lexical Analysis

The purpose of this stage of compilation is to translate the source text of the initial value problem into a sentence in the language defined above. It is logically a prepass of the source but for the Cambridge implementation it appears as part of the input subroutine. However, at this first stage it is convenient to perform certain manipulations of the source that greatly simplify the syntax analysis carried out at stage two. Consequently, while processing a differential equation or an identity, the analyser operates in two modes. In mode one, before reading the equals sign, the only sequence that is accepted is ⟨letter⟩ ⟨possibly null sequence of primes⟩. This sequence causes the analyser to assign names for the several variables that will be required during the later work, thus the sequence Y′ ″ causes the names $\underline{Y''}$, $\underline{Y'}$ and $\underline{Y}$ to be assigned for the quantities Y″, Y′, and Y, respectively. Then for a differential equation, where n is the number of primes occuring, the sequence ⟨letter⟩ ⟨n primes⟩ =, is translated to the sequence of basic symbols.

$$\langle\text{name for letter}\rangle \underline{=\int} \langle\text{name for letter}'\rangle \underline{=\int} \dots$$
$$\langle\text{name for letter followed by } n-1 \text{ primes}\rangle \underline{=\int}$$

while for an identity, the sequence ⟨letter⟩ =, is translated to the basic symbols ⟨name for letter⟩ =.

Thus the sequence Y′ ″ = is translated to $\underline{Y}\ \underline{=\int}\ \underline{Y'}\ \underline{=\int}\ \underline{Y''}\ \underline{=\int}$ and the sequence Y = is translated to $\underline{Y}$ =. Having read the equals sign, the analyzer changes to mode two, in which it accepts any sequence of characters and recognizes particularly the sequence ⟨letter⟩ ⟨primes⟩ and translates it to the appropriate name followed by the minimum sequence of prime operators. In mode two, numerical constants are also recognized and compiled, their translated value being their names. Finally, in mode two an explicit multiplication operator * is inserted between any two names found in juxtaposition and also, where appropriate, between parentheses and names. Thus the lexical analyzer translates the initial value problem given above into

$$\underline{\text{INTEGRATE}}\ \underline{\text{nl}}\ \underline{Y}\ \underline{=\int}\ \underline{Y'}\ \underline{=\int}\ \underline{2} * \underline{R} + \underline{\text{SIN}}\ (\underline{Y} + \underline{1}) + \underline{1} + \underline{Y}\ \underline{\text{nl}}\ \underline{R} =$$
$$(\underline{1} + \underline{Y}) \uparrow \underline{2}\ \underline{\text{nl}}$$
$$\underline{\text{WITH INITIAL CONDITIONS}}\ \underline{\text{nl}}\ \underline{Y} = \underline{Y'}\ \underline{\text{nl}}\ \underline{Y'} = \underline{1}\ \underline{\text{nl}}\ \underline{T} = \underline{0}\ \underline{\text{nl}}\ \underline{\text{END}}$$

where names and numerical constants are denoted by the corresponding underlined symbols.

Formal Syntax Analysis and Reduction to Matrix Form

This stage of compilation reads the output from stage one and translates it first to a syntax tree and then condenses it to an equivalent matrix form. It is this matrix form that is equivalent to the canonical form of the differential system from which the recurrence relations for the Taylor series method may be deduced. Algorithms for the reduction to a syntax tree and to matrix form are well known and we do not give a detailed description of them here (see Graham, 1964). First, those parts of the syntax tree that refer to initial conditions and second, those parts that refer to the identities and the differential equations are independently reduced to matrix form. The first of these two forms is later used to generate an initialization program and the second is used to generate the program to calculate Taylor series solutions of the initial value problem by means of recurrence relations. In Figure 8-2 is shown the syntax tree for our example and Figure 8-3 shows the two matrix forms.

Optimization of the Matrix Form

During the third and fourth stages of compilation the two matrix forms are treated independently; however, the same optimization procedure is used for both. Clearly the most fundamental form of optimization is the recognition and

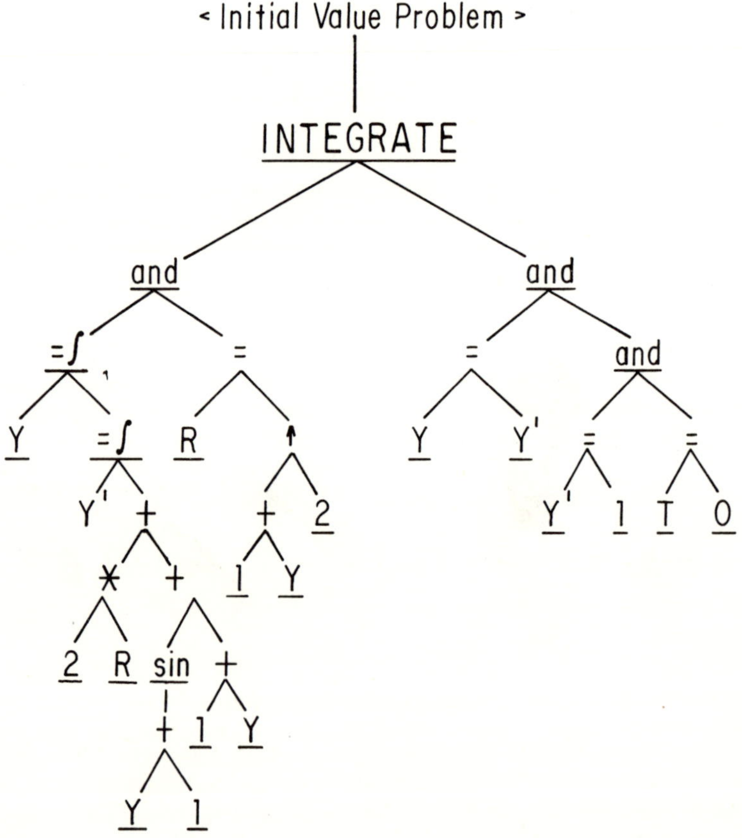

Figure 8-2.

OPN	ARG 1	ARG 2	RESULT
*	2	R	T1
+	Y	1	T2
sin	T2		T3
+	1	Y	T4
+	T4	T3	T5
+	T5	T1	T6
=∫	T6		Y'
=∫	Y'		Y
+	1	Y	T7
↑	T7	2	T8
=	T8		R

Figure 8-3. Recurrence Matrix

elimination of common subexpressions. This is of particular importance for the recurrence matrix (the matrix form of the differential equations), as it is from there that a program for the recurrence procedure is generated, and any redundancy there will have very serious effects on the runtime of the final compiled program. Common subexpressions are therefore detected by direct matching of the rows of the matrix and also by use of the commutative law for addition and multiplication followed by matching. The optimizer continues to work on the matrix until it fails to improve the representation in one entire pass through the matrix. The second type of optimization that takes place is the elimination of unnecessary operations between Taylor series. Thus the product of a constant and a series is marked as such and can be separately treated at the code-generation stage. We show the optimized matrix form in Figure 8-4. Operators between constants and series have been enclosed in circles. Finally, arithmetic between constants is carried out and the corresponding rows of the matrix are deleted.

Code Generation

The optimized matrix form of the recurrence matrix and the initialization matrix that results from stage three of the compilation is simply a representation of the canonical form of the initial value problem, and it remains to generate from it a program in the target language for use during the numerical

OPN	ARG 1	ARG 2	RESULT
=	Y'		Y
=	1		Y'
=	0		T

Figure 8-4. Initialization Matrix

integration. However, this task is not straightforward since the original equations may not have been presented in an order suitable for immediate evaluation and also because algorithms for the various elementary functions may not be available. In our example (Figure 8-5), if an algorithm is available to evaluate the the nth Taylor coefficient of sin (x) when those of both x and sin (x) are known up to the $(n - 1)$th coefficients and the nth coefficient of x is known, then the matrix form can be translated as it stands. However, if such an algorithm is not available, the system must append rows to both matrices (Figure 8-5), to correspond to the differential equations defining sin (x) and their initial conditions respectively. The code generator is provided with a list of elementary functions together with either the algorithm or the appropriate differential equations and deals with them according as either is known. For the present we assume that an algorithm is known and hence that the matrices (Figures 8-5 and 8-6) can be processed without modification.

OPN	ARG 1	ARG 2	RESULT
⊛	2	R	T1
⊕	Y	1	T2
sin	T2		T3
+	T2	T3	T5
+	T5	T1	T6
=∫	T6		Y'
=∫	Y'		Y
⊕	T2	2	R

Figure 8-5. Optimized Recurrence Matrix

OPN	ARG 1	ARG 2	RESULT
⊜	$\underline{Y'}$		$\underline{Y}$
⊜	$\underline{1}$		$\underline{Y'}$
⊜	$\underline{0}$		$\underline{T}$

Figure 8-6. Optimized Initialization Matrix

The code generator constructs three segments of program. The first of these is the initialization program and this is used just once to initialize the variables for the first step of the integration. For subsequent steps the variables are initialized by summing the previously generated Taylor series. To obtain the initialization program the code generator scans the rows of the initialization matrix until it finds a row corresponding to an operation that can be performed immediately. If the search is successful, the program appropriate to that row is generated, the row is removed, and the search continues. The program is complete when the matrix is totally deleted. If the procedure fails to terminate or if some of the variables defined by differential equations are not suitably initialized, then the problem is not well posed and the system rejects it. In our case the matrix (Figure 8-6) results in the following program being generated where, for convenience, we represent each variable by a vector whose elements are the coefficients of the Taylor series representing that variable and the target language is FORTRAN. The name YP represents Y′.

```
YP(1) = 1.0
Y(1) = YP(1)
T(1) = 0.0
```

It is, of course, found that our problem is well posed.

The other two segments of program that are generated are necessary to implement the recurrence procedure that will enable all the Taylor coefficients to be calculated in turn. One of these segments of program, the prologue, is concerned with the evaluation of sufficient terms in each Taylor series to enable the final recurrence procedure to be started. The other segment, the recurrence loop, simply advances each series by one term and continues until sufficient terms have been calculated in each Taylor series to give an accurate numerical representation of the associated function. At each step of the integration the prologue is first obeyed and then the recurrence loop completes the generation of the new Taylor series.

The need for the prologue is perhaps not immediately obvious; indeed, for many simple differential systems, it is null. However, if the differential operator ′ (prime) is present on the right-hand side of a differential equation or identity, the need for a prologue becomes apparent. Consider the equation

$$y' = y + (\sin^2 t)''$$

Before we can determine the first term of the Taylor series for $(\sin^2 t)''$ we must, in effect, compute the first three terms of the series for $\sin^2 t$. For this implementation it is the job of the prologue to calculate the first two of these and that of the recurrence loop to complete the evaluation of the series for y.

Before translating the recurrence matrix into its corresponding prologue and recurrence loop, it is obviously necessary to devise an effective ordering of the operations. As we have seen, this problem is complicated by the possible occurrence of differentiation operators in the recurrence matrix. Thus, for each dependent variable Y_j or each auxiliary variable R_j (including in both cases those that are introduced by the compiler) it is necessary to discover the other Y_i and R_i on which it directly depends. Once this is done, it is necessary to calculate, for a fixed number of terms in the series for the former variable, the number of terms needed in the series for the latter variables. We note that the auxiliary variables R_i on which a variable depends need to be known to one higher term than the dependent variables Y_i because the former do not occur as the result of an integration operation. An algorithm for deciding the relative number of terms needed in each series and for generating the prologue and recurrence loop is now described formally.

Let $\{Z_i\}$ be the set of variables that occur as the results of all operations in the recurrence matrix. Let $\{Y_i\}$ be the subset of $\{Z_i\}$ which are the results of an integration and $\{R_i\}$ be such that $\{Z_i\} = \{Y_i, R_i\}$. Consider the matrix D that contains a labeled row and column for each Z_i. We regard the rows of the matrix D as corresponding to the operations in the recurrence matrix that define the Z_i. To construct D_{ij} we first select the row of the recurrence matrix which has the result Z_i. Then we trace the arguments of this operation back through the recurrence matrix following each branch of the tree independently and stopping when we reach any Y or any constant or the independent variable t. Let n be the number of differentiation operators encountered enroute and provided that D_{ij} is increased by the operation, set $D_{ij} = n$ when a Y_j is encountered and $D_{ij} = n + 1$ when an R_j is encountered. Otherwise D_{ij} is set to negative infinity and can be omitted from further consideration.

Now let C be the set of integers i for which $D_{ij} \leqslant 0$ for all j. Thus, row i corresponds to an operation resulting in Z_i which *can* be used immediately. Let M be the set of integers j such that $D_{ij} \geqslant 2$ for some i, so that variable Z_j *must* be computed in the prologue in part. If $C \cap M \neq \emptyset$, choose the greatest $i \in C \cap M$ and compile program that corresponds to the operation yielding Z_i. This program is part of the prologue. Now, since D_{ij} can be regarded as the difference between the number of terms needed for Z_i and the number obtained by Z_j, we set $D_{ij} = D_{ij} + 1$ and $D_{ji} = D_{ji} - 1$ for all j. Then we recalculate the sets C and M and repeat the procedure until $C \cap M = \emptyset$ which occurs in a finite number of steps because no $D_{ij} > 0$ is even increased and some $D_{ij} \geqslant 2$ is decreased on each step. When $C \cap M = \emptyset$ we have either $M = \emptyset$ or $M \neq \emptyset$ and

$C \cap M = \emptyset$. In the latter case, the problem is not well posed, since no operation can be used that will result in those variables that must be computed in the prologue.

Consider therefore the case $M = \emptyset$ and $C \neq \emptyset$. We now generate the third segment of the program that is the recurrence loop. Choose the greatest $i \in C$ and generate program that corresponds to the operation resulting in Z_i, delete the row i from D and set $D_{ji} = D_{ji} - 1$ for all j. Then recompute C and continue until either $C = \emptyset$ or the matrix D is null. If $C = \emptyset$ before D is null, the problem is not well posed and if D becomes null the program for the recurrence loop is complete. It is of course understood that the program that forms part of the prologue and recurrence loop must be suitably indexed and the recurrence loop itself must be controlled by an appropriate count.

In the case of our example, the matrix D is

	T1	T2	T3	T5	T6	Y′	Y	R
T1		1					0	1
T2							0	
T3		1					0	
T5		1	1				0	
T6	1	1	1	1			0	1
Y′	1	1	1	1	1		0	1
Y						0		
R		1					0	

The prologue is therefore null and the program for the recurrence loop is shown in Figure 8-7.

Let us now consider the more complicated example of the equations

Y″ = (XR)″
R = XX
X′ = Y

The optimized recurrence matrix is

Opn	Arg 1	Arg 2	Result
*	X	R	T1
′	T1		T2
′	T2		T3
=∫	T3		Y′
=∫	Y′		Y
*	X	X	R
=∫	Y		X

and the matrix D is

```
      DO 6 I =1, N
C     THE INTEGRATION OF Y'
      Y(I+1) = YP(I) / FLOAT(I)
C     THE EVALUATION OF Y+1
      T2 (I) =Y (I)+ C1 (I)
C     THE EVALUATION OF R=(1+Y)**2
      R (I) = 0.0
      DO 3 J=1, I
3     R(I) = R (I) + T2 (J)* T2 (I+1-J)
C     THE EVALUATION OF SIN(1+Y)
      IF (I. NE.1) GOTO 4
      T3A(I) = SIN (T2 (1))
      T3B (I) = COS (T2 (1))
      GOTO 5
4     T3A(I) = 0.0
      T3B(I) = 0.0
      DO 5 J=1, I-1
      T3A (I) = T3A(I) + FLOAT (J)* T2 (J+1)* T3B (I-J)/(FLOAT (I)-1.0)
      T3B(I) = T3B(I)- FLOAT (J)* T2 (J+1)*T3A (I-J)/(FLOAT (I)- 1.0)
5     CONTINUE
C     THE EVALUATION OF SIN(1+Y) + Y + 1
      T5(I) = T2 (I) + T3A (I)
C     THE EVALUATION OF 2R
      T1 (I) = 2.0*R (I)
C     THE EVALUATION OF 2R+SIN (1+Y) +1+Y
      T6 (I) = T5 (I) + T1 (I)
C     THE INTEGRATION OF 2R+SIN (1+Y)+1+Y
      YP(I+1) = T6 (I)/FLOAT(I)
C     END OF LOOP
6     CONTINUE
```

Figure 8-7.

$$
\begin{array}{c|ccccccc|}
 & T1 & T2 & T3 & Y' & Y & R & X \\
T1 & & & & & & 1 & 0 \\
T2 & 2 & & & & & 2 & 1 \\
T3 & 3 & 2 & & & & 3 & 2 \\
Y' & 3 & 2 & 1 & & & 3 & 2 \\
Y & & & & 0 & & & \\
R & & & & & & & 0 \\
X & & & & & 0 & &
\end{array}
$$

The prologue generated is shown in Figure 8-8 and the matrix D before generation of the recurrence loop is

$$
\begin{array}{c}
 \\ \text{T1} \\ \text{T2} \\ \text{T3} \\ \text{Y}' \\ \text{Y} \\ \text{R} \\ \text{X}
\end{array}
\begin{array}{c}
\begin{array}{ccccccc} \text{T1} & \text{T2} & \text{T3} & \text{Y}' & \text{Y} & \text{R} & \text{X} \end{array} \\
\begin{bmatrix}
 & & & & & 1 & 1 \\
1 & & & & & 1 & 1 \\
1 & 1 & & & & 1 & 1 \\
1 & 1 & 1 & & & 1 & 1 \\
 & & & 0 & & & \\
 & & & & & & 1 \\
 & & & & 1 & &
\end{bmatrix}
\end{array}
$$

which yields the recurrence loop shown in Figure 8-9.

```
C      SECOND TERM IN X
       X(2) = Y(1)

C      FIRST TERM OF R
       R(1) = X(1)*X(1)

C      FIRST TERM OF T1
       T1(1) = X(1)*R(1)

C      SECOND TERM OF R
       R(2) = 0.0
       DO 1 J = 1, 2
1      R(2)=R(2) + X(J)* X(3-J)

C      SECOND TERM OF T1
       T1(2) = 0.0
       DO 2 J=1,2
2      T1(2) = T1(2) + X(J)*R(3-J)

C      FIRST TERM OF T2
       T2(1) = T1(2)
```

Figure 8-8.

That completes our description of the compiler and the reduction of a differential system to canonical form. We now discuss some points that have a marginal affect on the efficiency of the compiled program. We have, throughout this paper, referred to a ⟨numerical constant⟩ as simply a floating-point number identified by the input routine, and we have seen that operations between these quantities may be carried out at compile time and further, that arithmetic between them and bona fide Taylor series may, in certain cases, be carried out by a simpler program than that required for two Taylor series. It will, no doubt, have occurred to the reader that some of these remarks are also true of functions of the independent variable t. It is an open question whether it is better to treat, let us say, sin (t) as a function whose Taylor series about a given point t_0 can

```
      DO 5 I=1, N

C     THE INTEGRATION OF Y'
      Y(I+1) = YP(I) / FLOAT(I)

C     THE INTEGRATION OF Y
      X (I+2) = Y(I+1) /(FLOAT(I) + 1.0)

C     THE EVALUATION OF R=XX
      R (I+2) = 0.0
      DO 3 J=1, I+2
3     R (I+2) =R (I+2) + X (I+3-J) * X (J)

C     THE EVALUATION OF RX
      T1(I+2) = 0.0
      DO 4 J=1, I+2
4     T1 (I+2) = T1 (I+2) +R (I+3-J) * X (J)

C     THE DIFFERENTIATION OF (RX)
      T2 (I+1) =(FLOAT (I) + 1.0) * T1 (I+2)

C     THE DIFFERENTIATION OF (RX)'
      T3 (I) = FLOAT (I) * T2 (I+1)

C     THE INTEGRATION OF (RX)''
      YP (I+1 ) = T3 (I) / FLOAT (I)

C     END OF LOOP
5     CONTINUE
```

Figure 8-9.

be calculated by explicit techniques completely in the prologue or to allow it to be generated by recurrence relations by simply adding (internally) the equation $t' = 1$ with the appropriate initial condition, and so making the system autonomous. For the Cambridge implementation the latter view is adopted for simplicity.

The runtime speed of the compiled program is also to some extent affected by the representation of ⟨numerical constants⟩ and known functions of the independent variable. If they are represented as full Taylor series they are obviously wasteful of space, while the alternative is that more orders must be obeyed at runtime if another representation is chosen. Consider the operation $Y + t$ occurring in the recurrence loop. It is clear that for terms in the Taylor series of degree higher than one the operation need not be performed at all, and the function t need only be stored as two numbers. However, this would mean that the generated program must contain suitable tests to ensure that the operation of addition is carried out only for two terms and these tests could be omitted if the function *t* were represented as a full Taylor series filled out with zeros. The choice to be adopted here will depend mainly on the target language and for the Cambridge implementation we have chosen the latter alternative, the target language being Atlas machine code.

The efficiency of the system can be further improved by optimal treatment of non-rational functions. In our implementation we have found that some of these (sin, cos) are more efficiently generated from the defining differential equations than from the recurrence relation, but this may well not be true for them all. However, there is no doubt that the exponentiation operator must be carefully optimized to repeated multiplication whenever this is desirable.

Once the compiler has generated an efficient program that will discover a Taylor series solution to an initial value problem given the initial point, the speed of the step-by-step integration procedure is determined by the numerical techniques used to choose the step size and to ensure accurate evaluation of the generated series. These techniques, together with an evaluation of the Taylor series method, have been discussed in Barton, Willers, and Zahar (1970).

REFERENCES

1. Barton, D., Willer, I. M., and Zahar, R. V. M. (1970). Taylor series methods for ordinary differential equations–an evaluation, *Proc. Math. Software Symposium*, Purdue University, Lafayette, Ind.
2. Gibbon, A. (1960). A program for the automatic integration of differential equations using the method of Taylor series, *Comp. J.*, Vol. 3, p. 108.
3. Graham, R. M. (1964). Bounded context translation, *AFIPS, SJCC*, Vol. 25, pp. 17-29.
4. Moore, R. E. (1966). *Interval Analysis*, Prentice-Hall, Englewood Cliffs, N.J.

PART 5

THE INSTITUTE OF ELECTRICAL AND ELECTRONICS ENGINEERS

New York, New York

Two papers selected by the IEEE Computer Society as the best papers contributed by their members:

"The STAR (Self-Testing and Repairing) Computer: An Investigation of the Theory and Practice of Fault-Tolerant Computer Design"
by Algirdas Avižienis, George C. Gilley, Francis P. Mathur, David A. Rennels, John A. Rohr, and David K. Rubin

and

"Functional Memory and Its Microprogramming Implications"
by Peter L. Gardner

9 The STAR (Self-Testing And Repairing) Computer: An Investigation of the Theory and Practice of Fault-Tolerant Computer Design

by *Algirdas Avižienis, George C. Gilley, Francis P. Mathur, David A. Rennels, John A. Rohr, and David K. Rubin*

INTRODUCTION: CHRONOLOGY AND RATIONALE

This paper presents a summary of the theoretical results and design experience obtained in an investigation of fault-tolerant computing, which is being conducted at the Jet Propulsion Laboratory (JPL). Initial studies (1961-1965) led to the conclusion that dynamic (also called standby) redundancy offered the greatest promise in the design of fault-tolerant digital computer systems [1]. The *dynamic* redundancy [2] approach requires a two-step procedure for the elimination of a fault: first, the presence of a fault is determined; second, a corrective action is taken (e.g., replacement of failed unit, repetition of program, reconfiguration of systems, etc.). The alternative to the dynamic approach is *static* (masking) redundancy [2], which was already being utilized in existing component-redundant [3], [4] and triple-modular-redundant (TMR) [4]-[6] computers. Early analytic studies of dynamic redundancy with idealized series-parallel system models indicated that mean life gains of an order of magnitude and more, over a nonredundant system, could be expected from dynamically redundant systems with standby spares replacing failed units [7]-[10]. This gain compared favorably with the mean life gain of less than two in the typical TMR systems.

Other qualitative advantages of dynamic over static redundancy were: 1) greater isolation of catastrophic (nonindependent) faults, which is especially important for densely packed microelectronic circuitry; 2) survival of system until all spares of one type are exhausted; 3) ability to eliminate errors which are caused by transient faults by the use of program rollback; 4) ready adjustability of the number and type of spare units; 5) utilization of the potentially lower failure rate of unpowered components in spare units; 6) avoidance of the circuit-related problems of static redundancy: increases in fan-out, fan-in, power requirements, and the need for isolation and synchronization of separate channels; and

Editor's Note: From *IEEE Transactions on Computers,* vol. C-20, no. 11, November 1971. Reprinted by permission of the publisher, Institute of Electrical and Electronics Engineers, and the authors.

7) facilitation of the checkout of spare units by means of standard diagnostic programs.

The attainment of the apparent advantages of a dynamically redundant system had been shown to depend very strongly on the successful execution of the detection and replacement operations [9], [10]; these observations have since been formalized as the concept of "coverage" [12].

The second phase of the investigation (1965-1970) was focused on the identification and solution of the problems involved in the design of a general-purpose digital computer possessing the properties attributed to the abstract model of a dynamically redundant computing system. Three major areas of investigation were: 1) an investigation of fault-detection methods; 2) a study of computer architecture with emphasis on partitioning into subsystems with minimal interconnection requirements; and 3) a study of the "hard-core" problem, i.e., the alternate technologies and logic organizations for implementing the detection and switching functions. The choices among feasible alternatives in all three areas are strongly affected by assumptions on the available component technology and on the computing tasks to be required of the computer. In order to retain contact with the practice of computer design, it was decided to design and construct an experimental general-purpose digital computer which would incorporate dynamic redundancy (i.e., fault detection and replacement of failed subsystems) as integral parts of its structure. The design objectives have been carried out and the system, called the STAR (self-testing and repairing) computer, began operation in 1969. The modular nature of the STAR computer has allowed systematic expansion and modifications that are still being continued.

The first objective of the design is to study the class of problems encountered in transforming the theoretical model of a self-repairing system into a working computer. State-of-the-art integrated circuit and memory technology was employed in the design. The STAR computer characteristics were chosen to satisfy all predictable requirements of a spacecraft guidance, control, and data acquisition computer which would be used in the very long (ten years and more) unmanned missions exploring the outer planets of the solar system [13]. The second objective was to provide a tool for laboratory studies of fault-tolerant computing, including the injection of transient, as well as permanent, faults of catastrophic nature. Very extensive displays of registers, manually controlled clocking, and provisions for convenient modification of subsystems were incorporated into the experimental STAR computer breadboard.

The STAR computer employs a balanced mixture of coding, monitoring, standby redundancy, replication with voting, component redundancy, and repetition in order to attain hardware-controlled self-repair and protection against transient faults. The principal goal of the design is to attain fault tolerance for a variety of faults: transient, permanent, random, and catastrophic. The actual construction (rather than simulation) of the STAR breadboard has two significant advantages. First, the design process has uncovered interesting new hardware-related problems and led to numerous improvements. Second, the computer serves as a vehicle for further experimentation and refinement of the recovery techniques.

During the studies of fault-tolerant architecture and the design of the STAR computer, concurrent investigations were being conducted in other closely related areas of fault-tolerant computing, including studies of software, reliability prediction, and extension of dynamic redundancy to peripheral devices [14]. A complete redesign of the STAR computer is being performed to match the exact requirements of a control computer for the thermoelectric outer planet spacecraft (TOPS) [15]. This effort led to the evaluation of additional fault-recovery techniques. The results of the efforts described above are summarized in the sections below.

ARCHITECTURE OF THE STAR COMPUTER

Methods of Fault Tolerance

The STAR computer is a replacement system that provides one standard configuration of functional subsystems with the required computing capacity. The standard computer is supplemented with one or more spares of each subsystem. The spares are unpowered and are used to replace operating units when permanent faults are discovered. The principal methods of error detection and recovery are:

1. All machine words (data and instructions) are encoded in error-detecting codes and fault detection occurs concurrently with the execution of the programs.

2. The computer is divided into a set of replaceable functional units containing their own instruction decoders and sequence generators. This decentralization allows simple fault-location procedures and simplifies system interfaces.

3. Fault detection, recovery, and replacement are carried out by special-purpose hardware. In the case of memory damage, software augments the recovery hardware.

4. Transient faults are identified and their effects are corrected by the repetition of a segment of the current program; permanent faults are eliminated by the replacement of faulty functional units.

5. The replacement is implemented by power switching: units are removed by turning power off and connected by turning power on. The information lines of all units are permanently connected to the buses through isolating circuits; unpowered units produce only logic "zero" outputs.

6. The error-detecting codes are supplemented by monitoring circuits which serve to verify the proper synchronization and internal operation of the functional units.

7. The "hard core" test and repair processor (TARP) is protected by triplication and replacement of failed members of the triplet.

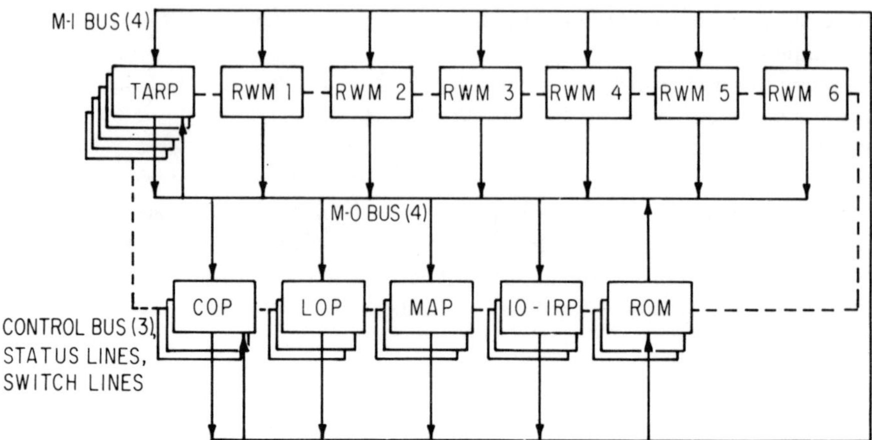

Figure 9-1. The STAR Computer Organization

Hardware System Organization

The block diagram of the STAR computer is shown in Figure 9-1. Communication between the units is carried out on two four-wire buses; the memory-out (M-O) bus and the memory-in (M-I) bus. The abbreviations designate the following units.

COP Control processor; contains the location counter and index registers and performs modification of instruction addresses before execution.

LOP Logic processor; performs logical operations on data words (two copies are powered).

MAP Main arithmetic processor; performs arithmetic operations on data words.

ROM READ-ONLY memory; 16,384 permanently stored words.

RWM READ-WRITE memory unit with 4096 words of storage (at least two copies powered; 12 units are directly addressable).

IOP Input/output processor; contains I/O buffer registers.

IRP Interrupt processor; handles interrupt requests.

TARP Test and repair processor; monitors the operation of the computer and implements recovery (three copies are powered).

The functional units (processors and memories) of the STAR computer communicate by means of the M-I and M-O (four-wire) information buses. The 32-bit words are transmitted on these two buses as eight bytes of four bits each. Three control signals are sent from the TARP on the three-wire control bus to synchronize the operations of the functional units and to initiate recovery. Otherwise the functional units operate autonomously. Unless otherwise noted, one copy of each unit is powered at a given time. The decentralized organization allows a standard interface between each unit and the remainder of the computer. Each STAR unit interfaces with the computer by the means of 14 signal lines. Eleven lines, both in active and spare units, are permanently connected to the

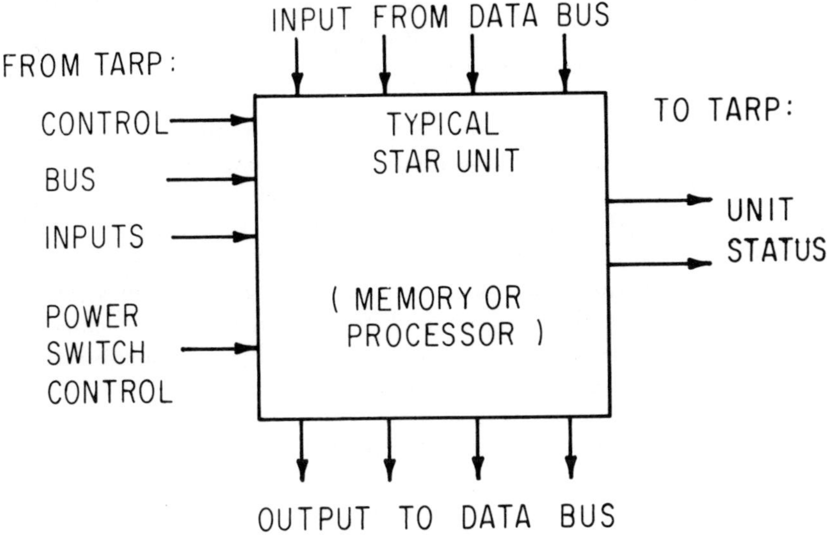

Figure 9-2. Functional Unit of STAR Computer

computer system buses, and three are connected to the TARP array. An unpowered unit cannot produce logic one outputs. The external connections of a STAR unit are shown in Figure 9-2.

The four input and four output lines are connected to the data M-I and M-O buses. They receive and send coded machine words in four-bit bytes. The power switch control input causes power to be applied to the unit. The three control bus input signals are: CLOCK, a basic timing input; SYNC, a periodic synchronization signal; and RESET, a signal that forces the unit into a standard initial state. Two unit status lines send information on the internal operation of the unit to the TARP. These lines carry multiplexed information, which will be discussed in a following section. Each functional unit is autonomous and contains its own sequence generator as well as storage for the current operation code, operands, and results. The internal design of a unit may be altered without affecting other units as long as the interface specifications are observed.

It is to be noted that the IOP and IRP units are shown combined in Figure 9-1.

Standard Operation

The STAR computer has two modes of operation, the *standard mode* and the *recovery mode* (under TARP control). During the *standard mode* the stored programs are carried out. The TARP processor issues the principal CLOCK signal and SYNC signal, which occurs when a new step is initiated in the execution of an instruction. Ten CLOCK periods form the basic time unit (cycle) of the computer. During the first period, a four-bit "step code" (in 2-out-of-4 encoding) is issued by the TARP to the M-O bus. The next eight periods are employed to transmit or manipulate one eight-byte-machine word. During the tenth period a four-bit "condition-code" byte may be broadcast by one of the functional units. The ten-period cycle is needed because of the series-parallel organization of the computer.

One instruction is executed in two or three steps. In the first step, the address of the instruction is sent from the location counter in the COP to the memory (ROM and RWM) units. In the second step, the addressed memory unit broadcasts on the M-O bus the operation code and address of the instruction to all functional units. The address is indexed in the COP which transmits it to the M-I bus if necessary. The appropriate units recognize the operation code, store the address, and initiate execution. In the third step the instruction is executed: an operand is placed on the appropriate bus and accepted by the destination unit. The first two steps require one cycle each; the duration of the third step depends on the instruction and requires 0, 1, or more cycles. Program interrupts begin without the first step. During the second step an instruction is broadcast by the interrupting unit (IO-IRP or TARP).

The instruction set consists of 180 single-address instructions, about one-third of which are indexable. It includes fixed-point arithmetic, maskable logic, and shift operations. Loop-facilitating and subroutine link register instructions are provided. There are 28 interrupts, which can be masked out and tested under program control. A special class of instructions aids in fault tolerance. They include diagnostic instructions which exercise unit status messages and the fault-location logic in the TARP. Others perform updating of the "rollback" register in TARP units, name assignment and cancellation of RWM units, power control of spare units, duplexing of ROMs and processors, and absolute read or write operations in RWM units.

Computer Words: Formats and Encoding

There are two possible effects of logic faults upon the operation of a digital computer. First, a data word or an instruction word may be altered during storage, transmission, or processing. The effect is a *word error.* Second, during the execution of an instruction a processor or a memory module may act incorrectly, act out of turn, or fail to act at all. The effect is a *control error.* Both classes of errors are detected in the STAR computer. The present section considers coding techniques for word-error detection; control errors are considered below.

Complete duplication offers the simplest word-error detection at the highest cost. Low-cost arithmetic error-detecting codes [16] are attractive because they are preserved during arithmetic processing and mandatory duplication of an arithmetic processor is avoided. An intensive study of error codes led to the choice of modulo 15 arithmetic checking which is especially effective for a byte-organized computer with four-bit bytes [17].

All words in the STAR computer are encoded as shown in Figure 9-3. The 32-bit numeric operand word (Figure 9-3(b)) consists of the 28-bit binary number *b*,

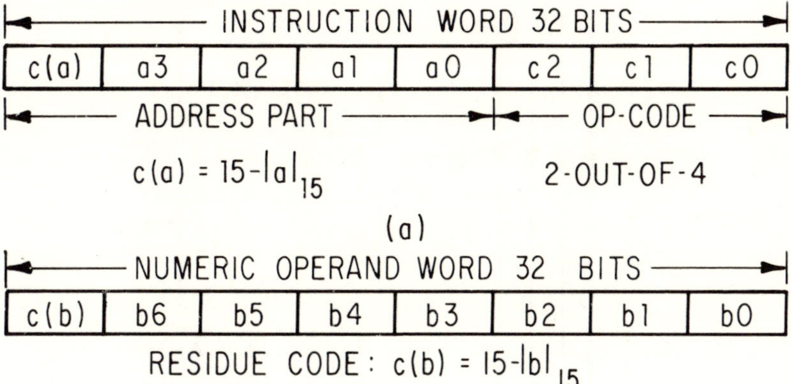

Figure 9-3. (a) STAR Instruction Word Format, (b) STAR Operand Word Format

and a 4-bit check byte $c(b)$. The check byte is a binary number which has the value

$$c(b) = 15 - |b|_{15}$$

where $|b|_{15}$ means "the modulo 15 residue of b." This check byte causes the 32-bit word to be a multiple of 15. The checking algorithm casts out 15s, that is, it computes the modulo 15 residue of the entire coded word. A zero residue, represented by 1111, indicates a correct word; all other values of the residue indicate a fault. The casting out 15s is implemented with a four-bit "end-around carry" adder and takes place concurrently with the transmission of a word on the bus.

The 32-bit instruction word (Figure 9-3(b)) consists of a 12-bit operation code and a 20-bit residue-coded address part. The 16-bit address is encoded in the same residue code as the operands, and the same checking algorithm is used. The operation code is divided into three bytes, and each byte is encoded in a 2-out-of-4 code. This code permits each byte to be checked individually. There are six valid forms of each byte, giving a total of 216 valid op-code variants. The structure of a bus checker circuit which performs word checking is shown in Figure 9-4. The single step-code and condition-code bytes also use the 2-out-of-4 code and are checked by the bus checker.

The initial choice of error codes in the STAR computer emphasized variety for the purpose of comparison and evaluation, and the arithmetic product (or AN) code was used for operands [16]. Two reasons for the change to the present encoding of operands were: 1) the residue code is separable and allows the use of the more efficient two's complement algorithms for binary arithmetic; and 2) multiple precision and floating-point arithmetic is much more readily implemented with residue encoding. Residue encoding is also suitable for operation codes in STAR instructions. Its advantage is that an identical checking algorithm is applied to instructions and operands; an explicit identification is not required

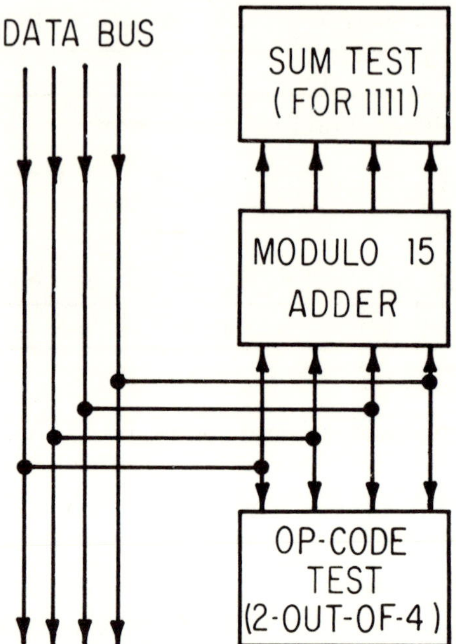

Figure 9-4. The Bus Checker Circuit

for checking, and loading of programs is facilitated. The drawback is that the bytes of the op-code cannot be checked individually as in the 2-out-of-4 encoding.

Control Error Detection

It has been observed that a large number of faults which cause control errors also cause word errors and are detectable by the use of error codes. Some critical control errors, however, do not fall into this category and therefore require other methods of detection.

The principal method of control fault detection in the STAR computer is the validation that every unit is active at the proper time and that the proper algorithm is carried out within the unit. The initial design [11] used a four-wire status line for every replaceable unit to transmit one of six possible 2-out-of-4 coded status messages. Experience has shown that the diagnostic logic in the TARP is significantly simplified when status messages are conveyed to the TARP at predetermined clock times within each ten-unit cycle of operation. In the revised design, each status message is conveyed on two wires (in 1-out-of-2 encoding) and each message covers the time interval between two messages of the same type. The status-message originating circuits are duplicated in each unit to allow the detection of a fault in the status message.

The "output active" message indicates that the unit has produced a nonzero output to the bus in the preceding time interval. It serves to identify improperly active units which otherwise would destroy the information being transmitted on a bus and make it impossible to locate the source of error. The absence of an expected active message is also a fault condition, since the all-zero word is not a validly coded operand or instruction. The checking of output activity is the most critical of all status-monitoring functions.

The other status messages are multiplexed and sent over the same pair of wires as the output active messages because the activity information is not required continuously in the byte-serial machine structure. The status messages, which are listed below, aid in increasing the probability of immediate detection of incorrect operation.

The "disagree with bus" message is needed for duplex operation (discussed in the next section). Two identical units produce outputs to a bus which acts as an OR gate. Each unit compares the bus word to its internally held output word and records a disagree message if a mismatch occurs. The message is conveyed to the TARP at a specified time. The bus checker result, together with disagree message, permits a rapid identification of a faulty unit. In simplex operation this message helps to identify improper activity of another unit.

The "complete" message is essential for functional units having variable-duration algorithms. Memory units issue "write complete" and "read complete" messages, which are essential for immediate detection of incorrect storage events.

The "internal fault" message is produced by internal monitoring circuits within each unit. Its function is to indicate incorrect internal algorithms detected by duplication of critical signals, special test circuits, and "inverse microprogramming" in which an operation is deduced from active gating signals.

In addition to the above listed four types of messages, time is provided for a "special" status message which varies for different units. For example, the IO/IRP uses it to report to the TARP the arrival of an external interrupt request.

Properties of Functional Units

The main arithmetic processor (MAP) input consists of an operation code followed by a coded operand, and the output is a coded result followed by a condition-code byte, indicating either one of three singularities (sum overflow, quotient overflow, zero divisor) or the type of a good result (positive, zero, negative). The control processor (COP) stores the condition code and uses it to implement conditional branches instructions. The COP also contains the location counter LC, two index registers, and a four-bit adder to implement indexing of residue-coded addresses and incrementing the LC. The logic processor (LOP) performs the bit-by-bit logic operations and code conversions on input words. The arithmetic coding is removed from the operand before the operation, since error codes are not preserved during logic operations, and the final result is again encoded. The LOP operation is checked by operating two copies which issue disagree status messages when their outputs differ. The IO/interrupt processor (IO/IRP) receives external interrupt requests, initiates allowable interrupts, and carries out input/output buffering functions.

The READ-ONLY memory (ROM) contains the permanent programs and the associated constants. The present machine uses a "braid" assembly of transformers and wires for the permanent storage of 16,384 words. Complete replicas of the ROM are used as replacements. Each 4096-word READ-WRITE memory (RWM) unit has two modes of operation. In the *absolute* mode a RWM unit recognizes its own wired-in absolute name. In the *relocated* mode a RWM unit responds to an assigned name. All relocated units with the same assigned name store and read out the same locations simultaneously. In case of a disagreement with the word on the M-O bus, the RWM unit sends a disagree status message to the TARP. The relocated mode provides duplicate or triplicate storage for critical programs and data. When a RWM unit fails, its replacement unit can be assigned the same name, avoiding a discontinuity in addresses. Assignment and cancellation of assigned names is performed under program control; this provision allows selective redundancy of storage. A record of RWM name assignments is retained (in nonvolatile storage) in all active TARP units. The accessing of storage locations within a RWM unit is checked by permanently storing the 4-bit check byte of its 12-bit internal address in every location. This byte is read out and checked against the contents of the address register during every read and write operation.

In the STAR computer only the logic processor and the RWM memory unit containing critical system programs are duplexed for normal operation. For experimentation, complete provisions have been made for optional duplex operation of all memory and processor units under program control. The combination of duplication and coding offers detection of all errors as well as a fast identification of one faulty unit. In order to permit duplex operation of processor and ROM units, active TARP units hold a record of units which are operating in duplex.

The Test and Repair Processor (TARP) and Recovery Mode

The "hard core" monitor of the STAR system is designated as TARP (test and repair processor) in Figure 9-1. The TARP monitors the operation of the STAR computer by two methods: 1) testing every word sent over the two data buses for validity of its code; and 2) checking the status messages from the functional units for predicted responses. An incorrect word or a deviation from predicted response causes an interruption of normal computing and an entry into the recovery mode of operation. The block diagram of one TARP is shown in Figure 9-5. It is functionally divided into two sections. One section provides standard mode machine control and fault location, and the other controls the recovery mode operation and effects the switching of replaceable units.

1. The Control and Test (CAT). This section contains the standard mode control logic consisting of an op-code decoder, a clock, and a counter which generates the step-code signals for standard mode operation. The machine-state prediction logic uses the current instruction and step-code to predict which status messages should be received from each powered functional unit. It also predicts the in-

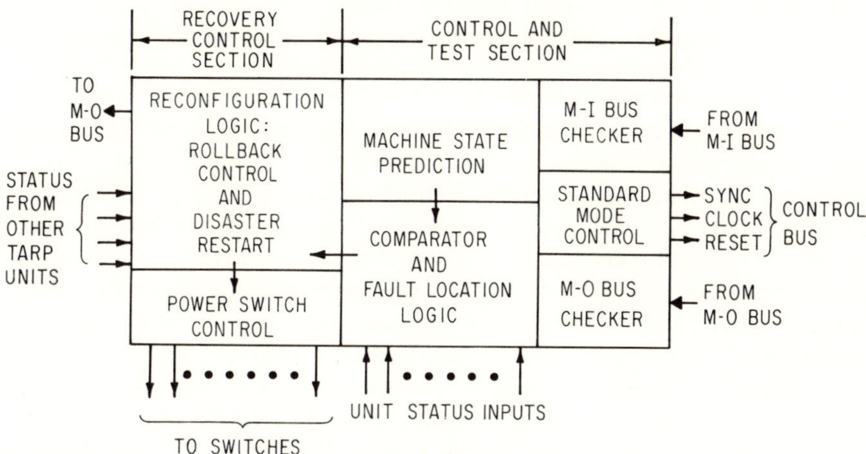

Figure 9-5. Test and Repair Processor (TARP) Organization

formation source and the type of encoding expected on each bus. The fault location logic compares the status and bus checker (Figure 9-4) results to the prediction. In most cases, it can localize an error to a particular functional unit. Upon detecting an error, the CAT section stops the machine and transfers its error information to the recovery control section.

2. *Recovery Control (REC).* This section of the TARP contains a "rollback point" address register which specifies the location of the instruction at which normal operation is to be resumed after a recovery. This register is updated under program control. Before every updating, the contents of all processor registers needed for recovery is stored in duplexed memory units. Upon receipt of an error message from the CAT section, the REC section issues the "reset" signal, which causes all powered units to be set to an initial state, then broadcasts an unconditional jump instruction, which causes the program to be resumed at the "roll-back" address. A repeated fault indication in the same unit leads to its replacement. The number of repetitions before replacement can be specified in the experimental TARP. To replace, power is turned off in the unit, a spare is turned on, and another reset (and jump) is issued. For cases of temporary power loss and other fault conditions which cannot be resolved by the fault location logic, the REC section contains a wired-in "disaster restart" procedure.

The TARP is the hard core of the system. Three fully powered copies of the TARP are operated at all times together with n standby spares ($n = 2$ in the present design). The outputs of the TARPs are decided by a 2-out-of-($n + 3$) threshold vote. When one powered TARP disagrees with the other two, the recovery mode is entered and an attempt is made to set the internal state of the disagreeing unit to match the other two units. If this TARP rollback attempt fails, the disagreeing unit is returned to the standby condition and one of the standby units receives power, goes through the TARP rollback, and joins the powered triplet. The computer is now restarted, a rollback performed, and standard operation continues. Because of the three-unit requirement, design effort has been concentrated on reducing the TARP to the least possible complexity. Experience with the present model has led to several refinements of the design.

The replacement of faulty functional units is commanded by the TARP vote and is implemented by power switching. It offers several advantages over the switching of information lines which connect the units to the bus. The number of switches is reduced to one per unit, power is conserved, and strong isolation is provided for catastrophic failures. Magnetic power switches have been developed, which are part of each unit's power supply and are designed to open for most internal failures. The threshold function is inherent in the control windings of the switch. The information lines of each unit are permanently connected to the buses through component-redundant isolation circuits. The signal on a bus is the logic OR of all inputs from the units, and unpowered units produce only logic zero outputs. The power switch and the buses utilize component redundancy for protection against fatal "shorting" failures.

COMPARATIVE RELIABILITY ANALYSIS

This section considers the reliability (with respect to permanent failures) which can be expected for the STAR computer. The approach is to estimate the relative reliability with respect to an existing reference system. An absolute reliability prediction is not made because the failure rates for components which are being developed for a flight model are not yet adequately established.

The reference computer for reliability estimation is the nonredundant Mariner Mars 1969 (MM'69) computer, which was the on-board computer for the successful Mariner 6 and 7 missions to Mars. It was chosen because a detailed description and extensive failure rate data are readily available. With respect to computing performance it must be noted that the MM'69 computer is a bit-serial machine with a bit rate of 2.4 kHz and an instruction set of 16 op-codes, whereas the STAR is a byte-serial machine with a 0.5 MHz clock and an instruction set of 130 op-codes. This gain in performance is not used as a factor in reliability estimation.

Reliability models 1) the MM'69 computer, 2) a simplex computer equivalent in performance to the STAR, and 3) the STAR computer are shown in Figure 9-6. The MM'69 computer (Figure 9-6(a)) is assigned a complexity of unity. It is assumed that the simplex computer (Figure 9-6(b)) consisting of eight functional units is $8 \times CF$ times as complex as the MM'69 computer. The relative complexity factor CF is defined as the ratio of complexity (component count) of a single STAR unit to the complexity of the entire MM'69 computer. The value $CF = 1/3$ was established by detailed comparison and is used in the subsequent analysis. The comparison is made with respect to MM'69 technology, i.e., it is assumed that the simplex and the STAR computers employ the same components and packaging techniques as the MM'69 computer.

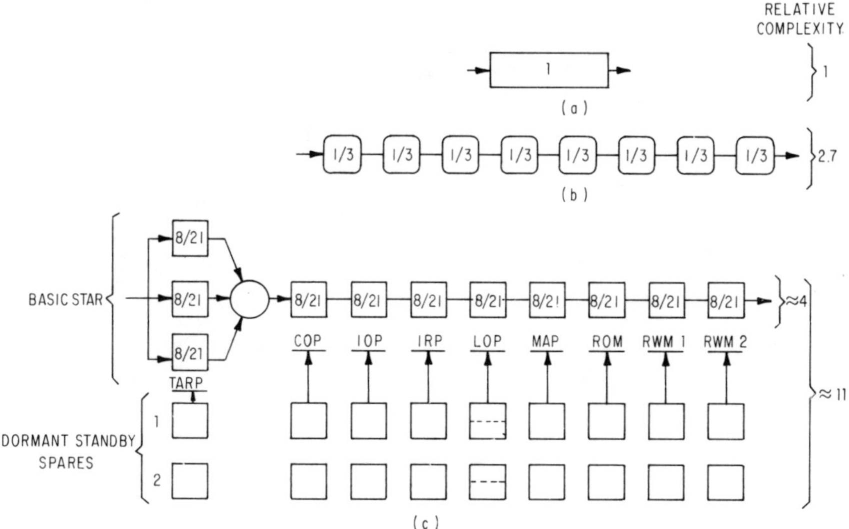

Figure 9-6. Reliability Models (a) Mariner Mars 1969, (b) Simplex Computer, (c) STAR Computer

The STAR model (Figure 9-6(c)) consists of eight functional units plus the test and repair processor (TARP) array in series reliability. All units are considered to be of similar complexity and are allocated an equal number of spares. Results for $S = 2$ and $S = 3$ are presented. The reliability model applied to all units except the TARP is the standby-replacement redundancy model with dormant spares [12], [19]. The TARP was modeled as a hybrid-redundant $H(3,S)$ system [18]. Details of the reliability models and measures are presented in [19]. The logic processor LOP is assumed to have an internal duplication of the circuits which are not protected by the error-detecting codes. Two sets of three RWM units each are shown; this is a pessimistic assumption, since the computer can function with only one of the six RWM units surviving.

The fault coverage factor [12] in the STAR model is taken into account in two ways: 1) by including the fault detector and recovery initiator as a separate processor (the TARP); and 2) by applying a self-testing factor (STF) to the relative complexities of the units. Note that the simplex computer (Figure 9-6(b)) does not contain a processor corresponding to the TARP in the STAR computer since the simplex computer is a computationally equivalent nonredundant machine without "test and repair" capabilities. Since 4 bits of the 32-bit STAR word serve for error detection, a STF equal to 8/7 was chosen. The STF expresses the overhead due to the self-testing and repairing features within each STAR unit, that is, a STAR unit has 8/7 of the complexity of the same unit in the "simplex" computer. Applying CF = 1/3 and STF = 8/7 a STAR unit has the relative complexity of 8/21 with respect to the entire MM'69 computer.

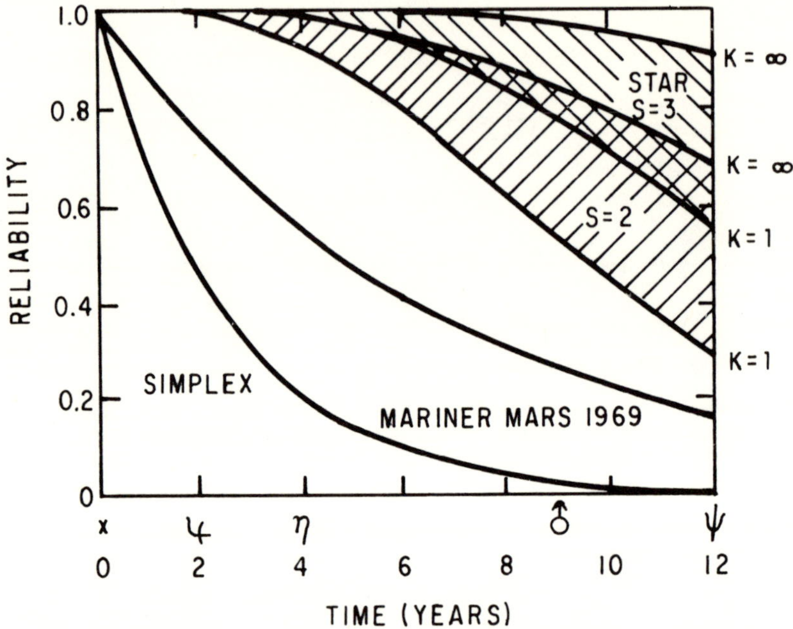

Figure 9-7. Reliability Versus Mission Time MM'69, Simplex, and STAR Computers

Examples of reliability predictions based on the MM'69 data are shown in Tables 9-1 and 9-2 and Figures 9-7 and 9-8. The *lower bound* $(K = 1)$ assumes equal failure rates of powered and spare units (K is the failure rate ratio). The *upper bound* $(K = \infty)$ assumes a zero failure rate of spare units. Two-spare $(S = 2)$ and three-spare $(S = 3)$ STAR systems are considered. Table 9-1 and Figure 9-7 show the predicted reliability as a function of time. Table 9-2 shows the time (in years) for which the reliability remains above a specified value. Figure 9-8 presents the predicted reliability gain, defined as the ratio STAR reliability/MM'69 reliability.

The computing operations for the foregoing analysis, the generation of tables, and the plotting of graphs was done with the aid of the computer-aided reliability estimation (CARE) program [21], which was developed as a design tool during the reliability study. CARE is a software package developed on the Univac 1108 computer system at JPL. CARE may be interactively accessed by a designer from a teletype console to calculate his reliability estimates. The input is in the form of a system configuration description followed by queries on the various reliability parameters of interest and their behavior with respect to mission time, fault coverage, failure rates, dormancy factors, allocated spares, and partitioning. The CARE program is extensible and may be updated to incorporate new reliability models as they become available.

Table 9-1. Reliability Versus Time for Various Configurations (CF = 1/3)

Mission Time (h)	*MM'69 Computer*	*Simplex Computer*	*STAR Computer with S Spares* *Upper Bound* (K = ∞) S = 3	S = 2	*Lower Bound* (K = 1) S = 3	S = 2
4368 (≈6 months)	0.928	0.82	0.9999998	0.99997	0.999995	0.99982
43 680 (≈5 years)	0.475	0.14	0.997	0.97	0.966	0.87
87 360 (≈10 years)	0.225	0.019	0:96	0.79	0.71	0.45

Table 9-2. Mission Duration for Specified Reliability (CF = 1/3)

Desired Mission Reliability	*Mission Duration in Years* *MM'69 Computer*	*Simplex Computer*	*STAR Computer with S Spares* *Upper Bound* S = 3	S = 2	*Lower Bound* S = 3	S = 2
0.9	0.7	0.3	12.5	7.5	6.7	4.5
0.8	1.5	0.6	16.0	9.7	8.5	6.0
0.7	2.4	0.9	18.5	11.7	10.0	7.0
0.6	3.5	1.3	20.5	13.5	11.3	8.3

STAR COMPUTER SOFTWARE SYSTEM

Early in the design of the STAR computer it became evident that the fault-tolerant architecture would impose unconventional constraints on its software. The development of the software system for the STAR computer was initiated in 1968 and closely followed the hardware development. It is partitioned into two subsystems. The programming subsystem consists of three modules: an assembler, a loader, and a functional simulator. An executive program facilitates coordinated use of these modules. The operating subsystem consists of two modules: the resident executive module and the applications program module. The programming subsystem has been implemented on the Univac 1108 computer of the Scientific Computing Facility at JPL. The first version of a resident executive for the STAR computer is nearing completion.

SCAP (the STAR computer assembly program) is the first module of STAR software. Programs for the STAR computer are written in the assembly language SCAL. SCAP is a traditional two-pass assembler incorporating machine instructions, pseudo-operations, and macrofacilities. A unique feature of SCAP is the encoding of instruction and data words as required by the STAR computer. SCAP calculates the code required and generates the encoded value of the word.

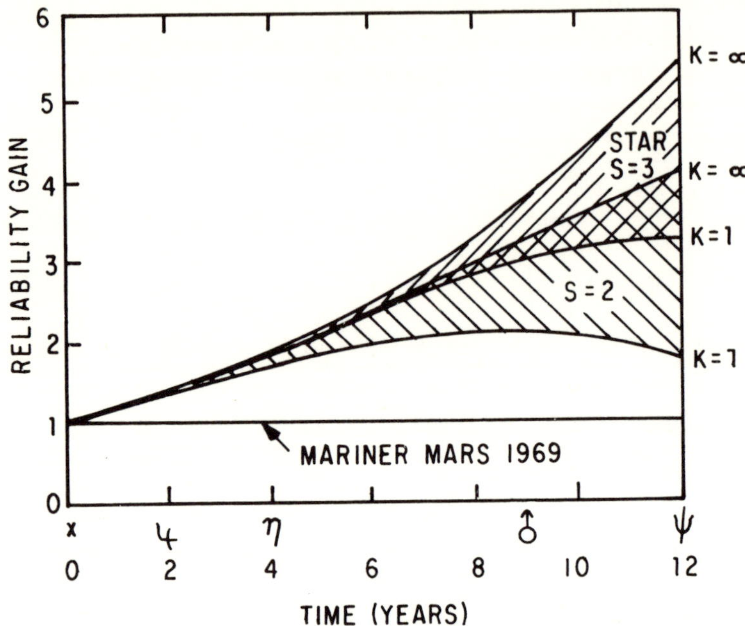

Figure 9-8. Reliability Gain of STAR Computer with Respect to the MM'69 Computer

Another feature of SCAP is the COMPILE pseudo-operation which implements automatic compilation of simple arithmetic statements by the assembler.

The second module LOAD (the loader) reads the program into the simulated STAR computer memory. After all decks have been read, a COMMON area is allocated, relocation is completed, and external linkage is accomplished. A map and cross-reference table are printed to aid in debugging and documenting the program. The third module of STAR software is the functional simulator, which is modular in nature and follows the latest STAR hardware configuration. Two special features are incorporated in the simulator. The first is the facility to simulate hardware errors in order to test the software aspects of error recovery. The second feature provides STAR register and memory dumps. An executive program facilitates the coordinated use of the assembler, loader, and simulator.

The modules of the operating subsystem of the STAR computer software system consist of the resident executive module and the applications programs module. The STAR resident executive augments the self-testing and repairing features of the hardware, in addition to its normal functions. The standard features include interrupt control, input/output processing, and job scheduling. Novel features incorporated due to the fault-tolerant architecture of the STAR computer include a "cold start" capability, reconfiguration processing, rollback assistance, and diagnosis of faulty units. The cold start capability resets the hardware and software after a disaster restart, as well as prior to an initial load. Reconfiguration processing is required for memory replacement, since software assistance is required to load a newly activated memory unit. All programs running on the STAR computer require rollback (recovery) points. The resident executive provides rollback status storage and controls events which are non-repeatable, i.e., they may not occur more than once even if a rollback takes place. Finally, it implements diagnosis for faulty units to determine the cause and extent of failures for possible partial reuse. The present application programs module includes floating-point arithmetic subroutines, and test and demonstration programs. The applications programs which will be required for space missions are a part of the TOPS control computer subsystem project discussed below.

EXTENSION OF STAR TECHNIQUES TO PERIPHERAL SYSTEMS

The STAR techniques of fault tolerance can be systematically extended beyond the boundaries of the computer to effect automatic maintenance of various peripheral systems that communicate with the computer. The case which was investigated in connection with the STAR computer development is the implementation of automatic maintenance for a simplified model of the JPL thermoelectric outer planet spacecraft (TOPS) which is being proposed for the exploration of the outer planets [15]. The potentially lower failure rates of unpowered spare units and the constant power demand of a replacement system are exceptionally important in missions requiring a ten-year survival of the spacecraft under very strict power constraints.

The methodology of extending the STAR techniques consists of several steps: 1) identification of the replaceable peripheral units; 2) selection of internal error detection functions which are economically feasible within the units themselves; 3) identification of possible functional redundancy, in which either another type of peripheral unit or the computer itself can take over the functions of a failed unit; 4) algorithmic description of the minitoring and recovery procedures to be performed for each unit by the computer; 5) development of fault-tolerant communication between the peripheral units and the I/O and interrupt processors of the computer; 6) translation of the monitoring and recovery procedures which have been assigned to the computer into computational requirements: speed, instruction set, storage size, input/output and interrupt system complexity; and 7) estimation of reliability and mean life attainable for each peripheral unit. Several iterations of the design process lead to a system for which a balanced gain in reliability has been attained by means of computer-controlled automatic maintenance. A detailed case study of the application of these techniques is presented in [20].

The investigation has identified and quantized the computing capability required from the STAR computer in order to effect the automatic maintenace of the TOPS spacecraft. Furthermore, the results have shown that the fully automatic maintenance of a complex long-life spacecraft is feasible through a systematic extension of STAR techniques and that the automatic maintenance requirements of the spacecraft systems can be algorithmically described to the detail required to produce computer programs for their implementation. The results of the investigation have systematically extended dynamic redundancy to various peripheral subsystems of an information-processing system. Beyond the specific example of a spacecraft, the methodology is applicable to computer-controlled automatic maintenance of other complex data processing, communication, and control systems.

DESIGN OF THE TOPS CONTROL COMPUTER

The most recent step in the development of the STAR computer concept has been the design of a control computer subsystem (CCS) for the thermoelectric outer planet spacecraft (TOPS) [15]. After the TOPS requirements were quantified, as described in the preceding section, the CCS design had still to meet four major externally imposed constraints: 1) the weight of the subsystem was not to exceed 40 pounds; 2) power consumption was not to be greater than 40 W; 3) probability of successfully completing a 100,000 h mission was to be equal to or greater than 0.95 (using TOPS-approved part-failure rates; and 4) it could not, as a consequence of any single internal fault, result in a failure mode catastrophic to the mission.

Because of these constraints, it was not possible merely to "shrink" the STAR computer into a flight package. The STAR design was simplified by retaining only the capabilities needed to meet the TOPS functional requirements. The entire self-test and repair ability of the larger machine has been retained; in fact, the TOPS CCS has expanded failure detection and recovery capability. A variety of advances arising from the years of work on the STAR computer that preceded the TOPS effort have been incorporated into its design.

The CCS operates at a clock frequency of 500 kHz. The CCS word is the same length as the STAR word—32 bits. The word-processing cycle, ten byte-times long in the STAR computer, has been reduced to nine in the CCS: eight for processing or transferring information and one (two in STAR) for the messages and decision making between words. The execution (including fetch) of an instruction requires one to three cycles. The STAR instruction set, with over 200 variants, has been reduced to less than 100. To detect word errors, the CCS uses the same residue code as the STAR computer. Unlike the STAR, however, the CCS employs the residue encoding also for operation codes of instructions. In addition to these failure-detection measures, the CCS incorporates dual control logic and clocking, memory address checking simultaneous with all memory accesses, and a nondestructive read-after-write option on all store instructions.

The CCS consists of the seven STAR computer functional units designated COP, LOP, IOP, IRP, ROM, RWM, and TARP (Figure 9-1). The IO/IRP has been split into independent IOP and IRP units in order to improve failure detection and isolation in a completely unattended environment. The MAP is deleted because software multiplication and division are sufficient, while addition and subtraction are done in the LOP. Simplifications in the instruction set have resulted in reduced hardware in the COP, LOP, IOP, and IRP. Conversely, there is increased hardware in the RWM and TARP for added failure detection. A 4096-word ROM and two 4096-word RWM units constitute the program storage capability of the CCS. In addition, another 4096-word RWM (designated SHM) is shared (by use of two independent ports) by the CCS and measurement processor subsystem (MPS). All the CCS RWM units are identical; any one of them can be assigned either as a CCS internal memory or as the SHM. The SHM contains the MPS operating program and the most recent samples of spacecraft variables gathered by the MPS. Because the SHM is available to the CCS as part of its own memory, these samples are conveniently available to it for fault diagnosis and monitoring of spacecraft activity [20].

CURRENT RESEARCH

The research and development program which led to the STAR computer is continuing in several directions. The design of several improved second-generation STAR functional units is under way, including a new arithmetic processor, a control processor for medium-scale integrated-circuit implementation, and the shared READ-WRITE memory unit for the storage of automatic maintenance information from the spacecraft telemetry system. Analysis of automatic maintenance algorithms and design of a command/data bus for their implementation are under intensive study. Other current investigations are concerned with the following areas: 1) hardware–software interaction in a fault-tolerant system with recovery, especially the interaction of the TARP and the operating system; 2) studies of advanced recovery techniques, i.e., post-catastrophic restart, TARP replacement schemes, recovery from massive interference, partial utilization of failed units; 3) advanced component technology, especially methods to attain bus and power switch (i.e., hard core) immunity to faults; 4) heuristic studies of fault tolerance by interpretation of extensive experiments with the STAR breadboard as the instrument; 5) design of a second-generation STAR-type computer with universal processor and storage modules, and their implementation by large-scale integration; 6) computational utilization of the spare units for supplemental tasks in a multiprocessing mode.

At the present time it is evident that the STAR computer design and construction effort has led to valuable new insights into the problem of fault-tolerant computing; further results in this field are expected from the research program in the future.

ACKNOWLEDGMENT

The research and development of the STAR computer has been performed in the Spacecraft Computers Section of the JPL Astrionics Division, and recognition is due to most of the Section's members for support in their respective specialties. The STAR concept of computer architecture is due to A. Avižienis, who has directed the overall research effort. The hardware design is directed by D. A. Rennels, the software effort by J. A. Rohr, reliability analysis by F. P. Mathur, and the implementation of peripheral automatic maintenance by G. C. Gilley. Technical contributions to the design have been made by P. H. Sobel and A. D. Weeks, and consultation has been contributed by R. K. Caplette, E. Greenberg, G. R. Hansen, E. H. Imlay, G. R. Kunstmann, J. Nievergelt, J. J. Wedel, and L. J. Zottarelli. The STAR effort has been administered by J. R. Scull, W. F. Scott, and J. J. Wedel. The power switch has been developed by the Stanford Research Institute, Menlo Park, California, and a fault-tolerant READ-ONLY memory has been designed by the M.I.T. Instrumentation Laboratory, Cambridge, Massachusetts, under subcontracts from JPL. Construction of the computer was performed by J. Buchok, J. L. Cline, N. B. Funsten, J. C. Schooler, and B. Stall. The design of the TOPS Control Computer is due to D. K. Rubin, with technical contributions by N. Deo, G. Milligan, and M. Vineberg. A special acknowledgment is due to R. V. Powell of the JPL Research and Advanced Development Program Office, and F. J. Sullivan, Director, Electronics and Control, J. L. East, J. I. Kanter, T. S. Michaels, and G. A. Vacca of the NASA Office of Advanced Research and Technology, Washington, D. C., for their continued support and encouragement of the STAR computer effort.

REFERENCES

1. A. Avižienis, "Design of fault-tolerant computers," in *1967 Fall Joint Comput. Conf., AFIPS Conf. Proc.*, vol. 31. Washington, D. C.: Thompson, 1967, pp. 733-743.
2. R. A. Short, "The attainment of reliable digital systems through the use of redundancy–A survey," *IEEE Comput. Group News,* vol. 2, pp. 2-17, Mar. 1968.
3. T. B. Lewis, "Primary processor and data storage equipment for orbiting astronomical observatory," *IEEE Trans. Electron. Comput.*, vol. EC-12, pp. 677-686, Dec. 1963.
4. R. E. Kuehn, "Computer redundancy: Design, performance, and future," *IEEE Trans. Rel.*, vol. R-18, pp. 3-11, Feb. 1969.
5. J. E. Anderson and F. J. Macri, "Multiple redundancy applications in a computer," in *Proc. 1967 Annu. Symp. Rel.,* Washington, D. C., pp 553-562, 1967.
6. R. E. Lyons and W. Vanderkulk, "The use of triple-modular redundancy to improve computer reliability," *IBM J. Res. Develop.*, vol. 6, pp. 200-209, Apr. 1962.
7. I. S. Reed and D. E. Brimley, "On increasing the operating life of unattended machines," RAND Corp., Memo. RM-3338-PR, Nov. 1962.
8. J. Kruus, "Upper bounds for the mean life of self-repairing systems," Coordinated Sci. Lab., Univ. Illinois, Urbana, Rep. R-172, AD-418 174, July 1963.

9. B. J. Flehinger, "Reliability improvement through redundancy at various systems levels." *IBM J. Res. Devel.*, vol. 2, pp. 148-158, Apr. 1958.
10. J. E. Griesmer, R. E. Miller, and J. P. Roth, "The design of digital circuits to eliminate catastrophic failures," in *Redundancy Techniques for Computing Systems.* Washington, D. C.: Spartan, 1962, pp. 328-348.
11. A. Avižienis, "An experimental self-repairing computer," in *Information Processing '68, Proc. IFIP Cong.*, vol. 2, pp. 872-877, 1968.
12. W. G. Bouricius, W. G. Carter, and P. R. Schneider, "Reliability modeling techniques for self-repairing computer systems," in *Proc. 24th Nat. Conf. Ass. Comput. Mach.*, pp. 295-309, 1969.
13. J. E. Long, "To the outer planets," *Astronaut. Aeronaut.*, vol. 7, pp. 32-47, June 1969.
14. A. A. Avižienis, F. P. Mathur, D. Rennels, and J. Rohr, "Automatic maintenance of aerospace computers and spacecraft information and control systems," in *Proc. AIAA Aerosp. Comput. Syst. Conf.*, Paper 69-966, pp. 1-11, Sept. 8-10, 1969.
15. "TOPS outer planet spacecraft," *Astronaut. Aeronaut.* (Special Issue), vol. 8, Sept. 1970.
16. A. Avižienis, "Concurrent diagnosis of arithmetic processors," in *Dig. 1st Annu. IEEE Comput. Conf.*, pp. 34-97, 1967.
17. ——, "Arithmetic error codes: Cost and effectiveness studies for application in digital system design," this issue, pp. 1322-1331.
18. F. P. Mathur and A. Avižienis, "Reliability analysis and architecture of a hybrid-redundant digital system: Generalized triple modular redundancy with self-repair," in *Proc. Spring Joint Comput. Conf., AFIPS Conf. Proc.*, vol. 36. Montvale, N. J.: AFIPS Press, 1970, pp. 375-383.
19. F. P. Mathur, "On reliability modeling and analysis of ultra-reliable fault-tolerant digital systems," this issue, pp 1376-1382.
20. G. C. Gilley, "Automatic maintenance of spacecraft systems for long-life, deep-space missions," Ph.D. dissertation, Dep. Comput. Sci., Univ. California, Los Angeles, Sept. 1970.
21. F. P. Mathur, "Reliability estimation procedures and CARE: The computer aided reliability estimation program," *Jet Propul. Lab. Quart. Tech. Rev.*, vol. 1, Oct. 1971.

10
Functional Memory and Its Microprogramming Implications

by *Peter L. Gardner*

FUNCTIONAL MEMORY AND LOGIC

Why Array Logic?

The problems of large-scale integration (LSI) have been stated many times, e.g., [1] and [2], and need not be repeated here. Suffice it to say that, because of these problems, the following properties are desirable for a logic module made in LSI:

1. high circuit density
2. regularity of interconnections between circuits
3. high circuit-to-edge connector ratio
4. loadable, i.e., have easily changeable personality; this is to ensure high usage of module type
5. easily testable.

The circuit organization that fits these requirements best is a storage array. Functional memory attempts to solve the problems of LSI by using a storage array to perform logic economically.

Conventional Array Logic

Traditional methods of performing logic on two operands by table lookup have been acceptable for narrow operand inputs, but have been prohibitively expensive for wide operand inputs because the number of words required has been related to 2^{2n}, where n is the operand width in bits (for example, related to 65,536 words for byte-wide operands). These methods have used either two-state directly addressed table lookup or two-state associative (content addressable) table lookup.

Assume that the Boolean OR function of bit pairs is to be performed on two two-bit operands, as represented in Figure 10-1. The two-state directly addressed memory would require 16 words of two bits, as shown in Figure 10-2. The two-state associative memory would require 15 words of six bits, as in Figure 10-3,

Editor's Note: From *IEEE Transactions on Computers,* July 1971. Reprinted by the permission of the International Business Machines Corporation, the Institute of Electrical and Electronics Engineers, and the author.

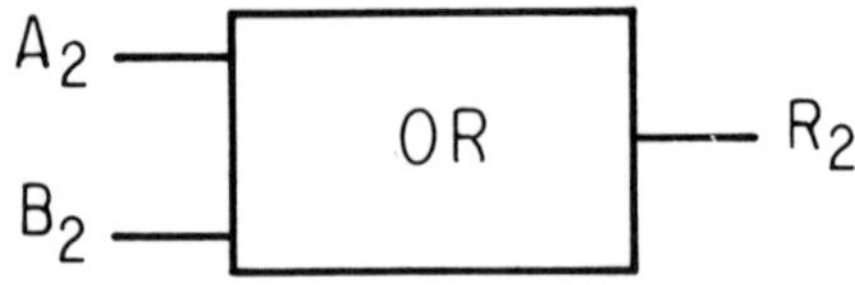

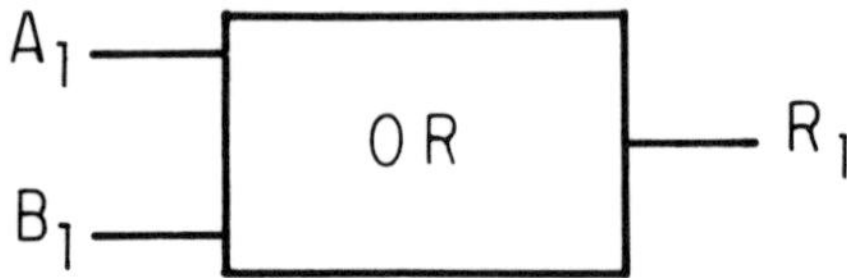

Figure 10-1. Bit Pair ORing of Two-Bit Operands

two bits for READ output, as before, plus four bits for SEARCH input in place of address decoder.

Note that, because the information stored in the table is not dependent on position within the memory, the search input 0000 can be omitted, since its READ output 00 is no different from the absence of output (unless checking is performed by a test on one and only one word selected).

Functional Memory Array Logic

In functional memory, where each cell position is capable of holding a binary 1 (matches a 1 input), a binary 0 (matches a 0 input) and a DON'T CARE (matches a 0 input or a 1 input), the same table compresses to four words, as in Figure 10-4. The DON'T CARE state is represented by X.

Note that in functional memory, multiple selection of words is possible. The associated READ outputs are ORed to form the result.

For the OR of bit pairs of two operands the number of words required is the following:

Operand Width (bits)	*Two-State Directly Addressed (words)*	*Two-State Associative (words)*	*Functional Memory (words)*
2	16	15	4
4	256	255	8
8	65 536	65 535	16
n	2^{2n}	$2^{2n} - 1$	$2n$

The number of words required varies per function. For example, the AND requirements are as follows:

Operand Width (bits)	*Two-State Directly Addressed (words)*	*Two-State Associative (words)*	*Functional Memory (words)*
2	16	7	2
4	256	175	4
8	65 536	58 975	8
n	2^{2n}	$2^{2n} - 3^n$	n

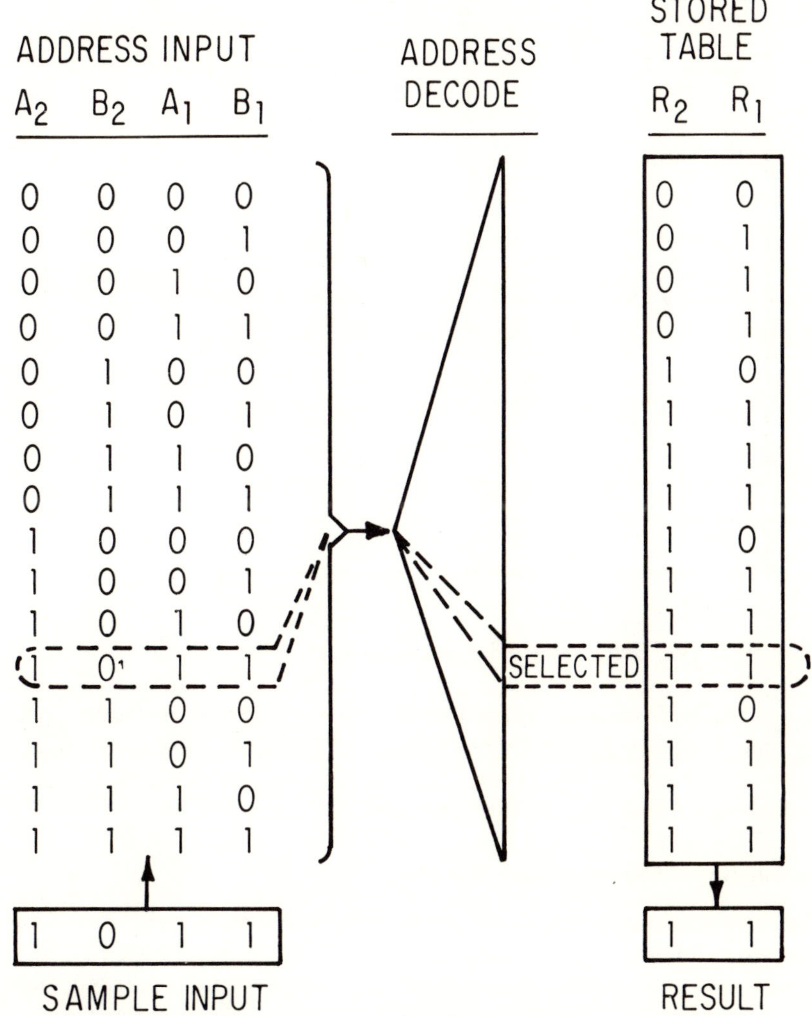

Figure 10-2. Two-State Directly Addressed Table Lookup

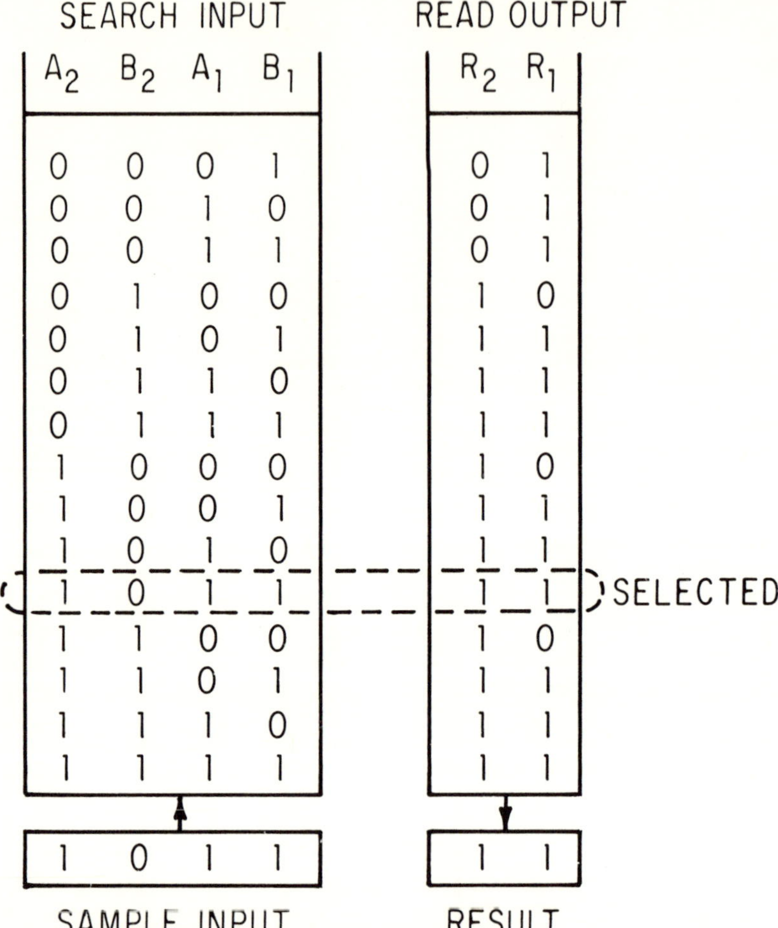

Figure 10-3. Two-State Associative Table Lookup

It can be seen from these figures that the degree of table compression possible with functional memory can be very significant. Before looking at the effect of functional memory on other, more complex functions, let us establish what it is that gives functional memory this advantage.

Why Functional Memory Tables Compress

The characteristics of functional memory that allow the compression of logic tables are as follows:

1. Independent Subfields. Each result output bit is treated separately. Only those input bits which *should* contribute to a particular result output bit are *allowed* to contribute. All others are deliberately excluded. The result output

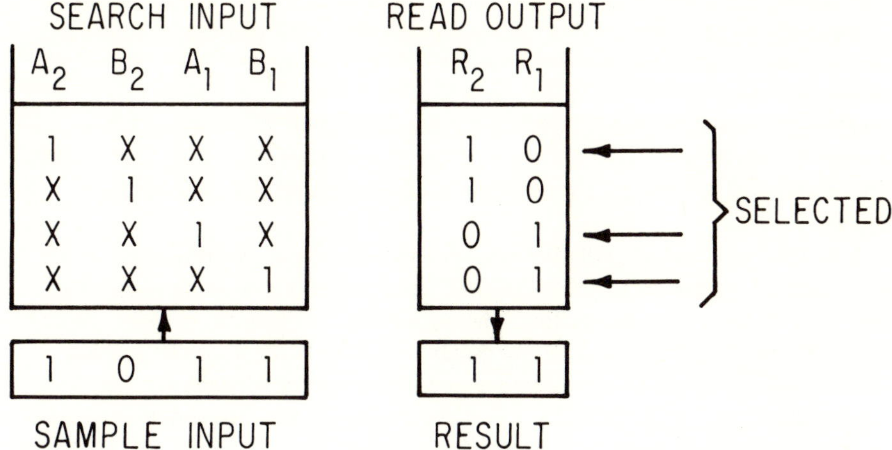

Figure 10-4. Functional Memory Table Lookup

bit with its relevent input bits together are regarded as a subfield and an independent table is built for each subfield. All subfields are processed simultaneously and the result output bits put together by concatenation. For instance, in Figure 10-1, A_2, B_2, and R_2 can be regarded as a subfield and A_1, B_1, and R_1 as another. The table could be represented as in Figure 10-5.

2. *Combinations of Interest.* Within each subfield only those combinations of input bits that actually produce an output are included. Combinations producing a 0 output are excluded.

3. *Compression of Combinations to Find Prime Implicants.* The combinations of input bits that produce an output within a subfield are examined to find the prime implicants. For instance, if from inputs A, B, C, and D combinations $A \cdot B \cdot C \cdot \bar{D}$ and $A \cdot B \cdot C \cdot D$ both produce the same output, then only one entry need be made for the two combinations. $A \cdot B \cdot C$ is entered and the D position is stored as a DON'T CARE. This is the obvious use for the DON'T CARE state of the cell.

Not all of these three characteristics are exclusive to functional memory (or to any other three-state associative organization). The first, independent subfields, is possible with both two-state directly addressed memories and two-state associative memories, and it is this characteristic, out of the three, that probably gives the greatest table compression.

Subfields *could* be processed independently by two-state directly addressed memory and two-state associative memory by providing a separate, smaller array for each subfield and concatenating the result output bits. The unwanted subfields would therefore be DON'T CARE by omission. Thus the total number of words required for a function would then be related not to the *product* of the number of words required for all independent subfields (as at present), but to the *sum* (as for functional memory).

However, there would still remain the problem of deciding on the number of small arrays to provide (i.e., how many independent subfields to allow for) and on their input width and number of words. This decision would vary according to function and would have to be made at manufacturing time. With functional memory, however, because one DON'T CARE is provided for each cell position instead of one for each subfield, no such decisions have to be made, and it is this factor which makes functional memory attractive as a general-purpose logic block.

With associative arrays, whether two- or three-state, some of this effect could be achieved by providing a DON'T CARE per column (i.e., one per each bit of width). This, of course, is masking. The problem would remain, however, of deciding at manufacturing time on the number of words over which each mask should have its effect, i.e., the number of words required for each subfield. It is interesting to note that the DON'T CARE state of the functional memory cell is in effect a SEARCH mask per bit position.

The second characteristic, the inclusion of only those combinations of interest, is common to any associative memory, whether two- or three-state.

The third characteristic, the compression of combinations to find prime implicants, is a function of the DON'T CARE state of the *cell* (as opposed to the DON'T CARE state of the *subfield*) and is not shared by the two-state memories.

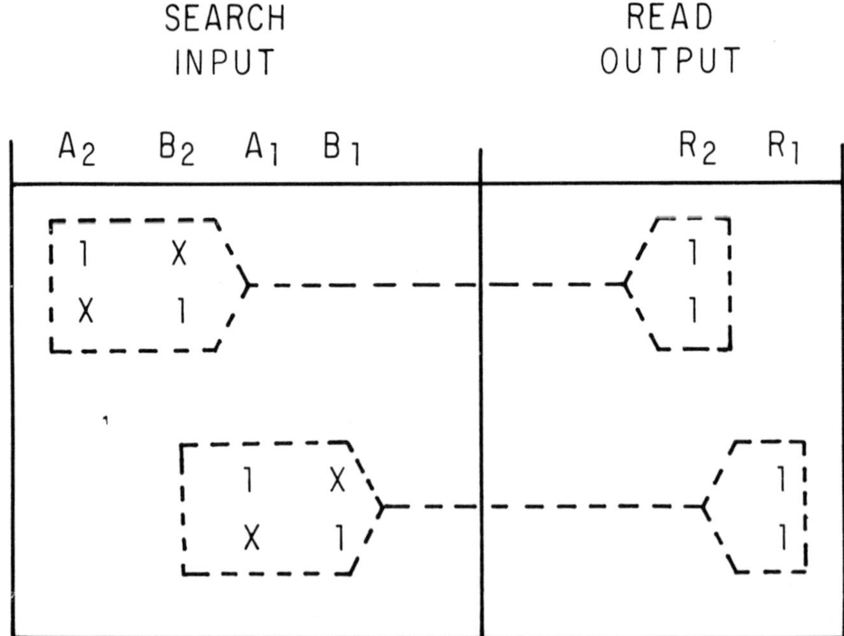

Figure 10-5. Illustration of Independent Subfields

The Functional Memory Module

Figure 10-4 showed the basic operation in functional memory whereby operands to be processed are presented as SEARCH input to the SEARCH input field of an array holding bit patterns appropriate to the function to be performed. The bits read from the READ output field are the result.

In functional memory a register, called an I/O (input/output) register, holds the SEARCH input during SEARCHing and the result during READing.

Although the SEARCH input field and the READ output field are shown as separated, there is no physical boundary between them inside the module. The SEARCH and READ fields can be of any width (within the limits of the module) and may overlap in any way. This gives generality and greater flexibility in choice of field widths than a fixed partition would allow. However, this generality must be paid for in two ways (see Figure 10-6).

1. Two-Phase Cycle. The result of the SEARCH is set into a register of latches, called *selectors.* There is one selector per word in the array. The process of searching the SEARCH input field of the array from the I/O register and of setting the result into the selectors is called the SELECT phase.

The second phase is the READ/WRITE phase. During this phase, if READing, the selector contents are used to access the array a second time and the result is set into the I/O register.

The module cycle is made up of a SELECT phase followed by a READ/WRITE phase.

2. Masking. The SEARCH input field and the READ output field are defined for each cycle by a pair of masks, the SEARCH mask and the READ/WRITE mask, respectively. The mask pair required for a given cycle is chosen from a mask stack by a set of mask address bits presented to the module at the start of the cycle. The mask stack is resident in the module and is loaded, together with the array, at initial load.

The selector register is defined as a shift register, the shifting being performed at the end of the SELECT phase by the external control NEXT, which is provided to the module at the beginning of the cycle. There are two important uses for NEXT.

a. Loading. During initial load, words to be loaded cannot be addressed by content. NEXTing is an alternative method of addressing.

b. Word Width. Should the total width of SEARCH input plus independent READ output exceed the total word width available in the module, then the SEARCH input patterns and the READ output patterns can be interleaved such that the READ output field for each table "word" is placed "next" to its corresponding SEARCH input field.

After a READ operation the result of the current cycle either remains in the I/O register of the same module or is passed via the *data bus* to another module for accessing another table in the following cycle. The functional memory system is therefore in three parts, as in Figure 10-7.

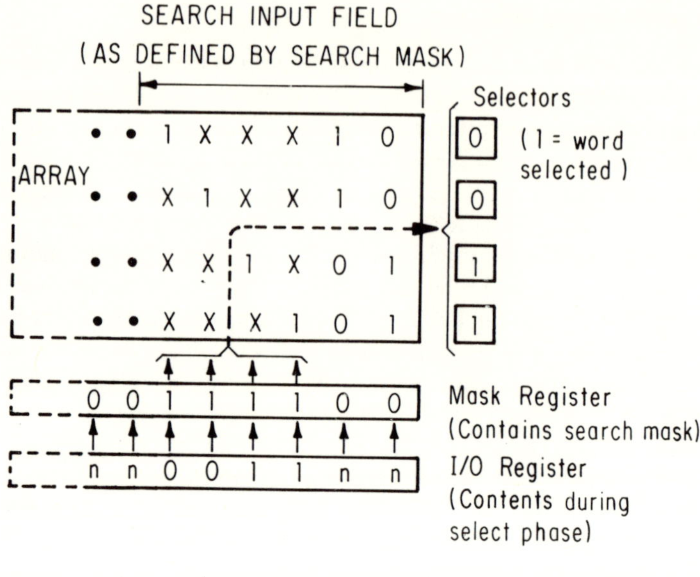

(a)

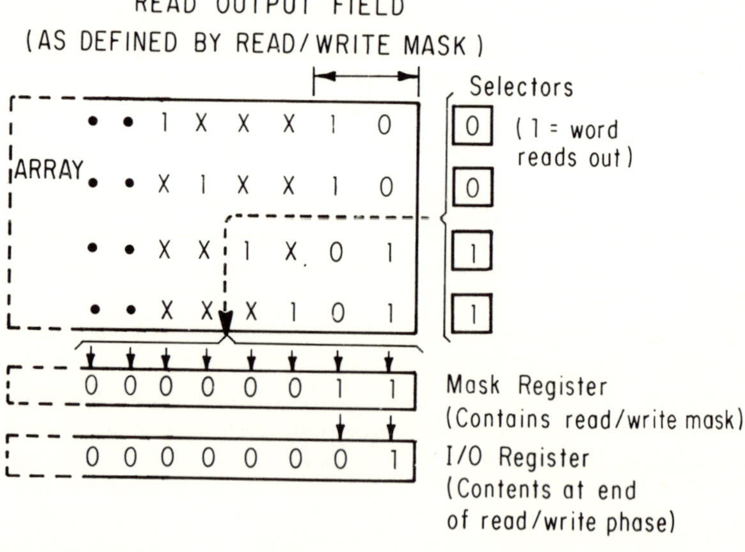

(b)

Figure 10-6. (a) SELECT Phase (SEARCH Operation), (b) READ/WRITE Phase (READ Operation)

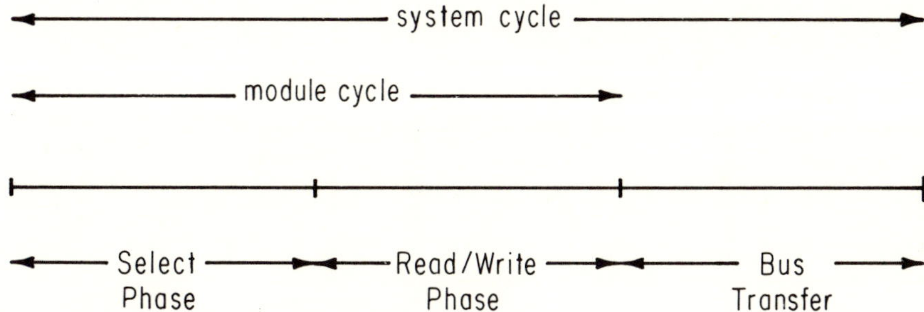

Figure 10-7. Functional Memory System Cycle

The I/O register communicates with the data bus by means of a set of bidirectional data pins. There is one data pin per bit position in the I/O register. Although only one I/O register and one set of data pins is necessary for the correct working of the functional memory module, it has been found that a significant improvement in array usage can be achieved by adding a second I/O register and a second set of data pins. The choice is made at the start of the cycle, under external control, as to which I/O register is to provide the SEARCH input and which is to receive the READ output. Pipelining through the array is thus possible.

In addition to the two sets of data pins, the module also has mask address pins (for addressing the mask stack), control pins (to control choice of I/O register for SELECT phase, choice of I/O register for READ/WRITE phase, whether to SEARCH, NEXT, READ, or WRITE, etc.), and pins to carry power and clock signals.

The data pins, mask address pins, and control pins all have compatible voltage levels on the bus. An FM data flow is composed of one or more FM modules with their data pins, mask address pins, and control pins connected together as required. Control of the data flow can be from either a control store or the data flow itself. The provision of the control from the data flow itself is known as autosequencing and is a powerful technique in functional memory.

Only those properties of functional memory necessary to understanding have been described above. Flinders et al. give a more detailed description of the module functions, together with a discussion of the checking, diagnosis, and recovery aspects.

Table Design in Functional Memory

Figure 10-4 shows a functional memory table for performing a bit-pair OR of two two-bit operands. When two or more tables exist simultaneously in the same module, or in the same group of modules common-wired (known as a "store"), they are distinguished from each other by means of a table name or "tag." This is a field of bits (0, 1, or DON'T CARE), stored in the array, together with the

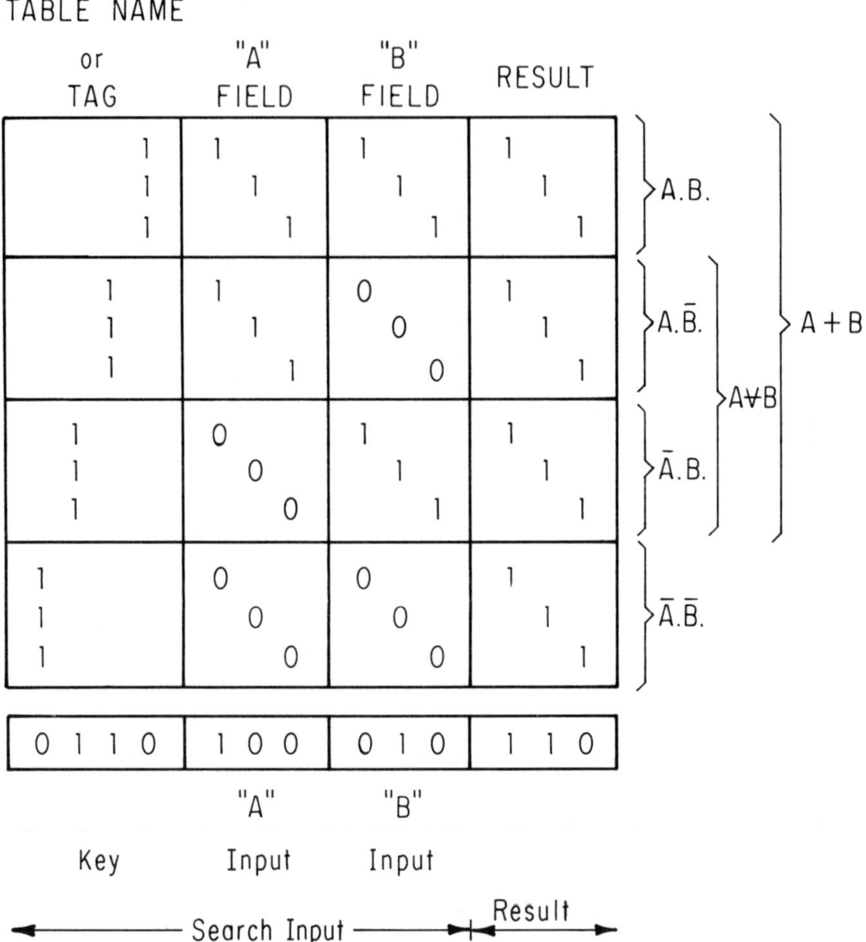

Figure 10-8. Complete Logical Table

tables at initial load, which form part of the search input field and which is searched by a "key" during the SELECT phase. Thus the relationship between the key in the current cycle and the tags stored beside the tables defines the function to be performed on the operand(s) in the current cycle.

The tables in Figure 10-8 (repeated from [1]) provide the four bit-pair products of two three-bit operands, $A_3A_2A_1$ and $B_3B_2B_1$ with their tags.

The tables can be used individually (for example, key 0010 will select table $A_n \cdot \bar{B}_n$ and exclude all others) or in combination to select any of the 16 possible logical functions of two variables. The contents of the I/O register in Figure 10-8 show the key and operand input bits (together forming the SEARCH input) and the result output for an XOR operation.

For clarity, the figures illustrating tables hereafter use blanks to represent those cells holding the X state. Only cells holding a 1 read out as 1; cells holding a 0 or an X read out as 0.

In designing a table for a particular function, it is necessary to express each result bit (in true form) as the logical sum of products of the input bits, all factors having been removed, and then map the equations into table form.

For instance, if the four-bit operand $A_4A_3A_2A_1$ is to be incremented by one in its least significant position (A_1) and the five-bit result $R_5\,R_4R_3R_2R_1$ is to be output, we would need to express the function as

$$R_1 = \bar{A}_1 \tag{1}$$

$$R_2 = \bar{A}_2 \cdot A_1 + A_2 \cdot \bar{A}_1 \tag{2}$$

$$R_3 = \bar{A}_3 \cdot A_2 \cdot A_1 + A_3 \cdot \bar{A}_2 + A_3 \cdot \bar{A}_1 \tag{3}$$

$$R_4 = \bar{A}_4 \cdot A_3 \cdot A_2 \cdot A_1 + A_4 \cdot \bar{A}_3 + A_4 : \bar{A}_2 + A_4 \cdot \bar{A}_1 \tag{4}$$

$$R_5 = A_4 \cdot A_3 \cdot A_2 \cdot A_1. \tag{5}$$

This is then mapped into a table such as Figure 10-9. Note that incrementing by means of this table requires only one cycle, since carry ripple is dealt with in the table.

INPUT				OUTPUT				
A_4	A_3	A_2	A_1	R_5	R_4	R_3	R_2	R_1
			0					1
		0	1				1	
		1	0				1	
	0	1	1			1		
	1	0				1		
	1		0			1		
0	1	1	1		1			
1	0				1			
1		0			1			
1			0		1			
1	1	1	1	1				

Figure 10-9. Increment

Note also that an increasing number of words need to be added to the table as each new bit of input width is added:

$$1 + 2 + 3 + 4 + \cdots n \text{ (+1 for carry)},$$

i.e., a total of

11	for a	four-bit operand
37	for an	eight-bit operand
137	for a	16-bit operand
$(n + 1) \times n/2 + 1$	for an	n-bit operand.

Provided that it can be written as the logical sum of products, any function *can* be mapped into a one-cycle functional memory table. However, some functions require a large number of words (such as 137 words for the 16-bit increment); for some other functions (such as binary ADD), the number of words required is so large that one is forced to design tables for two or more cycles, the intermediate results from the first table being passed as input to the second table.

It is reasonable, therefore, to search for additional module functions that can increase the logical power of the module while remaining generally useful. READ RIGHT XOR LEFT (XOR means EXCLUSIVE OR) has been found to be such a function.

Functional Memory Cell and READ RIGHT XOR LEFT

Before illustrating the uses of READ RIGHT XOR LEFT in the design of functional memory tables, a brief discussion about the FM cell is necessary.

The functional memory cell is composed of two bistables, named "left bistable" and "right bistable," each connected to its own bit line ("left bit line" and "right bit line," respectively), and both connected to a common word line. The cell states are represented as follows:

Cell State	*Left Bistable*	*Right Bistable*
0	1	0
1	0	1
X	0	0
Y	1	1

(The Y state is not essential to the functional memory concept, but can be useful, as in the use of READ RIGHT XOR LEFT.)

A column consists of a left bit line and its corresponding right bit line, together with all the bistables connected to them. A word consists of a word line, together with all the bistables connected to it. Columns and word lines, when put together as an orthogonal matrix, form the functional memory array (see Figure 10-10). Each column in the array is connected to a corresponding bit position in the I/O register.

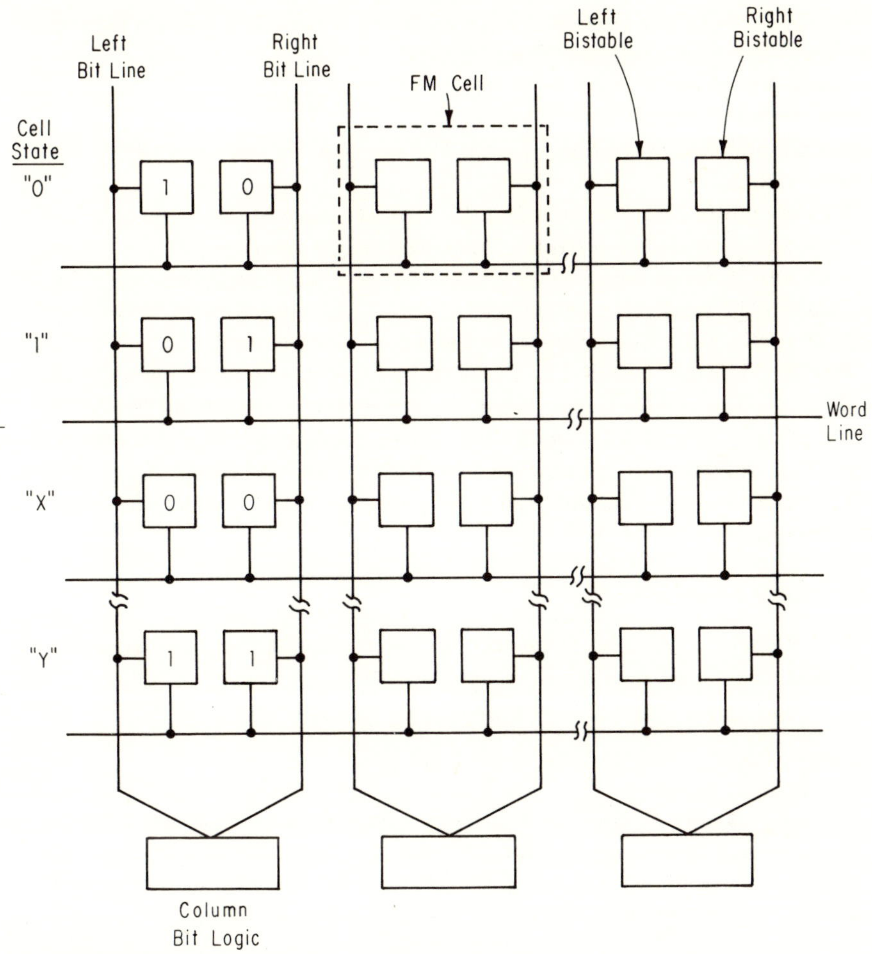

Figure 10-10. Functional Memory Cell and Array

During SEARCH the bit lines are driven according to the polarity of the corresponding I/O register bit and SEARCH mask bit for that cycle; thus we have:

I/O Register Bit	*SEARCH Mask Bit*	*Left Bit Line*	*Right Bit Line*
0	1	lower	raise
1	1	raise	lower
any	0	lower	lower

During SEARCH each bistable gates out a mismatch signal onto its word line if and only if it contains a one and its bit line is raised. Mismatch signals gated onto a given word line are ORed and the inverse of the OR is set into the corresponding selector to indicate "word selected."

During READ the selected word lines are driven and the bistables that are attached to them output onto their corresponding bit lines if and only if they contain a one and their word line is raised. The signals gated out onto a given bit line are ORed.

With the tables shown so far and in [1], the information ORed onto the left bit line was ignored during READ. The ORed information on the right bit line was set into the corresponding I/O register bit position (having been gated by the READ/WRITE mask). Hence only cell state = 1 had any effect on the result of a READ. (Cell state = Y read as = 1, and was therefore not used.)

With READ RIGHT XOR LEFT, the ORed information on the right bit line is XORed with the ORed information on the corresponding left bit line before being gated by the mask bit and set into the corresponding I/O register bit position. Thus cell state = 0 can now have an effect on the read result. Also, cell state = Y, if read out onto a column, can now be used to inhibit the output of that column (see Figure 10-11).

The Module Function

With READ RIGHT ONLY the result bits were expressed as the logical sum of products

$$R_k = (A_1 \cdot B_1 \cdot C_1 \cdot \cdots \cdot N_1) + (A_2 \cdot B_2 \cdot C_2 \cdot \cdots \cdot N_2) + \cdots + (A_n \cdot B_n \cdot C_n \cdot \cdots \cdot N_n) \tag{6}$$

where each element K_i could be true (=1), complement (=0), or ignore (=X). This equation was true whether the table was in one module or spread over several with the outputs of each being dot-ORed on the data bus. In abbreviated notation, the total module "function" could be expressed as

$$\cdot + \cdot + \cdot + \cdots + \cdot + \cdot \tag{7}$$

where · represents a product, i.e., one word's worth of matching and selection, and + represents the ORing of the READOUT, either onto the bit lines (right bit line only) or onto the bus.

With READ RIGHT XOR LEFT, the total module function can be expressed as

$$[\{\underbrace{(\underset{1}{\cdot} \underset{2}{+} \cdot + \cdots)}_{3} \underset{5}{\forall} \underbrace{(\cdot + \cdot + \cdots)\}\cdot]}_{4}\underbrace{(\cdot + \cdot + \cdots)}_{6}] + [\text{same}] + [\text{same}] \underset{7}{+} \cdots \tag{8}$$

where 1 represents a product, i.e., SEARCH and MATCH; 2 represents ORing of READOUT onto a given bit line; 3 represents ORed information on, say, right bit line; 4 represents ORed information on, say, left bit line; 5 represents RIGHT XOR LEFT, $\forall$ means EXCLUSIVE OR; 6 represents READing out the Y state

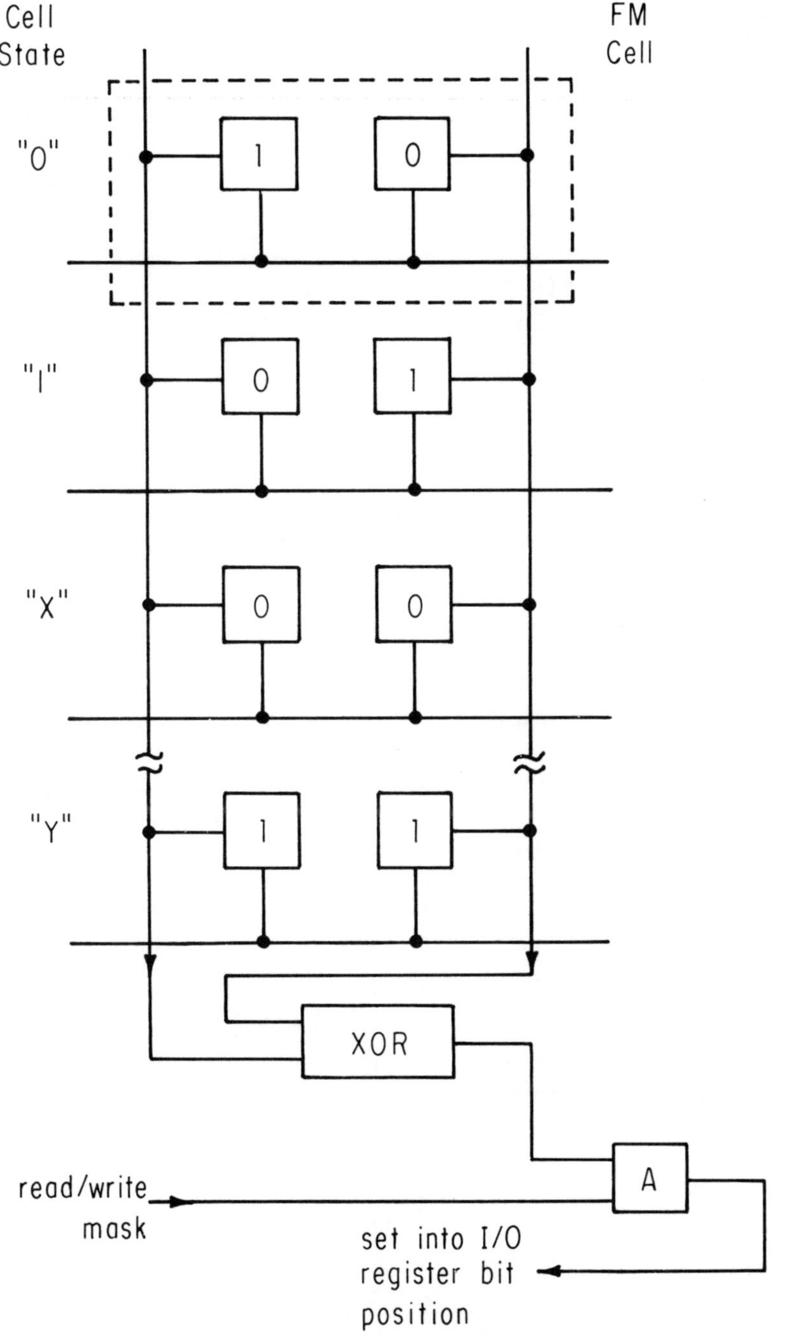

Figure 10-11. READ RIGHT XOR LEFT on Single Functional Memory Column

contained in one or more cells in a given column; ·⌉ means AND NOT; and 7 represents ORing of I/O register bits on the data bus.

The use of the Y state has been shown as separate in (6) (above) in order to show its effect more clearly. The physical operation is such that the logical sum of products in bracket (6) is actually included in brackets (3) and (4) at the same time.

READ RIGHT XOR LEFT Explained by Karnaugh Maps

The effects of READ RIGHT XOR LEFT can be demonstrated on Karnaugh maps in Figure 10-12. Case 1 is "complete." Case 2 is "nearly complete." Case 3 is "nearly complete plus a bit more." In all cases READ RIGHT ONLY requires

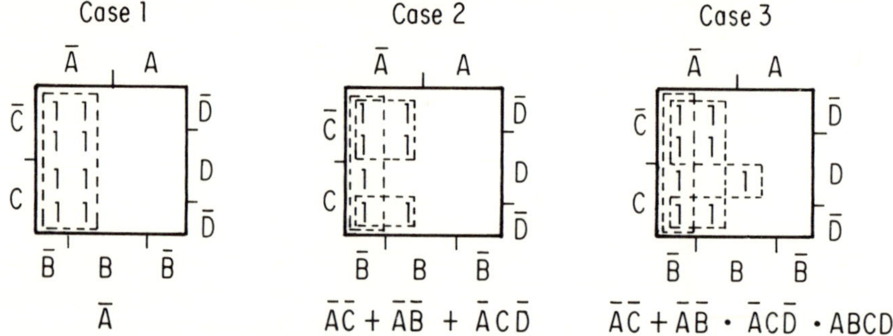

Figure 10-12. Karnaugh Maps for READ RIGHT ONLY

building up the function additively. For instance, Case 3 would map into a READ RIGHT ONLY table as the four words in Figure 10-13.

Whereas with READ RIGHT ONLY, the designer is obliged to build up the table additively, selecting only those prime implicants that he wants, with READ RIGHT XOR LEFT he has the option of building additively or selecting more than is wanted and removing the unwanted portions. For example, Case 1 re-

Input				Output
A	B	C	D	Result
0		0		1
0	0			1
0		1	0	1
1	1	1	1	1

Figure 10-13. Case 3 with READ RIGHT ONLY

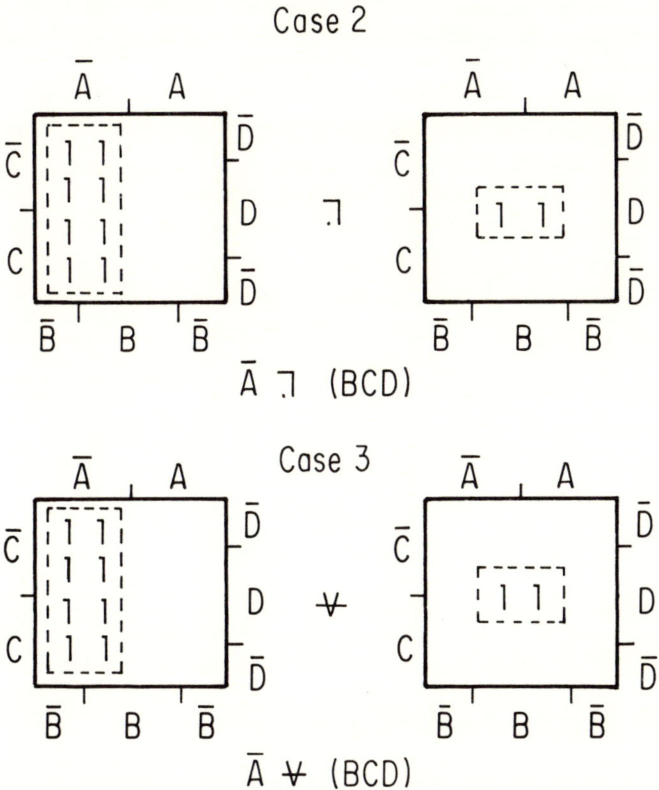

Figure 10-14. Using READ RIGHT XOR LEFT. ·⌉ Means AND NOT; ∀ Means EXCLUSIVE OR

mains unchanged since it is complete already. Cases 2 and 3, however, can be expressed as in Figure 10-14. Both Case 2 and Case 3 would map into only two words each with READ RIGHT XOR LEFT, as in Figure 10-15, contrasting with

Case 2

Input A	B	C	D	Output Result
0				1
	1	1	1	Y

Case 3

Input A	B	C	D	Output Result
0				1
	1	1	1	0

Figure 10-15. Cases 2 and 3 with READ RIGHT XOR LEFT

the three and four words, respectively, with READ RIGHT ONLY. Note that in Figure 10-15, Case 3, the result values 1 and 0 are interchangeable, provided that $\bar{A}$ outputs one value and $B \cdot C \cdot D$ outputs the other.

The most expensive function, for the logical sum of products method of table mapping and the function for which READ RIGHT XOR LEFT is most obviously helpful, is parity. This function can be represented as all the black squares on a chessboard, as in Figure 10-16. With READ RIGHT ONLY, the table designer

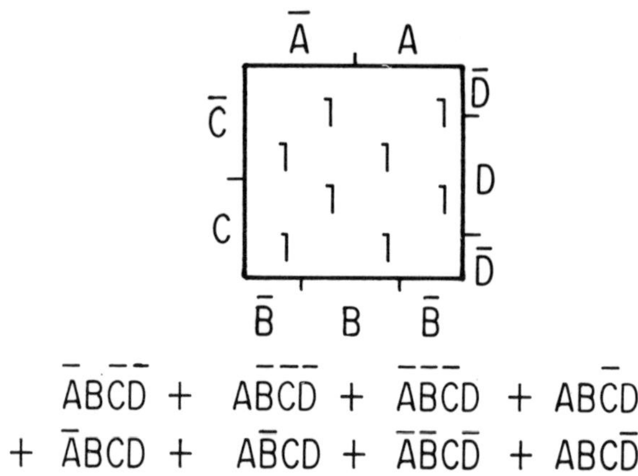

$$\bar{A}B\bar{C}\bar{D} + A\bar{B}\bar{C}\bar{D} + \bar{A}\bar{B}\bar{C}D + AB\bar{C}D$$
$$+ \bar{A}BCD + A\bar{B}CD + \bar{A}\bar{B}C\bar{D} + ABC\bar{D}$$

Figure 10-16. Odd Parity. READ RIGHT ONLY

must select individually every input combination which produces a certain parity (say, odd). No compression is possible and within the subfield the X state is useless. With READ RIGHT XOR LEFT, however, odd parity could be represented, as in Figure 10-17. The words required for a parity table are therefore the following where $n/2$ must be rounded up to the nearest integer.

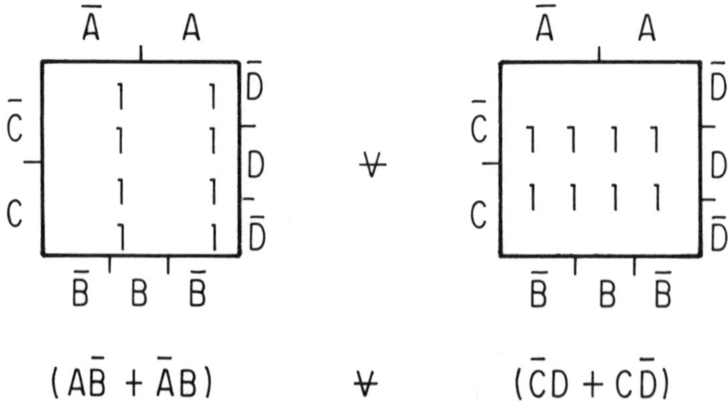

$$(A\bar{B} + \bar{A}B) \qquad \forall \qquad (\bar{C}D + C\bar{D})$$

Figure 10-17. Odd Parity. READ RIGHT XOR LEFT

(bits)	*READ RIGHT ONLY (words)*	*READ RIGHT XOR LEFT (words)*
4	8	4
8	128	16
n	2^{n-1}	$2^{n/2}$

Tables Using READ RIGHT XOR LEFT

The foregoing is an attempt to show the effects of READ RIGHT XOR LEFT in principle. Two examples should serve to show its effect in practice.

1. Increment. Four-bit operand $A_4A_3A_2A_1$ incremented by one: Equations (1)–(5) in the section "Table Design in Functional Memory" expressed each result bit as the logical sum of products, as required by READ RIGHT ONLY. With READ RIGHT XOR LEFT, the equations can become

$$R_1 = \overline{A_1} \tag{9}$$

$$R_2 = A_2 \forall A_1 \tag{10}$$

$$R_3 = A_3 \forall (A_2 \cdot A_1) \tag{11}$$

$$R_4 = A_4 \forall (A_3 \cdot A_2 \cdot A_1) \tag{12}$$

$$R_5 = A_4 \cdot A_3 \cdot A_2 \cdot A_1. \tag{13}$$

These equations can map into a $2n$ word table, compared with $(n + 1) \times n/2 + 1$ words required for READ RIGHT ONLY. For example, a 16-bit increment is now reduced from 137 to 32 words.

Although this reduction seems impressive, one can go further. Using the fact that $(a \forall b) = (\bar{a} \forall \bar{b})$, the equations for the increment result bits can now transform to

$$R_1 = \bar{A}_1 \tag{14}$$

$$R_2 = \bar{A}_2 \forall \bar{A}_1 \tag{15}$$

$$R_3 = \bar{A}_3 \forall (\bar{A}_2 + \bar{A}_1) \tag{16}$$

$$R_4 = \bar{A}_4 \forall (\bar{A}_3 + \bar{A}_2 + \bar{A}_1) \tag{17}$$

$$R_5 = 1 \forall (\bar{A}_4 + \bar{A}_3 + \bar{A}_2 + \bar{A}_1). \tag{18}$$

The table for increment now has the rather unexpected form given in Figure 10-18.

Final reduction figures for increment are at the top of page 206.

2. One-Cycle Compare. Comparison of two operands, $A_4A_3A_2A_1$ and $B_4B_3B_2B_1$, for $A > B$ can be expressed as

$$A > B = A_4 \cdot \bar{B}_4 + A_3 \cdot \bar{B}_3 \cdot (A_4 + \bar{B}_4) + A_2 \cdot \bar{B}_2 \cdot (A_4 + \bar{B}_4) \cdot (A_3 + \bar{B}_3) + A_1 \cdot \bar{B}_1 \cdot (A_4 + \bar{B}_4) \cdot (A_3 + \bar{B}_3) \cdot (A_2 + \bar{B}_2). \tag{19}$$

Operand Width (bits)	*Two-State Directly Addressed (words)*	*Functional Memory READ RIGHT ONLY (words)*	*Functional Memory READ RIGHT XOR LEFT (words)*
4	16	11	5
8	256	37	9
16	65 536	137	17
n	2^n	$(n+1) \times n/2 + 1$	$n + 1$

With READ RIGHT ONLY, the expression must be multiplied out, and $2^n - 1$ words are required for a one-cycle compare (where n is the width of each comparand). An additional $2^n - 1$ words are required for $A < B$, clearly unacceptable for medium to wide comparands.

With READ RIGHT XOR LEFT, the expression can be transformed to:

$$A > B = A_4 \cdot \overline{B}_4 + A_3 \cdot \overline{B}_3 \cdot \rceil (\overline{A}_4 \cdot B_4) + A_2 \cdot \overline{B}_2 \cdot \rceil (\overline{A}_4 \cdot B_4 + \overline{A}_3 \cdot B_3) + A_1 \cdot \overline{B}_1 \cdot \rceil (\overline{A}_4 \cdot B_4 + \overline{A}_3 \cdot B_3 + \overline{A}_2 \cdot B_2) \qquad (20)$$

where $\cdot \rceil$ means AND NOT.

By allowing a separate output column for each major conjunct, and by dot-ORing those columns on the data bus, the $2n + 1$ word table in Figure 10-19 will provide not only the required $A > B$, but $A < B$ and $A \equiv B$ as well.

Input				Output				
A_4	A_3	A_2	A_1	R_5	R_4	R_3	R_2	R_1
			0	0	0	0	0	1
		0		0	0	0	1	
	0			0	0	1		
0				0	1			
				1				

Figure 10-18. Increment. READ RIGHT XOR LEFT

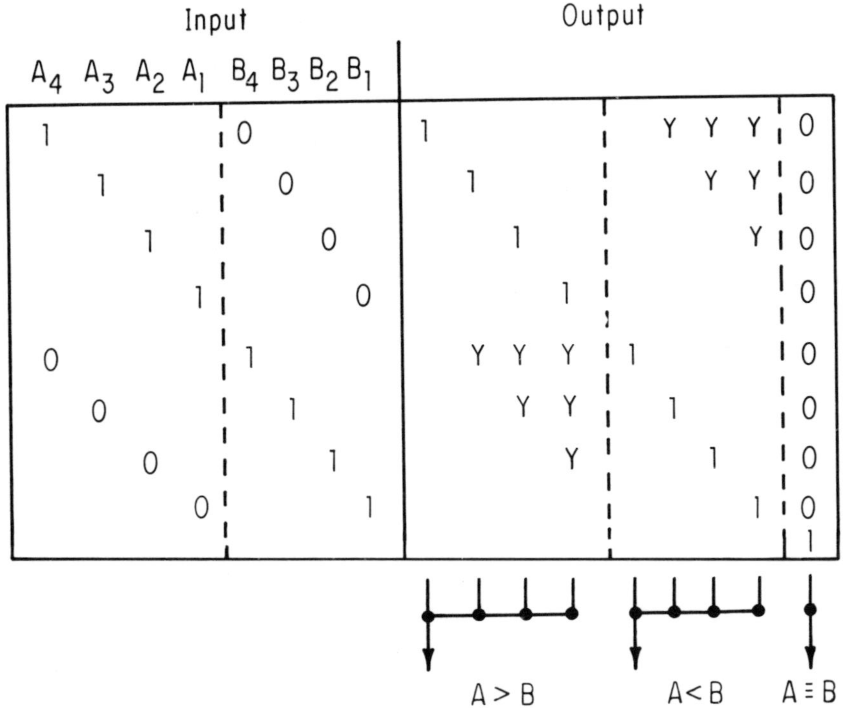

Figure 10-19. Compare. READ RIGHT XOR LEFT

The tradeoff is thus a small (linear) number of columns against a large (2^n) number of words. Nevertheless, although the tradeoff is clearly worthwhile, word width is valuable. Therefore the following refinement should also be adopted. Using the fact that $A_k \cdot \bar{B}_k$ can also be expressed as $A_k \cdot \bar{B}_k \cdot \rceil (\bar{A}_k \cdot B_k)$, (20) can be reexpressed as:

$$A > B = (A_4 \cdot \bar{B}_4 + A_3 \cdot \bar{B}_3) \cdot \rceil (\bar{A}_4 \cdot B_4) + (A_2 \cdot \bar{B}_2 + A_1 \cdot \bar{B}_1) \cdot \rceil (\bar{A}_4 \cdot B_4 + \bar{A}_3 \cdot B_3 + \bar{A}_2 \cdot B_2) \quad (21)$$

and the table in Figure 10-19 will reduce in width to that in Figure 10-20.

FUNCTIONAL MEMORY AND CONTROL

Introduction

The discussion so far has been about the logical aspects of functional memory—how tables can be designed to perform required functions. Most of the functions have been performed in a single cycle. However, some functions, such as binary addition, may require two or more cycles for the final result to emerge.

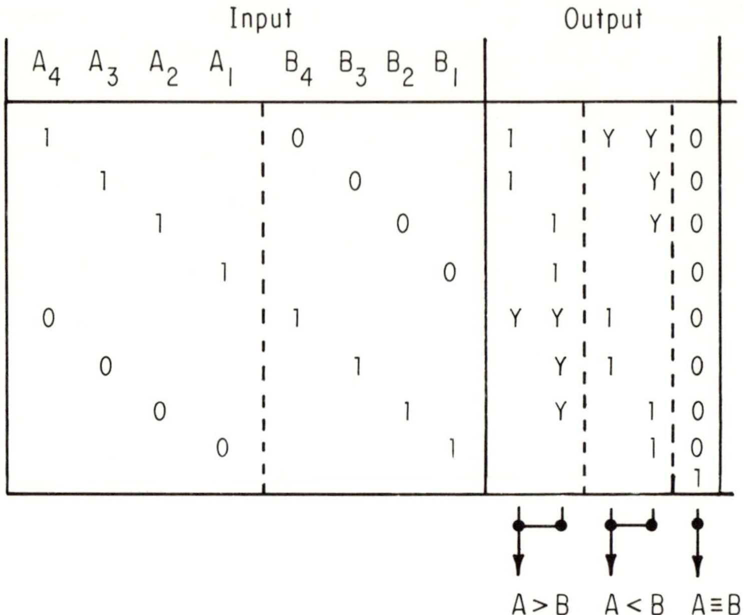

Figure 10-20. Compare. Reduced Width

This introduces the idea of time-dependent tables. The second table must wait until initiated by the output of the first table. Alternatively, the second table can be initiated after a certain interval of time (i.e., a certain number of cycles) relative to a reference point. In both cases the stimulus is fed either to the table as part of the SEARCH input or to one of the external control lines of the module. A functional memory data flow is a collection of modules holding single cycle or sequenced tables (together with locations used for data storage, status information, etc.), joined together on the data bus as required. The sequencing of the use of the tables is performed by microprogram.

The microprogram of a functional memory data flow could be in a conventional control store with conventional sequencing and with the functional memory external controls and table keys each having their own control fields in the control word. This would make a reasonable system, the functional memory having replaced the logic of a conventional data flow.

But what would be the effect if the microprogram itself were in functional memory? It *could* be used to provide a conventional control store organization, as in the previous paragraph. The sequencing could be explicit–some of the bits read out in the current cycle being used to address the immediate successor by content-addressing, or implicit–using NEXTing to address the successor by position. Two control words could be stored in each functional memory word and distinguished from each other by READ RIGHT XOR LEFT through an appropriate filter of all 1's or all 0's, or by using READ modes RIGHT ONLY and LEFT ONLY.

However, using functional memory in this manner would be an expensive way of providing a conventional control store (the extra expense might be justified by other considerations, such as wanting a unified procedure for loading, checking, diagnosis, recovery, debug, etc.). Furthermore, it would also be to ignore the interesting implications that functional memory has for microprogramming.

Only two of these implications are discussed here. These concern the branching delay problem and the field combination problem. In this discussion functional memory is seen not as the solution to the problems per se, but as clarifying the problems and making solutions easier to find.

Branching Delay Problem

The conventional procedure for a microprogram branch is for a condition or conditions from the data flow to be passed to a black box to modify in some way (it may be a transform or merely concatenation) the address produced at the end of the preceding cycle. The control for the current cycle cannot start until the modified address is formed and the required control word accessed. This means either that the data flow and control store cannot be run at full speed and must be interleaved to some extent (see Figure 10-21(a)), or that leap-frog branching must be accepted (see Figure 10-21(b)). In both cases delay is involved when an immediate branch is required.

This section does not attempt to eliminate branches that cause this delay, but to show that their inclusion in the microprogram is often unnecessary and can usually be avoided. In computer processing, decision making and branching are not synonymous. Consider the following three cases.

Case 1. When, in a conventional data flow, register P and Q are controlled to provide their contents to an ALU (arithmetic and logic unit) to be added together, no branching need take place while the data pass through the ALU. Nevertheless, decisions are being made in the logic of the ALU; in other words, there is a difference between the way the logic behaves when, say, $P = 3$ and $Q = 5$ and when $P = 3$ and $Q = 6$. In this case it is most unlikely that the microprogram would branch.

Case 2. A further input to the ALU is the carry in. Its value affects the decision making within the ALU in the same way as the values of P and Q. If the ALU is narrower than the data widths, then the data must be sectioned and the carry out of each section must be entered as carry in to the successor section. In this case it is quite possible that the decision to enter the carry or not might be made by a microprogram test and branch.

Case 3. Depending on the programmer instruction being performed, the control to the ALU may require to be add (as for ADD) or subtract (as for SUB-

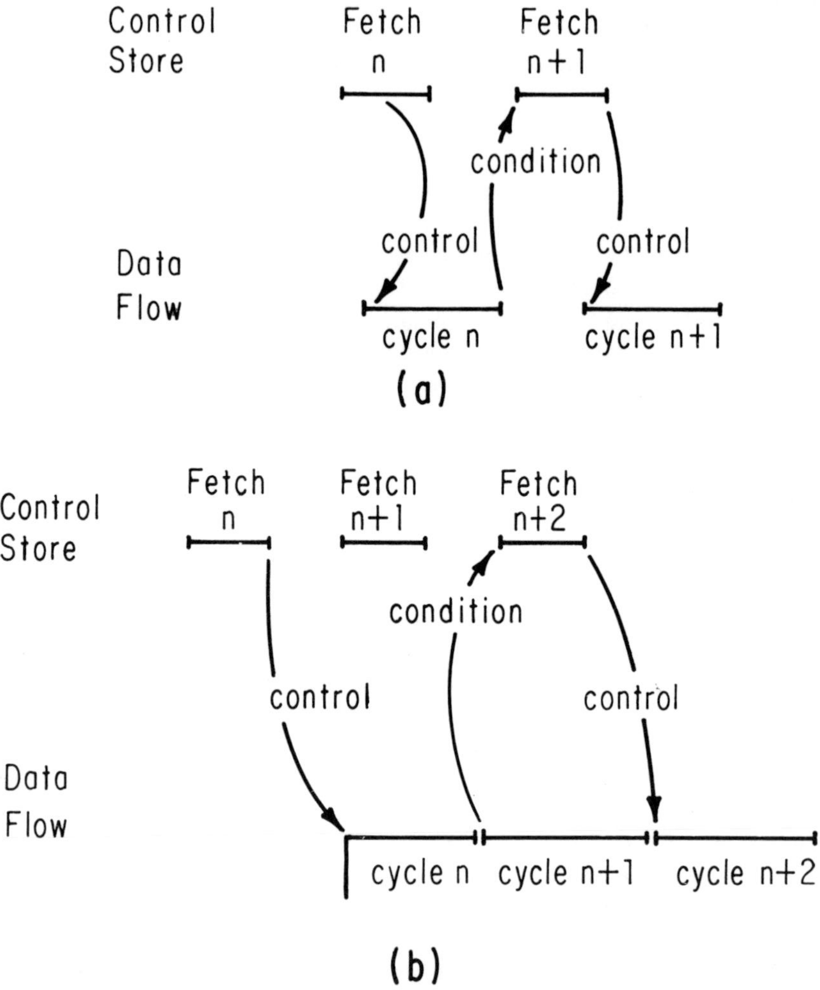

Figure 10-21. (a) Control Store and Data Flow Interleaved. (b) Leap-Frog Branching

TRACT or COMPARE) or some other function (e.g., as for LOGICAL INSTRUCTIONS). In this case it is very likely that the decision will be made by a microprogram test and branch.

As presented, these three decisions differ in the "level" within the machine control and hence in the degree of probability that, in a conventional data flow, they will be treated by microprogram test and branch.

In Case 1 the microprogram might read "take the values found in registers P and Q and add them together." Parameters are being used, in this case P and Q.

A (micro)program might be described as a sequence of steps to be taken by the unit being controlled, using parameters the values of which are not known when the (micro)program is written. It is the use of parameters instead of exact values that allows for variety and decision making within the same basic "shape."

There is nothing fundamentally different between Cases 1, 2, and 3. All three could use parameters and avoid branching. An example might read "If condition C exists, do function specified by value in F (register or data bus) to contents of register P and Q."

Whereas branching involves taking conditions from the data flow and returning them to the control store to modify the *address* of the succeeding control word, the use of parameters within a single shape could be regarded as keeping the conditions in the data flow to modify the *contents* of the succeeding word.

Thus, if parameters are used, the following is true:

1. The succeeding control word can be fetched before the value of the condition is known. This saves time.

2. The same control word will do for two or more different paths within the same basic shape. This saves control bits.

The system designer should pitch the level of his microprogram language to suit the system architecture according to the following principle.

Principle 1. Data flow conditions are of two types: those that give only minor changes in direction (e.g., the differences that exist between ADD, SUBTRACT, and COMPARE) and those that give gross changes in direction (e.g., differences between, say, ADD and EDIT). Minor conditions should be kept in the data flow; only gross conditions should be allowed to return to the control store.

Although any data flow organization can apply this principle, functional memory is particularly well suited to doing so. Much of the *function* performed in a functional memory data flow is already more diffused than in a conventional microprogram data flow. Now much of the *control* can also be integrated into the data flow. Decisions are taken close to both the place generating the conditions on which the decisions depend and the place where the action must be taken.

In this respect functional memory forms an interesting bridge between conventional microprogram-controlled and hardware-controlled machines, combining many of the advantages of both.

Field Combination Problem

Although not fundamentally different from each other, program and microprogram tend to differ in one important respect. In general, *program* is concerned with only one facility or element of the system at a time, whereas *microprogram* can be concernred with several at the same time.

Although in microprogram all the facilities or elements of the data flow may be contributing to the overall goal (for example, the particular programmer instruction being microprogrammed), the elements are often working in parallel on portions of the microprogram flow that can be considered independent of each other for the time being (say, for the following n cycles).

The truth of this is most obvious in a pipelined organization where there may be, say, three different programmer instructions in different stages of decomposition in the data flow at any one time. It is equally true, however, in a normal single-instruction stream, for instance with a System/360 RX instruction, where an operand from mainstore is processed with an operand from a programmer register. From the architecture point of view, there is no contraint on the order in which the operands are fetched: operand 1 could be fetched first, operand 2 could be fetched first, or both operands could be fetched at the same time. System/360 Model 40, for example, fetches both at the same time.

The control sequence for fetching operand 1 if therefore logically independent of the control sequencing for fetching operand 2, and this independence continues until the point where they are brought together for processing. However, unless each of the independent control sequences has its own independent addresing structure, the conventional single-addressing, single-control store organization can provide only pseudo-independence, and that at the expense of combination.

Consider a conceptual data flow for a CPU such as that shown in Figure 10-17 and repeated here as Figure 10-22. It was composed of five boxes and the interconnections between them which need not concern us here. The main functions of the five boxes were as follows:

1. Address store (functional memory): forms and increments addresses for main store.
2. Work store (functional memory): acts as ALU and op decoder.
3. Local store (functional memory): holds programmer's registers and provides work space.
4. Main store (conventional).
5. Control store (assume conventional).

The data flow could be divided, for control purposes, into three functional areas which we will call

A main store and addressing
W ALU
L registers and data.

In a conventional control store, each word would control all three functional areas for one cycle by having a control field devoted to each functional area and the appropriate values in each of the control fields, as in Figure 10-23. Each field will have a set of values used:

$$A_1;\ A_2;\ A_3;\cdots A_n$$

$$W_1;\ W_2;\ W_3;\cdots W_n$$

$$L_1;\ L_2;\ L_3;\cdots L_n.$$

It is likely that most of these values will appear many times in different combinations:

$$A_1, W_1, L_3$$

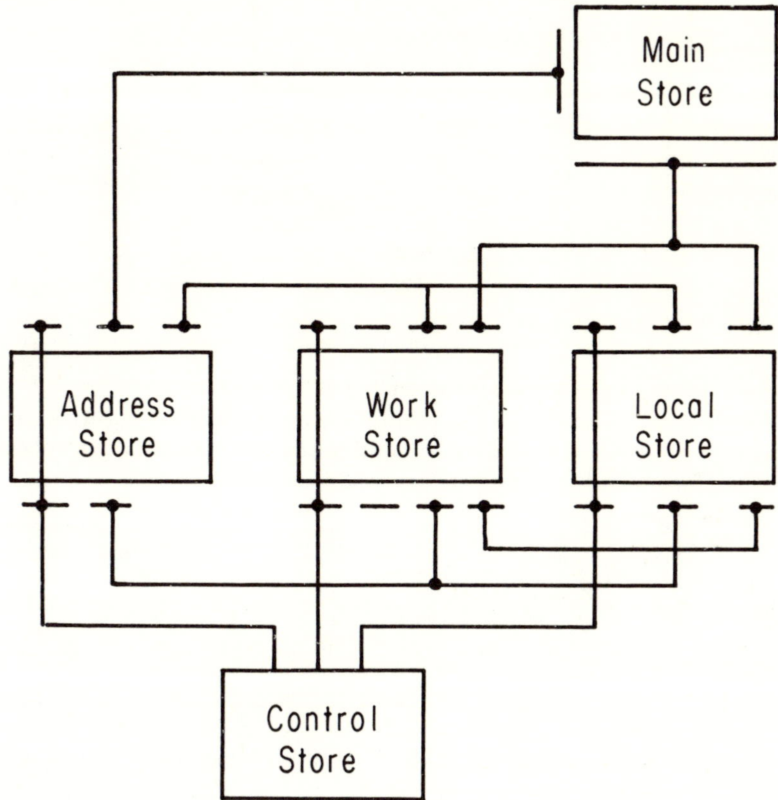

Figure 10-22. A Data Flow

$$A_1, W_7, L_5$$

$$A_2, W_7, L_3, \cdots.$$

Since one control word is necessary for each combination, the total number of control words necessary in the control is related to the *product* of the number of different values used in each field. This is seen as the field combination problem.

If, on the other hand, the control fields were to be separated from each other and each field given a separate control store, then the total number of control words necessary would be related not to the *product* of the number of different values used in each field, but to their *sum.*

Let us extract a second principle.

Principle 2. The system designer should attempt to identify those areas of control which, though concurrent, are architecturally independent of each other and provide a separate source of control for each independent area for the duration of their independence.

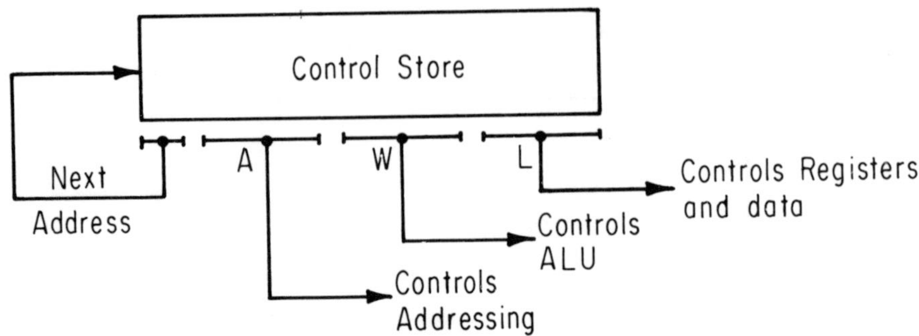

Figure 10-23. Control Fields

There are several arrangements for providing independence.

1. Each Control Store Full Width (Figure 10-24). Each control store is capable of controlling the whole data flow, but during any one cycle may control only one of the functional areas, thus we have the following:

	Control Store 1			*Control Store 2*			*Control Store 3*		
Cycle 1	*O*	*W*	*O*	*A*	*O*	*O*	*O*	*O*	*L*
Cycle 2	*A*	*O*	*O*	*O*	*O*	*L*	*O*	*W*	*O*
Cycle 3	*A*	*O*	*O*	*O*	*W*	*O*	*O*	*O*	*L*
etc.									

2. Each Control Store Only Field Width (Figure 10-25). Each control store is capable of controlling only one functional area of the data flow in any one cycle. The functional area to be controlled is determined by a field code which is read out with the field control value.

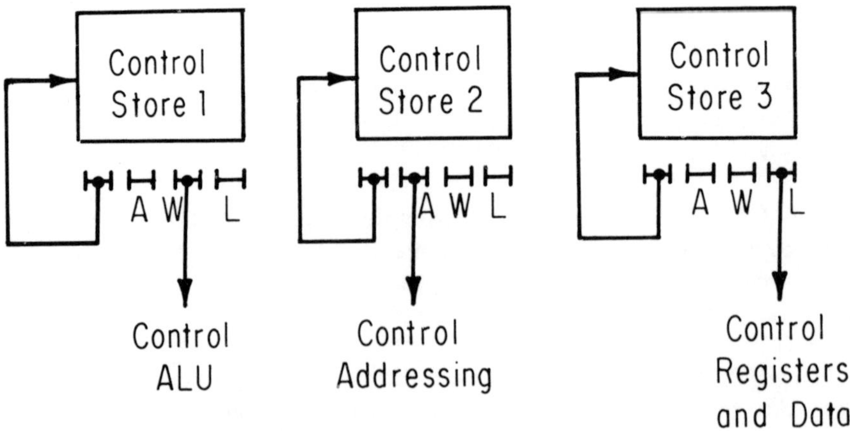

Figure 10-24. Multiple Control Stores, Full Width

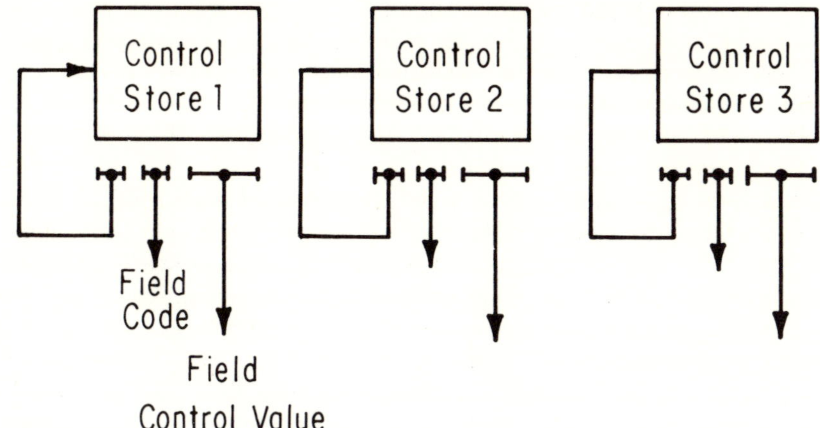

Figure 10-25. Multiple Control Stores, Field Width

3. Control Store Per Functional Area (Figure 10-26). Each control store is dedicated to a particular functional area. As data pass out of the control of one functional area, so too does addressing information from the control store of that functional area to the control store of the functional area to which the data are being passed. Each control store is thus sequenced not only by its own next address field, but also by next address information from the other control stores.

Of these three arrangements, the first and third seem of particular interest. The second arrangement would require an additional stage of decoding to decide which functional area is to be controlled. It is therefore not recommended.

An interesting difference, which can be illustrated in a pipeline organization, exists between the first and third arrangements. In the first, each control store could be devoted to a programmer instruction and could control it through the data flow from start to finish. (Clashes between instructions which cause hold-offs would presumably be detected in the data flow and returned to the control

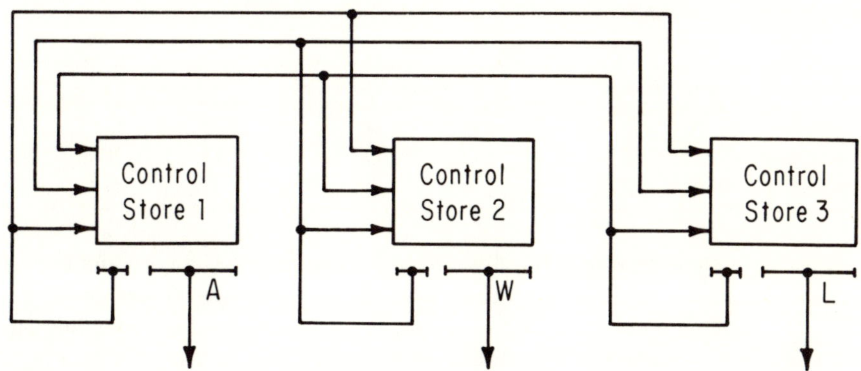

Figure 10-26. Control Store Per Functional Area

stores as holdoff or branching information.) There would, therefore, be as many control stores as the maximum number of instructions in the pipeline at any one time. With arrangement 3, on the other hand, since each control store controls a particular functional area, responsibility for each instruction is passed from one control store to another (one or many) as the information relative to that instruction passes around the data flow.

Although the conventional two-state directly addressed stores could be used to implement these control store arrangements, functional memory is particularly well suited to them. First, in its use in the data flow, functional areas are easier to define and isolate with functional memory than with conventional logic. This is because the elements of a conventional data flow tend to be defined according to their *logic* specialization (ALU, shifter, staticizers, etc.). With functional memory, on the other hand, logic function can be more diffuse and can be assigned to functional areas according to *architectural* requirements. Thus, for example, functional area *A* (main store and addressing) can contain tables for address formation, incrementing, and address specification testing, as required, and also locations for temporary storage of addresses. Second, in its use for control, arrangement 3 is well suited to the idea of integration of control into the data flow, as suggested in the discussion on the branching delay problem. However, it is in arrangement 1 that the implications of functional memory on microprogramming can be seen most clearly, even if not to best advantage (a mixture of arrangements 1 and 3 would probably be optimum).

It may seem wasteful to have only one third of each control store width active in any one cycle, but let us recall the discussion in Part I–D on the compression of tables. It was said there that probably the greatest degree of table compression results from the provision of independent logic subfields. What is being provided here by arrangement 1 is independent control fields, with no decision having to be made concerning the placing of those control fields.

It was suggested for arrangement 1 that each control store would control only one functional area in any one cycle. A natural extension is that in any one cycle any control store could control any number of functional areas from 0 to 3; thus we have the following.

	Control Store 1			*Control Store 2*			*Control Store 3*		
Cycle 1	*O*	*W*	*O*	*A*	*O*	*O*	*O*	*O*	*L*
Cycle 2	*A*	*O*	*L*	*O*	*O*	*O*	*O*	*W*	*O*
Cycle 3	*O*	*O*	*L*	*A*	*W*	*O*	*O*	*O*	*O*

A further extension is to place all three control stores into one functional memory store and read out up to three words at the same time. There could then be a *variable* number of control stores, the number provided depending on the number of independent functional areas required from cycle to cycle. For instance, in the System/360 RX example, a single control sequence, with only a single word being read out each cycle, might precede the fetching of the operands. At that point the control could split into two independent sequences, two words being read out for each cycle, until they come together again as a single sequence for processing.

In these examples the control fields being read out in a cycle are put together by concatenation. Yet a further extension is possible if the control fields are put together in some other way, for example by ORing the fields or XORing using the READ RIGHT XOR LEFT.

CONCLUSION

Functional memory is basically an array. The circuits are therefore densely packaged and the interconnections between them are regular.

The array is associative and the cells are able to hold a DON'T CARE state in addition to the normal binary 0 and 1. Functional memory is therefore able to perform logic by table lookup much more cheaply than conventional two-state table lookup methods. Techniques such as READ RIGHT XOR LEFT provide even greater table compression.

Logic personality is loadable and easily changed. Module manufacture is therefore independent of the function that it is to perform in a system. Because of this independence, because it is an array, and because it can perform logic, functional memory is an attractive way of applying LSI to the field of random logic.

Functional memory words can be written during processing. It can thus be used for local storage, working registers, status information, etc.

A functional memory data flow consists of a collection of functional memory modules connected together. Because the elements of the data flow are all operating synchronously, are all of the same type, and are distinguished from each other only by their position in the data flow and by their contents, the system designer has the following option: either to specialize the elements by logic function (as with a conventional data flow) or to diffuse logic function around the data flow and form "functional areas" that are related to architectural requirements. He will probably do both.

The voltage levels of the data pins and external control pins of a functional memory module are compatible. Therefore "autosequencing" is possible, whereby some functional memory modules control others or themselves. Again the system designer has the option of controlling his data flow by a separate control store (as with a conventional microprogram-controlled data flow), or integrating the control into the data flow and providing independent local control where it would be advantageous. He will probably do both.

Thus functional memory not only seems a good solution to the problem of applying LSI to random logic, but also opens up new possibilities in the field of microprogram control.

ACKNOWLEDGMENT

The author wishes to acknowledge ideas contributed by numerous colleagues.

REFERENCES

1. M. Flinders, P. L. Gardner, J. F. Minshull, and R. J. Llewelyn, "Functional memory as a general purpose systems technology," presented at the 1970 IEEE Computer Group Conference, June 1970.
2. J. P. Bartlett, "Processing memories," presented at the 1970 IEEE Computer Group Conference, June 1970.
3. B. T. McKeever, "The associative memory structure," in *Proc. Fall Joint Comput. Conf., AFIPS Conf. Proc.,* vol. 27. Washington, D.C.: Spartan, 1965.

PART 6

SIMULATION COUNCILS, INC.

La Jolla, California

Two papers selected by the Simulation Councils, Inc. as the best papers submitted during 1971:

"From Simulation Model to Public Policy: An Examination of Forrester's 'Urban Dynamics' "
by Leo P. Kadanoff

and

"Air Traffic Control System–Digital Simulation Facility"
by John R. Vander Veer and Louis J. Bona

11
From Simulation Model to Public Policy: An Examination of Forrester's "Urban Dynamics"

by *Leo P. Kadanoff*

INTRODUCTION

In his *Urban Dynamics* Jay W. Forrester constructs a simulation model of urban growth and then utilizes this model to assess and evaluate a variety of possible strategies for public policy [1]. This work is provocative in several respects. First, computations based on the model are used to reject as harmful or of mixed value a variety of the traditional "liberal" schemes for city improvement, including provision of jobs for unskilled workers, job training to increase the skills of the unskilled, financial aid for the city, construction of low-cost housing, and income maintenance schemes. Concurrently, Forrester presses for some policies which have considerably less appeal for the liberal thinker, including discouragement of the construction of housing for workers, destruction of low-cost housing, and encouragement of industrial growth to the further detriment of housing.

Even more provocative than these specific conclusions, however, is his explanation of why he reached the "result that past programs designed to solve urban problems may well be making matters worse . . . while policy changes in exactly the opposite direction from present trends are needed if the decaying inner city is to be revived" [2]. According to Forrester, he has gotten better results than his predecessor because planners and public policy makers have applied intuitive reasoning to the complex system that is a city. For this reason, their proposed policies turn out to be palliatives rather than cures. "With a high degree of confidence we can say that the intuitive solutions to the problems of complex social systems will be wrong most of the time. Here lies much of the explanation for . . . the troubles of the urban area" [3].

To reach a more effective treatment of city problems, Forrester proposes that we analyze them with the aid of the diagnostic techniques provided by simulation models. Public policies can be mathematically tested by working out the models and seeing all of the policies' effects, intended and unintended. In this way, one can reach conclusions unhampered by the defects and perils of intuitive thought.

Editor's Note: From *Simulation,* vol. 16, no. 6, June 1971. Reprinted by permission of the publisher, Simulation Councils, Inc., and the author.

But as Moynihan has pointed out, this point of view raises perplexing difficulties for planners, public policy makers, and ordinary citizens.* Must we all be experts in systems analyses before we can make intelligent conclusions about public programs and policies? Must we train all planners** and policy makers in computer programming so that they can avoid the necessary errors of "intuitive thinking?" Clearly these questions bear very seriously upon the educational experiences we propose for our future experts and our ordinary citizens.

To study this point, we shall examine Forrester's work in some detail and draw upon some earlier criticism [5, 6, 7]. The main conclusions of this paper are: (a) the main policy recommendations of *Urban Dynamics* are in no sense counterintuitive; they follow directly from Forrester's implied normative scheme and intuitive thought; and (b) some of the apparently counterintuitive features of this book result from questionable representations of urban dynamics and incorrect representations of proposed public policies. Despite these criticisms of Forrester's conclusions, I would argue that his model-making is so brilliant and beautiful that his ideas are certainly worthy of examination and further development. I would reject the conclusions, but accept the model as an appropriate basis for further work.

THE MODEL: FROM BASIC VARIABLES TO POLICY CONCLUSIONS

Forrester reaches his conclusions via a five-step process. First, he isolates a few basic variables which describe the social and economic composition of the city. Second, he writes down equations which describe the "natural" city development. These equations tell how the values of the variables at a given point in time determine their values at a later time. Third, public policies are introduced as modifications in these equations. Therefore, Forrester can as the fourth step find the composition of the city which results from each of the proposed policies, or from no policy at all. In the fifth and final step, he compares the resulting composition with his conception of a desirable city and thereby chooses the policies he would like to recommend.

The basic variables are chosen with an eye to city problems: the existence of large slum areas, the unemployment caused by industry's flight from the city, and insufficient tax revenue for city needs. The variables chosen are:

1. The numbers of people in various socioeconomic groups, namely:
   a. management and professional workers
   b. skilled workers (called Labor in the model)
   c. unskilled workers (called Underemployed in the model)
2. The number of acres of housing devoted to each of the above groups.
3. The number of acres devoted to business and industrial uses. Maximum economic activity occurs in the newer areas, called "New Enterprise." As the enter-

*R. Moynihan, from speech at Hendrix College, April 6, 1970.
**On this point see Ernest Erher, ed., especially the articles by Britton Harris, George M. Raymond, and Lawrence Mann.

prises age to "Mature Business" and then to "Declining Industry," the economic activity per acre declines.

4. Taxes. Here there are two important variables, the taxes needed and the actual taxes collected. The taxes the city needs to collect are assumed to be proportional to the number of people in the various social and economic groups, with the management and professional people requiring the least tax expenditure and the underemployed, the most. The actual tax collected usually lies below the taxes needed because the city can only respond imperfectly to an increase in its tax needs.

5. Land. The city is assumed to have a fixed area of 100,000 acres. Each unit of enterprise and housing subtracts from the pool of land available for further development.

Forrester's city, then, is a fixed land area, like an island, containing people, housing, and enterprises. It has a uniform tax rate. All the potential jobs and workers lie within this fixed area. Of course, this island-city is a poor representation [9] of either our central cities (which do have a fixed area but include many jobs filled by suburban workers) or of our metropolitan areas (which are continually growing). For this reason, this model does not include the effects of city-suburb interactions and in particular leaves out the influence of suburban growth on the central city [10].

In the model, the only interaction between the city and the outside world arises through the migration of people into and out of the city. Of course, the model includes the fact that a city which is more attractive for a given type of worker will have more immigration and less emigration of that group. Thus, the model includes the idea that—all other things being equal—a city which is more attractive for unskilled workers will tend to have more unskilled workers.

This point is important in understanding Forrester's conclusions, because his normative scheme seems to be one in which a "healthy" city contains relatively few unskilled workers. Forrester does not devote much attention to his goals, apparently because he does not consider them to be very controversial. Instead, he focuses attention on the model's predictive methods. "The approach presented in this book is suggested as a method for evaluating urban policies *once the proposed dynamic model or a modification of it has been accepted as adequate*" [11].

However, a careful reading does indicate the goals implicit in Forrester's work. These include the "minimization of the average per capita tax rate" [12] and "to diminish the population share of the underemployed" [13].

Given this point of view, the trend of Forrester's policy conclusions becomes obvious. Any policies which will make the city more attractive to unskilled workers will be classified under *Failures in urban programs* because of this normative framework. Under this category we find the provision of jobs for the unskilled, the provision of housing for them, a tax subsidy, and also job training to increase their skills. All these programs draw the unskilled to the city and hence "fail" in Forrester's terms. On the other hand, he applauds policies designed to force out the unskilled. His favorite scheme is to destroy their housing and limit the construction of new housing for skilled workers, thus preventing filtering down. The resulting reduction in unskilled worker population and in tax rates is described as "Urban Revival."

In short, Forrester's conclusions follow from his goals, without any counterintuitive steps.

DYNAMIC PROCESSES

Nonetheless, it is instructive to study the detailed logic which leads to these conclusions. The model focuses on rates of change. Each of the important variables change because of the flows which occur within the city and between the city and its external environment. For example, one of the key equations of the model calculates the number of "Underemployed"—that is, unskilled workers—as:

(Number of unskilled workers this year)
= (Number last year)
+ (Net flow into this group during year) (1)

Then each of the rates is further broken down into its component parts. For example:

(Net flow into unskilled group during year)
= (Migration of Underemployed into the city per year)
+ (People added to this category via births)
+ (People added via downward mobility from the skilled workers category during year)
– (People who have moved upward into skilled workers category during year) (2)

The determination of the various levels then depends on an accurate evaluation of the various component flow processes like those listed in Equation 2. All of the flows in the model have the same basic form:

Flow per year = (Rate constant) + (Some level) (3)

Equation 4 looks technical, but several examples should serve to illustrate its meaning. For example:

(People added to Underemployed category per year via births)
= (Birth rate) × (Number of unskilled workers) (4a)

The flow is the expression on the left, which is a rate constant (the birth rate) times a level (in this case the number of Underemployed). As another example:

(Workers added to the unskilled group via downward mobility from the skilled worker category during year) = (Rate of downward mobility) × (Number of skilled workers). (4b)

So far, we have seen how the job of determining levels—like the number of unskilled workers—can be reduced to a problem of determining rates of flow. Then the rates of flow are writtern in terms of the known levels and rate constants, as in Equation 4. To finish the story, we need to know the rate constants. Once the rate constants are known, the model is completely determined.

Some of the rate constants are rather easy to know. For example, the "birth rate" of Equation 4—which is actually a birth rate minus a death rate—can be determined from tables of vital statistics once the age of distribution of the unskilled workers is estimated. Others are harder. The "rate of downward mobility" of Equation 4 is not known. But Forrester makes a plausible guess by saying that this rate depends on the ratio of workers to available jobs. He writes this guess as a graph (see Figure 11-1), which is incorporated into the model. This graph says that for small values of worker unemployment, the downward mobility rate is very small, while for larger values of unemployment the ratio grows roughly in proportion to the amount of unemployment.

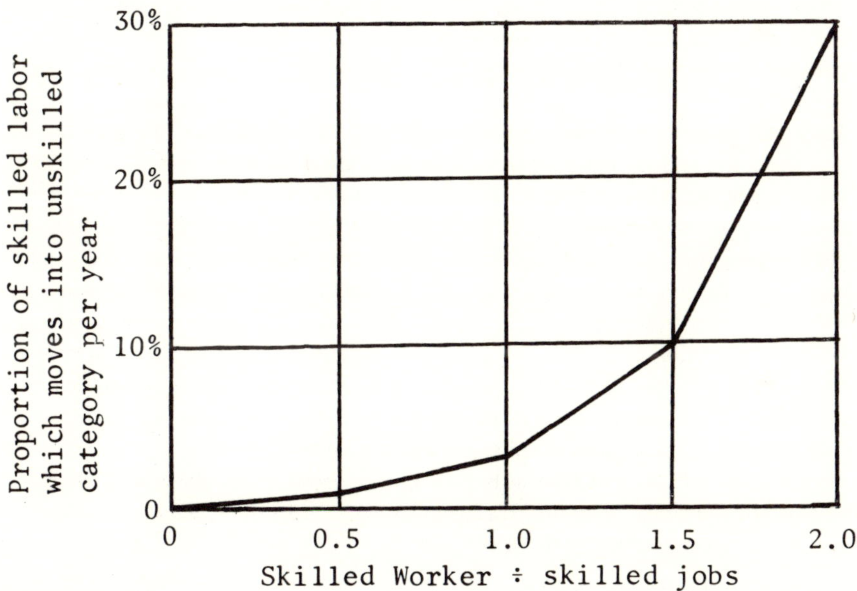

Figure 11-1.

If the aim of *Urban Dynamics* were an accurate prediction of the transition rate from labor to underemployed, the use of guesswork like that in Figure 11-1 would be unacceptable. However, the purpose is the comparison of different public policy alternatives. The model need only predict the kinds of changes caused by the different programs. In this case, it may be sufficient to obtain a qualitatively right form for the transition rate [14], for the relative effects of different public policies may well be quite insensitive to variations of curves like the one in Figure 11-1.

The most important flow rates are those due to the in-migration and out-migration of underemployed people. In this case, the flow rates are determined by rate constants which can be respectively interpreted as:

a. the attractiveness of the city as perceived by unskilled potential immigrants

b. the unattractiveness of the city for the unskilled. The relevant rate equations are:

$$\text{(Rate of in-migration)} = \text{(Perceived attractiveness for unskilled)} \times \text{(Number of skilled and unskilled workers)} \tag{4c}$$

and

$$\text{(Rate of out-migration)} = \text{(Unattractiveness for unskilled)} \times \text{(Number of unskilled workers)} \tag{4d}$$

"Unattractiveness for the unskilled" appears in Equation 4d as a rate constant, which determines the rate of out-migration from the city. Double the unattractiveness, while holding the number of unemployed fixed, and the rate of out-migration will double. Similarly, from Equation 4c, if you halve the perceived attractiveness, the rate of in-migration of the underemployed will go down by a factor of 2.

Forrester gives a precise numerical meaning to "attractiveness" by guessing the strength of the various forces which draw the unskilled to the city. Attractiveness for unskilled workers grows as their economic opportunity grows, as the density in their housing diminishes, as their unemployment rate diminishes, as the public expenditure per capita increases, and as the underemployed housing program produces superior housing units. Mathematically, the attractiveness is a product of separate factors describing each of these separate components of attractiveness. For example, Figure 11-2 gives the dependence of the attractiveness on residential density in the housing for the underemployed. This figure indicates that as the density rises from 120 people per acre to 180 people per acre, the attractiveness of the city diminishes by a factor of five.

By using guesses such as that in Figure 11-2, Forrester can give a numerical value to attractiveness. The unattractiveness which governs emigration is then given as the inverse of attractiveness

$$\text{(Unattractiveness)} = \text{(Attractiveness)}^{-1} \tag{5}$$

The perceived attractiveness which governs immigration of unskilled workers is assumed to differ from the actual attractiveness because people outside the city do not immediately find out about changed conditions within the city. The model assumes a 20-year time lag so that this perceived attractiveness at a given moment is approximately equal to the actual attractiveness 20 years before.

In this way, Forrester gives concrete mathematical expression to his ideas about the flow of people into and out of the city, and achieves a model in which an increased attractiveness for the unskilled will draw more unskilled into the city.

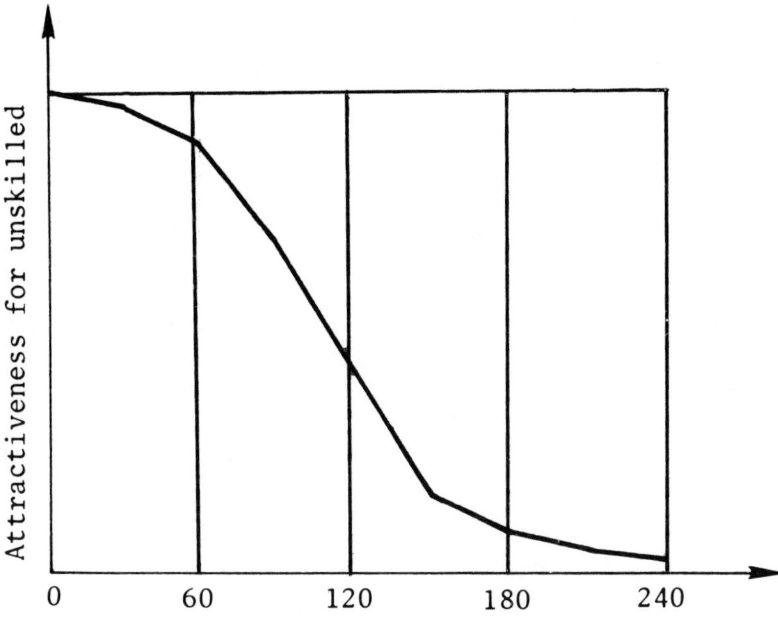

Figure 11-2.

Another key part of the model is the mechanism for producing new jobs via the creation of new enterprise. The rate constant for this kind of new job production is very sensitive to the amount of land still unutilized in the city. For the conditions most characteristic of the mature cities studied in the model, a 1% drop in the land occupied by housing will cause a 5% increase in this kind of new job formation.

Once the rate constants are specified, Forrester's model is complete. He can then set the city at some initial point, year zero, and let his rate equations calculate the changes in all the variables between year zero and year one. Successive applications of this procedure give the year-by-year growth of the city. At each point, the model calculates the values of all the level-variables. Eventually, the city begins to fill most of its available land area with housing and industry. Thereafter, the city begins to settle down to an equilibrium in which all the levels remain roughly constant. We then have a description of the mature city.

THE MATURE CITY: STAGNATION AND REMEDIES

As Forrester looks at the mature city of his model, he finds that it contains many of the defects of our real cities. The story is summarized in Table 11-1. Notice the high unemployment rate among the unskilled, the lack of skilled labor, and the high land fraction (31%) occupied by the unskilled and their

Table 11-1. Forrester's "Stagnant" City. The unemployment is calculated as the first row in the table minus the second

	Population Group			
	Unskilled workers = "Underemployed"	*Skilled workers = "workers"*	*Management + Professionals*	*Total*
Number of potential workers	377,300	403,500	71,100	841,000
Jobs for this category	208,300	392,600	51,800	663,600
Unemployed	169,000	10,900	19,300	177,400
Potential workers plus families	3,000,000	2,370,000	350,600	5,720,600
Land area occupied (acres)	31,000 "slums"	33,500	11,100	75,600
Density (people/acre)	98	71	32	76

families. Their area is identified as slums even though the residential density is rather low. As Forrester points out, these slums are harmful to the city because they occupy land which could be utilized by industry which, in turn, could provide more jobs. This condition is then termed "urban stagnation."

Next, Forrester examines a possible set of alternative strategies for city improvement; these strategies are inserted as changes in the model. For example, the underemployed job program simply provides jobs for 10% of the unskilled workers over and above those jobs naturally provided by the business sector. A job-training program moves 5% of the underemployed into the skilled worker group without changing any of the other flow processes. The tax subsidy program makes $100 per capita per year available to the city from outside sources. In the model, this permits extra tax expenditure, which then has the effect of increasing the upward mobility of the underemployed.

All of these "liberal programs" are directly designed to reduce unemployment among the poor. To evaluate how well they work, the model is run for 50 years. After this time, a new equilibrium is reached as shown in Table 11-2. From the data in the first three rows, all three programs seem to have failed. The training program seems to have had no effect. The job program and tax subsidy have increased the number of unskilled, the amount of unemployment in this group, and the amount of land devoted to slums.

If Forrester is right, the job program and the tax subsidy are harmful to the city. Those who have proposed them are the victims of "intuitive thinking" applied to a situation too complex for any simple method of thought.

The final liberal program in Table 11-2, low-cost housing, is inserted in the model as a simple addition to the stock of housing for the underemployed. Land available for industry decreases, jobs decline, and disastrous unemployment results.

Table 11-2. Effects of Programs in the Forrester Model. The programs are each run for fifty years. The numbers in parentheses are the changes produced by the programs in comparison to the results of no programs at all. The effects of the programs can be assessed by looking at the net upward social mobility (fourth from the bottom row) and at the resulting attractiveness of the city for various social groups (last three rows).

		Some "liberal" programs					*Some programs for city revival Demolition of slum housing*		
Program	*"Natural" development*	*Job program*	*Tax subsidy*	*Low-cost housing*	*Training program*	*New enterprise construction*	*Alone*	*+Discouragement of worker construction*	*+Encouragement of new enterprise construction*
Number of unskilled workers = underemployed (in thousands)	377	417 (+10%)	407 (+8%)	372 (−1%)	382 (+1%)	452 (+20%)	317 (−16%)	290 (−23%)	336 (−11%)
Unemployment in this group (in thousands)	169	173 (+3%)	201 (+19%)	214 (+27%)	168 (+0%)	152 (−9%)	57 (−66%)	4 (−97%)	22 (−87%)
Land area occupied by this group = slums (thousands of acres)	31.0	32.6 (+8%)	31.9 (+3%)	45.1 (+46%)	30.7 (−1%)	32.0 (+3%)	17.4 (−44%)	14.2 (−54%)	17.5 (−43%)
New upward social mobility (net flow underemployed to labor—thousands of workers per year)	5.5	6.8 (+24%)	7.6 (+38%)	3.8 (−31%)	16.8 (+206%)	13.0 (+136%)	5.6 (+2%)	7.1 (+29%)	9.2 (+68%)
ATTRACTIVENESS: Underemployed	1	1.03	1.05	1.01	1.25	1.16	.89	.91	.95
ATTRACTIVENESS: Labor	1	.90	.90	.91	.68	.78	1.08	1.03	.98
ATTRACTIVENESS: Management and Professionals	1	.98	.91	.94	.94	.95	.98	.98	.97

To replace these "unsuccessful" liberal programs, Forrester proposes a set of programs aimed at city revival. The most obvious, the direct encouragement of additional new enterprise formation, is inserted into the model as an increase in the rate constant for new enterprise construction. However, this program is rejected both because its effects are too small and because Forrester sees no direct way of bringing about this encouragement of new enterprise.

An indirect method is proposed: a program of slum housing demolition which removes 5% of the slum housing each year. This is most effective when it is coupled with diminished worker housing construction or with increased new enterprise construction. From Table 11-2, these programs seem quite successful in alleviating unemployment among the unskilled and reducing the size of slums.

Of course, the results of these calculations are in no sense counterintuitive. Each of the liberal programs increases the city's attractiveness for the unskilled (see row 5 of Table 11-2) and draws them to it. The programs for "city revival" are, as expected, unattractive for the unskilled. The model merely reproduces our intuitive expectations.

ANALYSIS OF BENEFITS: LOCAL VIEW

Each of the programs under consideration produces both gains and losses. For example, the demolition of slum housing, combined with the discouragement of worker housing construction, does decrease unemployment and diminish the area devoted to "slums." (The slum area goes down because houses are pulled down and because the "filtering down" of housing from the labor group to the underemployed group is inhibited). However, the density in the "slums" increases from 98 people per acre to 160 people per acre, while the density in the "labor" sections increases by 9%. How are we to balance the benefits of increased job opportunity against the disadvantage of more crowded housing?

Forrester does not exactly perform this balancing process. Rather, he has in mind an improved version of the city with fewer low-skilled workers, fewer slums, fewer people out of jobs, and more industrial growth. If a program produces results which approach these ends, he judges it to be successful. In essence, Forrester is working toward the goal of improving a given area of land—a city.

To see this reasoning at work, consider Forrester's evaluation of the training program. This program has the advantage that it increases the net flow of people from the "Underemployed" category to skilled "Labor." (This flow is recorded as the fourth row in Table 11-2.) However, Forrester focuses on the losses to the "city":

> The training program has created a flow through the area with a much increased underemployed-arrival rate and a much increased labor-departure rate. People come to the area because of the training program and leave when they find there is no use for the skills they have acquired. *As a service to society,* the program might be considered successful. But as a

> service to the city, its value is far less clear. The area is more crowded, the land fraction occupied has risen slightly, housing conditions are more crowded, the total of underemployed has risen very slightly, and the ratio of labor to jobs is higher, indicating a higher degree of unemployment [15].

Forrester's assumption that there is an object called "the city" to which we can assign benefits or debits is, I think, incorrect. We should only assign benefits and hurts to people, since the goals of our policies should be to enable people to live more satisfactory lives.

Is there anything in the model which would permit the estimation of benefits to the people involved? There is. The attractiveness functions give numerical estimates of the worth of the city as perceived by various groups. The model computes the changes in attractiveness resulting from each of the proposed programs. These attractiveness numbers are listed in the last three rows of Table 11-2. The numbers in each row are divided by a constant factor so that the attractiveness is unity in the absence of any public program. These attractiveness numbers provide a numerical way of estimating the worth of any public program for the various groups involved.

The benefits and losses to the unskilled have already been discussed. Each program which is attractive to the unskilled reduces the city's attractiveness for the skilled group. This effect occurs because the attractiveness for the skilled includes a "social attractiveness" which decreases as the city draws in a larger proportion of unskilled workers. Conversely, the reduction in the proportion of unskilled workers produced by the destruction of their housing increases the city's attraction for the skilled group. However, when this program is coupled with new enterprise construction, the increased attractiveness for the skilled group is cancelled because not enough land is available for housing.

From the point of view of the attractiveness concept, Forrester's favored program of slum-housing demolition plus discouragement of labor-housing construction does not look very good. The attractiveness for Labor increases only 3%, while Underemployed and Management are respectively 9% and 2% worse off than before. On this basis, we should probably reject this program. Furthermore, the last program in Table 11-2 is favored by Forrester even though it seems bad for everyone!

However, one might argue that this result is not really fair to Forrester. After all, there is more industry in the city. Is this not a gain? It is true that, in general, industry is good for a city by providing jobs and paying taxes. But the attractiveness measures already include these benefits. We cannot count them again. All the other beneficial effects of increased industry are harder to evaluate because they are largely benefits which accrue to the entire nation rather than to the city in question. However, it is possible that the appearance of this industry in this special city prevented the construction of competitive industry elsewhere. Perhaps the other location would have been better for the nation. We cannot know.

But there is one benefit which is possibly undervalued in the attractiveness measures. It is possible that the underemployed do not have a sufficiently long view to perceive the real value to themselves and their children of upward economic mobility. In the construction of city programs, we might consider the upward mobility from the low-skilled underemployed group to the higher-skilled labor group to be valuable in itself. In fact, one might argue that the main role of cities in American history has been to foster this upward mobility. Then, in evaluating the different proposed public policies in the context of this model, we should also consider—as Forrester does—the total number of potential workers who have been raised from the low-skilled group to the high. In the model the traffic goes both ways, from "Underemployed" to "Labor," and vice versa. The key number is the net flow from "Underemployed" to "Labor." Table 11-2 shows this number for the models under consideration. From this point of view, the "favorable" program has a much less favorable impact than the direct training program. Both seem preferable to the "stagnation" result.

It is true, nonetheless, that the programs favored by Forrester do increase the net upward mobility. Or at least the model says that they do so. This mobility increase is supposed to occur because the programs result in increasing industry, and the increased jobs help the upward mobility. Furthermore, the improved "social atmosphere" caused by an increased ratio of skilled labor to unskilled is also supposed to increase upward mobility.

It is, however, extremely dangerous to base any public policy decisions on the upward mobility predictions of this model. As Banfield has emphasized, we know very little about the conditions which help upward mobility. [16] Moynihan has suggested that this mobility might be tightly interwoven with family structure considerations which are certainly not in the model. [17] The mobility predictions of this model cannot be used to justify any public policy because they are completely unrealiable.

A NATIONAL VIEW

The most striking fact about the changes in attractiveness listed in Table 11-2 is that they are very small. If you momentarily increase the attractiveness for any group, more of that group will enter the city, consume jobs and housing, and thereby reduce the attractiveness. To see this result in operation, consider the attractiveness effects of the job training program as indicated in Table 11-3.

According to the following table, after the first 10 years, the training program produces a very large favorable effect for the unskilled in that the attractiveness for this group increases 68%. On the other hand, there is an immediate harmful effect to the skilled laboring population produced by the increased job and housing competition felt by this group. This effect is initially smaller than the benefit to the unskilled, being only a 26% decrease in attractiveness.

Table 11-3. Attractiveness Changes Produced by Training Program

		Before	After 10 years	After 50 years
Relative Attractiveness for	Underemployed	1	1.68	1.25
	Labor	1	.74	.68
	Management & Professionals	1	1.09	.95

Notice that after 50 years a large fraction of the benefits of this job training program for the unskilled group disappears, while the losses for the fully-skilled labor group increase. This kind of dissipation of benefits occurs because the increased attractiveness of the city draws more unskilled into the city so that a larger group of people must compete for a roughly fixed number of jobs. Hence, everyone is worse off at the year 50 compared to their state at year 10.

Forrester points out that this dissipation of benefits produced by increased in-migration is a general effect of all programs designed to give direct aid to any group of people. However, it is important to notice that this analysis only applies to a program which is applied only to the single city in question. If the program were applied nationwide, the attractiveness of all areas for the unskilled would increase equally. As a result, there would be no increase in the migration into any city. The long-term deterioration shown in the last two columns of Table 11-2 would then be replaced by a long-term improvement.

This discussion then leads us to the following conclusion: *Programs for improving the lot of the unskilled should be applied nationally rather than locally in order to prevent the partial neutralization of these policies as a result of the concentration of the unskilled in the program areas.* Forrester's model automatically assumes that all his programs are locally employed; hence, his work is simply inapplicable to the analysis of the long-range effects of any policy applied nationwide.

To see the striking effects of policies applied nationwide, imagine that nothing at all were changed within the city under study, but the rest of the nation improved its conditions suddenly to make its attractiveness for the unskilled group a factor of two better than before. Then immediately this group's in-migration decreases by a factor of 2. Even though nothing has changed within the city itself, the results of this nationwide change would be quite substantial, at least for the unskilled group. These changes are summarized in Table 11-4. The conditions of this group have bettered very substantially, without anyone else in the city being the worse off.

Naturally, the course we have just described is not a realistic policy alternative. Forrester's published analysis does not permit us to study and evaluate the results of realistic policies applied nationwide.

Table 11-4. Effects of an Increase in the National Level of the Attraction for Unskilled Workers on a City Which Itself Is Not Changed in Any Structural Sense. Numbers in parentheses refer to the percentage changes in this city caused by the change in the environment.

		Before nation-wide change	*After 10 years*	*After 50 years*
Number of unskilled potential workers = "Underemployed" (in thousands)		377	296 (−20%)	322 (−14%)
Unemployed in this category		166	86 (−41%)	102 (−39%)
Land occupied by "Underemployed" = "slums" (in thousands of acres)		31.0	29.5 (−5%)	28.7 (−8%)
ATTRACTIVENESS FOR	Unskilled workers ("Underemployed")	1	2.58	1.88
	Skilled workers ("Labor")	1	1.08	1.02
	Management	1	1.02	1.00
Underemployed to Labor net in thousands		5.5	5.9 (+8%)	5.6 (+2%)

REFERENCES

1. Forrester, J. W. *Urban dynamics,* MIT Press, Cambridge, 1969.
2. Forrester, J. W. *Urban dynamics,* MIT Press, Cambridge, 1969, p. 109.
3. Forrester, J. W. *Urban dynamics,* MIT Press, Cambridge, 1969, p. 110.
5. Kain, John F. *A computer version of how a city works,* Fortune, November, 1969.
6. Garn, Harvey A. *An urban systems model: A critique of urban dynamics.* The Urban Institute, Washington, D.C. Working Paper 113-25, unpublished.
7. Ingram, Gregory K. Book review, *AIP Journal,* May, 1970.
9. Ingram, Gregory K. Book review, *AIP Journal,* May, 1970, p. 207.

10. Garn, Harvey A. *An urban systems model: A critique of urban dynamics.* The Urban Institute, Washington, D.C. Working Paper 113-25, unpublished, p. 5.
11. Forrester, J. W. *Urban dynamics,* MIT Press, Cambridge, 1969, p. 2, italics added.
12. Kain, John F. *A computer version of how a city works,* Fortune, November 1969.
13. Ingram, Gregory K. Book review, *AIP Journal,* May 1970, p. 206, Garn also reaches similar conclusions about Forrester's goals.
14. Forrester, J. W. *Urban dynamics,* MIT Press, Cambridge, 1969, appendix B.
15. Forrester, J. W. *Urban dynamics,* MIT Press, Cambridge, 1969, p. 59, italics added.
16. Banfield, Edward C. *The heavenly city.* Little, Brown and Company, 1968.
17. Moynihan, R. As reported in Rainwater and Yancey. *The Moynihan report and the politics of controversy,* MIT Press, 1967.

12
Air Traffic Control System—Digital Simulation Facility

by *John R. Vander Veer and Louis J. Bona*

INTRODUCTION

Consider the following air traffic control/pilot conversation:

ATC: United Four Fifty-Six now 10 miles from outer marker. Turn right, heading two five zero. Cleared for ILS runway two seven left approach. Maintain one eight zero knots to the outer marker.

PILOT: Roger, cleared ILS approach.

PILOT: Chicago Approach, Clipper Thirty-Two on your frequency.

ATC: Clipper Thirty-Two, this is Chicago Approach, radar contact, reduce to two two zero knots, turn left heading one eight zero.

PILOT: Chicago Approach, United Four Fifty-Six passing through two hundred degrees, turning at reduced rate account CAS.

ATC: United Four Fifty-Six, say your altitude.

PILOT: United Four Fifty-Six passing three thousand five hundred.

ATC: United Four Fifty-Six maintain three thousand five hundred, advise when able normal turn.

PILOT: Chicago Approach, United Four Fifty-Six approaching the localizer, turning at normal rate.

ATC: Roger, United Four Fifty-Six, contact tower one one eight point one.

ATC: Braniff Forty-Five, turn right, heading two four zero, reduce to one seven zero knots. American Three Forty descend and maintain three thousand.

PILOT: Braniff Forty-Five, Roger, turning to two four zero.

PILOT: American Three Forty leaving five, descending 1000 feet per minute account CAS.

ATC: Roger, American Three Forty.

The foregoing air traffic control communication did not actually occur in the Chicago terminal air traffic control area, but took place in the Digital Simulation Facility of the Federal Aviation Administration (FAA) at the National Aviation Facilities Experimental Center (NAFEC) located near Atlantic City, New Jersey. This Digital Simulation Facility is now serving as a tool in research, development,

Editor's Note: From *Simulation*, vol. 16, no. 1, January 1971. Reprinted by permission of the publisher, Simulation Councils, Inc., and the authors.

and testing of futuristic air traffic control concepts and systems. It is also used to model various proposed Air Traffic Control (ATC) subsystems. The purpose of this article is to describe this simulation facility and some of the projects which are now utilizing it or are planned to utilize it in the near future.

FAA has been performing air traffic control and flight simulation for over 15 years using various analog devices as target generators. Several factors now dictate use of a digital simulator to evaluate advanced concepts:

a. Proposed ATC systems now include digital computers as essential components.
b. Increased air traffic throughout the country and the more complex problems arising as a result mean that more aircraft must be included in simulation studies.
c. Semiautomated systems to be studied require more realistic inputs for radar processing, automatic tracking, and driving alphanumeric digital displays.
d. The modeling of airborne or ground-based computerized subsystems to be tested also adds to the requirement to perform ATC simulation on a digital computer.

This new Digital Simulation Facility is not the first that NAFEC has had, but it is a much larger and more complete facility than its predecessor, which was developed by Thompson Ramo Wooldridge Inc. for the FAA. The previous facility was used for terminal air traffic control studies, and proved the feasibility of the digital approach.

Currently the new facility is being used for two projects. The first is the evaluation of the interaction between the ATC system and the proposed airborne Collision Avoidance System (CAS). The second is the validation of the Automated Radar Terminal System III (ARTS III). These projects will be discussed below.

DIGITAL SIMULATION FACILITY

The Digital Simulation Facility, which has been designed for expansion, currently has 12 alphanumeric digital displays, a Keyboard Data Entry System, an XDS Sigma 5 computer, a High-Speed Multiplexor, two Communication Systems, and a Data Link Subsystem. Five displays are used as pilot consoles, each one capable of serving up to three pilots. Seven displays are used as controller consoles, each usable for two controller positions.

An XDS 910 computer is used in the Keyboard Data Entry System as a buffer for receiving keyboard messages for later interrogation by the Sigma 5 computer. The heart of the system is the Sigma 5, which is used to simulate the aircraft flights, the radar and beacon data acquisition system, radar and beacon tracking, and the airborne collision avoidance computer of each aircraft. In addition, it is used to interpret pilot and controller keyboard messages, to drive the pilot and controller displays, and to record data for off-line processing. Air-to-ground and ground-to-air communication lines, plus controller interphone lines, provide communications similar to real-world conditions. The physical layout of this facility is shown in Figure 12-2. Figure 12-3 and Figure 12-4 show the pilot and controller consoles used in the system.

Figure 12-1. Control Area of the Digital Simulation Facility

All ATC simulation studies do not call for the same analytical approach or equipment configuration. With this in mind, the system was designed to be flexible and to have three different modes of operation. In one mode the computer and software can be operated without the keyboards and displays, thereby serving as a fast-time analytical tool. Initial studies may be performed using this mode of operation. Promising concepts may then be tested in either or both of the other two modes, both of which utilize the displays and keyboards. In this configuration, the capability exists to run the system in either the real-time mode or in compressed time, referred to as the analytical mode.

The analytical mode is useful for the many human engineering studies performed by the FAA in developing future ATC systems. In a number of these studies it is not necessary to have a full complement of controllers and pilots. An analyst may merely wish to observe traffic flows on the display in compressed time. Then, as interesting situations occur, time may be slowed or even stopped to allow him to study the situation. Time compression is limited by how much work the computer must do and is related to the number of simulated targets, number of subsystems being simulated, and the number and complexity of operational and ATC systems being simulated. The realism desired in simulating these also limits the amount of compression.

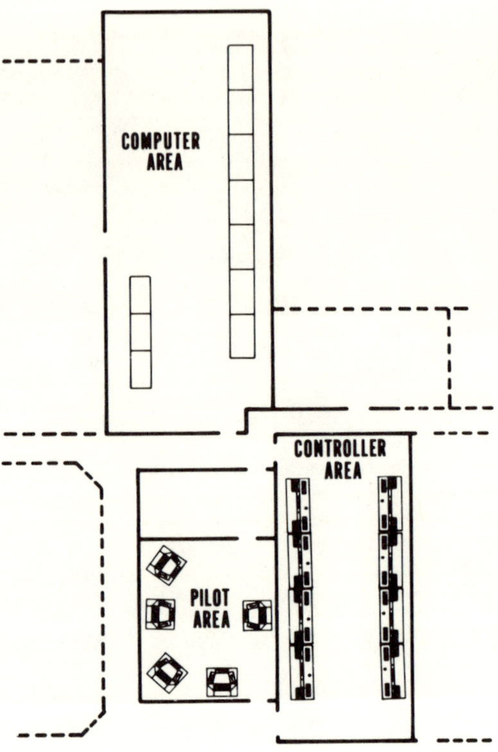

Figure 12-2. Physical Layout of the Digital Simulation Facility

The simulator may be manned with a complete complement of controllers and pilots and be used as a real-time simulation facility to study the many ATC system problems. Real-time simulation studies normally require a traffic build-up period prior to the actual data collection so that realistic traffic conditions exist at the start of the test. The compressed-time feature is used for the traffic build-up, and then time is slowed to real time for the test period.

The simulation software has been designed to accommodate up to 500 simultaneous simulated tartets, 5 radars, 500 navigational aids or fixes, and 500 route segments, a route segment being a portion of an airway defined by as many as 20 fixes along its path. An aircraft's flight path is described by up to four segments: namely, a departure segment, en route segment, transition segment, and arrival or approach segment. The 500 route segments can be combined to form all the routes needed for a very complex simulation.

The constraints of currently installed hardware limit the number of controlled active aircraft to 150. Each of the five pilot displays serves three pilots, each of whom may "fly" up to 10 aircraft. Future hardware expansion will allow for 480 controllable aircraft targets. If core space is available, the software will allow simulation of additional aircraft that can serve as uncontrolled, or "ghost," traffic.

Figure 12-3. Pilot Console

Figure 12-4. Controller Console

Total capacity of the system is difficult to state because of the variety of intended uses of the facility and the varying numbers of programs used in different simulations. The facility may be used merely as an aircraft target generator to supply targets to another system being tested in which case 150 simultaneous active controllable aircraft can be simulated. With present core limitations, an additional 100 ghost or uncontrollable targets can also be simulated when the facility operates in this manner. In its current configuration the facility has the capacity to simulate 150 targets for simulations of the present ATC system.

In the Collision Avoidance System project, the amount of core required for the CAS model and tables, the CAS pilot display, and the tag information on the controller displays reduces the memory available for simulating targets. The maximum number of simultaneously active aircraft for this project is 75, the same number as are being used in the ARTS III simulation.

The entire simulation facility has been designed for a quick changeover of projects being simulated, so it may be used for several projects during one day. The displays are interchangeable and can be changed in 15 minutes, as can the communications setup. The software system tape and new adaptation data for geometry, pilot assignments, etc., required to run the simulation can be loaded in about five minutes.

Another feature of the facility is that if projects do not require the full amount of hardware, more than one simulation can be run at a time, each with its own geometry and route structure. The software simulates the flights and operates on the inputs, even though they represent diverse areas.

HARDWARE

Computer

The Sigma 5 Computer is a medium-size, general-purpose computer. It is fully integrated and modular and has 48K of word-oriented memory divided into three equal banks. Three-way access is provided on one bank and two-way access on the others. The memory has a cycle time of 850 nanoseconds and a word length of 32 bits plus parity.

Other features included are floating-point arithmetic, memory protection, 16 priority interrupts, two real-time clocks, a Multiplexor Input-Output Processor (MIOP) with 16 channels, and a Direct Input-Output Channel (DIO).

Two magnetic tape drives, a line printer, a card reader, and a teletypewriter comprise the peripheral equipment in the computer system.

A block diagram of the Computer System and interface connections is shown in Figure 12-5.

Displays

The displays used in the Digital Simulation Facility are capable of presenting digitally coded information in the form of alphanumeric characters, symbols, and lines on the face of a 19-inch cathode ray tube. The displays use a P-28 phosphor, a stroke writing technique, and have 1024 possible discrete positions. A character repertoire of 64 characters, A through Z, 0 through 9, and special symbols, is provided on each display. A blink feature of two cycles per second on individual selected characters is also available.

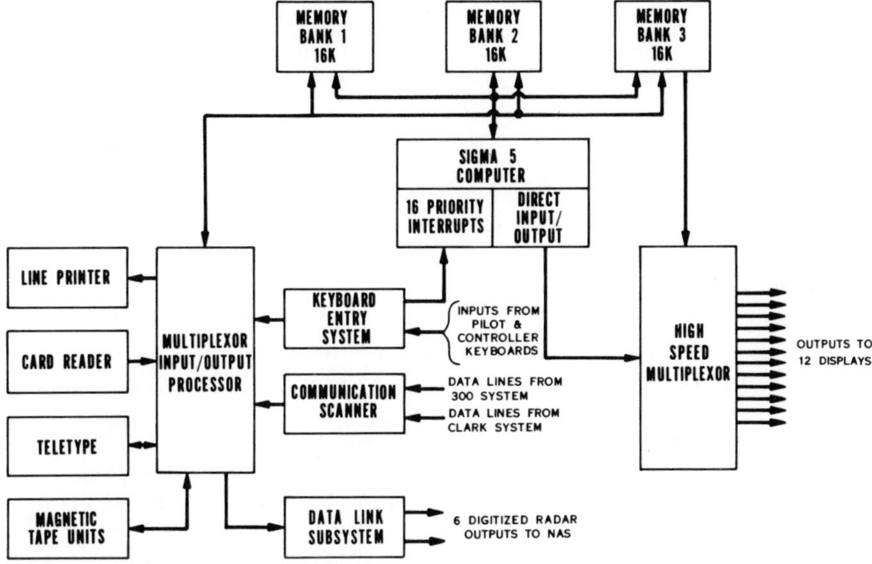

Figure 12-5. Computer System Block Diagram

The pilot displays have a 48-microsecond character write time, of which 24 microseconds are used for positioning and settling and 24 microseconds for write time. These displays (built by Radiation, Inc.) use magnetic deflection for positioning and electrostatic deflection for writing.

The controller displays were built by International Telephone & Telegraph Co. (ITT) and have a maximum character write time of 24 microseconds. These displays use magnetic deflecting for both positioning and writing. The positioning and settling time is a maximum of 14 microseconds, and the write time is a maximum of 10 microseconds. These times can be shorter, depending on the distance the beam must move and on the number of strokes required to write the character.

The hardware has the capability of displaying up to 4095 characters, with the refresh rate being a function of the number and type of characters being written. At a refresh rate of 30 times per second, approximately 1400 characters can be written on the ITT displays and 700 characters on the Radiation Displays. Below this refresh rate flicker becomes noticeable.

The data presented by each display is refreshed from one memory bank of the Sigma 5 Computer. Each character on the display is derived from a computer word coded as follows:

Bits	*Function*
0–5	character code
6	vector unblank
7	blink
8–17	X-deflection
18–27	Y-deflection
28–29	trackball flags
30–31	unused

High-Speed Multiplexor

The High-Speed Multiplexor (HSM) was constructed with commercially available T-Series Logic and is interfaced between one memory bank of the Sigma 5 and 12 digital displays. Its function is to independently transfer data at the maximum write rate of each display.

The main units of the HSM are a static memory, an active memory, an incrementing register, a decrementing register, and control logic. A block diagram is shown in Figure 12-6.

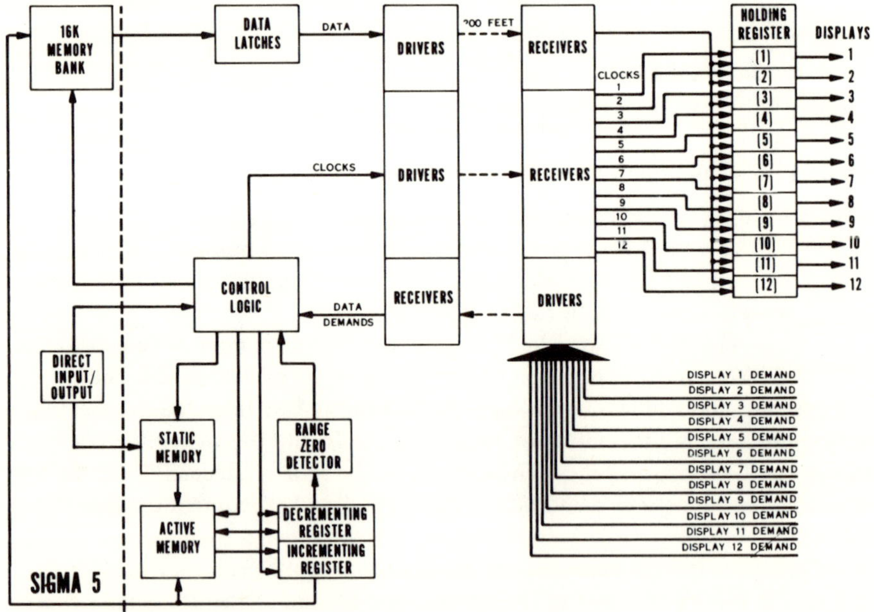

Figure 12-6. Block Diagram of High-Speed Multiplexor

The HSM is fully buffered, with a maximum output rate of 800,000 words per second. Its outputs are asynchronous and variable, depending on the particular display being serviced. Each output channel of the HSM is capable of transferring a variable block of data to a display, starting at any address within the 16,384 word memory bank. The data transfer is a full word and unidirectional. Once initiated by the computer, there is no attention required by the compute module for recycling of the data unless the programmer wants to change either the starting address or the number of words being transferred.

Keyboard Entry System

The Keyboard Entry System consists of 42 controller and 15 pilot keyboards, 14 trackballs, a keyboard multiplexor, a keyboard monitor, an XDS 910 computer, and an Multiplexor Input-Output Processor (MIOP) channel. See Figure 12-7. The keyboards and trackballs serve as input devices which modify data tables while the program is being executed.

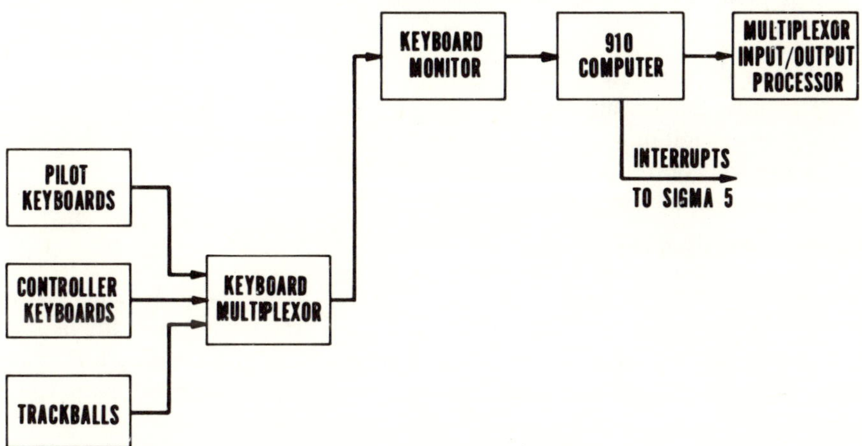

Figure 12-7. Keyboard Entry System Block Diagram

Communications

A Bell No. 300 Switching System and Clark Communications Equipment provide the communication positions utilized in the Digital Simulation Facility. In the present configuration, the No. 300 System supplies eight radio positions which serve as the controller-to-pilot communications and eight interphone lines for controller-to-controller communications. The Clark Communications Equipment supplies 15 radio positions for the pilot-to-controller transmissions.

Activating a push-to-talk key at any position allows for voice transmission and simultaneously enables a unique data line (one per position). On command from the Sigma 5, usually once per second, these data lines are scanned and read into memory through the Communication Scanner and MIOP (Figure 12-5) and used for communication analysis.

Data Link Subsystem

The Data Link Subsystem transmits digitized and formatted data from a channel of the MIOP to any of six Data Receiving Equipment (DRE). The DRE is input equipment to the National Airspace System (NAS) and serves as the receiver for all radar data. The basic data formats transmitted are the 52-bit "Search/Sector" message and the 91-bit "beacon message."

SOFTWARE

The software for the system was developed in a FORTRAN IV framework. The off-line programs were written mainly in FORTRAN and the on-line real-time programs in SYMBOL, the assembly language of the Sigma 5 Computer. Tables were defined as labeled COMMON in FORTRAN BLOCK DATA subprograms so that their addresses would be available to both FORTRAN and SYMBOL programs.

The programs which comprise the software can be grouped into five major areas:

1. Test input preparation programs
2. Executive and system routines
3. Target generation
4. Air traffic control or operational
5. Data collection and analysis

Test Input Preparation Programs

The test inputs preparation programs (TIPP) were developed to generate traffic samples and the associated flight strips, flight plan cards, event tapes, and listings necessary to perform an ATC simulation. They are used for generating test inputs for both the new Digital Simulator and the older analog simulators that are still in use.

The system of programs allows an analyst several options in creating a traffic sample, depending on the needs of the project. First, traffic samples and associated outputs may be obtained by collecting flight strips (controller's records) from an actual field facility to be studied, keypunching the information on data cards, and running them through the TIPP system.

Second, the system also has the capability of reading flight strip information and creating a master file of flight plans on magnetic tape. Traffic samples with given characteristics can then be selected from the master file by requesting given traffic characteristics.

The third and most commonly used way of generating traffic samples is to create synthetic flight plans by statistical generation, using random-number generation techniques in conjunction with traffic mix and route density data. It is also sometimes desirable to include a set of flight plans developed by the analyst so that special situations may be studied. This option has been included. TIPP can be used to prepare a traffic sample by any one of these techniques or by merging flights generated by any combination of these techniques into a final traffic sample. Fix posting times or estimated times of arrival (ETA) are precalculated by the program and printed on the flight strips.

Executive and System Routines

The fast-time and real-time executive routines and routines which facilitate compilations and loading of the system comprise the second group of programs.

Various simulations require different table sizes and memory allocation. In order to make effective use of the memory available, table sizes in COMMON storage must be changed. The many tables used in the simulation system have sizes which are related to a relatively few key parameters such as numbers of aircraft, controllers, fixes, routes, pilots, displays and radars, so a program to change COMMON was developed. Instead of assigning numerical sizes to tables in labeled COMMON, each is defined by the variable name of the key parameter. The program reads the key parameter values from a data card, reads the COMMON statements, substitutes numerical table sizes for names, and writes the BLOCK DATA subroutines on tape. The BLOCK DATA subroutines, with labeled COMMON changed, are then used in the simulation system compilation.

The executive routine is organized in two links, Link 1 and Link 2. Link 1 inputs the initial data values for tables and then is overlaid by Link 2, which is the executive routine for the simulation.

The basic differences in the executive routine for fast-time and real-time operation of the system is that in fast-time the keyboard and display programs are not called and time is advanced when the program cycle is completed rather than waiting for the real-time clock interrupt. A sense switch controls whether the clock interrupt and timing loop is used to control real-time or if it is bypassed to allow the system to run in compressed time.

Target Generation

The target generation group of programs include those programs necessary to operate the facility as a target generator only, supplying simulated radar and beacon information to another system being tested such as the NAS en route system or the ARTS III terminal system. Included are a program to simulate the aircraft flights, a program to simulate the data acquisition system including radar and beacon acquisition and digitizing, a program to format and transmit digitized radar and beacon information to the test system, and the programs necessary to operate the pilot keyboards and displays.

The aircraft flight program updates the aircraft positions each cycle. For the initial real-time simulations, an update interval of one second has proven satisfactory for accuracy and timing. The aircraft flight model includes pilot and aircraft response distributions and navigational distributions for altitude, heading, and velocity variations. The errors are defined as normal distributions with mean and standard deviation being input parameters so that varying navigational accuracies can be simulated.

Aircraft have a predetermined flight path generated by TIPP. This includes their horizontal path traced over the ground, plus the vertical profile. When the system is run in fast time the aircraft will automatically follow this flight path. This is known as the flight-plan mode of operation. In real-time the aircraft are controlled through inputs from the pilot keyboard in response to controller instructions, or in the CAS simulation from inputs received as a result of the airborne CAS computer's ordering evasive maneuvers or restrictions. In real-time, "ghost" or uncontrolled traffic will automatically follow the TIPP route.

The aircraft can perform all the maneuvers as directed by air traffic controllers in real life, for example, standard instrument departures, entering and leaving holding patterns, intersecting and following the Instrument Landing System (ILS) to touchdown, etc.

Future aircraft maneuvers and pilot reports are controlled by storing events. Those which are to occur at a given time are listed in a time event table. Those occurring at a given position are stored in a position event table and are triggered when the aircraft reaches the position. Position events make possible the flight-plan mode of operation. Other maneuvers and reports which are dependent on heading, altitude, velocity, etc., become monitor events with the given argument being monitored until it equals, within limits, the desired value. The event is triggered at this time.

The aircraft flight program contains 1686 instructions and the necessary associated subroutines contain 3654 instructions; it takes an average of one millisecond to update an aircraft position. Thirty-one data words are needed to describe the flight data of each aircraft.

The data acquisition program which simulates radar and beacon returns has been designed for flexibility. Depending on the realism desired for a given project, any combination of the following features may be selected to be simulated:

1. Up to 5 radars and Radar Video Digitizer Processors (RVDP) or Common Digitizers (CD)
2. Radar scan (RPM input)
3. Quantization rationale of RVDP/CD
4. Capacity, delay, and discrimination characteristics of RVDP/CD
5. Probability of detection as a function of range, line of sight, and cone of silence
6. Rho, theta errors of beacon, and primary radar
7. Elevation errors of beacon
8. Beacon garble
9. Target splitting
10. False returns due to weather
11. Loss of targets due to weather
12. Blanking out of storm areas
13. Map outline messages

The data acquisition program contains 530 instructions and requires 700 words for data. Based on 75 aircarft, the program takes 92 milliseconds to execute.

A data link program is included when the facility is being used as a target generator. It provides radar and beacon inputs to another system being tested. The program assembles messages in the format of a Radar Video Digitizer Processor or Common Digitizer for transmission to the Data Receiver Equipment of the test system. Plans call for use of the facility as a target generator in testing both the NAS en route and ARTS III terminal ATC systems.

Figure 12-3 shows a pilot console with three pilot positions sharing one display. Each pilot has his own keyboard and predefined position on the display. Figure 12-8 is a close-up of the pilot display. It shows that the display contains a single digital clock at the top showing time in hours, minutes, and seconds and for each of three pilots an aircraft tabular list, message preview area above the list, and report area below the aircraft list.

Typical pilot input messages are shown above each aircraft list. The message associated with the upper left aircraft list means, "American 119, transfer to frequency 127.4." The one with the upper right means, "Northwest 213, reduce speed to 200 knots," and the one with the lower means, "United 334, turn left to a heading of 249°." Validity checking is performed by the keyboard program. When an error is made, an error message is displayed to the pilot. An aircraft-identification error message which occurred on a previous attempt to enter the message for United 334 is shown (this is on the line numbered "3" on the lower area

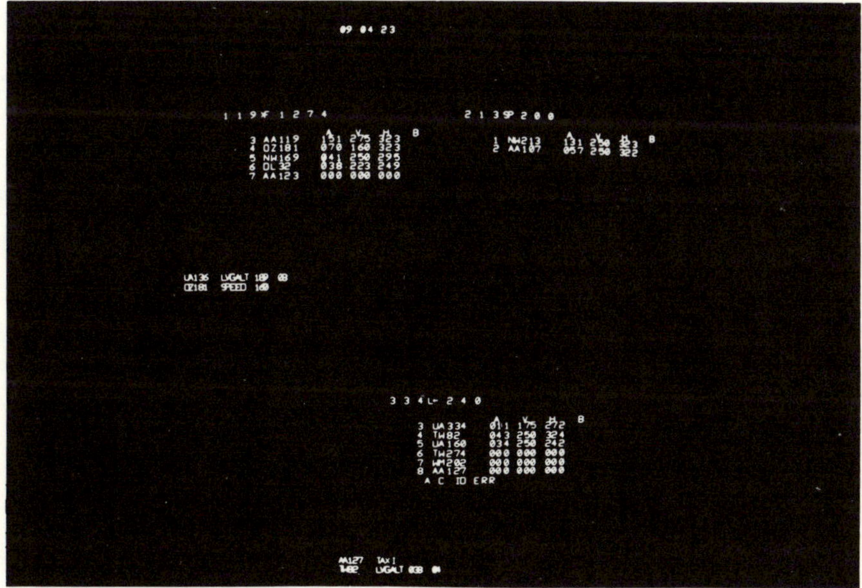

Figure 12-8. Pilot Display

of the display). It still shows because the entry key for the current message has not been depressed signaling the computer to interpret and validate the message.

The basic update of display information is once per second. The only variation to this is in the preview area where, as the keys are depressed, they are displayed on an interrupt basis from the 910 computer. The keys have dual meanings, depending on whether a mode shift key has been depressed. A two-letter code is shown in the preview area representing the key's function. "Backspace" and "clear message" keys are included. After the pilot has edited the previewed message, it is entered by depressing the enter bar.

The program which controls the display was designed to offer flexibility in display content. Information contained in the aircraft tabular list may be varied according to project requirements. For example, in the CAS project, the display which appears in Figure 12-9 shows that the aircraft tabular list includes communication line number, aircraft identification, altitude, velocity, and heading. The CAS status is displayed to the left of the normal tabular list.

It is possible to display aircraft identity only, and when information is requested of the pilot, the computer is interrogated through keyboard entry to provide the answer in the report area. This feature enables data collection of all controller-initiated requests for information from the pilot, which allows for automated communication content analysis by correlating communication contacts with information requests of the computer.

The report area of the display can contain up to four messages at a time. Messages are displayed for 15 seconds in a first-in first-out order. When the first message in the list disappears, other messages move up in the list. A queue of messages to be displayed, beyond the four being displayed, is maintained in a buffer in memory. As space becomes available, additional messages are displayed. Messages appear in abbreviated ATC terminology so that the pilot merely reads the message back to the controller. Certain messages blink to attract extra attention.

In Figure 12-8 the upper left pilot has two messages to report. The first appeared as a result of an aircraft maneuver and states, "United 136 leaving altitude 18,900 feet at 3 minutes past the hour." The second is a reply to a speed request and states, "Ozark 181 at a speed of 160 knots."

For an aircraft entering the system as a departure, two minutes prior to the proposed departure time a TAXI message for the aircraft will appear and blink in the report area. The pilot reports taxiing to the controller. At proposed departure time a TAKE OFF message appears and blinks and the pilot requests clearance to take off. When it is granted, he enters a TAKE OFF message through the keyboard and the aircraft starts its roll on the runway and accelerates to take off speed and then begins its climb. For aircraft entering the system airborne, an ENTRY message appears blinking two minutes prior to entry. At entry time, a POSITION REPORT message appears and the pilot reports position to the controller who must now control the aircraft.

The pilot keyboard program is the largest in the simulation system and contains 5000 instructions. One hundred and ten different pilot messages can be

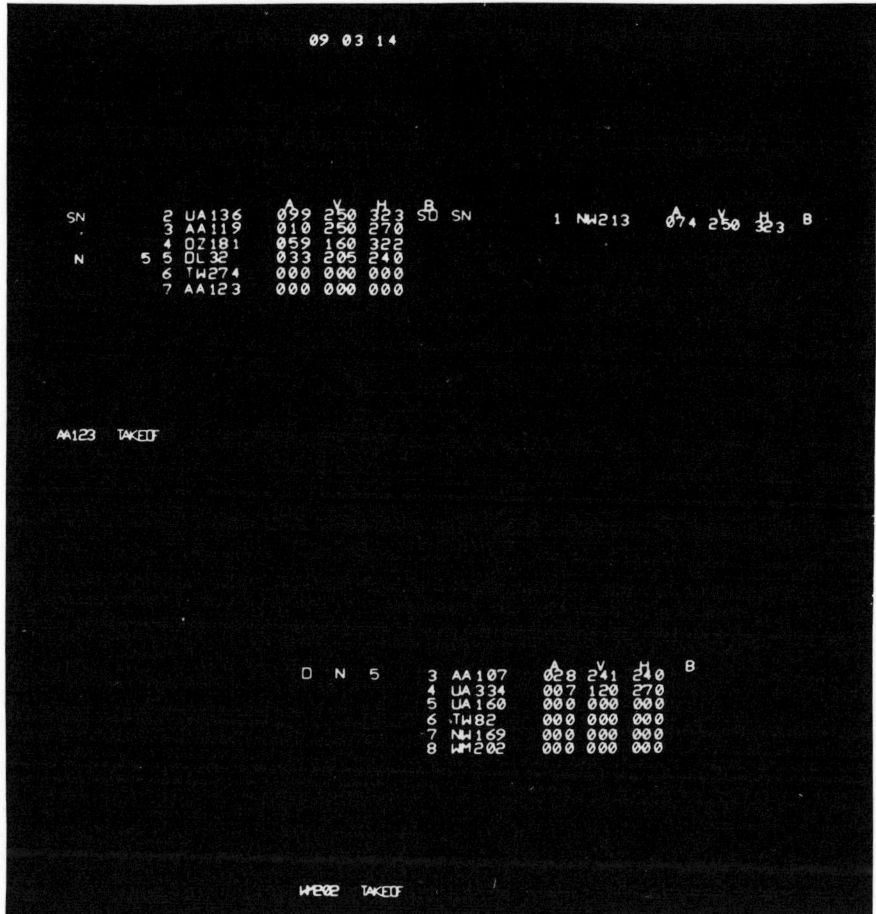

Figure 12-9. Collision Avoidance System (CAS) Simulator–Pilot Display

entered through the keyboard, making it possible for the controller to request the pilot to take almost any action that would occur in real life.

The major categories of pilot functions are as follows:

1. Flight plans and IFR clearances
2. Route assignments
3. Vector instructions
4. Speed adjustments
5. Altitude assignments and changes
6. Departure instructions
7. Holding instructions
8. Departing fixes
9. Approach clearances
10. Reporting instructions

Air Traffic Control and Operational Programs

The Air Traffic Controller's consoles, which are part of the facility, are used to test various ATC systems. Figure 12-4 shows the console configured for two controller positions. Each controller has two keyboards and a trackball for data entry and modification. The keyboard layout has been configured similar to the ARTS III layout.

The information on the controller display is selectable and normally includes a digital clock, a map, controller keyboard message preview area, aircraft symbols, aircraft data tags, and leader lines to the data tags. In some cases, a tabular aircraft list is also provided with its location being controlled through a keyboard entry. An example of information displayed to the controller is shown in Figure 12-10.

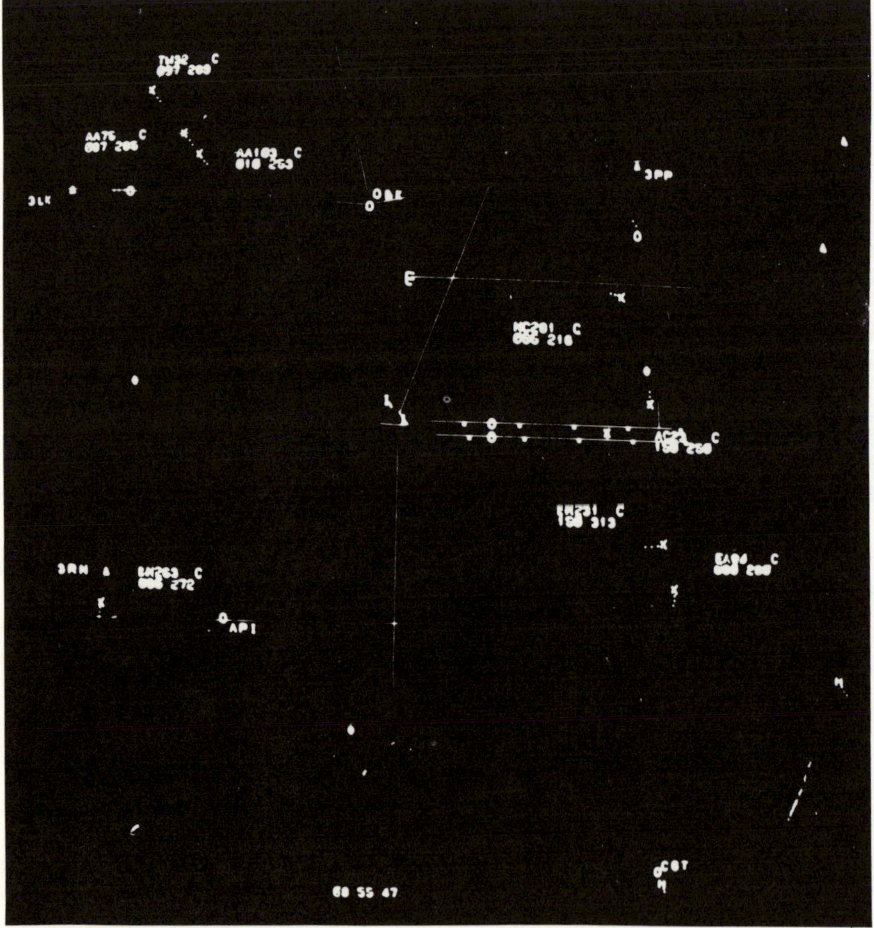

Figure 12-10. Controller Display

The program which generates this display contains 1000 instructions and takes 20 milliseconds per display when generating displays as shown. Basic update rate for the display in present projects is once per second. When radar scan is being simulated, aircraft position symbols and tags become the exception and are updated only if they are scanned by the radar during the second.

Information for the map is read in by LINK 1 and stored in a memory area reserved for map data. In order to reduce cluttter, the map normally contains only the essential information from an aeronautical chart required to control traffic. The display map in Figure 12-10 can be compared to the detailed aeronautical chart (Figure 12-11) which is located directly above the display for reference.

Several options are available for displaying the aircraft position symbol. If the present ATC system is being simulated, the program simulates target positions by a series of dots to represent the radar and beacon broad band image that

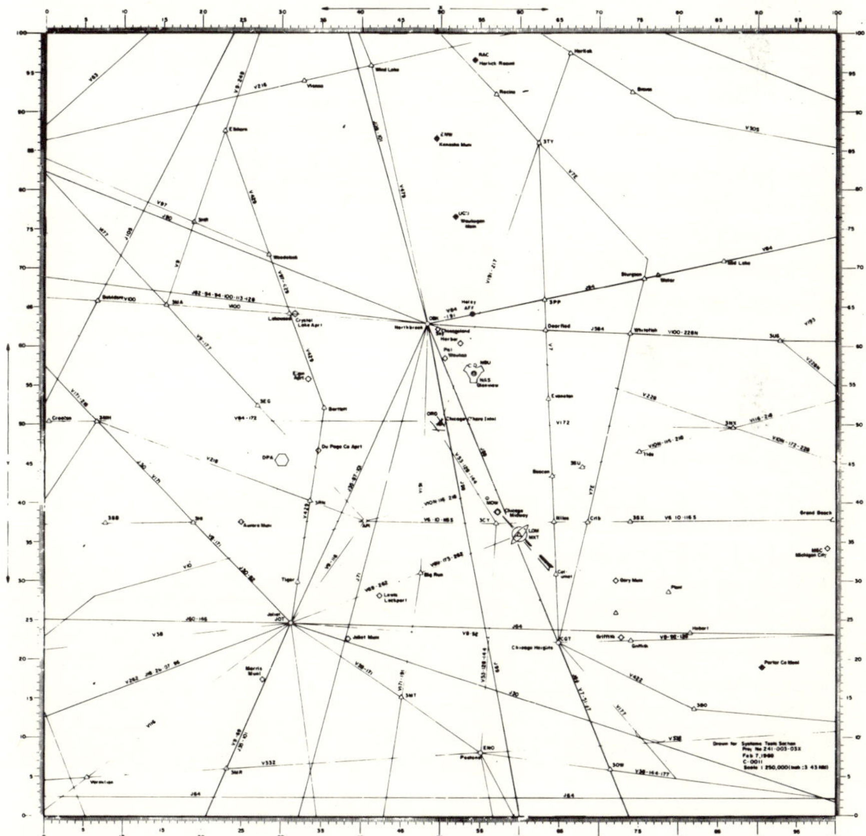

Figure 12-11. Aeronautical Chart

would be seen on a radar scope. Positional information from several previous scans is shown with dots gradually being attenuated to simulate the decaying intensity in the trail.

If a digital system is being simulated, as in the CAS and ARTS III projects, the target positions displayed are those resulting as output from a tracking program. Discrete symbols are used to display the aircraft under control of a given controller. In Figure 12-10 the symbol "X" indicates aircraft under control of this position, while other symbols, for example "0," indicate aircraft being controlled by another controller. Dots are displayed showing the the three previous track positions of the aircraft thus providing trail information to the controller.

Aircraft alphanumeric tags can also be provided to include information such as aircraft identification, beacon code, assigned altitude, ground speed, and mode C (beacon encoded) altitude. The tags are connected to the symbol by a leader line and may be repositioned by a keyboard entry to avoid clutter and overwriting. Combinations of eight leader lengths and eight angles are available for repositioning the tags.

Functions currently available to the controller through keyboard entry are similar to those proposed for the ARTS III system and pertain mainly to tracking, hand-offs, and control of the display. These are:

1. Initiate track
2. Drop track
3. Suspend track
4. Track follow
5. Missed approach
6. Track reposition
7. Initiate handoff
8. Recall handoff
9. Acknowledge handoff
10. Change offset direction
11. Change offset distance
12. Altitude assignment
13. Beacon code assignment
14. Transfer track
15. Recall track
16. Track readout
17. Erase track readout
18. Code readout
19. Erase code readout
20. Display next code
21. Erase next code
22. Quick look
23. Erase quick look

24. Display mark
25. Erase display mark
26. Change tabular list coordinates
27. Change preview coordinates
28. Inhibit controls
29. Display controls

Four ways of referring to an aircraft are available for functions requiring aircraft identification—positioning the trackball symbol over the aircraft symbol or by entering the aircraft identification, track number, or discrete beacon code through the keyboard.

Two radar and beacon-tracking programs have been written for the system. The first, known as the "perfect tracker," assumes perfect correlation. With this program, tag switching and lost tracks do not occur unless the results are deliberately degraded by included probabilities for switched and lost tracks. Positional variations are generated by applying errors to the actual aircraft positions generated in the aircraft flight simulation routine. The second is the ARTS III tracking program and has been written for projects requiring more realism in tracking. Lost tracks, tag switching, and position variation occur as a function of the simulated radar and beacon inputs to the program.

CAS Logic Program

In the Collision Avoidance System project, the final operational program is the CAS logic program which simulates the airborne computer of each aircraft. When a CAS condition is detected, an interface program automatically sets status bits and table values which cause the aircraft flight simulation routine to make the aircraft automatically respond to the restriction or maneuver and causes the CAS display program to yield the proper indications to the simulator pilot. Further discussion of the CAS model is contained in the section, "Projects of the Facility."

Data Collection and Analysis

Data collection for the simulations is performed on a per-cycle basis with all data reduction and analysis being performed off-line. Due to the vast quantity of data which must be collected, the data for a given cycle is recorded in one large record rather than several smaller records, reducing both write time and the amount of tape used.

Both magnetic tape drives are used for data collection in a buffered operation. One is used for data collection while the other is being rewound and a new tape mounted. A data tape is written approximately every 30 minues in the CAS and ARTS III projects.

Data reduction and analysis is performed off-line and is somewhat cumbersome, due to having only two tape drives. The data reduction program reads the first record on tape, which contains the write commands used to generate the tape. These commands are then modified to be read commands and used to read the data tapes. Saving the I/O commands eliminates confusion in setting up the input to the data reduction system.

The data reduction programs can provide:

1. Test input parameter listing
2. Aircraft position history listing
3. Aircraft delay listing
4. Holding listing at fixes
5. Communication listing and summary
6. Pilot data entry listing and summary
7. Controller data entry listing and summary
8. Controller activity analysis
9. Radar and tracking data listing
10. Conflict listing and summary
11. CAS alarm listing and summary
12. Operations summary
13. Fix activity summary
14. Plots of aircraft positions plus CAS alarm status

Programs to perform various statistical analyses on selected measures are also available.

FEATURES OF DIGITAL SIMULATION

The advantages of the digital simulation over the old analog facility include the standard considerations of accuracy and repeatability of experiments. In addition, digital simulation affords a general-purpose and flexible tool that is easy to use and can easily be changed to meet project needs. The laboratory can be reconfigured in 15 minutes to run another project and in some cases, if projects do not demand the full capacity of the system, more than one project can be run at a time.

The digital approach now allows for a greater number of aircraft, reduced operating cost per target hour, and less overall floor space requirements. The cost per target hour in the present projects is one-fifth the cost per target hour in the old analog facility. Floor space requirements per target are about one-tenth that required using the old target generator.

Precise control of error parameters is an important aspect in modeling subsystems, which makes it possible to perform sensitivity studies. Accuracies of subsystems such as navigation or data acquisition can be varied systematically to ascertain the effects on the ATC system and to point out areas where a concentrated effort for improvement is worthwhile.

The fact that the model may be run in either fast or real time affords a more powerful tool for investigation. Initial studies cna be run in fast time, trying many approaches quickly and inexpensively without requiring controllers, pilots, and a complete laboratory configuration. Those approaches that show promise can then be investigated and verified with real-time simulations.

Another advantage of the digital system is that it affords an automatic means of obtaining a complete controller workload record. Keeping track of the controller's data entry functions makes it possible to measure his data entry activity. The number of aircraft under his control can be deduced by analyzing the hand-off information.

The method of communications analysis also assists in developing controller workload information. Controllers and pilots have a "push to talk" button which activates signals indicating the communication line is in use. The communications data can be saved and analyzed to determine the number and length of communication contacts. If the pilot is forced to request all flight information from the computer, it is then possible to correlate message content to the communication contact, thus providing automatic communication analysis without having to listen to voice tapes.

Use of the digital computer for target generation in ATC simulations allows the additional capacity to be used to simulate the computer functions of future automated ATC systems. The surplus capacity can also be used to simulate various airborne computer systems such as CAS or proximity warning indicators.

PROJECT OF THE FACILITY

CAS Simulation

As previously mentioned, evaluation of the interaction between the ATC system and the airborne Collision Avoidance System was the first project to use the new Digital Simulation Facility. It is also the most complex simulation study to be attempted by the FAA because so many different subsystems must be modeled. The purpose of the study is to determine the interaction and, if necessary, recommend revisions to ATC procedures or CAS logic so as to enhance system compatibility. In the first series of simulation runs, all flights are CAS equipped. The objective is to gain insight into the frequency-of-occurrence of the several CAS conditions, where they occur in the environment, and the effect their occurrence has on the air traffic flow. Subsequent testing will be addressed to investigating certain ATC/CAS effects when only part of the flights are CAS equipped.

CAS is a cooperative airborne system utilizing time-frequency techniques to exchange range, range rate, and altitude information. It is cooperative in that protection is offered only from other CAS equipped aircraft. A three-second time period (epoch) is divided into 2000 time slots, each of 1500 microseconds duration. Each aircraft assumes a previously unoccupied time slot and transmits at this time each epoch. Fifteen microseconds after the start of the time slot a 200-microsecond doppler burst is transmitted. Receiving aircraft evaluate the time of signal reception to get a range measurement. The doppler frequency shift is used to derive range rate. Aircraft altitutude is transmitted by positioning a pulse in the 400-724 microsecond band of the time slot.

The CAS makes use of "tau zones" (tau equals range divided by range rate), the evaluator's altitude and altitude rate, and the altitude of the intruder in assessing the situation. Figure 12-12 indicates how tau zones are determined. The maneuvers and restrictions shown in the matrix (Figure 12-13) result when a pair of aircraft fall in the corresponding tau zones and altitude bands.

The CAS status portion of the pilot display conveys to the simulator pilot the information which in real life would be available to the pilot. In the aircraft the display of CAS conditions is on the vertical speed indicator, as shown in Figure 12-14. Lights on the indicator come on to indicate to the pilot the vertical velocity restrictions of 2000 fpm 1000 fpm, or 500 fpm; or maneuvers of of climb, dive, level off, hold altitude, or do not turn.

In simulation, when a CAS condition is found which affects the aircraft's flight path, a blinking symbol is displayed to the pilot notifying him to report the condition to the controller. The pilot then enters a message that the alarm has been reported and the symbol stops blinking. If the alarm does not affect the flight path, the symbol is steady and the alarm need not be reported. When in the real world the light would disappear in the cockpit, the simulated display

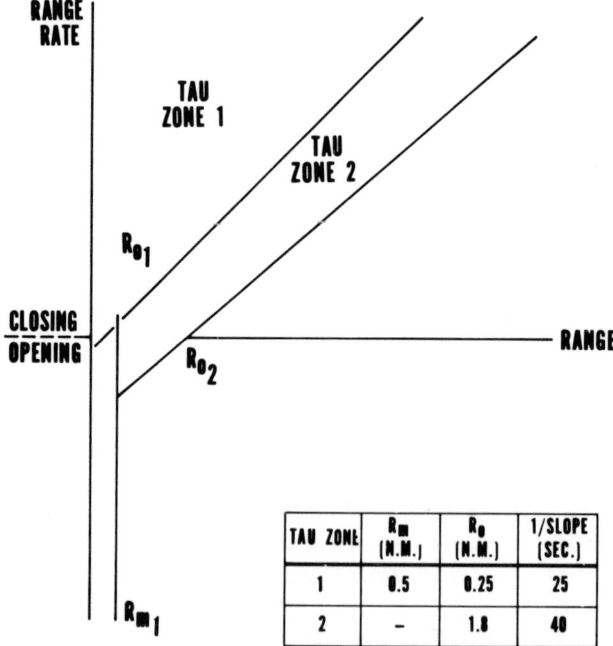

TAU ZONE	R_m (N.M.)	R_o (N.M.)	1/SLOPE (SEC.)
1	0.5	0.25	25
2	-	1.8	40

Figure 12-12. Threat Evaluation Range and Range Data

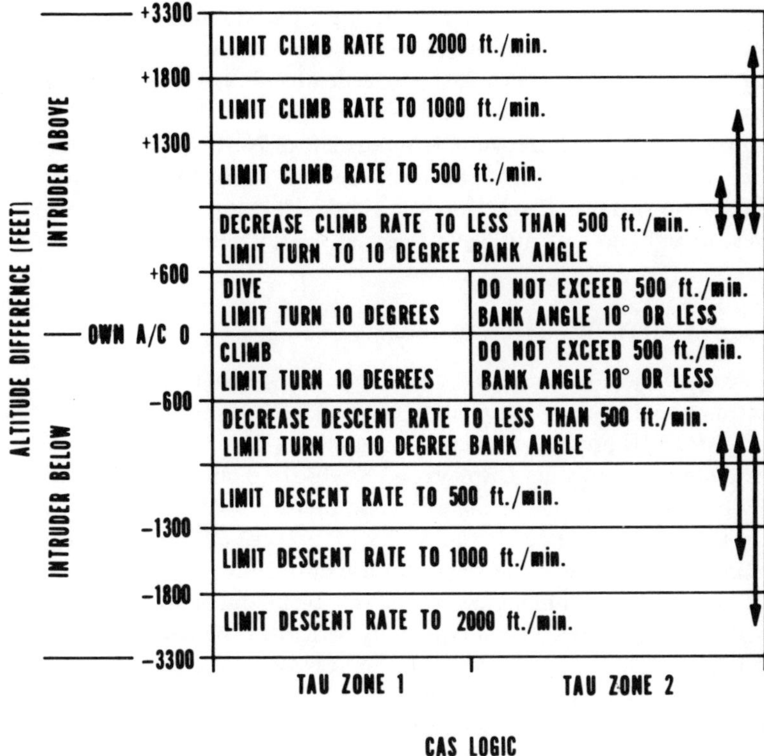

Figure 12-13. Threat Evaluation Matrix

precedes the symbol with an S and blinks both the S and the symbol to indicate to the pilot that the light has gone out. The pilot then reports this information to the controller and enters a message indicating to the computer that he has

Figure 12-14. Collision Avoidance Systems Cockpit Display

done so. The symbol then disappears from the CAS pilot display area. Vertical speed limitations of 2000 fpm and 1000 fpm do not cause blinking. When vertical restrictions disappear, they are not preceded by an S, but merely disappear because the pilot is not expected to report.

In Figure 12-9, SD and SN symbols appear left of Northwest 213, indicating that the "dive" and "no turn" lights in the cockpit would have gone out. Delta 32 is indicating "no turn" and "500 fpm climb rate" restrictions. American 107 indicates "dive," "do not turn," and "restrict vertical descent to 500 fpm."

Validation of ARTS III Functional Levels

The second project running on the facility is a cost-benefit study of the various functional levels of automation in the ARTS III terminal automation program. ARTS III provides beacon and radar tracking plus the controller functions listed in the Controller Displays and Keyboard section. The controller consoles in the facility and the Sigma 5 computer are used to simulate the stages of automation planned in the ARTS III terminal automation program.

The simulation facility is also slated for use in the second phase of this project in developing automated metering and spacing techniques and other automated ATC functions which will ultimately be part of the ARTS system. Later, when an actual ARTS III system is installed at NAFEC as a system support facility (where new systems and features are tested), the Digital Simulation Facility will be used as a target generator to simulate radar and beacon information in support of ARTS III system testing.

National Airspace System (NAS) Test Support

The target generator capability of the facility is also scheduled to provide digitized radar and beacon information as input to the support facility for NAS, the enroute ATC system being installed at 21 ATC Centers in the country. NAS relieves the controller of much of the clerical functions by providing flight plan data processing and by transferring data on flights automatically between facilities. ETA's and altitude information are calculated by the computer and flight strips are automatically printed. Data eventually will be transferred not only between ATC Centers but also to air terminals, when both NAS and ARTS III are operational. NAS also provides for radar and beacon tracking.

Communication Switching

Plans call for providing targets to a NAS configuration to test a new communications switching system that allows an aircraft to remain on the same frequency for an entire flight. The communication switching system automatically selects the proper frequency for the controler.

In-Service Improvement Projects

In addition to supporting the major automation efforts, the facility is scheduled to be used for in-service improvement projects. These are projects which are scheduled to support studies of problems of a more immediate variety that face facilities within the ATC system. The effects on ATC of relocating navigational aids, new routes, multiple runway configurations, noise abatement procedures, etc., are examples of problems in this category.

Airport Simulations

Another important aspect of improving air traffic operations is in improving the surface movement of aircraft at the airport. The Digital Simulation Facility is slated to play an important role in such airport studies. The aircraft characteristics values can be changed so that aircraft taxiing and other surface vehicular movement can be simulated.

For the coming year, 13 different simulation projects have been scheduled on the new facility, with the demand for future years appearing even greater.

FACILITY EXPANSION AND IMPROVEMENT

The development of the Digital Simulation Facility was planned as a three-phase program because of economic considerations and the need to expedite simulation support for ATC system studies before the total system could be procured. The intent of Phase I was to procure the equipment which would provide the most immediate simulation capability for the limited funds available. Phases Two and Three will allow for expansion of the system to accommodate larger projects resulting from increasing demands of the FAA technical programs.

Phase Two will include the addition of 24 display terminals to be used as individual pilot consoles. These terminals house a cathode ray tube for readout, a keyboard for data entry, and memory for data refresh.

The addition of the 24 pilot consoles will release the present pilot consoles for use as controller consoles. The consoles released along with the spares on hand will exceed the capacity of the present system for memory and data transfer. Therefore, an additional 16K memory bank and another High-Speed Multiplexor will be added to the system.

Other items that will be introduced to the system during Phase Two include two nine-track magnetic tape units, a seven-track magnetic tape unit, and a Rapid Access Disc (RAD). The nine-track tape units will enhance the data collection and reduction capabilities of the system because fewer passes will be required on the data tapes and output listings will be produced in a more orderly sequence. The seven-track tape unit will allow adaptation data and TIPP flight plans to be entered more efficiently than by the present use of punched cards. The RAD will be useful in data reduction as well as in real-time simulation in which it will be used to store infrequently used tables and programs, thereby freeing core for other uses.

The RAD will make available more powerful system programs and better assemblers and compilers, and will make it possible to add remote terminals to the system.

At the completion of Phase Two, the total system will consist of 24 individual pilot displays and 16 controller displays with a capacity for simulating 240 simultaneously controlled aircraft. The third phase of development will include the purchase of an additional 24 pilot terminals and eight alphanumeric digital displays, bringing the total system capacity to the planned 480 controlled targets. Another Central Processing Unit and two additional 16K memory banks will also be installed. This addition will permit simultaneous operation of ATC simulation and flight simulation.

A Radar/Beacon Simulator will complete Phase Three of the expansion. This subsystem will provide a broadband environment through the conversion of digitally generated targets.

The FAA expects that the present facility and the two add-on phases will allow it to perform the systems studies necessary to develop ATC systems to meet the future demands of air transportation for years to come.

ACKNOWLEDGMENTS

The authors wish to acknowledge the contributions of the many individuals at NAFEC involved in the implementation of the Digital Simulation Facility; in particular, Mr. Arthur G. Halverson for his continuing effort in recommending the establishment of the facility and his contributions to it, and Mr. John Zappacosta who as Chairman of the Digital Simulation Implementation Task Group was responsible for managing the system development.

PART 7

NUMERICAL CONTROL SOCIETY

Princeton, New Jersey

Three papers selected by the Numerical Control Society as the best papers submitted during 1971:

13
Developments in DNC

by *Edward E. Kirkham*

DEFINITIONS

As in any new field, each new word has been used in a variety of contexts. In this paper, the following table of acronyms and definitions will be used.

CAM: Computer Assisted Manufacture. The application of computers to any aspect of the manufacturing process. This term includes DNC.

DNC: Direct Numerical Control. The application of computers to multiple numerically-controlled manufacturing machines.

NC: Numerical Control. The application of electronics to receive tape data and cause a single machine to complete a series of operations.

SWC: Soft-Wired Control. The application of a computer to a single machine to perform NC functions.

BTR: Behind the Tape Reader. A general-purpose device that permits a computer to feed EIA tape data directly to a controller (NC or SWC).

SYSTEM PLANNING

It is unrealistic to hope that all computer applications to manufacturing processes (CAM) can be dealt with here. Instead, attention will be limited to DNC, and even then it will be necessary to brush lightly over the uncontroversial fact that the computer applied to numerically controlled machine tools contributes in a very positive way to the efficiency of the manufacturing processes; there will be a tremendous payoff to each user who installs the necessary equipment and refines the software to fit his individual requirements. He can then expand his knowledge of those factors which influence productivity so that a regenerative improvement cycle is initiated.

Editor's Note: From *NC; 1971: The Opening Door to Productivity and Profit* (1971). Reprinted by permission of the publisher, Numerical Control Society, Princeton, N. J., and the author.

COMPONENTS OF COMPUTERIZED MANUFACTURING

Following is a discussion of several components of a computerized manufacturing system.

DNC Functions

The DNC computer can be used in many, many ways; here are a few:

1. To provide a library of machine language tape data.
2. To provide a file of tape data in source language.
3. To provide a way of editing tape programs (machine or source) so that they may be readily optimized during proveout.
4. To monitor machine operation and keep a utilization log.
5. To provide a scheduled maintenance reminder and record those procedures as they are performed.
6. To provide a terminal whereby a large APT computer can be used to convert source files to machine language.
7. To eliminate tape and tape reader maintenance.

NC Functions

Here are some of the features that a numerical controller needs:

1. A tape reader.
2. An operator's control station.
3. An interpolator.
4. Position servo loops.
5. Velocity servo loops with compensation.
6. Special cycle control logic (magnetics).
7. An executive controller for all of the above.
8. Power amplifiers for servo and logic outputs.
9. Interfaces for limit switches and pushbuttons.
10. Transducer.

Soft-Wired Controller

The first seven of the above functions are candidates for implementation by a computer. The combination of a computer, software, power amplifiers, and interfaces is called a soft-wired controller, or SWC. This brings the economy and versatility of the computer to bear on the entire NC. The downward spiral in computer prices had made this approach attractive; several SWC's are now in field use.

It has been shown that SWC provides many NC options conveniently. It is attractive to the machine tool builder and the control builder because it permits a high degree of control hardware standardization. Control inventory can be reduced, since any control can be fitted to any machine and provide any set of options.

The evaluation of such control is relatively easy because each feature can be compared in cost and performance with its hard-wired counterpart. Certainly the SWC will win easily today for the most sophisticated controls having the greatest number of options. As computer costs continue to fall, the number of economic applications will increase.

DNC, NC, and SWC Combined

If the computer simply replaces the NC unit on each machine (SWC), what is to be the role of the DNC computer? In order to provide all the good services listed in the previous section on DNC Functions, a common data base must be made available to all people and machine controllers. A DNC minicomputer is installed to deliver data to the manufacturing area from a mass storage. Any NC machine may be supplied using an adapter connected in place of the tape reader. The interface equipment for this purpose is called a BTR since it couples to the controller "behind the tape reader." One type of BTR, once satisfactorily designed, is useful for all machine tools that use the same number of tape levels. EIA Standards for 8-level tapes are universally followed. Thus, the BTR can be very highly standardized needing only versatility in the signal levels delivered by it. It can interface all NC machines of any make or age, be they hard-wired or soft-wired.

Reduced Tape Reader Maintenance

DNC eliminates the routine use of the tape reader and its attendant maintenance problems. In some applications, this factor is of importance; but the dollar justification of a DNC computer cannot be completed on this basis alone. One must look to other advantages.

Tape Editing

In the past, when punched tapes were used, the initial proveout at the machine resulted in a list of modifications to be made in the tape. The replacement tape would be produced one to three days later, at which time the alterations would be tested on the machine. Meanwhile, the machine setup was removed and time lost in a repeated setting up for the next proveout. Also the programmer and machine operator must then reacquaint themselves with the original problems (and successes) so that a new evaluation of the tape program may be made.

Several repetitions of this long cycle result in a "final" tape that will make the part; but ultimate machining efficiency is not obtained. Only a limited number of trials of feedrates have been made.

The installation of a CRT (cathode ray tube) terminal at the machine permits rapid changes to the parts program right in the magnetic disc library. Such changes may be immediately tested and rerevised. The gains in efficiency of a medium-sized NC installation brought about by this improved optimizing process will readily justify the DNC installation. NC machine output is improved at least 20 percent.

ADVANTAGES OF MULTIPLE COMPUTERS

The use of a single, central computer to do all the logic and arithmetic for any given company is assumed by many to be the only possibility. Using several minicomputers is now a more satisfactory arrangement. What led to this new conclusion?

Single-Computer Prejudice

In data processing, the use of a single large computer has been promoted in preference to several smaller units. One reason given is that a single data base is desirable; but let us separate the processing unit from the mass storage. Then the question is deeply rooted in semantics.

Computer manufacturers in the early days stated quite accurately that the most expensive part of a computer was that portion used for arithmetic, logic, and control. This processing unit was so expensive that it was commonly assumed that no company could afford to have more than one such unit. Further, it would have sufficient speed to accommodate all the processing requirements of any company. For this reason, that device was called a *central* processing unit and dubbed with the abbreviation CPU. The abbreviation remains with us today, and the assumption that there can be only one *central* processing unit is implied by it.

What are the consequences of that assumption? A large operating system is resident in the computer to time-share the CPU among many programs, memories, and input/output devices. A large computer may have one-third of its core and processing time devoted to its own operating system. In addition, a staff of people hover nearby to maintain the operating system.

New Axioms

Now, however, the basic assumptions may be challenged. A processing unit is now available for a very few dollars, having plenty of speed to do whatever is required in the way of control, logic, or arithmetic. These devices are so plentiful that it is more economical to apply one to each requirement than to provide the necessary operating system to time-share many tasks to one CPU.

The use of a minicomputer at each machine to replace the hard-wired NC has already been discussed and justified.

The DNC computer has several requirements. It needs for each machine:

1. Time to deliver data
2. Room for temporary data storage
3. A sufficient number of connecting wires

Any one or all of these needs may become a limitation if a sufficient number of machines is connected. The time, storage, and connections can all be greatly expanded by the use of several DNC computers, each connected to a single supervisory computer. These individual DNC computers are then called satellite computers.

Data received by a satellite can be verified and retransmissions requested if necessary; data is buffered and fanned out to the various machines. The satellite greatly reduces the number of times the central supervisory computer must be interrupted since it buffers larger data strings for each machine and then pays them out as the machines require.

Gains Provided by Multi-Computer Technique

Here are the features provided by this multi-computer approach:

1. All possible computer applications to the control of an individual machine can be achieved by the SWC.
2. Any NC or SWC machine can be connected to the NC system, regardless of make or age, via a BTR.
3. Long, high-speed transmission lines can be time-shared among several machine tools, saving cable installation cost.
4. The BTR is actually a two-way device so that automatic data acquisition is possible.
5. Each satellite has bulk memory and can operate its battery of machines independently of the complete DNC system, maintaining continuity of operation.
6. A company can start small applying, progressively, NC, SWC, SATELLITE, and then complete DNC.
7. Any machine may be operated independently by reconnecting its tape reader; it is available for transfer or sale to another plant.
8. Added costs for interfacing and debugging extra control-machine combinations especially for DNC are avoided.
9. Each computer application may be justified on its own merit.
10. Unlimited vertical and/or horizontal integration may be implemented at will.
11. Conventional computer interfaces exist to couple CRT's to the system for shop floor control.

CONCLUSION

It is hoped that this analysis of existing DNC systems will stimulate constructive thought and lead to the revelation of pertinent facts which will be the basis for a winning second generation of DNC.

14
Computer-Aided Manufacturing for the 70's

by *John B. Peterson*

As we enter the 1970's, we are entering the era of computer-aided manufacturing.

Looking back to the 1950's, there was a manufacturing emphasis placed on high-production, low-flexibility transfer lines that were intended to solve the manufacturing manager's problems. It became quite evident that these systems could only be applied to automotive-type industries where the enormous quantities of a particular part could justify the investment in the system.

The problem with transfer lines, of course, was the fact that they did not provide flexibility. Changeover time from one part to another–if indeed possible at all–could take anywhere from 24 to 40 hours or more.

The aerospace industry, with the advent of the jet aircraft shortly after World War II, developed a need for machining complex parts in very, very low production quantities.

The government supported the development of a new concept of machine control, which resulted in the emphasis in manufacturing on numerical control during the 1960's.

The numerically controlled machining center has provided the ability to produce low quantities of parts economically. Now, entering the 1970's, there is a need for systems which expand capability to produce low quantities of parts on a random basis, and a need to expand these capabilities into medium-quantity lot sizes.

COMPUTER-AIDED MANUFACTURING

It appears certain at this point that computer-aided manufacturing will approach a solution to this manufacturing problem. Computer-aided manufacturing will effect not only the fabrication area of the manufacturing facility, but also production planning, production control, material management, and quality control.

Probably the production area has been affected more up to this time than the other areas. It is estimated, however, that manufacturing is only using 25 percent of the computer application potential at this time. Two of the main reasons for

Editors Note: From *Management Guide to NC* (1971). Reprinted by permission of the publisher, Numerical Control Society, Princeton, N.J., and the author.

greater use of the computer in the manufacturing facility are the continually reduced costs of the computer hardware and the fact that technology is giving us more and more reliable hardware.

It has been stated that the cost per gate is 10 percent of what it was five years ago, while the speed of the computer has been increased by a factor of 10 in the past 10 years. One of the necessary elements enabling the computer-aided manufacturing concept to become a reality has been the advent of direct computer control of the machine tools themselves.

There are basically six reasons which have been identified for the development of DNC. All of these are aimed at improving the operating efficiency of the system.

- First, the tape input medium itself has been eliminated.
- The DNC systems provide a by-product in the form of management reports.
- Use of the computer allows conversational reprogramming capabilities.
- Elimination of the tape reader, along with integrated circuit hardware, increases reliability.
- Lower costs can be expected in the initial system as well as operationally.
- Software modifications can be added to the system.

To present a better understanding of DNC, take a closer look at one of the operating systems.

THE OMNICONTROL SYSTEM

The OMNICONTROL System was initially designed to operate from the IBM 360 family of computers. The minimum requirements specified a Model 30 with 64K, which would be capable of handling up to 16 machine tools.

The maximum technically feasible arrangement would require an IBM 360 Model 50 capable of controlling up to 256 machine tools. The choice to go to the IBM computer was partly based on the fact that IBM manufactures some 70 percent of the computers on the market today.

Also, the basic concept was also to use the existing computer in the user's facility to run the machine tools, so as not to encumber the system with unnecessary costs.

Since the design of the system permits operation of a full complement of machines while only using 5 percent of the throughput capability of the computer, this means that 95 percent of the computer's throughput can still be used for data processing work such as payroll, inventory, machine scheduling, etc. Since introduction of the system almost three years ago, most computer facilities have been administered by accounting-oriented data processing people who do not have an appreciation for manufacturing's problems.

Therefore, the same OMNICONTROL System has been made available on a dedicated computer, the PDP-11, manufactured by Digital Equipment Corporation.

The dedicated system provides the same capabilities, except that additional data processing work cannot be accomplished. On the IBM 360 system, a disk drive unit and disk pack storage capability for the computer program library are required, as well as the parts program library.

The same Model 2311 disk pack which contains the Disk Operating System (DOS) for the computer can also provide storage for approximately 600 parts programs—each of which would be the equivalent of 600 feet of tape.

A second disk drive could provide capacity for an additional 1,000 parts programs.

On the in-house computer system, the model 2314 disk drive is used, which is capable of storing approximately four times the amount of data of the 2311.

It is important to note that sufficient parts program storage can be a major problem in a DNC system, since one must have availability to any one of his parts programs on demand.

The OMNICONTROL System makes use of either the SPLIT programming language or APT, in which the parts programs are stored in source language and CL data, respectively.

Storing the information in the form of machine language, that is, EIA formatted data, would require that the storage capacity be increased by a factor of 10 or more to accommodate the same quantity of parts programs. The conventional NC tape control unit, as known today, has been eliminated and replaced by two complements of boards—one of which resides in the computer room itself in specially provided cabinets; the other set is contained in a small enclosure at the machine tool.

These units provide the interpolating function and are capable of transmitting 1,000,000 data points per minute, per axis, to the machine tool. This equals being capable of driving any number of axes at 1,000 inches per minute at .0001 resolution.

The unit also has the capability of handling up to 96 auxiliary commands as well as up to 64 machine sense bytes. The latter capability provides capacity for the future addition of adaptive control units.

The control will be capable of accepting information from transducers and either feeding the information directly into the servo loop or back to the computer to bias succeeding blocks of information being transmitted to the machine tool.

Also resident in the computer room environment is a multiplexer control unit which is capable of controlling up to 42 terminal devices. In the OMNICONTROL System, cathode ray tubes (CRT Display Units) are used for the communication function with the computer itself. A CRT provides conversational reprogramming capabilities in either the SPLIT or APT programming language. The significance of this is that the program can be changed or corrected, essentially instantaneously, at the machine tool, rather than having to wait for a new tape to be produced by flexowriter or computer—which may involve hours or even days in some facilities.

Since the program can be altered at the machine tool the first time a part is run, the program is optimized by correcting feeds and speeds and removing false moves so that the program will run in the least possible time.

Optimizing the parts programs via the CRT has resulted in 20 to 50 percent reductions in run time over programs previously considered acceptable on punched tape.

The OMNICONTROL System, as was pointed out earlier, operates in the source language of SPLIT or in the CL data level of APT to provide true reprogramming capabilities, as opposed to editing EIA coded machine language. The CRT is programmed also to provide the capability of calling for a printed manuscript or punched tape for operation on other machine tools not equipped with DNC as the programmer desires.

On-line diagnostic programs are also available for viewing on the CRT by the maintenance personnel. The particular problem area is identified by the maintenance man from the list provided on the CRT; through a series of questions posed by the program and responses from the maintenance man, the CRT leads him down the logical path and pinpoints the particular component which requires replacement.

Other programs illustrate the set-up procedures for servo drives and spindle speeds.

At the present time, most of the diagnostic programs are related to the OMNICONTROL System hardware itself. However, these can easily be expanded to incorporate the hardware for any particular machine tool. Direct numerical control of machine tools is only one of the necessary elements for the computer-aided manufacturing facility, but it is a very important one and the technology is available today.

PROGRAMS IN USE

At the 1970 NMTBA show in Chicago, at least six operating systems were shown.

Sundstrand presently has 14 systems operating in production environments. These systems involve some 70 to 80 machine tools. Some of these machines have been running under DNC for as long as three years. Basically, the CRT used as a part of the DNC system is a terminal device attached to the computer. To illustrate some of its further potential in the computer-aided manufacturing facility, here are some of the programs which are presently being displayed in the Sundstrand installation.

There are approximately 14 CRT's in various areas of the plant, such as the production control department, repair parts order department, marketing department, and assembly areas. They are capable of interrogating 22 different files.

Not all CRT's are programmed to receive information from each of these files, but, as a security measure, can only view those files which would be of interest to the particular department. Of particular interest in the computer-aided manufacturing vein are the inventory inquiry files, the order files, and work-in-process files.

The inventory file shows the current status of some 70,000 various items.

A listing of the orders outstanding against any particular part is available, as well as the reservations or requirements for that particular part.

Complete bills of material are available and can be expanded up to the complete machine tool on which the particular part will be used, or conversely, the machine tool can be broken down to the smallest screw used in the assembly.

Orders which are in process can be interrogated as to the exact location, as well as material and labor costs compiled against the particular order. The purchasing department has access to vendor information files on the CRT and also has the capability of writing purchase orders from the CRT. These are later printed in a batch mode in the computer room and automatically sent to the vendors involved. The repair parts department can input customer orders for parts through the CRT, and the computer produces all necessary paperwork and automatically distributes it to the correct departments.

The inventory records for the part are depleted by the quantity ordered. A requisition is sent to the stock room and the necessary shipping papers are sent to the shipping department. Also within our own corporation, there are two examples of manufacturing systems which illustrate the computer-aided manufacturing approach.

One of these facilities incorporates eight NC machine tools, which are connected for material-handling purposes by means of a powered conveyor. Palletized parts are delivered to any one of the eight machines in the line for the necessary machining operations. Each machine may be operating on an entirely different part number or all machines can be performing the same operation on a particular part.

Typically, the part will be scheduled to go to two or three various machines in the line.

Common bolt hole patterns are machined on multispindle drilling and tapping units.

Inspection and gauging stations are also provided. While this particular facility (which has been operational for over four years and predates OMNICONTROL) is not computer-controlled, this same concept has been applied to a new facility which is presently being installed. The new facility, which does not happen to be within the Sundstrand Corporation, involves a total of six computer-controlled machine tools of three different configurations which, again, are tied together by means of a powered conveyor. In this instance, the conveyor, as well as the machine tools, are under control of the computer. This enhances the versatility and flexibility of the manufacturing system considerably. Parts ranging in size from a six-inch cube up to a three-foot cube can be machined in the system. The original complement of parts involves some 120 variations.

Technically, the parts can be run on a completely random basis. Tooling requirements, however, place some constraints on this; in an actual operation, the line will be manufacturing parts in batch lots. However, these will be quite small.

It may be easier to visualize this concept if you think of an automotive spare parts machining system in which any part configuration from a carburator or fuel pump housing up to the V-8 engine block can be manufactured on demand. The process can be controlled by the computer all the way from the triggering of the order for the part from a dealer in Iowa through its manufacture, inspection, and shipment.

Another system incorporates approximately 70 machine tools which are fed tooling and parts by means of a computer-controlled stacker crane. The stacker crane also provides in-process work storage. The system employs a computer-aided quality control assurance program through statistical analysis of the parts in process. Over 700 different parts are produced in job lot quantities ranging from 75 to 2,500 per order.

As you can see from these examples, the necessary hardware items, as well as the technical knowledge, is available today to create manufacturing systems capable of using the full potential of a computer in the manufacturing area.

15
Computer and Numerical Control—A Shotgun Marriage

by *E. R. Reese*

The term "computerized control," as presently used, brings to mind an efficient system controlling a complex process, several machine tools, or a complete factory, in an efficient, error-proof, ultra-reliable, unmanned way. It implies a foregone conclusion that any system or process that is not under computerized control is behind the state-of-the-art. It is true that there are a number of computerized systems in operation which to some degree are functionally successful. These systems are gaining considerable publicity and present a very attractive approach to automation. However, there is another side of the story that should be presented, to point out the possible pitfalls that one could encounter, before DNC can be assumed to be the answer to all aspects of automation.

There is considerable talk, and, of course, literature has filled the desks of numerical control users and control manufacturers on the NC-computer marriage. This literature has been very well received because it points out the obvious compatibility between the two technologies. The reader, therefore, concludes that the result must be a happy marriage. Perhaps there is no disputing this—all marriages are happy; it is the living together afterwards that causes the trouble.

It seems that the old saying, "necessity is the mother of invention," has in this case been reversed. Rather, the industry is trying to mother a necessity for what has been invented. It is not unusual to hear comments such as, "Here is a programmable 4K memory; there must be an application for it in the NC industry." It is also very common to hear statements such as, "Computers can do anything." The subscript that should be added is, "as long as they can be interfaced and programmed."

DEVELOPMENTS

The reasons behind these comments are not difficult to understand. Developments in the last five years, particularly in the area of peripheral equipment, interface equipment, software techniques and, of course, the minicomputer, have been staggering. Further, numerical control is, in fact, a special-purpose computer.

Editor's Note: This article reprinted from *NC Scene,* November 1970. Reprinted by permission of the publisher, Numerical Control Society, Princeton, N.J., and the author.

The multitude of types of machines and applications has restricted the conventional NC controller somewhat because it is difficult to respond economically to the many requirements. Since NC and computer technology are similar, it is natural to approach the problem of customization through the use of a general-purpose computer. The idea behind this is to eliminate hardware changes in order that all systems can be identical, thus reducing all costs associated with the production of numerical control equipment.

The potential contribution the minicomputer has made to the NC industry has not gone unnoticed. However, the advantages the computer has offered have been almost exclusively in the area of programming and applications where pattern storage, error correction, and recordkeeping functions are required.

PROBLEMS

With on-line applications, where a computer is used exclusively to control a machine in real time, there are problems. It is not a question of whether or not the technology exists for computerized control, nor is it a question of hardware availability. The problem falls into two basic categories: (1) economic, and (2) training.

The attractive cost of $5,000 for an all-purpose computer makes it hard, at first glance, to understand why it cannot take the place of a $7,800 conventional system. It seems that a computer should be able to replace a simple NC control and at the same time add versatility and increased capability. There are many reasons why this cannot be done. The $5,000 initial investment for the computer is misleading because this price does not include the non-recurring costs such as the design of the interface equipment and software. It also does not include the recurring costs of peripheral equipment and interface hardware.

Training becomes a big factor in added costs. There exists a language barrier between the computer manufacturer and the original equipment manufacturer (OEM) supplier of NC equipment. This language barrier is a more significant problem between the computer engineer and the end user. Therefore, the OEM supplier of controls utilizing computers must first educate his designers, and then field service engineers must be trained in the ways of computer technology. This training must in turn be passed on to the end user. Anyone who has been through this experience will fully understand the problems involved.

Aside from the economic reasons and the problems in personnel training, is it really practical to replace portions of the NC system with the minicomputer? There are, of course, many ways of integrating a computer into a control system—most of which have been tried and either are in the experimental stage or are being sold to a limited degree. A close examination of some general forms of these types of systems makes it readily apparent that the economics are not justified and, further, that the computer is capable of much more than just controlling X, Y, and Z, plus a few other functions. At this point the system "grows" to make it economically justifiable and to utilize better the computer's capability, which in turn takes it out of the financial reach of the majority of potential users.

THE SYSTEM

Typically, a conventional NC system consists of three major subsystems: (1) the servo system, (2) the I/O units and peripheral equipment, which includes the control panel, tape reader, dials, etc., and (3) the logic control or arithmetic unit. The single item of least cost on this sytem is the third subsystem, the logic control. In order to "computerize" this system, only the logic control can be replaced. The two high-cost systems (servo and I/O control) remain unchanged.

Actually, the hardware has been increased, not only in the logic control unit (now a computer), but a Teletype or some other input device has been added, as well as the intangible and undefinable (graphically) software. Justification for this type of system usually is attempted by pointing out that it is capable of doing a certain amount of part programming or on-line program corrections and block insertions.

This illustration might be an oversimplification, since the computer system usually is designed to include some limited part programming and to perform some recordkeeping. But these functions are not the functions of NC or part-producing equipment and are normally of no interest to a job shop machinist. Perhaps the addition of linear and circular interpolation becomes a relatively simple software addition so far as the computer is concerned; but this capability also can be added comparatively inexpensively by present hardware techniques. Is the price for this versatility worth the initial investment? Some may point out that an example like the one above is not practical and should not even be considered. Perhaps so. The consideration of a one-to-one relationship between machine and computer is not a practical system, so the next justification usually is made by controlling two machines, three machines, or even five. At first, this concept seems ideal. The elimination of the logic of five controllers, the possible elimination of five unreliable tape readers, the reduction of operating personnel from 5 to 1 and, additionally, centralized control of the shop are all obtained. This seems to be the answer to a manufacturer's dream. If this is true, where are the problems?

First, for the computer to be marketable, the customer must be convinced that the computer will not fail, or that it can be repaired in a very short time, or that redundancy (twice the cost) has eliminated the problem that if the computer is down, the complete shop is down. If this is accomplished, consideration must be given to the fact that in order to make this kind of a system economical, the operation of each machine must be independent of the other. This is a requirement in order to utilize the system's maximum capability. This presents a significant computer programming problem. Perhaps "problem" is the wrong word; programming "challenge" is better suited since it certainly is not an impossible task or even a problem. It does, however, represent high cost, and it is very doubtful that the program could be implemented in a 4K memory. This may, or may not, take the system out of the minicomputer classification, depending upon the current definition of a minicomputer.

In addition, this systems utilizes a disk or a drum memory for part programs. While this approach is ideal for storing part programs, there is that ever-present fear of what happens if the information on the memory is lost for whatever reason. There goes the advantage of ridding the controllers of the punch tape readers. The user will need these readers for backup or redundancy.

The size of the drum is limited so that work must be very carefully planned for a given period to ensure that proper programs are put on the drum.

The biggest disadvantage of this type of system is the revolution it produces in the shop, mainly in the type of personnel that are required. It may not be required to retrain operators to any large degree, but a new type of person must be added to the staff to take care of software maintenance. Further, hardware maintenance no longer can be left in the hands of the very capable electronic technicians (who know logic and can trace a signal from input to output and locate a malfunctioning board). This system requires a new breed of technician, who not only must have competence in electronics, but must also be trained in and have a thorough knowledge of software techniques and computer technology in order to be able to distinguish between a hardware problem and a software problem.

Anyone who would make an all-inclusive statement that this type of system will never succeed certainly would be less than informed. Systems such as this will be demonstrated soon and in all probability will be functionally successful. However, the problems discussed above still exist and only large companies with adequate resources will be able to afford these systems and obtain the appropriate personnel to maintain and operate them.

If the computer adds costs by requiring sfotware, interface equipment, extra peripheral equipment, more highly trained personnel, such as programmers and both hardware and software maintenance personnel, what has it contributed? It has not increased cutting speed, chip production, or spindle horsepower; it has not added another axis to the machine, nor has it added any other useful machine characteristic. It has not contributed to less expensive production, faster production, or allowed us to do something we could not otherwise do with conventional equipment. What, then, is the answer? It has been stated that these systems will succeed in the large companies, but what will make the computer approach practical or obtainable for the small user?

NEW APPROACH

The answer to DNC must start at the machine. This approach will not utilize the conventional NC controller as we now know it, but rather a computer compatible controller that does not suffer from increased cost. In fact, it should cost less, and it will not lose any capability inherent in conventional NC. This system must also be within the small shop's present capabilities to operate and maintain.

This new approach would, perhaps, make use of read only memory components, computer flow logic, and algorithm specifically derived for control design. The concept of the 4K memory as a requirement should be eliminated; and, most importantly, the computer industry must dig out the problems and requirements of the machine tool industry, and the machine tool industry must educate itself to the capabilities of the computer industry, and both must rid themselves of the concept that the "computer can do anything."

This effort would not result in a system under the present definition of the general-purpose computer–dedicated computer or special-purpose, perhaps, but remember the restrictions. It must be competitive with present NC. It must be computer-compatible by not requiring any additional interface equipment or any modifications to the unit and require no personnel upgrading. This may sound like the idealistic system that would never reach the practical stage. This is not true. The term "computer compatible" is over-used these days and is precisely what this paper has criticized; but if a new approach is taken, a different type of system that is truly computer compatible will certainly evolve. This approach will combine present computer and NC technology in such a way as to produce this practical system.

A system such as this could grow into the automatic factory. A conventional work station manned by machinists or assemblers would be replaced by the new type controller. The necessary part programming capability will be included as an off-line function. The next step in computerization would include the use of dedicated minicomputers to control each manufacturing subgroup. Additional programming functions would also be included. Following this, a centralized computer for control of the automated factory could be incorporated. After this plateau has been reached, functions such as material control, production control, and accounting features could be programmed into this total system concept.

It is readily apparent that one could stop it at any place along this type of development and still be completely within the state-of-the-art for one's operation and, more importantly, would not have a large initial outlay of capital funds.

In summary, at the present time there are several total DNC systems either in the proposal stage, in the design stages, or on the market. These approach the automatic factory concept or a machine control programming center and are not generally available to anyone except the large manufacturer–not available insofar as the cost of the systems or the trained personnel to maintain them is concerned. Because of this, only the aerospace industry, the automobile industry, and other such large industries can utilize these systems, and they are also the reason for so much publicity being given to them. There are, of course, no arguments with the fact that these large systems may operate efficiently and economically. However, a recent survey shows that 80 percent of our metal cutting is done by smaller job shops. This is the market that requires considerable attention, and it is also the market that has been neglected and frustrated by the DNC publicity.

The computer is, of course, the obvious next step up in the state-of-the-art of manufacturing. The minicomputer makes a great contribution to the automated factory, but it must be developed with the smaller user in mind and not be limited in approach to large industries—to those that can take a giant step or can purchase a computerized control as a curiosity item or a toy.

PART 8

FORECAST

Isaac L. Auerbach
Philadelphia, Pennsylvania

This paper was presented by Isaac L. Auerbach, President, AUERBACH Corporation, to the IFIP Congress 71–Ljubljana, August 1971:

"Technological Forecast 1971"
by Isaac L. Auerbach

16
Technological Forecast 1971

by *Isaac L. Auerbach*

INTRODUCTION

In attempting to forecast the development of information systems technology during the remainder of this decade, we must be sensitive to three primary influences.

First, we must recognize that the information processing business has reached economic maturity. From an economic viewpoint the computer field is no longer the tottering infant of the 1950's nor the impetuous adolescent of the 60's. The worldwide population of computers now exceeds 70,000 installations. The ranks of computer professionals and technicians are numbered in the high hundreds of thousands and we have invested well in excess of one million man years in developing system designs and computer software. In short, our worldwide investment in hardware, software and manpower development now approaches the $100 billion mark. Clearly, the magnitude of this investment will serve as a major constraining influence on the rate at which information systems technology is permitted to develop.

The second major consideration—and one which appears paradoxical in terms of the first—is an evident lack of maturity in the effective application of computers to the social, economic, scientific and commercial problems which confront us. After 25 years of dramatic progress in hardware development, we continue for the most part to apply computers to scientific and commercial workloads in a piecemeal fashion, tending to view them merely as efficient replacements for the calculators and accounting machines of the past. Certainly, there is an enormous opportunity for progress in the design of coherent information systems and in the effective application of computer technology. Despite the economic constaints cited above, and despite our dubious record in the past, I find myself decidedly sanguine regarding our ability to make notable progress in applications development during the remainder of this decade.

The third influence which will play a major role in the future development of the information systems field is a continued rapid rate of progress in hardware technology—particularly in the solid state field. We are just beginning to experi-

Editor's Note: From *IFIP Congress 71,* August 1971. Reprinted by permission of the publisher, North Holland Publishing Co., and the author.

ence the impact on the computer field of advances in the large scale integration of solid state circuitry. It is clear that continued progress in large scale integration, as well as in other areas of solid state technology, will potentially exert a dramatic influence on the design and cost effectiveness of information systems during the remainder of this decade.

As I look at the future today, I will be doing so with the belief that the growth of information systems during the remainder of this decade will be subject to these primary influences. Let me restate them: (1) the economic maturity of the computer industry and our increasingly massive investment in computer systems will certainly act as a contraining force on the rate at which technology is permitted to advance; (2) we should recognize the shortcomings of our present information systems and the increasing need for improvement in applications development; and (3) we must acknowledge a continued steady rate of progress in hardware technology, particularly as a result of advances in the solid state field.

The challenge I face is to place these somewhat oppositional influences into a proper perspective and to gauge their combined effect on the development of the information processing community. For the sake of order I will progress by organizing my remarks into three broad categories: hardware, software, and systems.

HARDWARE

Turning to the hardware field, let's consider the matters of solid state circuitry and central processor logic, then proceed to a discussion of memory devices and, finally, peripheral equipment.

Arithmetic and Control Elements

Semiconductor technology, and the supporting technology in physics, chemistry, optics, and computer-aided design, have now developed to the point where it is possible to design and build nearly any circuit configuration that can be conceptualized and to achieve volume production at an increasingly small manufacturing cost. Manufacturing techniques are approaching the point where the cost elements of design, packaging, and testing comprise the major part of the semiconductor device cost; in effect, the actual fabrication cost of semiconductor logic is approaching zero. The amount and complexity of circuits that can be packaged are approaching the limitations imposed by the economies of the package itself and the interconnections to it. In short, the contents of the package are strongly controlled by its electrical connectors.

As a consequence of the above, we are rapidly approaching the point where an entire computer (of the 16 bit × 4000 word class) can be fabricated in a few LSI packages at a cost on the order of a few hundred dollars. Compared to two years ago, let alone 20 years ago, the cost elements of computer power are becoming a relatively inconsequential factor in the economics of information processing.

Achieving these economics, as in any other mass production industry, requires a massive engineering and tooling investment and large volume production runs. The key question is where can such a cheap computing power be effectively used in these large volumes. Furthermore, we must not overlook the applications cost of such cheap computer power. The costs to apply a computer to a specific problem and to develop the associated application programs are relatively independent of the cost of the computer itself. Thus, as in the case of the engineering and tooling costs, it is necessary to find the high volume, identical applications over which to amortize the applications development and programming costs.

Finally, we must view such technical achievements in the context of existing investments in information systems; for it is patently clear that any engineering solutions which would render obsolete current investments in system designs, manpower development, data files, and application programs would lack commercial viability.

Keeping these constraints in mind, we can proceed to consider some of the likely consequences of the availability in large volume of very inexpensive computational elements.

In the first place, the availability of such computing elements suggests a trend away from massive, centralized computational facilities of a very general purpose design and toward a dispersion of computing power among the peripheral elements of an information system. Such a trend might manifest itself in two years.

First, we could expect a proliferation of specialized processors for the performance of such functions as channel and device control, data file management, communications line control, remote multiplexing, system monitoring and similar functions which presently entail either time sharing of a central processor or rigid and costly hand-wired control methods. A trend in this direction can be discerned from some recent product introductions.

Second, we can envisage the development of inexpensive intelligent terminals and satellite processors which would permit the user to perform routine computational tasks on a localized basis so that access to a central computational facility would occur only if communication with a central data base is required or if massive computational power is needed.

The above comments are focused on the availability in large volume of inexpensive, complete basic computers. It is also reasonable to consider the construction of a large computer out of many small, identical computational elements, or to allocate simple tasks to individual computational elements, rather than to time-share a large computing device. Indeed, it might be possible to couple individual computers with parts of programs, somewhat in the same way as analog computer elements are interconnected. Other interlocking programs then become the interconnections. Thus, a computer might become a collection of processor elements, each of which is "statement effectuating. . ." and which are linked together by a switching intelligence directed by the flow chart.

The chief obstacles which must be overcome if such solutions are to be viable relate to questions of applications and applications programming. Whenever a highly parallel machine organization is proposed, the problem immediately arises of mapping the user's application to the topology of the system—a question which does not arise when we proceed to solve a computational problem in a serial fashion. Second, assuming that satisfactory approaches to program design can be effected, present investments in programmer training and applications program development must not be ignored. Certainly any engineering solutions along the lines discussed above must be achieved in such a manner that reasonable compatibility with present-day programming techniques is maintained or practical conversion tools are provided.

Each of the approaches discussed above is predicated on the availability of increasingly low cost computing logic and related memory and the associated attainment of mass production volumes. Such production volumes, in turn, will be highly dependent on the standardization or universality of hardware designs, which further increases the already evident trend toward microprogramming and the development of so-called "firmware" technology. The basic computing unit (with a function-defining memory) could be implemented in the following manner. The operational function of each computing element would be entirely defined by the program resident in its associated memory. The program could be built in or could be read in at run time to define the operational function of each computing unit.

We might expect such a trend to manifest itself in the availability of standard "computer component"—analogous to our present-day standard logic elements—which would be manufactured at very low cost in high volume and then used in a variety of ways by system vendors. The unit would be a plug-in sub-assembly without external packaging or power supply—just a memory and processing logic—which would be applied at the user's direction. The need for large production volume to achieve low production cost would result in few minicomputer manufacturers surviving in their present form. In effect, the minicomputer processor will eventually become a standardized component, which will be produced as a high volume OEM package, sold primarily to system builders.

Memories

Turning next to the subject of computer memories, my previous comments with regard to the low cost of logic are generally applicable. Magnetic core memories of the conventional type will reach an irreducible cost level on the order of 2¢–3¢ per bit. Most of this cost will consist of peripheral electronics and packaging and other non-stack costs. Further reductions must come from reducing the cost of the physical package and the peripheral electronics. Little reduction is expected in price or increase in the speed of magnetic core memory in the future. Consequently, the market share of these memories will gradually decline.

The next memory technology to briefly consider is magnetic thin film of the planar and plated wire types. As recently as three or four years ago it was believed by many that thin film memories—particularly the platted wire variety—would succeed core memories as the primary storage medium of our digital computers. However, such has not proven to be the case. In the first place, the magnetic core memory has proven to be a much more tenacious survivor than seemed likely several years ago, having achieved costs in the order of 3¢ per bit and cycle speeds on the order of 600 nano-seconds. Secondly, the thin-film memories have proven difficult to manufacture at projected costs, due largely to unresolved yield problems. Finally, and most importantly, the monolithic semi-conductor memory has arrived on the scene as a practical entity much sooner than was anticipated several years ago. As a consequence, the future of the thin-film memory does not appear to be bright.

The announcement by IBM in 1970 of a bipolar monolithic memory on the 370/145 appears to be a strong indicator of the role of semiconductor memories during this decade. Large scale integration techniques make it possible to treat memory subarrays like logic arrays and to achieve increasingly higher speed and lower prices as production volume increases and process quality and yield improves. Although the semiconductor storage cell is more complex than a ferrite core or a magnetic film region, the compatible techniques used for storage and access, both physically and technologically, result in a great simplification in peripheral circuit costs and elimination of specialized packaging and handling. Thus, it is fairly evident that the monolithic semi-conductor memory will predominate as the primary computer storage medium during the remainder of this decade.

In addition to its use as a conventional memory element, the integrated circuit memory offers the potential for the incorporation of logic functions by the addition of logic in memory. An associative memory organization—based on monolithic integrated circuit technology—is just one possibility.

The continued development of integrated circuit memories suggests other possibilities. For example, one can visualize the use of LSI memory/logic arrays as the target of emitting devices, such as light-emitting diodes, thus permitting the emitted beam to interact with the stored data and logic functions on the LSI array. It is interesting to speculate on the possibilities of such an arrangement to modify the logic functions, programs, or data resident in an LSI array. The photon beam noted above could be scanned, or directed, and might contain pictorial as well as digital information. Thus, these are the means for causing an image scanner to interact directly with a memory or logic processing array.

The magnetic bubble memory is a major technique now being developed by Bell Laboratories, North American Rockwell, and others, which bears close watching. Bell Laboratories has discovered that when a monolithic single ferrite crystal is put into a magnetic field, it is possible to enable portions of it to alter their magnetic spin direction. This can be done to particles of less than ½ mil in dimension. It is then possible to control the reading in and out of this "bubble" within the crystal. As a result, a very high capacity memory can be built with the permanent storage characteristics of the magnetic core and the potential of the integrated circuit memory for the application of sophisticated manufacturing techniques. Should this magnetic bubble development activity progress to the point where volume production can be achieved with acceptable yields, widespread application within the commercial computer field can be expected.

Proceeding next to a consideration of bulk or mass devices, the potential for significant cost or performance achievements is less evident than in the case of primary memory devices discussed previously. Even at the limits of large scale integration technology it may not be possible to effectively compete in mass memory applications with the various continuous magnetic surface recording media, exemplified today in drum, tape, disk, etc. where the storage element is transported to the input/output device. The characteristics of such large volume memory are determined almost entirely by the methods used to transport the medium and the ways in which it is subdivided. The speed, cost, and information storage density of bulk magnetic storage are almost entirely determined—not by the medium itself—but by the supporting hardware. The storage density of the medium is far from being used effectively (by 2 or 3 orders of magnitude) due to shortcomings in the external machinery.

There are many current efforts to improve mass memory performance by changing to other media with better inherent storage element density. However, progress has been quite slow in relieving the shortcomings of magnetic memory machinery and recent improvements have been relatively marginal. Furthermore, significant advancements are expected in mechanism dynamics—since this is a very mature discipline—so that progress in magnetic bulk memory technology is expected to be evolutionary during the remainder of this decade.

Exploration of other mass storage media is expected to continue at an increasing pace, with photon-interactive types being the prime candidates. Synergism between integrated photon-responsive and photon-emissive arrays and various types of photon interactive chemical materials is likely to be productive. The problem of bringing the medium into registration with the electronic devices will continue to be the primary limiting factor, but possibly limiting at higher levels of storage capacity—rather than higher dynamic speed. The use of photon-deflecting techniques may have application as a level in the access hierarchy but will not be a fundamental breakthrough.

The use of holography in bulk storage applications will continue to be explored. Holographic recording not only may yield very high storage density, but in addition uses an area approach to recording a bit rather than a spot approach. This can result in higher reliability and may obviate the need to periodically re-record magnetic tape files.

Peripheral Devices

In discussing likely technical advances in the peripheral device field we should first distinguish between those devices which are primarily electromechanical in nature and those which are susceptible to advances in electronic technology.

Among the former class of devices are the various card readers, punches, impact printers, and similar mechanical devices which presently play such an important role in data processing installations. It is apparent that improvements in the performance of such devices will be limited during the future since the applicable engineering disciplines are quite mature and advances in the state of the art are achieved only in a gradual and evolutionary fashion.

The important advances in the peripheral device field during the remainder of this decade will occur as a result of the application of electronic technology. For this reason we can expect major efforts to be expended in attempting to displace electromechanical devices with alternative devices which have a stronger electronic orientation.

A prime example is the computer printer field. At present the impact line printer is the primary output device in most computer installations with printing speeds on the order of 2000 lines per minute representative of the current state of the art. To illustrate the evolutionary nature of advances in the printer field, consider that since 1965 computer printer speeds have increased only about 30% from a level of 1500 lpm to the present level of 2000 lpm. In the previous five years (1960–1965) a gain of 150% was achieved as speeds increased from 600 lpm to 1500 lpm. Finally, during the five year period from 1955 to 1960 a 200% increase was achieved as speeds advanced from 150 lpm to 600 lpm. If we merely extrapolate from this trend, it is unlikely that impact printing speeds much in excess of 2500 lpm can be achieved during the remainder of this decade.

A straightforward solution to the printer "bottleneck" which confronts so many present-day computer installations would be to replace current impact printers with higher speed non-impact printers or microfilm recorders. Indeed, during the past two or three years there has been a fair amount of progress along these lines, particularly through the application of computer output microfilm techniques. Furthermore, continued significant progress will be realized during the 1970's and I can visualize flexible and cost-effective non-impact computer printers—employing electrostatic imaging techniques and operating at speeds in the order of tens of thousands of lines per minute—in widespread use during the latter part of this decade.

Despite this, it is unlikely that the non-impact printer or microfilm recorder will completely replace the impact line printer during the foreseeable future—particularly for those commercial applications which require the immediate production of multiple copies of printed documents.

An indirect, and often proposed, solution to the computer printer bottleneck is to reduce the hard-copy output of computer installations through more efficient information system designs. Indeed, the concept of "management by exception" is a well-known step in this direction. Although this concept has been accepted in principle for perhaps 15 years, progress to date has been generally disappointing. However, as a result of continued advances in the development of centralized data bases and data mangement systems, as well as an expected proliferation of CRT displays and other "soft copy" devices for the remote interrogation of a data base, I am hopeful that significant progress will be made in stemming the outflow of printed documents from our data processing installations.

Turning to other segments of the peripheral device field, it is apparent that source data entry devices and systems will be particularly subject to advances in technology and a rapid rate of product improvement. Since the earliest days of the data processing industry, the punched card has been the predominant medium for the recording of source data and the basic keyboard-driven card punch has been the primary tool for source data entry. During recent years, the primacy of the card punch has been challenged by a wide variety of source data entry devices and systems, including key-to-tape and key-to-disk units, OCR readers, point-of-sale recorders, and a variety of on-line terminals for source data entry.

This upsurge of new product announcements in the source data entry area can largely be explained by two factors. First, the efficiency and responsiveness of data processing systems are being increasingly hampered by a lack of adequate source data input facilities and hence an increasing demand exists for improved data entry devices. Second, as a result of advances in the solid state field, it has become increasingly possible to produce sophisticated systems for source data capture at a cost which competes favorably with older key punching methods.

I do not believe that the complete demise of the punched card will occur during this decade, nor would I favor such an occurrence. However, data entry methods will be subject to dramatic improvement over the next several years with strong emphasis on the capture of data at the point of origin and on line entry from remote terminal devices. Furthermore, a strong trend can be expected toward the development of specialized, application-oriented devices for source data entry, such as retail point of sale recorders, factory data collection devices, and hospital terminals. Finally, during the latter half of the decade the availability of relatively low cost OCR document readers used as remote terminals, featuring improved flexibility and reliability, can be anticipated. Certainly, the availability of such devices and systems for source data entry will exert a dramatic influence on the efficiency and responsiveness of future information systems.

The final category of peripheral devices I will discuss is perhaps the most important in terms of improving the effectiveness of our future information systems. I refer to remote terminal devices which will serve to establish a vital interface between future information systems and the user community. Remote terminals of various classes will play an increasingly important role in future systems and will be subject to major technological advances during the remainder of the decade.

To a large extent, my remarks concerning source data entry devices also apply to the remote terminal field since many of the source data entry devices of the future will, in fact, be remote terminals which are in direct communication with a central processing facility. However, it is apparent that the application of remote terminal technology will also extend into many application areas outside the source data entry field.

A relatively recent trend in remote terminal design, which will undoubtedly become increasingly important in the future, is the concept of an intelligent terminal—that is, a terminal equipped with certain logical and processing capabilities. I previously mentioned the dramatic reductions in processing costs which are occurring as a result of advances in integrated circuit technology and of the expected widespread distribution of processor elements in future information systems. Certainly, this concept of distributed intelligence will have a significant bearing on the remote terminal field and suggests some powerful terminal configurations. It is easy to visualize, for example, that source data capture terminals of the future will be equipped with specialized processor elements to provide advanced formatting, editing, and error control capabilities, thereby improving the integrity and accuracy of the recorded data. Remote batch entry terminals of the future can be expected to be equipped with increasingly powerful processing capabilities, including source language translators, data compression/expansion functions, and similar pre-processing and post-processing services. Finally, there will be the development of low cost, keyboard-operated computational terminals with sufficient processor and memory capabilities to permit the processing of routine computational tasks on an autonomous basis so that access to a large scale central processor need only occur to interrogate a data base, to retrieve library programs, or to obtain sufficient processing power to handle significant computational problems.

SOFTWARE

Now let us turn to the subject of computer programming. In order to discuss this subject properly, I will divide it into the very imprecise and overlapping categories of applications programs and system software. Without pretending to be precise, applications programs are user- or end-use-oriented, whereas systems software is oriented toward the utilization of the data processing system.

The primary problem to be solved with respect to application programming is to cope with the continued proliferation of computers and their intrusion into virtually every aspect of our civilization. The pressure of time and the urgency of the data processing demands will not afford us the luxury of measured growth. In order to contend successfully with these demands, we must learn how to produce applications programmers at an increasingly high rate. This, in turn, means that languages and applications programming tools must be developed which will serve to increase the productivity of our applications programmers, while keeping the entry level for apprentice programmers at or near its present level.

As a starting point, several things must be provided. For example: better procedure- or problem-oriented languages, such as COBOL and FORTRAN, ALGOL and PL/I, SIMSCRIPT, and LIPS; efficient compilers for both testing and production runs; appropriate program diagnostic tools including test data generators, program traces and symbolic jump routines; and the implementation of generalized sort/merge programs, report program generators, linear program packages and regression routines which are required so frequently by various communities of application programmers.

However, to merely improve upon present programming tools will not relieve the applications programming bottleneck which confronts our industry and which is rapidly approaching crisis proportions. To achieve truly effective and lasting solutions, the applications programming question must be approached from a fresh perspective, and bold and innovative approaches to the design and coding of applications programs must be sought.

To cite but one example, the possibility of making greater use of the computer for programming design should be considered. Significant use of the computer has already been made in the design of such things as transformers and motors, as well as in logical design; but it has not been successfully utilized adequately in the programming process itself. Such a breakthrough would greatly decrease the time required to develop a program and would, at the same time, greatly increase the efficiency of the program. In short, computer-aided program design would help overcome the problem of a desperate shortage of programmers—a situation which has become a crisis and which has driven the cost of programming to staggering proportions.

Now let us turn to system software. By most measures, the status of software development is the most troublesome aspect of the computer business. Software history today is being written in terms of large scale schedule slippages, vastly underestimated costs, and significant cutbacks in functional specifications. Computer users continue to be plagued with severe operational problems with residual bugs in the operating systems, compilers, and other essential software. Successive versions and releases of software systems often remove some errors, but only at the hazard of introducing new sources of trouble.

Examination of these systems and their internal architecture is not reassuring. In many cases, they lack a basic coherence or design integrity; instead, they appear to have grown through a series of ad hoc solutions rather than by a process of directed growth. Coherence between systems is lacking, and the problems involved in converting even from one operating system to another on the same machine can be costly and time consuming.

The unsatisfactory state of software today is a reflection of the current state of the art. "State of the art" is a deliberate term, because software development is still an art and not a science. It has no basic principles of organization; it has no well-recognized standards of performance; it appears impossible to forecast as to cost, length of development cycle, or core requirements; and is currently incapable of objective measurement or quality control.

These problems exist even though the people who have been developing software have been working no less diligently and with no less intelligence creativity and imagination than those in the fields of computer architecture, hardware, or peripherals. The hardware-oriented technologists have their roots more firmly planted in the classical engineering tradition than do the software developers. Software and its development represents a greater departure from conventional engineering practice and is thus more vulnerable to the growing pains of emerging technology.

While acknowledging the high caliber of its best practitioners, it is also true that the software field has attracted many individuals whose performance is most charitably described as marginal. The booming demand for programmers of all types has forced salaries upward at an astonishing rate. This fact, coupled with relatively modest educational and experiential entry requirements, has created the sellers' market that most programmers now enjoy, and which has attracted many individuals with little aptitude or training into the field.

In short, then, of all the fields of computer technology, that of software developments is the last to mature. Can we look forward to something better in the future, or will the software problems of today persist into the seventies and beyond?

There is some reason for optimism. There are some indications that system software development is beginning to emerge as a technology and not as an art form. Work has been done under Lincoln Laboratory sponsorship on coherent programming which shows an awareness of program organization problems. Similar work from Carnegie Institute can be cited. The development of improved program maintenance methodology is the subject of a current U.S. Government research study. These few examples from the work in progress indicate a growing interest in the development of the systematics of software development.

We are beginning to move in the direction of increasing formalism of software structures as well as improved discipline of the software development progress, and by moving in this direction, the quality of the software produced, its durability and its adaptability to change will be upgraded. Program modularity and interchangeability must be regarded as more than catchwords or slogans in the future. Just as hardware systems can be built from components developed by different manufacturers, software systems from separately developed components should be able to be produced and integrated. If we can agree on how to define system functions and functional program modules and how they relate to each other, we should be able in the future to select a resource allocator from one supplier, a data management system from a second, an I/O control system from a third, and a command language processor from a fourth.

This degree of modularity is impossible to achieve today, but I believe that by the end of the 1970's the technology of software system development will have progressed to the point that such interchangeability will be common.

Closely allied to the emergence of software development as a technology will be a substantial increase in the professionalism of the software development personnel. Already, significant upgrading of the educational curricula for system and software designers is taking place, and there is a corresponding sharp increase in the requirements for entry into the profession. This trend shows every sign of continuing and in fact deserves encouragement. The end is near for the era in which software implementers are recruited from the ranks of the chemists, the psychologists, and the mathematicians. The university graduate in the field of computer sciences is no longer an oddity; and it can be expected that the majority of future entrants to the software profession will come from this source. Moreover, there will be less variation in the quality of the curricula they have undergone, as standards within the profession are established and strengthened and the educational requirements for the profession become more universally recognized.

In an address before the IFIP 10th Anniversary Celebration in Amsterdam in October, 1970, I spoke of the need for an information systems theory to provide a firm intellectual base for continued progress in our field. I suggested that "too often trial and error is the practiced methodology to match an information processing system to the need. The heuristic approach is still the rule rather than the exception in computer system design."

As the end of the 1970's nears, I believe that we will begin to observe the formation of a scientific base for the information processing industry and the formulation of an effective information systems theory. As a practical consequence, signs should begin to appear that the software development field, with all its imprecision and inefficiency—as we know it today—is disappearing.

I believe that by the 1980's, significant progress will have been made in learning to specify the requirements, characteristics, and parameters of a program with sufficient clarity to enable a program to be independently designed according to specifications and within a time and cost agreement. I further believe that by the 1980's, information handling systems will begin to be built from a wide variety of elementary modules, including control units, memories, peripheral units, communications gear, microprogramming modules and software.

Interchangeability will be possible not only among alternative software modules, but also between software modules, microprogrammed modules, and hard-wired instructions. The interchangeability of hardware and software will not be a universal phenomenon by the 1980's, but it will by then exist in some early stage of development, and it will take hold and grow strongly in the years that follow.

SYSTEMS

We have previously examined expected advances in various areas of computer technology, including processors, memories, peripheral devices, application programs and systems software. These individual technologies can be viewed as the building blocks of our future information systems. Now let us turn our attention to the systems themselves and probable trends in system architecture during the remainder of the decade.

To predict with any degree of specificity the structure and performance of information systems eight or ten years hence is at best an exercise in prophecy, which I will not impose upon you here. However, it is practical for us to identify some important technical, economic, and procedural trends which are likely to exert a formative influence on the design and behavior of future information systems.

Economic Constraints

The first influence which I should like to consider is the matter of the growth toward economic maturity of the information processing business and the impact of this maturity on future system designs. In an address to the Information Processing Association of Israel in October, 1970, I stated that the byword in the decade ahead will be *economic payoff.* The size of the information processing business today and its rate of growth will establish it as the first or second largest world industry by the end of this decade. When an industry has matured to this extent and has achieved this importance, it is axiomatic that economics will govern its future development, not new techniques or clever engineering phenomena.

As a consequence of this economic maturity, progress in the architectural development of future information systems will, of necessity, occur at an increasingly evolutionary pace. In spite of the great potential for hardware cost reduction and performance improvement which we have discussed at some length, the rate at which these technological advances are reflected in the design and structure of information systems will be strongly tempered by economic considerations. Certainly, our existing investments in computer hardware, data bases, applications, and programming skills are of such a magnitude that it would be disastrous to permit an abrupt and massive displacement of our existing systems in order to capitalize on some engineering breakthrough.

Can we legitimately infer from the above that progress in system design throughout the remainder of this decade is likely to be inconsequential? It is my firm conviction that this need not happen and I am hopeful that we will experience substantive advances in information systems architecture which will serve to complement and extend the effectiveness of our existing systems, rather than render them obsolete.

I expect, first of all, that technological innovations will find their early implementation in new, unexploited application areas and will gradually find their way into more mature applications. Considering the myriad applications in such diverse fields as education, health care, industrial control, urban systems, science, and finance which have thus far had minimal exposure to information systems technology, the possibilities appear virtually limitless. It is in such virgin areas that the most dramatic and important innovations in information system design may be expected.

Increasingly greater attention in future systems engineering can be expected to be devoted to methods of affording compatibility and ease of conversion with earlier systems. Certainly, the computer system announcements in 1971 confirm this view with their strong emphasis on compatibility with predecessor systems through the use of advanced emulation techniques. In fact, one might persuasively argue that the key to success in future systems development will be to seek technical solutions which strike a proper balance between advancements in the state of the art and compatibility with existing systems.

I am confident, moreover, that through the development of innovative compatibility and conversion techniques, including a reliance on flexible microprogramming, we will be able to effectively safeguard our immense investments in system designs while at the same time providing a strong—if not startling—rate of technological progress through the remainder of the decade.

Distributed Intelligence

Having briefly considered the constraining effects of economic maturity on technical progress in the information processing field, let us consider some of the technical forces which are likely to influence future system designs.

In discussing expected advances in hardware technology, I dwelt at some length on the potential which exists for dramatically lower processor and storage costs during this decade. Also considered was the need to identify large volume applications for standardized processor and storage elements in order to maximize this potential for lower costs. I believe that a major consequence of this will be a a proliferation of processor modules in future information system networks and a strong trend toward *distributed intelligence* in systems architecture.

This does not mean that in future system designs there will be a trend completely away from the powerful centralized processing complexes of the present and an exclusive reliance on small scale, special purpose, decentralized processors. Future information system designs will continue to include a powerful central processing kernel with extensive computational and storage capabilities. They will be needed in order to permit the management of central data bases, to provide for the solution of computational problems of significant proportions, to provide an effective interchange of data and programs among decentralized elements and, finally, to effect centralized supervisory control of the total information systems complex. We can look forward to continued progress in central processor performance during this decade and we should see the construction of some super scale central processor complexes before 1980 with throughput rates approaching one billion instructions per second.

What the distributed intelligence concept does mean is that in the future the central processor complex will provide service to a network of decentralized processors organized in a hierarchical fashion. At the periphery of such systems would be the intelligent terminal devices, discussed previously, which will be required with microprogrammed processor elements to provide an intelligent, applications-oriented man/machine interface between the end user and the information system. These intelligent terminal networks will be linked with arrays of satellite processors which might provide communcations control capabilities, regional data files, as well as the next higher level of computational, or data processing, power. The satellite processors might in turn be linked with an intermediate level of processors until finally the central processing complex is accessed.

The byword of such distributed intelligence systems will be *responsive customer service.* Today's monolithic, centralized computer systems can be highly cost-effective if cost-effectiveness is simply measured in terms of instructions executed per dollar. However, if our present systems are evaluated in terms of service to the end user and their adaptability to the end user's specific needs, more often than not they will fall far short of the mark. A distributed intelligence system, of the type under consideration, promises significant relief to these shortcomings. First, the availability of inexpensive, microprogrammed processor modules makes it economically feasible to provide specialized, or applications-oriented, service to the end user, rather than force-fitting the user's problem into the confines of a general purpose, centralized system. Second, by providing intelligence, or processing, capabilities in proximity to the end user, it becomes possible to provide user services on a much more timely basis, while maintaining a powerful reservoir of centralized processing capabilities for those functions where centralized service is warranted.

Data Communications

It is evident that information systems based on these distributed intelligence concepts will require cost-effective data communcations facilities in order to provide suitable transmission links among the decentralized system elements. In fact, a strong data communications orientation will be a hallmark of future information processing systems.

For more than 15 years, industry observers have been predicting that data communications would soon play a dominant role in our information processing systems and that the preponderance of our data processing installations would include data communications facilities. Although advances in the application of data communications techniques during the past 15 years have been significant, I think that it is fair to say that progress has in general fallen short of most predictions.

There are a number of factors which explain the slower-than-expected development of communications-based information processing systems. Certainly, there have been unforeseen problems in the design and implementation of adequate executive software for communications-based systems. Similarly, our ability to produce sufficiently low cost terminal devices with suitable functional capabilities has been somewhat disappointing. However, the overriding problem has been an almost blind faith in public telephone systems as a foundation for data communications requirements. I am convinced that data communications will not come into its own until digital transmission networks are developed which are specifically designed to handle data traffic with all its specialized requirements. I predict that such digital networks will come into widespread use during this decade and will play a major role in the implementation of the distributed intelligence system architectures which I have previously discussed.

The first steps toward the development of broad based data transmission networks are already being taken. In the United States a number of independent firms have petitioned the Federal Communications Commission for the development of data transmission systems using microwave links. For example, Datran, a subsidiary of University Computing, is planning a switched data transmission network providing service to 35 cities in the United States.

American Telephone and Telegraph will have a digital network serving 60 major cities by the middle of the decade. This digital network will include long haul digital carriers using microwave links and coaxial cables. The service provided by these new facilities should be greatly superior to that presently provided using the switched telephone network. For example, call completions will be made within a few seconds and error rates are expected to be reduced to one in ten million bits.

The use of the public telephone networks for data communications will not be totally eliminated by the end of this decade. The construction of digital networks of sufficient capacity to completely handle our rapidly expanding data workloads seems out of the question. However, I am confident that we will have at least taken significant steps in this direction prior to the end of this decade and that our major cities will be linked by a flexible switched data network, featuring a variety of bandwidths and user services.

System Design and Management

The information systems which I have been discussing are complex structures—considerably more so than today's data processing installations. In view of this complexity, it is appropriate to briefly consider the manner in which these future systems will be designed, implemented and managed.

At present, the system design and management functions are largely a joint effort on the part of the computer manufacturer and the end user. Working in concert with the manufacturer, the user generally selects a hardware configuration which appears to meet his needs from the manufacturer's product catalog. Similarly, the system software required for operation of the system is generally selected from the manufacturer's standard offerings, and the applications programs are frequently a joint effort on the part of the user and computer supplier. In short, the present system design and implementation process is more often than not a loose, collaborative effort with ill-defined spheres of responsibility and ambiguous goals and objectives. Needless to say, this lack of definition and ambiguity are often reflected in the end product.

Clearly, this approach to system design and management will not suffice as system structures become increasingly sophisticated and geographically dispersed. Therefore, I expect to see increasingly widespread acceptance of professional system management firms that are fully equipped to provide the user with a broad range of services, including problem definition, system design, implementation, and programming, and operational management. An early indication of this trend is the recent emergence in the United States of facility management companies which purport to assume total system design and management responsibilities for computer users.

As this trend matures and as information systems increase in complexity to the extent that present-day system management practices become patently unworkable, I foresee some fundamental changes in the traditional role of the computer manufacturer in the information systems business. I believe that the day is not far off when the user can no longer afford his present almost blind reliance on the computer manufacturer as an all-knowing information system architect. Certainly, the emergence of a new breed of "system companies" will in turn create its own set of problems for the user community. However, on balance, I feel that a restructuring of the information processing industry will ultimately be of great benefit to the user and will enhance the effectiveness of his information processing systems.

CONCLUSION

In a paper such as this, I can only hope to highlight the salient trends and influences which are likely to determine the future course of information processing technology. The spectrum of technical disciplines which comprises the information processing field has become astonishingly broad and varied and is increasing in breadth each year. Consequently, I have attempted to provide an overview of those key trends in hardware, software, and system technology which I believe to be particularly significant. Certainly, a number of important areas have not been covered and some crucial technical issues were not discussed.

In concluding, I want to stress the single issue which ultimately transcends all others in importance when dealing with information processing technology. I am referring to the effective *application* of this technology to the social, economic, scientific, and commercial problems which confront us.

Few professionals will take issue with me when I say that our accomplishments in the effective applications of computers have simply not kept pace with our progress in hardware and software technology. In the field of computer technology it has become fashionable to speak in terms of fourth generation computing systems. In the field of applications development, it may not yet be appropriate to speak of a second generation.

Clearly, the reasons for this lack of suitable progress in applications development are varied and complex. I will mention only one of these reasons—which I believe to be particularly pernicious—and I will suggest at least a partial solution which I expect will result in a substantive improvement in the effectiveness of our information systems within this decade.

At present, those responsible for computer applications development seem to fall into two major camps. At one extreme are the "machine accountants"—by far the largest of the two groups. Members of this persuasion tend to view the computer as a super accounting machine which is best suited for the brute force mechanization of our record-keeping functions. The results of this approach to applications development are only too well known and the resultant computer installations can best be described as paperwork factories.

The other major camp in applications development might be termed the "total systems school." Members of this persuasion—perhaps in over-reaction to the machine accountant approach—appear to be content with nothing short of a total corporate management information system, featuring a massive centralized data base, which attempts to integrate the totality of a firm's business activities in a central computing complex. The problem with this approach is simply its ambitiousness. To put it bluntly, we do not know how to construct an effective system of this complexity and I doubt that we will learn how within this decade. As a consequence, we have all seen a large number of well-intended system development programs fall of their own complexity after a massive financial outlay—only to reenforce people's allegiance to the machine accounting approach to computing.

Fortunately, within recent years a third school of applications development appears to be emerging. Members of this school are acutely conscious of the primacy of the end user in information processing. Recognizing that the present state of the art will not permit the construction of a highly centralized "total system" which is at the same time responsive to the service needs of end users, they are quite willing to abandon this approach as impractical. At the same time, they are not willing to revert back to the piece-meal methods of the machine accountant.

The solution which appears to be emerging is to construct a set of reasonably autonomous sub-systems, which are decentralized to permit highly responsive and customized service to end users. At the same time a centralized facility would be provided to serve as a coordinating element, to provide those data files which must be maintained centrally and to provide massive computing power for those tasks which are beyond the practical scope of a satellite subsystem.

Throughout this paper, I have repeatedly stressed the concept of "distributed intelligence" as the key development in information processing technology during this decade. I believe that the emerging trends in application development which I have just discussed will flourish as the distributed intelligence architectures become increasingly cost effective.

In effect, I am saying that for the first time we are beginning to see an emerging climate in the computing field where the user needs will determine the structure of our information systems rather than the present force-fitting of user requirements into a general purpose centralized monolith. I am convinced that the end result will be a major step forward during this decade in the effectiveness and responsiveness of our information system.